Forschungen zum Alten Testament

Herausgegeben von

Bernd Janowski (Tübingen) · Mark S. Smith (New York)
Hermann Spieckermann (Göttingen)

39

Patrick D. Miller

The Way of the Lord

Essays
in Old Testament
Theology

Mohr Siebeck

Patrick D. Miller, born 1935; Ph.D in Near Eastern Languages and Literatures at Harvard University; currently Charles T. Haley Professor of Old Testament Theology at Princeton Theological Seminary.

ISBN 3-16-148254-9
ISSN 0940-4155 (Forschungen zum Alten Testament)

Die Deutsche Bibliothek lists this publication in the Deutsche Nationalbibliographie; detailed bibliographic data is available in the Internet at *http://dnb.ddb.de.*

The book was printed by Gulde Druck in Tübingen on non-aging paper and bound by Spinner in Ottersweier.

To

Wallace M. Alston, Jr.

Robert W. Jenson

and the members and staff of the

Center of Theological Inquiry

Foreword

The essays presented here are largely the product of the last decade, most of them published previously but several appearing here for the first time. They represent my endeavors to carry out an ongoing theological interpretation of Scripture, particularly the Old Testament, in three broad areas. In the course of teaching Old Testament ethics over a period of time, I realized I was taking up the pertinent issues and texts increasingly in relation to the Ten Commandments. I have pursued that line of direction more thoroughly through various lectures and essays seeking to uncover the rich complexity of the Commandments as they are elaborated in the whole of Scripture. The result, as represented in the first section of this book, is a broad rather than a narrow reading of the Commandments.

The Psalms provide the second area of focus. While the essays take up both individual psalms and wider themes, my interest is a theological reading and one that, like the study of the Commandments, opens a way of believing and acting that is compelling and rewarding. The possibility that the Commandments and the Psalms together can point the way of faith and life is suggested by the presence of a previously unpublished essay on the Psalms and the First Commandment.

The third group of essays is more wide-ranging. They take up topics and issues that have to do largely with theology and anthropology. Included here also are some modest efforts to think more methodologically about theological interpretation of Scripture, including listening to the Old Testament in the context of God's redemptive word in Jesus Christ.

There are many persons who have assisted in the writing and publishing of these essays, including those who have listened to their presentation and responded with helpful criticisms. In this context, however, I want particularly to thank Prof. Dr. Bernd Janowski and Prof. Dr. Hermann Spieckermann, the editors of the series Forschungen zum Alten Testament, and Dr. Henning Ziebritzki, editor of Mohr Siebeck, for their interest and support in bringing this volume into print. My special gratitude goes also to Amy Erickson, who has taken time from her doctoral studies to help prepare these essays for publication, and to J. P. Kang, who prepared the final form of the manuscript and the indices and without whose combination of scholarly and computer competence this project could not have been completed. On two separate occasions, I have had the opportunity to do my research and writing as a member of the Center of Theological Inquiry in Princeton. While most of the essays collected here have appeared elsewhere, a number of them, both published and unpublished, were prepared during my time at the Center. My gratitude to the Center and those who participate in its life and leadership is reflected in the dedication of this volume to all my friends there.

Princeton, New Jersey, 2004   Patrick D. Miller

Table of Contents

Old Testament Theology

The Commandments

1. The Place of the Decalogue
in the Old Testament and Its Law

A number of years ago a committee in the Presbyterian Church U.S.A. was charged with preparing a draft of a new confession of faith for that denomination. When it first sent out its draft for initial reaction, the responses were, as one would expect, many and varied. One of the strongest criticisms of the draft, both in terms of frequency and intensity, was that the proposed confession did not contain an exposition of the Ten Commandments. That response was in part a reflection of the particular tradition of that church, in which exposition of the Commandments has historically been a part of major confessional statements. Yet many of those who raised this objection, particularly lay people, were not that cognizant of the tradition but felt somehow that the Commandments are so central to the Bible's teaching and fundamental to life and faith that they must be included in any effort to say who and what we are as a community of faith. Whatever uncertainties and ambivalences we may have as Christians about the place of law in the Christian life, most of us understand that the Ten Commandments are basic and not abrogated in any final way by the Christ event. While we may not always know what they mean for our conduct or how literally or strictly they are to be obeyed, there is some sense that they transcend the normal limitations, restraints, and temporality of most of what we call law, within the Scriptures and beyond. That sensibility is certainly on target, not only in relation to the Reformed tradition, but in light of the place of the Decalogue in the Scriptures.

Within the Bible, the Ten Commandments are at one and the same time both the starting point of the law and of our thinking about the law and the one part of the legal material of the Old Testament that least resembles law as we are accustomed to understanding it. Both of these facts are important for understanding the place of the Decalogue. It stands at the beginning of all the legal material and as such occupies primary place in the divine instruction that comes through the laws or laws of Scripture. The contexts in which the Commandments appear give significant and obvious clues that these words are special.

The first clue is in the very fact that there are two accounts of the presentation of the Decalogue. Exod 20 tells of their initial transmission to Israel, and in Deut 5 Moses restates them to the people, reminding them, at the boundary of the Promised Land, that these words are the basic charter of their life together in the land that the Lord is giving. The foundational character of the Commandments as the essential obligations of the community of faith is thus reinforced at a critical moment in history.[1] Deuteronomy calls attention to this understanding of the Commandments when, in chapter 4, Moses alludes to Sinai and states: "He declared to you his *covenant*, which he commanded you to perform, that is, the *ten words*" (Deut 4:13). To the extent that the covenant provides the framework for the relation of the people to God and to each other, its contents or requirements as far as the people are concerned are to be found in these ten words or commandments.

A second clue to their special place is found in the fact that the narrative around the giving of the Commandments clearly presents their transmission as something that happened directly between God and the people. It is only after the Commandments have been given that the people explicitly ask Moses to stand in their stead and receive the rest of the law. The Decalogue is thus perceived as direct revelation of God to the people, while the rest of the law is mediated through Moses. That does not mean that the rest of Old Testament law is unimportant. It is all God-given; but the story wants to single out the Decalogue as the starting point, separating it and lifting it to a higher level by distinguishing between the modes of transmission of the Commandments and the rest of the laws.

A third indicator of the significance of the Decalogue as the starting point for the understanding of law is the fact that the two presentations of the Decalogue in Exod 20 and Deut 5 are essentially the same. They perdure unchanged.[2] However the rest of the laws that are presented by Moses at Sinai (Exodus and Leviticus) and on the plains of Moab (Deut 12–26) form two quite different collections. They do deal with common subjects at various points, but even then they handle them differently. Deuteronomy picks up some of the matters that appear in the Book of the Covenant (Exod 21–23) but seems to reflect a different economic and social situation, the circumstances of a later time in Israel.

All of this suggests that there is something going on with the Decalogue that is akin to what we encounter in constitutional law. The foundations are laid for the order of the community. Those foundations do not change. They continue in perpetuity to be the touchstone for all actions on the part of the people as they seek to live in community and order their lives. The

---

[1] The moment is critical whether one has in mind the stated setting of the Commandments, that is, the early history when Israel was coming into the land, or the likely actual setting at the time of Josiah or the Exile.

[2] There are some differences, particularly in the form of the Sabbath commandment, but the differences are slight compared to other laws that are present in more than one tradition.

specifics of those basic guidelines, however, need to be spelled out again and again in changing circumstances and as new matters come up in the community. So a body of precedents or cases is built that is based upon the directions laid out in the foundational law. With regard to the Commandments, the link between the basic guidelines and the body of precedents is most strongly indicated in Deuteronomy, where a number of interpreters have seen in the Deuteronomic Code of chapters 12–26 a structure that is based upon the Decalogue.[3]

While the analogy to the Constitution of the United States should not be carried too far, that analogy is nevertheless further suggested by the fact that neither the Constitution nor the Ten Commandments is strictly law. The former sets forth basic principles and rules in a broad sense. The Commandments do the same thing. The main terms for referring to them are not words that really have to do with legislation and community regulations in the usual sense and do not arise out of the activities of legislating or administering justice. The specific terms used for the Decalogue are, of course, "command/commandment" and also "word." In both cases we are told something about these entities that points primarily to their origin. They are the "words" of God, and they are imperative and commanding in nature. One receives them, therefore, not as a body of law that has been worked up to cover all sorts of situations and matters that may arise, but as direct address from God about the most basic things in life. They are, like the Constitution, the fundamental principles. They do not, however, simply sit out there like a body of law to which one can refer as one would to a manual or a textbook. They are connected. Their source is always in view. They are the word and command of God. Their direction is also always indicated: "*You* shall not . . . ." The continuing force and power of these commandments is not unrelated to these facts. They are not heard or read simply as a body of Canaanite or Israelite case law, precedents arising out of Palestinian tribal or urban judicial activity in the Late Bronze Age and Iron Age. They are properly, that is, by every intention of the text, identified as God's word addressed directly to the individual who hears or reads them. In the Commandments, therefore, we encounter law that is *personal*. It does not assume an unidentified amorphous body, either as the originators or the recipients, but a relationship between two parties – no, more accurately, between God and "you" – in which these words or commands make sense and construct or maintain the relationship. Neutrality, indifference, or objectivity are difficult responses to the Commandments. Because

---

[3] For example, Stephen A. Kaufman, "The Structure of the Deuteronomic Law," *MAARAV* 1 (April 1979), 105–158.

they have been addressed to "you," "you" must do something about them, that is, obey them.

Their dissimilarity from precedent law and other forms of legislation is reflected also in the general absence of sanctions and punishments, that is, indications of the consequences of failure to keep the Commandments. Although sanctions may be implied, the focus is not on the penalty. Where the consequences of obedience or disobedience are in view, as in the commandments prohibiting images and the misuse of the name, they are there in terms of relationships (loving and hating).

In addition to their being characterized as "commandment" and "word," the Commandments do belong to the body of material commonly called *torah*. That is the word most often translated as "law," but it, too, does not strictly mean that. It actually means "instruction," which is what the Commandments are, instruction for life, the teaching of God about what is necessary to do in order for the community to live according to God's way and in harmony with one another. That understanding of the commandments has implications for the way in which we receive them. To perceive the Commandments as instruction rather than law, or to comprehend the law as instruction that enhances and provides for life and harmony, is to view them quite positively. Teaching is meant to guide us and enable us in some fashion to be better, and better off than we would be without it, not to undo us. To the extent, therefore, that the Ten Commandments have become law or are to be understood under that rubric, it is law in this sense, as the instruction of God.

The foundational character of the Decalogue as the basic principles and norms shaping and undergirding the rest of the legal material of the Old Testament is seen also in the *order* or *structure* of the Decalogue. It is careful and comprehensive, clearly meant to bring together all that is important for Israel's life – religious, familial, social. It moves from the fundamental requirements of Israel's relation to God to the basic guidelines for life in community. Thus like the Great Commandment, the Decalogue deals with responsibility to God and neighbor and in the same order. Yet that distinction or division in the Decalogue must be understood in the context of the form and character of the Decalogue as *covenantal*, which is the biblical language for the definitive relationship of human existence, the binding together of God and human community on the basis of the prior redeeming grace of God and in the expectation of a human response that will order life as God wills it. That means that the two parts of the Decalogue have to be held together as the one word of God. That is, the relation to the neighbor is both a divine command and explicitly a matter of the relationship with God by being set as a part of the covenant with *God*, not simply a matter of what is good for the community. Keeping this teaching does bring harmony in the human community, but it is also essential for harmony with God. So the Decalogue begins at what is in fact the starting point of the law, the grounding of the relationship and the identification of the covenantal parties, especially the identification of the One who by delivering Israel from oppression claims its response.

The fundamental stipulation of that response and of the covenants is the exclusive worship of the Lord commanded in the first two commandments and carried further in the third and fourth. The Sabbath commandment, particularly in the Deuteronomic formulation, is the *bridge* from God to neighbor, in that it deals in some sense with relations to God and responsibilities in the human sphere, and also the *center* of the Decalogue. The Fifth Commandment is also transitional in that it moves into the human community by dealing first with the closest community, that is, family, and with persons who, like God, are authority figures. The remaining commandments also manifest an order, moving from the taking of life to the taking of spouse and the taking of property. From there the commandments move from act against the neighbor to word against the neighbor (false witness) that can accomplish the same kinds of harm as the preceding commandments seek to prevent and, finally, to internal attitudes (covetousness) that may – and do – come out in action, such as killing, adultery, stealing, and false witness.

As the Decalogue functions in the Old Testament as the basic guidelines for the life of Israel, three different but related developments may be said to characterize the way in which the Commandments are carried forward, explicated, and developed. There are indications that the Decalogue is in some ways capable of being *summarized*, so that the essential matter or matters are set forth in shorthand or succinct fashion. It is also, as we have already noticed, subject to *elaboration* and *specification* in the legal codes that appear elsewhere. Finally, one can discern a kind of *trajectory* for each commandment as it is carried forward, a trajectory that holds to the intention of the particular commandment but also creates a dynamic of new or broader meanings that are seen to grow out of its basic intent. This includes the elaboration in other laws but is not confined to that.

The Summarization of the Commandments

The clearest effort to *summarize* the Commandments is found in the Shema (Deut 6:4–5): Hear, O Israel, the Lord is our God, the Lord alone.[4] You

---

[4] This clause may also be read as: The Lord is one.

shall love the Lord your God with all your heart, and with all your soul, and with all your might. More specifically, the Shema is a summary of what Israel heard commanded of them in the Prologue and the First and Second Commandments, the exclusive and total commitment of one's whole being to the Lord alone, the one who had been seen to be their God powerfully in the Exodus from Egypt. The primacy of these parts of the Decalogue is indicated by the fact that they are embodied in the most enduring brief statement of Israel's covenantal obligation in the Old Testament and that they provide the main theme for the whole Book of Deuteronomy. These were the most important words that God gave the people, the touchstone for Israel's faith and life, one of the plumb lines by which the people were constantly being measured. Story after story in the Old Testament bears witness to the significance of the demand for Israel's exclusive and aniconic worship of the Lord. It is surely no accident that in Israel's memory the first act of covenantal disobedience on the part of the people was a violation of the primary commandments when they made and worshiped the golden calf (Exod 32). From Elijah's contest with the prophets of Baal through the extensive use of the image of harlotry in Hosea, Jeremiah, and Ezekiel to speak about the people's pursuit of other gods to Josiah's removal of the images and paraphernalia of the Canaanite and Assyrian gods from the temple, obedience to the First and Second Commandments was one of the fundamental tests of faith for the covenantal community, a test that seems often to have been failed.

Other summaries of the beginning of the Decalogue appear in Deuteronomy, for example, in 6:13 and 10:20, where the first three commandments are set forth in positive rather than negative form and in a context (vv. 12–15) that is filled with decalogical language.[5] The Prologue and the first two commandments appear together as a summary of the law also in Ps 81:8–10, a psalm that may have been a festival liturgy in which the people were admonished to obey the law as it was embodied in the opening address and injunctions of the Decalogue.

In some cases, one finds a summary or collection of other commandments, as in Lev 19:3–4, where the Fifth, Fourth, First, and Second Commandments are gathered together. Indeed, Lev 19 contains many of the commandments in some form or other. Its character as the chief statement of the requirement that Israel conform to the holiness of God brings the Commandments formally into the definition of what is meant by holiness as a way of characterizing the moral life. A similar perspective is discerned in the prophetic indictment of Ezek 22:1–12. The indictments of this chap-

---

[5] Cf. Deut 11:13–16; 13:4–6.

ter reflect some of the specification and extension talked about below, but all of them have some connection to the Decalogue, particularly as it is reflected in and spelled out in Lev 18–20; idolatry, dishonoring of parents, profaning the Sabbath, slander, adultery and the related sexual sins (see below), and theft by extortion.

Ps 81, which, like Ps 50, seems to be a liturgy for some sort of covenant renewal ceremony, castigates those who observe religious ritual and recite the Commandments with great ease but do not in fact keep them. In this case, the Decalogue is summarized or represented by reference to the Seventh, Eighth, and Ninth Commandments (Ps 50:18–20). The wicked are admonished for the casualness with which they treat adultery, theft, and slander. Such prophetic indictments on the basis of the Ten Commandments are found also in Hos 4:2, where the *absence* of the knowledge of God in the land is manifest in the *presence* of (false) swearing, lying (see below on this as an extension of the Ninth Commandment), murder, stealing, and committing adultery, and in Jer 7:9: "Will you steal, murder, commit adultery, swear falsely, burn incense to Baal, and go after other gods that you have not known?" The Ten Commandments therefore, could be called upon and set before the people for various reasons or purposes by citing the primary commandment as spelled out in the Prologue and the first two commandments or by referring to a group of any three to five commandments. When the latter is done, we may assume that the commandments referred to are at issue but not necessarily those alone.

The Elaboration and Specification of the Commandments

Elaboration and specification of the force of the Commandments in particular laws, whether apodictic or casuistic, takes place rather extensively. For example, the First and Second Commandments are reiterated in Exod 20:23; 23:24; 34:14, 17 and given specificity in the prohibition of sacrifice to another god (Exod 22:20). Other examples are the exclusion of any mentioning of the names of other gods (Exod 23:13); the requirement of execution of a false prophet, or a member of the family, or a base fellow who leads the people to go after other gods (Deut 13); the prohibition of divination (Lev 19:26; 20:6, 27, 31; Deut 18:10) and the burning of children (Lev 20:1–5; Deut 12:31; 18:10); the command to destroy all the cultic paraphernalia of the other gods (Deut 12:1–4); and the command to worship and sacrifice to God only at the divinely chosen place (Deut 12).

The force of the Third Commandment is clarified by those injunctions to swear only by God's name (Deut 6:13; 10:20) and not to do so falsely (Lev 19:12; cf. 6:5). Any misuse or empty use of God's name is prohibited, and that is particularly likely to take place when that name is invoked in oaths to validate what is said. When that is done for evil purposes, that is, when the oath taker makes false statements and then claims they may be accepted because their truthfulness and integrity are a matter of relationship to God, then the Lord's name has been used vainly.

Specific laws governing the use of the Sabbath appear in Exod 23:12; 31:12–17; Lev 19:3; 23:3; and 26:2. In Exod 34:21 the prohibition of work on the Sabbath is spelled out in terms of plowing and harvesting, and in Exod 35:1–3 specific reference is made to kindling fires. Such activities were obviously seen as ones that people were likely to continue to do on the Sabbath and thus needed specific prohibition. The narratives of Exod 1:22–30 (harvesting) and Num 15:32–36 (gathering of sticks for a fire) indicate that lapse in these areas did in fact happen.

The commandment requiring the honoring of parents is spelled out in those laws that prohibit striking or cursing father or mother (Exod 21:15, 17; Lev 20:9; Deut 21:18–21; 27:16). The Sixth Commandment against killing is dealt with specifically a number of times (Exod 21:12; Lev 24:17, 21). In Num 35:30–34 and Deut 19:11–13, the commandment is modified to allow for some protection in cities of refuge for those who did not kill treacherously or with malice aforethought. Prohibitions against adultery appear in Lev 18:20; 20:10 and Deut 22:22. A body of legislation is created also that seeks to deal with some of the different situations that might come up relative to adultery, such as intercourse between a man and a betrothed virgin or one who is not betrothed (Deut 22:23–29) as well as a fairly extended presentation of what one is to do with a wife "under her husband's authority" who is suspected of adultery (Num 5:11–31).

Specifying and spelling out of the commandment against stealing is done in Exod 22:1–12, where various possibilities are envisioned and addressed, for example, the penalties if an ox is stolen and found dead or alive, or if a thief is killed during a burglary, or when an ox grazes in another's field or someone's fire consumes another's goods. This section is one of the clearest cases of the need to spell out the casuistry of the basic guidelines, that is, the great variety of possible things that could happen that would come under the general guideline of the commandment. The Ninth Commandment against false witness has its most detailed spelling out in Exod 23:1–3, 6–9 and Deut 19:16–19. It is clear from the specification that the particular concern of the community as it followed this command was to guard against false witness in the court with its obvious outcome of judicial murder.

The elaboration in specific instances of the force of each of the Commandments does, however, contribute to the opening up of each of them, to the creation of a kind of *trajectory* for each one, so that as they continue to function as direction for the conduct of individuals in the community, the possibilities or implications of the Commandments begin to broaden. To some extent that has already happened in the process of the formation of the Decalogue itself. The commandment prohibiting images may have originally enjoined against representations of Yahweh, but it clearly came to prohibit images of any deity. Because of its formulation, that is, because it prohibited making "a graven image, or any likeness of anything" (Exod 20:4), it eventually came to be understood by some as a general restriction upon artistic representations of human beings and to some degree of animals.

One of the obvious cases of a trajectory that opens out of the basic commandment is in regard to the Sabbath commandment. The extension of this commandment into a kind of "sabbatical principle" providing for relief and humane treatment in various aspects of community life can be seen in Deut 15 and elsewhere. The association of a sabbatical release with the provision of the weekly Sabbath is made explicit in the Book of the Covenant, where the law of the Sabbath is preceded by the law calling for a sabbatical fallow year (Exod 23:10–14). It is also made explicit in the Holiness Code, where the seventh year of release is called "Sabbath" and "the Sabbath of the land" (Lev 25:2–7) and is followed immediately by provision for the jubilee year, which is first described as "seven sabbaths of years" (Lev 25:8).

The "release" first appears in Exod 23:10–11, where the land is "released" and lies fallow in the seventh year, presumably for the sake of the land but expressly for the sake of the poor and the wild beasts who are allowed access to what grows of its own.[6] The Deuteronomic sabbatical release is seen as analogous to the Sabbath rest. As one "does the sabbath day" (Deut 5:15, RSV: "keep the sabbath day"), so one "does a release" (Deut 15:1, RSV: "grant a release"). As the Fourth Commandment calls for "a sabbath to the Lord" on the seventh day (Deut 5:14), so Deut 15:2 calls for "a release to the Lord" every seven years. The force of the sabbath rest is now carried forward from the agricultural sphere of Exod 23 into the economic sphere to say that the burden of debt can be stopped (Deut 15:1–6) and even that bond slaves gain release and freedom (15:12–18). The latter provision is specifically grounded in the same motivation or aim as the Sabbath commandment: "You shall remember that you were a slave in the land of Egypt" (15:15). Jer 34:13–15 recounts a prophetic condemnation of

---

[6] Cf. Lev 25:2–7, where, like the Sabbath, the sabbath of the land is a provision – in this case food rather than rest – "for you, for yourself and for your male and female slaves and for your hired servant and the sojourner who lives with you; for your cattle also and for the beasts that are in your land . . .."

king and people for failure to carry out the law of release and then for pro-
claiming a release that was immediately followed by taking back into
bondedness those who had been released.

The Sabbath trajectory continues on in the jubilee year (Lev 25) as provision is made for the return of land to those to whom it was originally
granted. The complex of laws centering around the jubilee year in Lev 25
is very explicit that the intent of the requirement is to provide for the weak
and the poor and those who have had to go into indenture to regain the
possibility of a sufficient livelihood and access to the goods of the land.
The sabbatical principle prohibits a permanent slavery or an enduring poverty. It resists the acquisitive instinct that would keep others from having
the opportunity to live good and satisfying lives in God's creation.

The direction set by the Sabbath commandment continues on in the
word of Jesus, both in his recognition that the Sabbath was made for human beings, not human beings for the Sabbath, and in his reading from Isa
58 and 61 in the synagogue at Nazareth (Luke 4:16–20). The central and
definitive term combining those two texts is the word "release" or "liberty," which combines the various kinds of release of which the Old Testament law and prophets have spoken with Jesus' release of people from
their sins, that is, forgiveness.[7]

The Fifth Commandment, as it enjoins an attitude toward parents that
parallels one's attitude toward God (honor, fear, reverence), demonstrates
the appropriateness of the ordering of this commandment at the point of
transition from those instructions that have to do with relationships to God
and those that have to do with relationship to other members of the community. It also suggests why there is a long tradition in both Jewish and
Christian understanding of this commandment that has seen it instructing
not only in the proper attitude to actual fathers and mothers but in the right
approach to *authorities in general.* Martin Luther, in his *Larger Catechism,*
states explicitly: "Out of the authority of parents all other authority is derived and developed."

Such an understanding of the wider force of the commandment is
largely an inference, but it receives some indirect confirmation from the
biblical text in that to the extent that the Deuteronomic code of chapters
12–26 is structured to some extent according to the Ten Commandments,
the laws that have to do with the leaders of the community (judge, prophet,
king, and priest) appear in Deut 16:18–18:22. This material closely follows
the laws having to do with release in chapter 15 and the festivals in chapter

---

[7] For a more extended discussion of the sabbatical principle growing out of the Sabbath
commandment, see P. D. Miller, "The Human Sabbath: A Study in Deuteronomic Theology,"
The Princeton Seminary Bulletin 6 (1985), 81–97.

16, laws that clearly are related to the Sabbath.[8] This association of laws identifying the leaders of the community and their responsibilities or qualifications with the commandment calling for the honoring of parents suggests that filial responsibility to respect father and mother is in some sense the starting point of the human experience with persons who exercise a proper authority over others by reason of relationship, wisdom, and experience.

The commandment against killing, the extension of which into the morality of various forms of taking life has been a matter of long discussion and debate, does immediately begin to broaden out. The verb that is used in the commandment, *rṣḥ*, can refer not only to high-handed killing or murder, including judicial homicide as in the case of Ahab's execution of Naboth (1 Kgs 21),[9] but also to unintentional homicide or simply accidental killing, as one sees in Num 35:25–28, where the word "manslayer" translates *rṣḥ* (cf. Deut 4:41–42; Josh 20:3).[10] The clearly broader force of the commandment in prohibiting other forms of killing opens up its instructive impact to ask about other ways in which persons are harmed, indeed killed, and how these relate to this commandment of God. This openness is seen explicitly in Jesus' extension of the prohibitions against killing to guard against anger and insults with its positive corollary in active movement toward reconciliation (Matt 5:21–26). Thus manifestations of anger and hatred at a less extreme level than murder are seen to flow out of the Sixth Commandment to represent an intensification of its force. This is not foreign to the Old Testament, which also has injunctions against hating a brother or neighbor that may be seen as extensions of the Sixth Commandment (Lev 19:1–18).

There is a broadening of the impact of the commandment against adultery, particularly in priestly legislation (e.g., Lev 20:10–21) through laws prohibiting all unnatural sexual unions and especially sexual relations with any near relative, whether within marriage or not. Here there is a clear intent to guard and affirm the sexual relations of a man and woman in the

---

[8] See Kaufman, "The Structure of the Deuteronomic Law," 133–134. Kaufman notes that the motivation clause in the Fifth Commandment, "that you may live long," appears also as a motivation in two forms in Deut 16:20 and 17:20.

[9] Note that the Lord tells Elijah to say to Ahab: "Have you killed (*rṣḥ*), and will you also take possession" (1 Kgs 21:19).

[10] Kaufman, "The Structure of the Deuteronomic Law," sees in Deut 19:1–22:8 the various laws that specify what the Sixth Commandment has to do with. The specific topics covered all have to do with *rṣḥ*, the taking of a life: homicide (19:1–13; 21:1–9), those institutions – war (Deut 20) and criminal justice (19:15–20; 21:18–21; 21:22–23) – that constitute the only legitimate procedures for taking a human life, and the prevention of unnecessary loss of life through intentional oversight (22:1–4) and neglect (22:8).

marriage relation against its violation by sexual activity unrelated to the marriage commitment and covenant. Again there is a further explicit move in Jesus' teaching, extending the trajectory of the commandment toward a more radical and internal understanding of it, one that may be difficult to obey but one that at least shows the seriousness and sanctity of the marriage relationship that is intended in the Seventh Commandment: "You have heard that it was said, 'You shall not commit adultery.' But I say to you that every one who looks at a woman lustfully has committed adultery with her in his head" (Matt 5:27–28). Not only the act but the thought breaches the marriage vow.

The commandment against theft, like the commandment against images, reveals a broadening of its application within the very process of its formulation. At its earliest stages, it may have been a guard against enslavement, that is, the theft that was prohibited under absolute sanction was the stealing of persons, kidnapping. In Exod 21:16 and Deut 24:7 laws are found referring to stealing a person for slavery or for selling; and the punishment is death, the type of punishment appropriate to the laws of the Decalogue. The form of the commandment now, however, has no object (whether or not it ever did), and the verb "steal" is used with things or property as its object as much as persons. So the prohibition is more inclusive in its directions, prohibiting property theft as well as theft of human beings.

In Israel, however, such protection of property was not intended as a means of developing and accumulating masses of wealth and squeezing out others from a place at the table of resources in the land. Property was provided for each in the allotment of land. Even kings could not legally take that away, as clearly indicated by the story of Ahab's theft of Naboth's vineyard in 1 Kgs 21 and Nathan's recounting to David of the story of the rich man's taking the single lamb of a poor man to avoid using his own (2 Sam 12:1–6). Laws allowing gleaning of leftovers by the poor as well as those prohibiting usury and extortion and requiring the return of garments taken in pledge all were aimed at protecting property while resisting the exploitative and accumulative possibilities that can arise out of a system that permits private property, possibilities that themselves can turn into forms of stealing.

The dangers against which the Ninth Commandment stands as a shield are well illustrated in the Old Testament. The lament or complaint psalms are often petitions to God for help against persons who have endangered the petitioner by false accusations (e.g., Pss 4:2; 5:6, 9–10; 7:12–16; 10:7–9; 27:12). The story of the trial of Naboth in 1 Kgs 21 is a vivid example of the violent possibilities when the court is perverted by lying witnesses. Ahab and Jezebel are able to have Naboth judicially murdered and his coveted vineyard confiscated simply by having two hoodlums falsely accuse him in court of having cursed God and the king.

The question naturally arises: Do we hear in this commandment a more general injunction against lying and in behalf of truth-telling? The Old Testament does indeed expand the force of this commandment by connecting the witness in the court with more general practices of lying, particularly slander. That is probably seen in the false report of Exod 32:1a and clearly in Lev 19:11 and 16. Lev 19:11 shows why this commandment is placed between those having to do with stealing and coveting. Both lying and coveting are forms or aspects of stealing or getting at what belongs to one's neighbor, whether it be life, property, or reputation. Hos 4:2 also suggests this broader understanding, as does Prov 30:3–10. Negative judgments against the false witness are set alongside positive statements about the truthful witness in Prov 14:5 and 25, and Ps 15:2–3 sets among the criteria for temple entrance speaking truthfully and not slandering with the tongue.

The commandment against coveting is by its very character the vehicle that opens up the Commandments as a whole to a broader understanding. It is a guard against an internal, private attitude or feeling that tends to erupt into public and violent acts against one's neighbor. The Bible is full of examples of such feeling and behavior, notably David's lust for Bathsheba that leads to adultery and murder and Ahab's desire for Naboth's vineyard to make for himself a better vegetable garden. Amnon's rape of Tamar and Shechem's rape of Dinah are acts that arose from ardent desire.

As it moves into the sphere of attitudes and inner desires and their capacity to lead to harmful acts, the commandment sets the mind and heart as subjects for moral direction and ethical reflection. Not simply what one does but what one thinks and feels may have – and often does have – moral effects. It is certainly the case that character and virtue are affected by the workings of the mind/heart. Disposition as well as action is important. Yet even as character and virtue are hardly explicable at any length apart from life and acts in community, that is, in relationship to others, so the disposition of the heart is a neighbor issue also. At this point, the commandment against coveting creates a bridge, or inaugurates a trajectory leading directly to Jesus' internalization of the commandments in the Sermon on the Mount (Matt 5:21–30). The observation that anger and lust are feelings that cannot be controlled in the way in which murder and adultery can be is to an extent true, but that is inadequate as a sole response to Jesus' injunctions against those emotions as well as the acts of killing and adultery, which the Ten Commandments prohibit. Already in the commandment against coveting, the connection between internal feelings and external acts, between private attitudes and public deeds, is explicitly recognized.

The point is clear. The inner attitudes and feelings potentially also have to do with the well-being and security of one's neighbor, and they are subject to a degree of control for the good of the community. Jesus' teaching, therefore, like that of the rabbis and philosophers, is an extension of the instruction clearly set forth in the last commandment and illustrated negatively so often in the Scriptures and human life.

2. The Sufficiency and Insufficiency of the Commandments[1]

The centrality of the Decalogue for the moral life of those within the Christian community – and indeed beyond – is a claim that is easily documented in the history of the church. In some traditions, the Commandments have encapsulated the wholeness of the sanctified life that is lived in obedience to God and in proper relationship with other persons. Will such a claim about the role of the Commandments stand up? Are they a sufficient guide for the Christian life or not? To explore those questions, I want to do three things in this essay. First, and most important, my aim is to identify clues *within scripture itself* that the Commandments are an *adequate* definition of what is needed for life, adequate in the sense of being *fundamental, comprehensive,* and *sufficient.* In the Preface to his Larger Catechism, Martin Luther says "anyone who knows the Ten Commandments perfectly knows the entire Scriptures." I think he was serious about that and believe there are reasons why his comment should not be passed over as simply or largely hyperbole. Second, I want to point to some indicators that I see, or that others have noted, suggesting the Commandments are in themselves *not* an adequate and sufficient ground and definition of the life of the Christian community in relation to God and to others, that they leave out some things or approach matters in a particular direction while neglecting other things. Then, finally, I want to offer some *response* to those counter-indicators to reassert the adequacy and the significance of the commandments, if now in a more qualified way.

---

[1] Earlier forms of this essay were presented as public lectures at Austin Presbyterian Theological Seminary (Currie Lectures), San Francisco Theological Seminary (Moore), Columbia Theological Seminary (Smyth), United Theological Seminary of the Twin Cities (Gustafson), Southern Methodist University (Tate-Willson), Anderson School of Theology (Newell), Central Baptist Theological Seminary (Spring), Union Theological Seminary-PSCE (Sprunt), and Louisville Presbyterian Theological Seminary (Caldwell).

The Sufficiency of the Commandments

The primary impetus for giving preeminent place to the Ten Commandments and for seeing encapsulated in them the fullness of divine teaching
about the way to live comes *from within scripture* itself, as suggested both
by the *presentation* of the Commandments *in their contexts* and *by intertextual connections and resonances between the Commandments and the
rest of scripture.*

I want to focus attention primarily on the *contextual* clues, that is, on
the way in which the literary context of the Commandments, as they are
presented in Exodus and Deuteronomy, lifts them up and underscores their
significance and comprehensiveness. That is done in part by their presentation as the *first* words of the Lord to the people of Israel and as the explicit
content of the covenant. While there is already a covenantal history with
Abraham and his descendants – and there are indications of divine commands that function as basic directives – the narrative of Exodus makes it
clear that the formation of a people to be the people of the Lord and to live
in covenantal relationship with God begins with the encounter at Sinai and
God's first words. Those words are the Commandments. Israel's vocation
as a holy nation and a priestly kingdom is grounded in, effected by, and
given its content in the Commandments: "If you obey my voice and keep
my covenant, you shall be my treasured possession" (Exod 19:5). Deuteronomy explicitly identifies the Ten Commandments as the covenant that
the people are to keep, as in 4:13–14:

"*He [the Lord] declared* to you his *covenant*, which he charged you to
observe, that is, the ten commandments [literally "ten words"]; and he
wrote them on two stone tablets. And the Lord charged *me* (i.e., Moses) at
that time to *teach* you statutes and ordinances for you to observe in the
land that you are about to cross into and occupy." In Deuteronomy, "the
sole content of the covenant law at Horeb" is found in the Commandments.[2] In Deut 9, the tablets are called "the tablets of the covenant," a
term that is then taken over in Exod 34:28–29: "He wrote on the tablets the
words of the covenant, the ten words....as he came down from the mountain with the two tablets of the covenant in his hand" (cf. Exod 25:16, 21;
31:18).[3] There are thus *two* designations of the Commandments, one focus-

---

[2] Ernest W. Nicholson, "The Decalogue as the Direct Address of God," *VT* 27 (1977),
422.

[3] For the likelihood that this terminology in Exod 34 represents a Deuteronomic redaction,
see the discussion in Brevard Childs, *The Book of Exodus* (The Old Testament Library; Philadelphia: Westminster, 1974), 614–617. In Exod 25:16, 21; 31:18; and 34:29, the term for
covenant is *ʿēdût*, rather than the customary Deuteronomic *běrît*. See with regard to the

ing upon them as the direct *words* of the Lord and the other focusing upon them as the content of the *covenant*. While both ways of labeling the Commandments may have their origin in Deuteronomy, they are now carried over into Exodus as well.[4] The Mosaic injunction in Exod 19:5 to "keep his covenant" and "listen to his voice" further suggests these two understandings of the Commandments, as the words of the deity and as the content of the covenant.[5]

The explicit identification of the Commandments as the direct revelation of God to the people in distinction from other teaching and instruction is indicated in various other ways as well:

- Deut 5:4 reinforces the point by saying that the Lord spoke "*face to face*" with the people at the mountain. This is probably an intentional correction of the reference in verse 5, which is an anticipation of Moses' role and probably alludes to Exod 19:3–25. In both cases, there is some ambiguity about Moses' intermediation, an ambiguity that the final form of the text has sought to override. That is, Deut 5 creates a narrative report that is unambiguous and the present location of the Decalogue in Exod 20 conforms to that separation of the Commandments as the direct speech from the later reception of further divine instruction only through Moses. Elsewhere the Lord speaks "face to face" with Moses (Exod 33:11; Num 12:8; Deut 34:10; Sirach 45:5).
- The description of the Commandments as *written* by the Lord (Deut 4:13; 5:22; 9:10; 10:2, 4; cf. 34:1, 17) is underscored then with reference to the *finger* of God as doing the writing (Exod 31:18; Deut 9:10).
- A distinction is made between the Commandments that are on *stone* (Exod 24:12; 31:18; 34:1, 4; Deut 4:13; 5:22; 9:9–11; 10:1, 3) and kept *in* the Ark of the Covenant (Exod 25:16, 21; Deut 10:2, 5) and the law that is written down by Moses on a *scroll* (*sēper*) and placed *beside* the Ark (Deut 31:9, 24–26).[6]
- Deut 5:3 suggests the way that the direct words of the Lord in the Commandments open up their continuing force by regarding the pre-

---

Priestly use of *ʿēdût* in this context, Norbert Lohfink, "Kennt das Alte Testament einen Unterschied von 'Gebot' und 'Gesetz'? Zur bibeltheologischen Einstufung des Dekalogs," *JBTh* 4 (1989), 82–84 (= idem, *Studien zur biblische Theologie* [SBAB 16; Stuttgart: Kath. Bibelwerk, 1993]).

[4] Note the designation of the Commandments as "these words" in Exod 20:1.

[5] Here again there may be Deuteronomic influence on the Exodus formulation.

[6] See Lohfink, "Kennt das Alte Testament einen Unterschied von 'Gebot' und 'Gesetz'? Zur bibeltheologischen Einstufung des Dekalogs," 63). It should be noted that the term *torah* in Deut 31 probably has in mind the whole of the Deuteronomic polity, including the Commandments, so the differentiation is more mixed in this instance. But the Commandments alone are placed in the Ark, not the whole of the torah.

sent listeners as the ones to whom the Commandments are addressed. The emphatic form of the sentence "...with us, we, these ones, here, today, all of us, living" stresses in an extraordinary way the claim that the words are directed to the present generation, to "us," to those who are living right now, to whoever is present in reading and hearing these words. This is the strongest example of Deuteronomy's contemporizing of the divine teaching. Here with the Commandments, the word is given that they are always addressed to those living, present, and here.[7]

What is also indicated by these and other texts is that the Commandments are not only God's first and primary words, they are virtually God's *only* words direct and unmediated to the whole community, a point Thomas Aquinas underscores in the Summa, along with many other interpreters, as a significant distinction between the Decalogue and the rest of the laws. The point is implicit in that the Lord does not speak again to the people,[8] but it is made explicit by the Deuteronomist: "These words the Lord spoke with a loud voice to your whole assembly...and *he added no more*" (Deut 5:22), the Hebrew syntax emphasizing the point. The presentation of the Commandments in Deuteronomy gives an extended narrative rationale for that being the case as it tells in chapter 5 of the people's fear – after receiving the ten words – of not surviving any further direct encounter with the Lord and so they ask Moses henceforth to mediate the word to them, to listen to the Lord and then "you tell us everything that the Lord our God tells you" (Deut 5:27). In the Sinai pericope of Exodus, the redaction of the text has followed this line of thought also by inserting the Commandments roughly between chapter 19 and the words of 20:18–20 where the people in fear of the theophanic thunder, lightning, and smoke say to Moses, "You

---

[7] Lohfink refers to this move as "a cultic identification of the generations." It is indeed that, but it moves beyond the cultic as the assertion becomes a part of the narrative and the book and is received in various ways that are not simply cultic (N. Lohfink, "Reading Deuteronomy 5 as Narrative," in *A God So Near: Essays on Old Testament Theology in Honor of Patrick D. Miller* [eds. B. A. Strawn and N. R. Bowen; [Winona Lake, IN; Eisenbrauns, 2003], 266).

[8] There is a prior possible address directly to the people, and that is at the very beginning of Deuteronomy, the initial address to the people: "The Lord our God spoke to us at Horeb, saying, 'You [plural] have stayed long enough...'" (1:6; cf. v. 19). In the rest of this speech, one may assume that the Lord's words are to Moses and through Moses to the people. Verses 34–40 are ambiguous. The speech starts out to Moses, but the last part speaks to the people as "you." In 2:3, the text is explicit: "The Lord said to me..." but then it follows with plural "you," and it stays that way through verse 7. From chapter 2 on, it is clear that the speech to the people is through Moses. Only 1:6 is ambiguous, and it may well be understood as speech through Moses to the people. For the possible narrative connections between 1:6 and 5:1–4, see Lohfink, "Reading Deuteronomy 5 as Narrative," 265–268.

speak to us, and we will listen, but do not let God speak to us, or we will die."[9] Thus *explicit texts*, such as Deut 4:13-14, which I quoted a moment ago, distinguishing between the *Commandments directly declared* and the *statutes and ordinances* communicated by God *through Moses' teaching*, join with the shape or movement of *the narrative* to present the Commandments: a) *first* of all the law, the divine instruction; b) as *the only direct words* of God to the people;[10] and c) to *separate* them from all the laws that follow – and there is a lot more to follow.[11] This move "established a sharp distinction between the Decalogue and the Book of the Covenant which appears again in 24:3,12."[12] Exod 24:3 states: "Moses came and told the people 'all the words of the Lord' (*kol dibrē yhwh)* and 'all the ordinances' (*kol hammišpāṭîm*)." The distinction is made between the "words" (Exod 20) and the "ordinances" (Exod 21–23). Further, in Deuteronomy, where the emphasis is placed on the rest of the divine instruction as teaching by Moses, "[w]ith the exception of the 'ten words,' ... Moses does not formulate the legal legacy he received at Horeb by quoting God (no stipulation is prefaced with 'YHWH said: . . .')."[13]

The marking off of the Commandments is thus both literary and redactional. While this lifting up of the Commandments is smoothly a part of the narrative as in Deut 5:22ff. and Exod 24:3, elsewhere one can see the rough redactional moves and the tensions in the text created in order to bring off the necessary result of a special weight and distinction for the Commandments. The announcement of the Commandments directly by Yahweh to the people runs counter to the expectation created by chapter 19 that Moses would be mediator. Even the terminology follows these leads as the Commandments in Deuteronomy are not called commandments but "words," "Ten Words." The more legal rubrics, such as statutes, ordinances, and even commandments, generally are reserved for the laws in the other collections that follow the Decalogue.[14] In several strong ways,

---

[9] For more detailed analysis of the development of the text at this point, see, e.g., Childs, *The Book of Exodus*, 351–360.

[10] For other discussions of the Commandments as the direct speech of God, see Nicholson, "The Decalogue as the Direct Address of God."

[11] Exod 33–34 in its earlier stages did not reflect the distinction being described here. There has been redactional work to cement the distinction, probably Deuteronomic.

[12] Childs, *Exodus*, 350–351.

[13] Jean Sonnet, *The Book within the Book: Writing in Deuteronomy* (Biblical Interpretation Series 141; Leiden: Brill, 1997), 47.

[14] There is some exception to this point. The Commandments may be referred to in 4:44; 6:17, 20 as ʿēdôt. For discussion of the possible uses of the term *miṣwôt* ("commandments") with reference specifically to the Decalogue, see Georg Braulik, "Die Ausdrücke für 'Gesetz' im Buch Deuteronomium," *Biblica* 51 (1970), 56–57; repr. in *Studien zur Theologie* [SBAB 2; Stuttgart: Katholisches Bibelwerk, 1988], 28–29; and Norbert Lohfink, "Prolegomena zu

therefore, the Ten Commandments are placed in a separate category as the primary summary of the requirements for life in the covenant.

Insufficient attention has been given to the fact that, to the best of my knowledge, these are the *only* words that the Lord speaks to the whole community in *all* of the Old Testament. Never again does God speak directly to the whole community. All other words are spoken to individuals or mediated to the people through prophetic and priestly figures. The *whole of scripture* serves, therefore, to lift up these words to a special place, separating them off from all other divine instruction. There is a sense in which the Bible tells its readers: "These are the most important words; Moses will fill you in on all the rest of my instruction."

The point being made by the immediate context and the whole of scripture is then reinforced and carried further by the fact that this body of divine instruction, the commandments, *is the only body of divine instruction in the Old Testament that is repeated*. When at the beginning of Deuteronomy, Moses recapitulates the story of Israel's deliverance from slavery and wandering through the wilderness, he restates the Commandments to the people, reminding them – now not at the mountain in the wilderness but at the boundary of the promised land – that these words are the basic charter for their life together in the place the Lord is giving them.

The *narrative location* of the two presentations of the Commandments thus serves to give them gravity and centrality. The initial giving of the Decalogue is at the mountain of God, the moment when the people appear before the God who has liberated them from Egyptian slavery. The worship of the Lord at Sinai has been identified from the beginning of the Exodus story as the penultimate destination of the people (Exod 3:12). The recall of the Commandments is on the boundary of the promised land, the ultimate destination of the people (Exod 3:8).[15]

As the Commandments are presented *first*, *repeated*, *strategically located*, and singled out by *separating* them off from other instruction and making them alone the direct words of the Lord to the people while also *following* them in each case with an extended body of particular statutes

---

einer Rechtshermeneutik des Pentateuch," in *Das Deuteronomium* (Österreichische Biblische Studien 23; Frankfurt: Peter Lang, 2003), 26, n. 58.

[15] Note the comment of Sonnet: "[T]he efficiency of Deuteronomy's plot derives to a great extent from the distance created between God's and Moses' respective writings. The former belongs to the foundational revelation event at Horeb; the latter is reported as late as possible, well beyond its point of occurrence in the chronological sequence." Sonnet notes that in recording God's "words" in the "book" of the covenant in Exodus, "Moses intervened as a writing character before any mention of God's own writing. Not so in Moses' retelling in Deuteronomy: Moses establishes God's absolute primacy in the recording process and passes over his own scribal activity in silence" (*The Book within the Book*, 48).

and ordinances – the Book of the Covenant (Exod 21–23) and the Deuteronomic Code (chaps. 12–26) – a clear distinction is made between the commandments and all the rest of the laws. That marked distinction raises the question, then, of the *relation* of the *Commandments* to the *rest* of the laws, to the statutes and ordinances.

Elsewhere, I have suggested the function of the Decalogue may be understood to some degree as analogous to the function of the American constitution.[16] The Commandments serve as a kind of constitution for this covenanted community, and they stand in relation to all further direction for life, more specific and contextual, that is, the Mosaic teaching, roughly as the constitution stands in relation to the later history of legal and judicial issues and cases that have come up in the history of this nation. Unlike the two forms of the Decalogue, the Book of the Covenant that follows the Commandments in Exod 20:22–23:33 and the Deuteronomic Code in Deut 12–26, are very different from each other, although they share a lot of common subject matter. They represent *cases* that have come up that serve to spell out the way in which the Commandments are to work in the life of the community. They *specify* and *illustrate* the force of the Commandments. They are clearly time and case bound, differing at times in their presuppositions from each other, Deuteronomy representing a body of statutes that seems to reflect a later more moneyed economy and a developing legal tradition than the Book of the Covenant, both of them serving to give, in effect, specific interpretations of the meaning and implications of the Commandments in specific circumstances.[17]

An important tension thus arises between the Commandments and the statutes and ordinances. On the one hand, the statutes and ordinances are time and place specific and do not operate in the permanent constitutional way that the Ten Words do. On the other hand, they are to be connected to the Commandments so that disobedience of one of these statutes is to be

---

[16] See above, 3–16.

[17] There is considerable discussion of the way in which dependence runs between the Book of the Covenant and the Deuteronomic Code. A number of scholars have argued for the Deuteronomic Code as a revision of or dependent upon the Book of the Covenant and so later. See in this regard Gerhard von Rad, *Deuteronomy* (The Old Testament Library; Philadelphia: Westminster, 1966), 12–15; Eberhard Otto, "The Pre-exilic Deuteronomy as a Revision of the Covenant Code," in idem, *Kontinuum und Proprium: Studien zur Sozial-und Rechtsgeschichte des Alten Orients und des Alten Testaments* (OBC 8; Wiesbaden: Harrassowitz, 1996), 112–122 (and the bibliography included there); Bernard Levinson, *Deuteronomy and the Hermeneutics of Legal Innovation* (Oxford: Oxford University Press, 1997), especially 3–13 and the bibliography cited there. For a recent and vigorous counter argument, see John Van Seters, *A Law Book for the Diaspora: Revision in the Study of the Covenant Code* (Oxford: Oxford University Press, 2003), especially chapter 1 on the history of research on the Covenant Code (or Book of the Covenant).

seen in some sense as disobedience of what the Commandments are after. One is both freed from and tied to the statutes and ordinances.

So while the Commandments are *separated* from the statutes and ordinances, they are also *related* to them, and one cannot comprehend how the Commandments are sufficient without perceiving that relationship. Two particular expressions of the relationship may be discerned in the text. One is the way in which, as Deut 4:13–14 indicates, the "statutes and ordinances" are specifically given to be done "in the land that you are about to cross into and occupy," while no such restriction is given for the commandments. They are lasting and unchanging.[18] The statutes and ordinances are for a particular time and place, a spelling out of the specifics of the perduring Ten Words in that circumstance. And those specifics will vary from one time and place to another, as the significant variations between the Book of the Covenant and the Deuteronomic Code implicitly suggest. Further, the presence of two bodies of explication, specification, and illustration of the force of the Commandments, coming from different times and circumstances and providing differing formulations indicates that the community that lives by the basic stipulations of the Decalogue will have to continue to work out the specifics in new times and places.[19]

The formal and material connection between the Ten Commandments and the other laws is indicated in Deuteronomy in yet another way, that is, *structurally*. The statutes and ordinances of the Deuteronomic Code are brought together in "a highly structured composition whose major topical units are arranged *according to the order of the laws of the Decalogue*...an expanded Decalogue," so that the first group of chapters in the Code, specifically 12–14 have to do with the worship of God, the subject of the First Commandment, chapter 15 has to do with the sabbatical principle set forth first in the Sabbath Commandment, and so on.[20]

---

[18] "Denn der Dekalog verpflichtet immer und überall, die Gesetze dagegen gelten nur in Israels eigenem Land (4,5; 12,1)" (G. Braulik, *Die deuteronomischen Gesetze und der Dekalog: Studien zum Aufbau von Deuteronomium 12–26* [SBS 145; Stuttgart: Katholisches Bibelwerk, 1991], 11). Cf. N. Lohfink, "Die *ḥuqqîm wĕmišpāṭîm* im Buch Deuteronomium und ihre Neubegrenzung durch Dtn 12,1," in idem, *Studien zum Deuteronomium und zur deuteronomistischen Literatur II* (SBAB 12; Stuttgart: Katholisches Bibelwerk, 1991), 229–256; idem, "Dtn 12,1 und Gen 15,18: Das dem Samen Abrahams geschenkte Land als Geltungsbereich der deuteronomischen Gesetze," in *Die Väter Israels: Beiträge zur Theologie der Patriarchenüberlieferungen im Alten Testament* [FS Josef Scharbert], ed. Manfred Görg (Stuttgart: Katholisches Bibelwerk, 1989), 183–210; idem, "Kennt das Alte Testament einen Unterschied von 'Gebot' und 'Gesetz'?

[19] Cf. Lohfink, "Kennt das Alte Testament einen Unterschied von 'Gebot' und 'Gesetz'? 87.

[20] Stephen Kaufman, "The Structure of the Deuteronomic Law," MAARAV 1,2 (1978–79), 105–158. For further analyses of ways that the Deuteronomic Code may be seen as

But this way of understanding the relation between the Commandments and the other laws, the statutes and ordinances, has much earlier antecedents, in the Jewish tradition, for example, reaching back to Philo of Alexandria, who argued that the "Decalogue encompasses the whole of the Torah, for all of the [laws] simply elaborate in detail what the Ten Commandments say in compressed form."[21] And the rabbinic midrash to Deut 32:10 – "He cared for him" or "He watched over him"– says that this was "through the Ten Commandments," which "shows that when the pronouncement came forth from the mouth of the Holy One, blessed be He, Israel perceived it, acquired wisdom through it, and knew what interpretations were contained in it, what rules were contained in it, what inferences from the minor to the major were contained in it, what analogies were in it." (Piska 313). Michael Fishbane, comments with regard to this interpretation:

As a fixed and final formulation, the tablets [that is, the Commandments] are therefore a canon-before-the-canon. That is to say: just as the closing of Scripture in later times

structured along the lines of the Decalogue, see Braulik, *Der deuteronomischen Gesetze und der Dekalog* and the bibliography cited there. Cf. Braulik, "Die Abfolge der Gesetze in Deuteronomium 12–26 und der Dekalog," in *Das Deuteronomium: Entstehung, Gestalt und Botschaft*, ed. N. Lohfink (BETL 68; Louvain: University Press, 1985), 252–272; repr. in "The Sequence of Laws in Deuteronomy 12–26 and in the Decalogue," in *A Song of Power and the Power of Song: Essays on the Book of Deuteronomy*, ed. D. Christensen (SBTS 4; Winona Lake, IN: Eisenbrauns, 1993), 313–335; idem, "Die dekalogische Redaktion der deuteronomischen Gesetz: Ihre Abhängkeit von Levitikus 19 am Beispel 22,1–12; 24,10–22 und 25, 13–16," in *Bundesdokument und Gesetz: Studien zum Deuteronomium*, ed. G. Braulik (HBS 4; Freiburg, 1995), 1–25; repr. in Braulik, *Studien zum Buch Deuteronomium* (SBAT 24; Stuttgart: Katholisches Bibelwerk, 1997), 147–182; Dennis Olson, *Deuteronomy and the Death of Moses: A Theological Reading* (OBT; Minneapolis: Fortress, 1994); and Frank-Lothar Hossfeld, "Das Dekalog als Grundgesetz – eine Problemanzeige," in *Liebe und Gebot: Studien zum Deuteronomium*, eds. Reinhard G. Kratz and Hermann Spieckermann (Göttingen: Vandenhoeck und Ruprecht, 2000), 46–59.

The argument makes much sense of the data but is hardly a definitive one, as evidenced in the differences of opinion among the various scholars who hold to the relation between the Decalogue and the structure of the Deuteronomic Code as to which statutes in the latter fit with which commandment in the Decalogue. For a critique of Braulik's analysis in the monograph mentioned above, see Frank Crüsemann, *The Torah: Theology and Social History of Old Testament Law* (Minneapolis: Fortress, 1996), 204–207. [Translated from the German edition: *Die Tora: Theologie und Sozialgeschichte des alttestamentlichen Gesetzes* (München: Chr. Kaiser, 1992).]

[21] Yehoshua Amir, "The Decalogue According to Philo," in *The Ten Commandments in History and Tradition*, ed. Ben-Zion Segal (Jerusalem: The Magnes Press, 1985), 126. Cf. Gunter Stemberger, "Der Dekalog im frühen Judentum," in *JBTh* 4 (1989), 91–94; and Ulrich Kellermann, "Der Dekalog in den Schriften des Frühjudentums: Ein Überblick," in *Weisheit, Ethos und Gebot: Weisheits und Dekalogtraditionen in der Bibel und im frühen Judentum*, ed. H. Graf Reventlow (BThS 43; Neukirchen-Vluyn: Neukirchener Verlag, 2001), 161–170.

meant that "all" was "in it" (as an old epigram put it) and nowhere else, so too is "every-thing" already on the tablets."[22]

And in the tenth century, Saadia Gaon classified all the traditional 613 mitzvot (or commandments) of Judaism under one or another of the Ten Commandments,[23] while Numbers Rabbah 13:14–16 says that the rest of the law appeared "between the lines" of the Ten Commandments.

In the Christian tradition, Aquinas, argues that all the moral precepts of the old Law are reducible to the ten precepts of the Decalogue, quoting approvingly one of the early Patristic glosses on Matthew:

On the other hand, on the text, *Blessed are ye when they shall revile you* [Matt 5:11], etc., the *Gloss* says that *Moses, setting forth the ten commandments, goes on to expound them in detail.* Therefore all the precepts of the Law are so many parts of those of the decalogue.[24]

The identification of the rest of Deuteronomy after the Ten Commandments as a homiletical and legal spelling out of the meaning and implications, the details and specific cases, of the Ten Commandments, was set forth in less technical ways but with much theological acumen by both Martin Luther and John Calvin. For Luther, the whole of Deuteronomy is a development of the meaning of the Commandments, so that he begins each of his lectures on a chapter of Deuteronomy by identifying the commandment that chapter develops.[25] Calvin developed his *Harmony of the Pentateuch* largely around the Commandments, connecting not only Deuteronomic statutes and ordinances but those in Exodus and Leviticus with the appropriate Commandments.[26] The "harmony" of the Pentateuch is found in the meshing of all its detailed laws with the basic chord of the Commandments.

---

[22] Michael Fishbane, "Midrash and the Meaning of Scripture," in *The Interpretation of the Bible: The International Symposium Slovenia*, ed. J. Krasovec (JSOTSup 289; Sheffield: Sheffield Academic Press, 1998), 551.

[23] Amir, "The Decalogue According to Philo," 159.

[24] Thomas Aquinas, *Summa Theologiae*, Vol. 29, The Old Law (1a2ae. 100, 3) (New York: McGraw Hill, 1969), 65.

[25] See Martin Luther, *Lectures on Deuteronomy*, vol. 9 of *Luther's Works*, eds. J. Pelikan and D. Poellot (Saint Louis: Concordia, 1960). See also Lothar Perlitt, "Luthers Deuteronomium-Auslegung," in *Vergegenwärtigung des Alten Testaments: Beiträge zur biblischen Hermeneutik*, eds. C. Bultmann, W. Dietrich, and C. Levin (Göttingen: Vandenhoeck und Ruprecht, 2002), 211–225, esp. 216–217.

[26] John Calvin, *Commentaries on the Four Last Books of Moses, arranged in the Form of a Harmony* (Grand Rapids: Eerdmans, 1950).

The intertextual way, therefore, by which the Commandments are seen as *fons et origo*, as the whole of the instruction of God in its most basic and sufficient form, is found *as a trajectory of meaning and action* is created out of the Commandments, that is, as a dynamic flows out of the Commandments and runs through *law* and *narrative*, developing and explicating in specific cases and particular stories the actualization and specification of the Commandments in the life of the people.[27] As Torah in the Old Testament is the conjoining of law and story, so the unfolding of the force and significance, of the meaning and applicability, of the Commandments is found as one moves through the laws and reads the stories.

The Insufficiency of the Commandments

At this point, however, one needs to ask if, despite all these indications from scripture that the Commandments are the primary, inclusive, and foundational instruction of God for the community of faith, are there ways in which the Commandments are *not fully* sufficient to guide our life under God and in relation to neighbor? It is already clear from what I have been saying that many other laws, many other pieces of instruction are provided as God's will for the people's lives. But that is not a sign of the insufficiency of the Commandments. On the contrary, I have been suggesting the *connectedness* of these other statutes and ordinances to the Commandments is a fundamental clue to the *foundational* and *comprehensive* character of the Commandments. For however indirect the connections may seem at times, the manner of their presentation alerts us to the fact that these statutes and ordinances are part of the stream of the Commandments, important and specific points on their trajectory of meaning.

But there are other indications from Scripture that the Commandments may not be wholly adequate in themselves as a moral and theological foundation or framework:[28]

1. Within the prophetic tradition, the Commandments are present and their obedience a matter of concern, especially the First Commandment. But equally prominent in the oracles of the prophets is the concern for *justice* and *mercy* for the poor, the weak, and the oppressed. In Jeremiah's

---

[27] On the image of trajectory as a way of understanding the complex outflow of the Commandments in effecting a rich description of the character of the Christian life, see below, 37–50.

[28] For a thoughtful argument claiming the "insufficiency of the Decalogue alone," see Waldemar Janzen, *Old Testament Ethics: A Paradigmatic Approach* (Louisville: Westminster/John Knox, 1994), 89–96.

famous Temple sermon, he lays two demands upon the people. He says, "Will you steal, murder, commit adultery, swear falsely, make offerings to Baal, and go after other gods that you have not known" – apparently references to the Commandments and the moral and theological issues they address. But he also says, "if you truly act justly with one another, if you do not oppress the alien, the orphan, and the widow, or shed innocent blood in this place..." He thus joins Commandment concerns with other matters that do not seem to be present in the Commandments: the oppression of the stranger, the orphan, and the widow. In his words to the Pharisees, Jesus accuses them of careful tithing of mint, dill, and cumin while neglecting the weightier matters of the law: justice, mercy, and faith (Matt 23:23). Is this an implicit accusation of strict obedience to the Commandments that does not carry with it a concern for mercy and justice? Whatever shape a biblical ethic takes, there is no question that at its heart is this concern for compassion and justice for the weak and the marginal. Indeed, in the prophetic books, the treatment of the marginal members of the community is the primary criterion of justice.[29]

2. There is also that large body of law in the Pentateuch that has to do with *holiness* and *purity*, something that does not seem to be a concern of the Commandments. The identification of holiness as a dimension of who God is – the Holy One of Israel – that is to be reflected in some way within the life of the community is a major motif in scripture and thus a necessary part of a biblical ethic.[30]

3. Perhaps the most significant suggestion of the inadequacy of the Ten Commandments as a basis and framework for biblical ethics is that such a move leaves out the New Testament. In his book, *The Moral Vision of the New Testament*, one of the important works on New Testament ethics, Richard Hays makes only a *single* reference to *one* of the Commandments in some *500* pages of text and that precisely to indicate its insufficiency (the commandment against murder does not help us on abortion because everyone is against murder).[31] The point is perhaps most dramatically identified in the six antitheses of the Sermon on the Mount, where Jesus says

---

[29] See, e.g., James L. Mays, "Justice: Perspectives from the Prophetic Tradition," *Interpretation* 37 (1983), 5–17; repr. in *Prophecy in Israel*, ed. David L. Petersen (Philadelphia: Fortress, 1987), 144–158.

[30] See the focus on the continuing trajectories of justice and holiness as central to the depiction of the God of Israel in Walter Brueggemann, *Theology of the Old Testament* (Minneapolis: Fortress, 1997), 187–196. On the central place of holiness and purity in the religion of Israel, see Patrick D. Miller, *The Religion of Ancient Israel* (Library of Ancient Israel; Louisville: Westminster John Knox, 2000), chap. 4.

[31] Richard B. Hays, *The Moral Vision of the New Testament: A Contemporary Introduction to New Testament Ethics* (San Francisco: HarperSanFrancisco, 1996), 446.

with reference to particular commandments and statutes of Old Testament law, "You have heard that it was said...but I say to you...," where one hears the teaching of Jesus in some sense over against the Commandments and laws of the Old Testament. And even when Aquinas sees all the moral law caught up in the Commandments, it is the "Old Law."

4. The character of the Ten Commandments as law and their consequent failure to evoke an *ethic of love* is a charge that has long been made but was popularized in modern times in Joseph Fletcher's famous little book, *Situation Ethics*, where the Commandments are seen as in danger of leading to legalism, to an ethic of obedience to rules rather than to an ethic of love, always asking what love requires.[32] The development of an ethic of love is customarily rooted primarily in the New Testament and the teaching of Jesus and Paul.

Or, from a somewhat different context, the Jewish scholar, Moshe Weinfeld makes a similar point:

[T]he Decalogue does not include any generalized or abstract moral laws such as "Love your neighbor" (Lev 19:18), "Befriend the stranger" (Deut 10.19) or "Justice, justice shall you pursue" (Deut 16:20). Hence there is no justification for the statement that the Ten Commandments represent the highest moral achievement of ancient Israel.[33]

5. Yet another possible inadequacy of the Commandments as a basis and framework for a biblical ethic may lie in the very community context that seems so important to their functioning. For it suggests that the Commandments are for a *community* ethic, a *covenantal* ethic, that tells us how we live together within the community but does not really work for the relationship of communities to each other or for dealing with persons outside the community.

6. Further, more than one Old Testament scholar has criticized the adequacy of the Commandments on the grounds of their social location, that is, that they were aimed at a class of free, propertied persons, "the elites and powerholders in Israelite society,"[34] and are applicable only to such a class, not really providing an ethic for the underprivileged, for slaves and the poor, the propertyless.

---

[32] Joseph F. Fletcher, *Situation Ethics: The New Morality* (London: SCM Press, 1966).

[33] Moshe Weinfeld, "The Uniqueness of the Decalogue and Its Place in Jewish Tradition, in *The Ten Commandments in History and Tradition*, 11.

[34] David J. A. Clines, "The Ten Commandments, Reading from Left to Right," *Interested Parties* (Sheffield: Sheffield Academic Press, 1995), 26–45.

The most extensive argument in this direction may be found in the work of Frank Crüse-mann.[35] Crüsemann's monograph is a strong critique of all claims about the Command-ments as being broadly foundational, perduring, and widely applicable. He argues that they had to do with a particular class of persons at a particular time (eighth century B.C.) and dealt with only particular, albeit important, matters and left many things untouched, including some of the matters discussed above.[36] He has carried this argument further in his later extensive treatment of the legal traditions in ancient Israel, *The Torah: Theology and Social History of Old Testament Law*.[37] There he argues primarily with Lohfink's interpretation in his essay "Kennt das Alte Testament einen Unterschied von 'Gebot' und 'Gesetz'," In the former work, Crüsemann orients his discussion around the content of the Decalogue and what that does and does not show about those for whom the Com-mandments are intended and the issues with which they do and do not deal. In the latter work, his argument is about Lohfink's strong claims concerning the way in which the redactional work and the final shape of the biblical text give primary place to the Deca-logue. In sum, Crüsemann sees the Decalogue as time-bound, narrowly addressed, and limited in its subject matter, a clearly insufficient basis for complex theological and ethi-cal discussion. While the whole of this essay is addressed to such a point of view as Crüsemann represents and so it is not necessary to address his discussion in detail in this context – see the next section in this essay – a few matters merit brief comment:

1. The argument about the Commandments transcending a particular time and place and representing the basis for all the rest of the legal instruction, is worked out in detail above and by Lohfink in his essay. It is evidenced in both the redactional activity and the narrative presentation. The differentiation and singling out of the Commandments and giving them first and special place is carried out by all the moves indicated in the first part of this essay. Crüsemann is right that the rest of the legal material is also to be un-derstood as the will of God, but his argument that the difference between the Decalogue and the rest of the Torah lies exclusively in the mode of transmission, whose significance is revealed in the history of composition, presumes that being able to uncover the history of transmission and suggest motivations behind it invalidates the final outcome. In fact, the contrary is the case. The redactional work is a tutor to the reader indicating how the text is to be understood.

2. The assumption about the limited focus of the concerns of the Decalogue presumes that its force is to be understood only within its own content when the argument that is being made here and by many others is that the presentation of the text makes it clear that one is to view the rest of the law and many other things as specifying and developing and elaborating what the Commandments are about.[38]

---

[35] Cf. Frank Crüsemann, *Bewahrung der Freiheit: Das Thema des Dekalogs in sozial-geschichtlicher Perspektive* (Kaiser Traktate 78; München: Kaiser, 1983), 28–35.

[36] See Crüsemann, *Bewahrung*, 8–11

[37] *The Torah: Theology and Social History of Old Testament Law* (Minneapolis: Fortress, 1996), 351–357.

[38] For further modes of arguing the significance of the Decalogue for matters presumably not covered by it, see the next section of this essay. For further argument about the limited or "sampling" character of the content of the Decalogue, see Janzen, *Old Testament Ethics*, 92–96. Janzen undercuts his own argument seriously by comparing the Commandments to the Apostles' Creed, regarding it and the other creeds as having a central place (like the Deca-logue) but leaving out many things (like the Decalogue). Of course, the point of the Creed is precisely to identify the basic framework of faith, which then is elaborated in much more de-

3. Crüsemann claims to be making an exegetical argument, but it is primarily a historical critical argument, or the exegetical work is primarily at that level of the text. More specifically, he seems to regard genetic arguments, that is, those that uncover what is going on behind the present form of the text as controlling its interpretation. These are complex matters, and the history of the text is part of the argument presented in this essay, but the combination of redactional and literary reading of the text as attempted in these pages leads to quite different results than those reached by Crüsemann.

Reasserting the Sufficiency of the Commandments

These are all rather telling blows against a claim that the Commandments are sufficient as a ground and framework for a biblical ethic. Most of them come from within scripture itself or from critical analysis of scripture. Nevertheless, in this last part, I wish to reassert my original claim about the sufficiency of the Commandments. The points identified above are serious and important. A return to the Commandments, however, suggests, I would contend, an openness within them to the issues that would seem to point to their insufficiency. Or to put the matter in another way, the Ten Commandments are the *starting point* and *ground* for scripture's dealing with such matters as compassion for the weak and the poor, the holiness and purity of life, an ethic of love, and the possibility of an ethic that transcends class and communal boundaries. Let me suggest how that may be so.

1. The biblical concern for justice and compassion for the marginal members of society begins in the story of the Exodus and God's compassionate listening to the cries of Hebrew slaves. The single ground on which obedience to the Commandments is laid is the liberation from the house of bondage. More specifically, the *Deuteronomic* form of the Decalogue is clearly a *Sabbath*-centered Decalogue that identifies the *whole purpose* of the Sabbath as *providing release for slaves*, that is, persons economically squeezed, forced by debts into bonded servitude.[39] The Sabbath commandment sets forth and sets loose a sabbatical principle that is worked out in the Deuteronomic Code and the Book of the Covenant precisely to provide compassionate relief and support for not only the slave and the poor but also for domestic and even wild animals:

For six years you shall sow your land and gather in its yield; but the seventh year you shall let it rest and lie fallow, so that *the poor of your people may eat*; and what they

---

tail in the faith and practice of the church, just like the Decalogue. One of the primary ways of teaching the faith is instruction in the Creed.

[39] Patrick D. Miller, "The Human Sabbath: A Study in Deuteronomic Theology," *The Princeton Seminary Bulletin* 6 (1985), 81–97.

leave the wild animals may eat. You shall do the same with your vineyard, and with your olive orchard. Six days you shall do your work, but on the seventh day you shall rest, so that your *ox* and your *donkey* may have relief, and your *homeborn slave* (*ben ᵓămâ*) and the *resident alien* (*gēr*) may be refreshed. (Exod 23:10–12)

Here is the starting point, both for an ethic of *compassion* for the poor and the powerless and also for an *ecological compassion*, the trajectory of which runs through the Commandments into the Psalms and the peaceable kingdom of the prophet Isaiah's vision. Scripture's framing of an ethic of justice and compassion is rooted and grounded in the Commandments where the impetus for that compassion and that justice is identified and the specification of which in the statutes and ordinances sets the particularities for such justice and compassion to which the prophets later appeal. The prophetic concern for justice and mercy does not arise *de novo*. It begins in the Ten Words and the moral space and moral flow they create.

2. The world of the Holiness Code in Leviticus and the legislation having to do with purity and sacrifice seems a long way from the Commandments. But once again, a careful look at scripture suggests that the concern for holiness begins at Sinai. Apart from God's sanctification of the creation, which is clearly to be associated with the sanctification of the Sabbath – Rashbam [Samuel ben Meir] argued in the Middle Ages that the whole account of the creation in Genesis is to serve as an introduction to the Sabbath commandment[40] – the concern for sanctification and holiness does not even come into the biblical story until the encounter with the holiness of God at Sinai, where the community is told that its keeping of the covenant, that is, of the Ten Words, makes them into "a holy nation" (Exod 19). As in so many other matters of life with God and the neighbor, the *Sabbath* is the center. Rabbi Judah said, "The Sabbath Commandment equals all the other commandments of the Torah put together...(Neh 9:14)."[41] The sanctification – making holy – of a day to the Lord is the *opening* of a trajectory of holy times, holy places, holy lives, and holy things.

In the Holiness Code of Leviticus, the various statutes are framed with self-presentation formulae that parallel the decalogical declaration, "I am the Lord who brought you out of the land of Egypt" with a comparable formula, "I am the Lord who sanctifies you." Lev 19 is the charter chapter of the Holiness Code and the rabbis claimed – with good reason – that it

---

[40] Ezra Z. Melamed, "'Observe' and 'Remember' Spoken as One Utterance," in *The Ten Commandments in History and Tradition*, 210.

[41] Ibid., 213.

contained the essence of the Ten Commandments.[42] The sanctification, the holiness, of the people is thus effected and demonstrated in their living by the Commandments.

In this connection, I would call attention to the argument that Dean McBride has made, following Jewish tradition – and somewhat the converse of Rashbam's reading of the creation story as a way of introducing the Sabbath – that the ten archetypal injunctions in the *creation* story, each introduced by "and God said," which "invoke structural cosmos out of chaos" may be compared to the ten words of the Decalogue "that define Israel's covenantal society," invoking community out of the chaos of slavery.[43] The words of creation and the words of commandment echo each other as parts of God's creation of order in the world and in human society.[44] Conversely, the Sabbath commandment, which is the center of the Decalogue and the transitional Commandment between the two tables, roots the ethics of the Commandments in God's work of creation (the Exodus version) and in God's work of redemption (the Deuteronomic version).

3. It should be clear to the careful reader of scripture that the separation of a love ethic from the Commandments can only be done by a misreading of them or by an inattention to their force and context. Not only is the love command of the New Testament the result of the conjoining of two Old Testament commands, the Shema, "You shall love the Lord your God with all your heart, and with all your soul, and with all your might," is itself the *positive* form of the First Commandment and occurs in the context of an extended commentary or sermon in Deut 6–11 on the beginning of the Decalogue. Further, one notes that the *first time in scripture* that the *love of God* is identified as a fundamental responsibility of the community is in the Second Commandment prohibiting the making and worshipping of images, and there it is explicitly defined by the keeping of the commandments: "showing steadfast love to the thousandth generation of those who *love me and keep my commandments*." It is the Commandments, as Paul recognizes in Rom 13, that initiate, flesh out, specify, and make concrete

---

[42] David Flusser, "The Decalogue in the New Testament," in *The Ten Commandments in History and Tradition*, 229, 232.

[43] S. Dean McBride, Jr., "Divine Protocol: Genesis 1:1–2:3 as Prologue to the Pentateuch," in *God Who Creates: Essays in Honor of W. Sibley Towner*, ed. W. P. Brown, et al. (Grand Rapids: Eerdmans, 2000), 10 and n. 16.

[44] See W. G. Braude, *Pesikta Rabbati:Discourses for Feasts, Fasts, and Special Sabbaths* (New Haven: Yale University Press, 1968), I, 444–445 (Piska 21): "The Ten Commandments were intended to be paired off with the ten words whereby the world was created" (444). Without the Ten Words, the world would have gone under. For further discussion of this connection in rabbinic interpretation, see Stemberger, "Der Dekalog im frühen Judentum, 102–103.

what a love ethic is all about and give it material substance that does not let it dissolve into a situationally controlled moral chaos rather than a shaped and molded moral space. "The commandments, 'You shall not commit adultery; You shall not murder; You shall not steal; You shall not covet'; and any other commandment, are summed up in this word, 'Love your neighbor as yourself'" (Rom 13:9). The Commandments also are the first time in scripture that we encounter the explicit moral obligation *to the neighbor*. The internal structure and movement of the Commandments – as widely recognized – moves from the first words, "I am the Lord your God," to the last words, "everything that is your neighbor's."[45]

4. The apparent limitation of the Commandments to a community-bound rather than a trans-community ethic or to a class and socially restricted group fails to take account of the way in which the Commandments are separated from their context, even as they are found within it.[46] That is, the restrictions that operate within the particular statutes and ordinances, set for the life of the people in the land, do not hold for the Commandments. The Commandments are for all times and places, and they open up a dynamic of understanding of *the neighbor* that cannot be restricted to the social location of the persons who first received them.[47] That dynamic of understanding of the neighbor that flows out of the Commandments is still going on when one moves into the New Testament with the question of the lawyer, "Who is my neighbor?" and Jesus' telling a story about a man going down to Jericho, thereby expanding and particularizing once more the meaning of the Commandments, enabling the cove-

---

[45] See, e.g., Amir, "The Decalogue According to Philo," 158.

[46] Even within the framework of the Commandments themselves, one cannot argue a highly narrow point of address. Both the setting, that is, the assembly of the people as a whole – and there is no indication that this is simply a part of the people – in which the divine words are spoken and the clear evidence from other Old Testament texts that various commandments have their play on women and children and the like suggest that the Commandments were not understood as narrowly applicable. See the discussion of Werner H. Schmidt in Zusammenarbeit mit Holger Delkurt und Axel Graupner, *Die Zehn Gebote im Rahmen alttestamentlicher Ethik* (EdF 281; Darmstadt: Wissenschaftliche Buchgesellschaft, 1993), 33–34, 92, 117–118. Schmidt shows how not only do the prohibitions against having other gods or making and worshipping images address women as well as men, as many texts indicate, but other commandments, such as keeping the Sabbath, honoring parents, and not committing adultery are also to be understood, either with reference to the way they are framed or by their connections to other texts, as applicable to women.

[47] Note Schmidt's discussion of Joseph's encounter with Potiphar's wife and what it suggests about the prohibition of adultery as being something that is valid with foreigners and persons outside the group. The Commandments he argues, citing Hermann Gunkel in support, are not simply a group morality but precisely relative to the neighbor identity transcends the group and extends beyond it (*Die Zehn Gebote*), 6–8.

nanted community to learn further what obedience to the Commandments involves – in this case, specifically who is your neighbor – and in so doing breaking open any ethnic or other restricting definitions of the neighbor.

5. As for the antitheses of Jesus, these are not to be read as relegating the Ten Commandments to a secondary position; nor are they to be seen as fundamentally counter to the Commandments. They are rather an extension of them into a deeper level of meaning and action, but a meaning that is *initiated* and *guided* by the *Commandments.* Jesus' is teaching the law in the Sermon on the Mount, referring to interpretations of the Commandments and other pieces of torah, often to literal interpretations, which he does not think get at the radical intention of the Commandments properly. The analogy to Moses that is suggested here is appropriate in that the New Testament understands such teaching of Jesus to have the kind of authority that was also given to Moses. In that respect, he is not just another rabbi, but a new Moses. This does not mean a new law but authoritative interpretation of how it works out, which is what Moses did in the statutes and ordinances of the Torah. Further, the interiorizing of the force of the Commandments that is so associated with Jesus' teaching, so that mind and heart and attitude are also under direction, is already prepared for in the Tenth Commandment with its focus on desire.

A number of years ago, the then Presbyterian Church in the United States[48] prepared an extended document of moral reflection on a number of controversial issues: abortion, euthanasia, suicide, capital punishment, and war.[49] Following the clues from scripture and the tradition, this study, titled "The Nature and Value of Human Life," let the Sixth Commandment, "You shall not kill," be the starting and guiding point of its theological argument, regarding the commandment as "the central explicit biblical assertion of the comprehensive value (respect for life)." The commandment, "You shall not kill," became the basis for sophisticated and developed moral reflection as the ground for discussing and deciding about abortion and other issues having to do with human life and death. It was exactly the reverse of Richard Hays' decision that there is nothing helpful that this commandment brings because we are all agreed not to murder. That point of agreement, given to us in the Commandment, is the critical point from which all further discussion flows.

In conclusion, therefore, I would submit that claims about the foundational and formative character of the Commandments, the implicit judg-

---

[48] That denomination merged with the then United Presbyterian Church in the USA in 1983 to become the present The Presbyterian Church USA.

[49] "The Nature and Value of Human Life" (Atlanta: Office of the Stated Clerk, The Presbyterian Church in the United States, 1981).

ment about their sufficiency for creating the moral space to live under God and in relation to neighbor, what I am calling their sufficiency, is well-grounded. Understanding the Commandments as the foundation and framework for biblical ethics and sufficient for the moral life does not mean there is nothing more to be said. The sufficiency claim is made only in light of the way the Commandments are to be understood, as being constantly fleshed out, specified and particularized, extended and developed – what I have called a dynamic or trajectory of meaning and action, one that begins with the statutes and ordinances of Exodus and Deuteronomy but does not stop there or even with the instruction of the Sermon on the Mount, but continues in the moral deliberation and acting of the community of faith.

3. Metaphors for the Moral

In order to comprehend how the Commandments function in the life of faith, a number of metaphors or models can be identified to suggest different but complementary ways of discerning the force of the commandments and the way they operate to guide the moral life of those for whom these formulations are instructive and to be obeyed. The metaphors or models suggested here are surely not exhaustive, but they all assume that the Commandments belong in some context of life and literature. That is, they all assume that the Commandments are relational and to be interpreted and attended to in relation to their context in human experience, in the history of the community's experience with these Commandments as bearing moral force, and in their literary setting within Scripture. In what follows, it is not my intention to develop a full-scale interpretation of the Commandments via the metaphors and images I am suggesting but to show how they may provide ways into interpreting and appropriating the Commandments for moral direction and ethical reflection.

Trajectory

The metaphor that is most influential in my analysis of the way the Commandments are to be viewed in relation to the rest of the biblical legislation and indeed in most of my arguments for the full adequacy of the commandments is the metaphor of an *arc* or a *trajectory*. Borrowing a phrase from William Schweiker, I would call it an "arc of moral understanding" that is created out of the Commandments, one that begins in the Commandments in their context and continues out from there.[1] The variation on the image of the arc that I would propose as most appropriate to the way the Commandments function is to speak of *a trajectory of meaning, action, and effect* projecting from the Commandments as they are carried through various vectors. That is, we learn something about what the Commandments *mean*, what they are after, what their particular force is. We also learn about the *actions* that are in some way envisioned by or spoken

---

[1] William Schweiker, "Divine Command Ethics and the Otherness of God," in *Power, Value, and Conviction* (Cleveland: Pilgrim, 1998), 157.

against, the behavior that these Commandments are meant to evoke, something that the contemporary reader may learn about more in the negative than the positive, that is, in the recollection of disobedience more than of obedience. And we learn *what happens* when these directives guide the life of the community or are ignored in the life of individuals as well as the community. What effect does living this way have upon folk?

The vector on which the trajectory of the Commandments moves includes first of all the *context of Scripture*. That is, the meaning and effect of each commandment and of the whole begins with its formulation in the Decalogue and the understanding provided by that immediate context and by the collection as a whole for understanding what the particular commandment meant, what sort of actions were expected by its formulation and presence in the Decalogue, and finally what happened, that is, what sort of effect resulted from obedience or disobedience of each Commandment. While the Commandments begin in the revelation of the divine will at Sinai in the stipulations of the Decalogue, they do not end there, at least not in terms of their meaning, what the members of the covenant community are to do, and what will happen dependent upon the people's attention to the Commandments. The trajectory of the Commandments continues through the whole of the Mosaic legislation, as it provides case laws and other forms of legislation or direction for developing and explicating the actualization and specification of the Commandments in the life of the people.

If, however, the arc of understanding and specifying what the Commandments mean individually and collectively goes through the other forms of biblical legislation and they provide a way of informing and spelling out for us how the Commandments work and what are the issues and concerns that grow or "project" – to keep the imagery of trajectory before us – out of each commandment, the trajectory does not only or simply flow through the legislation. It incorporates also narrative and prophetic oracle, psalm and wisdom, story and teaching. Particularly in the stories we learn about the effects of the trajectory of the Commandments, of the outcomes when commandments are kept and when they are broken. But the stories also tell us something of what a commandment is getting at, what its powerful force is to which we must pay attention. Thus, one is led to read and think about the experience of Egyptian slaves and the "service" that was laid upon them in order to comprehend fully the force of the insistence on the inclusive worship and "service" of the Lord of Israel as it is set forth in the first Commandment.[2]

---

[2] See below, 68–79.

The trajectory of the meaning, action, and effect of each commandment does not really stop at any point, however. This arc of understanding is not even confined to the context of Scripture. The transition by which this point is scored, however, is found within Scripture itself. That is, the arc of understanding of the Commandments is not confined to the Old Testament and to the story of Israel. That trajectory continues on directly into the New Testament, explicitly in the Sermon on the Mount and Jesus' teaching about the Commandments but by no means confined to that. For Paul and other New Testament voices take up the Commandments and their place in the life of Christians. But the trajectory of the Commandments does not even stop with the New Testament. It moves through the continuing story of God's people and the way of the Lord with those on whom these obligations are laid, those who have been freed to live in this way. So if one wants to understand the force of particular commandments, we should go on to read the stories of other figures of faith in the history of church and synagogue and listen for the way that the Commandments have been interpreted in theological and ethical discussion and in the concrete acts of human beings who have taken the Commandments seriously.

The point of the imagery of the arc or the trajectory is that, ironic as it may sound, while the Commandments were written in stone, they are very lively and there is a lot of "paperwork" that goes along with the Commandments before one can fully understand what they are about and how specifically they are to be followed. As cases and stories articulated the force of the Commandments in the past, so they still do. Indeed, the history of interpretation shows frequent interpretive moves that rely heavily on stories for illuminating the particular force of a commandment.[3] Rather than being rigid, fixed, archaic, and obvious, the Commandments open up a moral and theological arc or movement that began long ago and is still going on. They are dynamic, open in meaning and effect, and uncovering many dimensions subtle and obvious of the moral life for the community that lives in covenant with the Lord of Israel who is known to us in Jesus Christ.

The result of perceiving, tracing, and appropriating such a trajectory or arc of moral understanding flowing out of the Commandments is, in effect, a "thick description" of the morality or the ethics of the Commandments.

---

[3] For examples from the teachings of the Rabbis, see *Rabbinic Fantasies: Imaginative Narratives from Classical Hebrew Literature*, eds. D. Stern and M. J. Mirsky (Yale Judaica Series, 29; New Haven: Yale University Press, 1990), 91–119. In the medieval period, St. Bonaventure used anecdotes and stories in his sermonic Collations on the Ten Commandments. See *St. Bonaventure's Collations on the Ten Commandments*, introduced and translated by Paul J. Spaeth (Works of St. Bonaventure, 6; St. Bonaventure, NY: St. Bonaventure University, 1995), 6–7 and *passim*.

The apparent "thinness" of the Commandments becomes a rich description of the way in which all sorts of situations and all sorts of issues are dealt with from the starting point, that is, from the beginning of the arc of meaning and action evoked by the Commandments. Part of the problem that is often felt in the effort to live by the Commandments is not their difficulty but the fact that if they are "sign posts on the margins of a wide sphere of life," as Gerhard von Rad described them, a lot of things get through between the few posts that are given to mark out the moral life, between the cracks, so to speak.[4] The thick description of the life under God set forth by the Commandments and their trajectories of meaning and effect covers a much wider territory than the frequent thin interpretation often suggests, as the Reformers and others have rightly recognized.

In that connection, then, one notes a further figure or image for the moral meaning of the Commandments, a figure of thought related to the image of the arc or trajectory of meaning. It is one that played a significant role in John Calvin's interpretation of the Commandments and shows how well he sensed the way in which the Commandments connect with all sorts of texts and issues that are not immediately obvious in the brief formulations of the Commandments.[5] For Calvin, the primary figure operating in the Commandments and in our understanding of them was *synecdoche*, a standard figure of thought familiar to those who study literature and deal with metaphor, simile, metonymy and other figures by which meaning is conveyed in literary texts.[6] Calvin defined synecdoche as others have done: "By synecdoche the whole is sometimes taken for a part, sometimes a part for the whole."[7] He noted, with some accuracy, in my judgment, that this figure of thought "is constantly occurring in Scripture"[8] but found it most extensively in the Decalogue, where, he argued, there are "such manifest synecdoches" that "the commandments and prohibitions always contain more than is expressed in words."[9] With his typical forceful expression,

---

[4] Gerhard von Rad, *Old Testament Theology* I (New York: Harper, 1962), 194.

[5] See below, 133–134.

[6] While my own reading of Calvin's commentaries on the Pentateuch has depended for some time upon the recognition of the way in which Calvin read the legislation of the Old Testament in relation to the Commandments, in this discussion of Calvin's treatment of synecdoche I am particularly indebted to an essay by Roland M. Frye, "Calvin's Theological Use of Figurative Language," *Calvin Studies IV*, eds. J. H. Leith and W. S. Johnson (Davidson, NC, 1988), 73–94. Frye calls attention to the wide use of figurative tropes, especially metaphor, metonomy, and synecdoche, in Calvin's theological work and exposition.

[7] John Calvin, "Psychopannichia," in *Tracts and Treatises in Defense of the Reformed Faith* (Calvin's Tracts and Treatises, III; Grand Rapids: Eerdmans, 1958), 458.

[8] Ibid.

[9] *Institutes of the Christian Religion*, Book II.8.8. (All quotations from Calvin's *Institutes of the Christian Religion* are taken from the translation of Ford Lewis Battles in *The Library of Christian Classics*, ed. J. T. McNeill [Philadelphia: Westminster, 1960]).

Calvin said: "Obviously, in almost all the commandments there are such manifest synecdoches that he who would confine his understanding of the law within the narrowness of the words deserves to be laughed at."[10] A careful interpretation of the law, therefore, will always and *necessarily* "go beyond the words."

Calvin took a further step in establishing a trajectory of meaning and action out of the Commandments, one that has been central for the Reformed and indeed wider Reformation interpretation of the Commandments. He argued that, as a matter of common sense everyone would concede "that when a good thing is commanded, the evil thing that conflicts with it is forbidden."[11] His cardinal example was critical to the formulation of a Presbyterian study paper on "The Nature and Value of Human Life" that set the commandment against killing as the biblical basis for a comprehensive theological and ethical study of abortion, euthanasia, suicide, capital punishment, and war.[12]

Calvin exemplified this form of his synecdoche, that is, the prohibition of the vice implies the practice of the virtue and vice versa, as follows: "Therefore in this commandment, 'You shall not kill,' men's common sense will see only that we must abstain from wronging anyone or desiring to do so."[13] By means of synecdoche, simply stated in this prefatory way, Calvin begins to open up the trajectory of meaning in two ways. First of all, the Commandment directs us against "all acts of injury," that is, against *any* physical endangerment of the neighbor, not just killing, much less just murder. And second, every prohibition in the Commandments is seen to have a positive implication. This is a major move, for the Com-

---

[10] *Institutes* II.8.8.

[11] *Institutes* II.8.9. Such an interpretation is not peculiar to Calvin. It is inherent in the New Testament's interpretation of the prohibitions of the second table as exemplars of the command to "love your neighbor" (e.g. Rom 13:8–10), and it may be found in various of the church's teachers through the ages. In his Collations on the Ten Commandments, for example, St. Bonaventure sees the negative and the positive forms of the Commandments in the requirement to love God and to fear God: "It is impossible that a person would avoid evil except through fear, and that he would do good except through love" (*Collation* 2.14). He spells this out more specifically in his concluding remarks on the Commandments as a whole: "We should understand that although some commandments are called positive and some negative, nevertheless all of them contain positive and negative elements. When God prohibits something in any commandment, he commands its opposite. This is clear." Then Bonaventure goes on to illustrate his point with reference to each commandment (*Collation* 7.8).

[12] "The Nature and Value of Human Life" (Atlanta: Office of the Stated Clerk, The Presbyterian Church in the United States, 1981).

[13] *Institutes* II.8.9.

mandments are often interpreted with particular attention to the *restricted* character of the *negative* formulation. That is, they are seen to be limited to certain areas and leaving a wide area of moral freedom. That is, much that has to do with the moral life is not seen to be addressed by the Commandments. On the basis of the synecdoche, the part tells about the whole, and on the basis of common sense, Calvin rejects such a narrow understanding of the Commandments and points us toward a very expansive moral trajectory, one that requires some serious moral thinking and acting as one tries to understand the present force of the Commandments.

To illustrate more specifically with reference to the Sixth Commandment, Calvin saw here, by means of the figure of synecdoche, a directive against "murder of the heart," hatred and anger, for "hatred is nothing but sustained anger."[14] Killing is a terrible outcome of uncontrolled anger. Anger – and Calvin is not talking about general indignation but about animosity toward a neighbor – too often moves from the mental and emotional state to the act of injury and killing of the object of one's anger. Then on the principle that the prohibition of a vice assumes the practice of its opposite virtue, Calvin taught that the commandment against killing requires us to protect the lives of our neighbors, to procure those things that are conducive to their tranquility, to shield them from harm, and to "lend a helping hand" in cases of danger.[15] So interpreted, the commandment "you shall not kill" is "extended to mean the exclusion of all forms of ill will and violence and the encouragement of all forms of social peace."[16] It is not surprising, therefore, that when Calvin turned to writing commentary on the legislation of the Pentateuch, he did so by interpreting that legislation as itself commentary and explication of the Commandments. So his interpretation is not simply a working through of the Pentateuch verse by verse in typical commentary fashion but an arrangement of the laws in relation to the Ten Commandments.

Contingency, Complexity, and Coherence

A second way of viewing how the Commandments work to give moral direction to the Christian life is to see in them a threefold interaction, including some clear tensions, among *contingency*, *complexity*, and *coherence*. That is, one reckons in the Commandments with features that call attention a) to their contingent, rather than permanent and eternal, character; b) to

---

[14] *Institutes* II.8.39.
[15] Ibid.
[16] Frye, "Calvin's Theological Use of Figurative Language," 86.

their complex rather than simple character; and c) to their coherent wholeness rather than to their apparent fragmentation by the contingency and
complexity that belongs to their functioning.[17] Such a way of seeing the
Commandments seems inherently contrary to their very character. That is,
we read them as eternal and unchanging, as simple rather than complex,
and as a list of prohibitions rather than a coherent moral philosophy. All of
those traditional views of the Commandments are true, and important for
understanding them. But they do not uncover all that the Commandments
are about as a framework for the moral life and a constitution for the covenant community without comprehending also their opposites as features of
the Commandments: contingency, complexity, and coherence.

By the *contingency* of the Commandments, I do not mean that one can
take or leave them willy-nilly or that they are applicable some of the time
but maybe not at other times. I mean that the Commandments are to be understood as operative in a context, that context being both communal and
situational. The communal is self-evident in that these are stipulations for
those who identify with the slaves who came out of Egypt and committed
themselves to serving the God who had freed them, the same God whose
redemptive work in Jesus Christ was a further salvific work in our behalf.
(There are signs that the Commandments may have a broader applicability,
but that is something always to be argued whereas their applicability to the
covenant community is a given out of the story of Israel and the instruction
of Jesus.)[18] Further, situational contingency does not mean that the situation determines whether or not one obeys. Rather it determines the particular way in which the Commandments come to bear on the moral life. That
is what is indicated by the development of a large body of law in the Old
Testament, teaching that serves to spell out the way in which the Commandments function, though usually indirectly and without any specific
reference to the Commandments themselves. The very presence of this legislation and its changing character is a testimony to the contingency of the

---

[17] For an example of the interplay of contingency and coherence, see the work of J. Christiaan Beker, especially his most famous work *Paul the Apostle: The Triumph of God in Life
and Thought* (Edinburgh: T. & T. Clark, 1989). For discussion of his appropriation of these
categories as central to his reading of the apostle, see Patrick D. Miller, "A Theocentric Theologian of Hope: J. Christiaan Beker as Biblical Theologian," *The Princeton Seminary Bulletin*
16 (1995), 22–35. For the interplay of complexity and coherence as central to the theological
and hermeneutical task, see the introductory essay of William Schweiker and Michael
Welker, "A New Paradigm of Theological and Biblical Inquiry," in *Power, Powerlessness,
and the Divine: New Inquiries in Bible and Theology*, ed. C. L. Rigby (Atlanta: Scholars
Press, 1997), 3–20. See also Gerhard Sauter, *Gateways to Dogmatics: Reasoning Theologically for the Life of the Church* (Grand Rapids: Eerdmans, 2003), 41–43.

[18] See below, 136–163.

Commandments, the need to determine the contingent factors and how the moral direction in the Commandment is to come to bear in a particular instance and situation.

It is this same relationship to a body of legislation that makes us immediately aware that the *simplicity* of the Commandments is in tension with their highly *complex* nature even as their *contingency* is in tension with their *eternal and unchanging* character. The complexity is not a negative, for life is complex and moral values, decisions, and acts are complex. That one is not to have sexual relations with the spouse of another is a straightforward and clear moral direction, one that is freeing and helpful. It is not complex and difficult to figure out. But the ramifications of that for relationships with one's spouse and with other persons, for thinking about sex and sexuality, for figuring out how one relates to a neighbor's spouse in appropriate ways that protect the marriage relationship of the neighbor, who is the true beneficiary of this commandment (not the one who obeys it – as in all the commandments). If Calvin is right that the prohibition of a vice implies the nurturing of its opposite virtue, then the Commandments are indeed quite complex. An excellent illustration of that is the Presbyterian study of "The Nature and Value of Human Life," referred to above, where the simple prohibition, "You shall not kill" – whose apparent simplicity is deceptive from the very start[19] – became the basis for thinking in complex ways about various significant moral issues.

One of the requirements for a realistic theology is the resistance to oversimplifications and the need for awareness of complex relationships in which the moral life and the devotion to God are marked out.[20] When the trajectory of the Commandments, either as a whole or singly, is charted – and such articulation of the trajectory will always be partial and incomplete – it is clear that they incorporate a variety of complex relationships and systems: power relationships (e.g., king and subject, master and slave, husband and wife, employer and employee, parent and child), family relationships, communal relationships, property definition, systems of loans, systems of welfare, and the like.[21] One may properly speak about the

---

[19] Some indication of the complexity of this "simple" commandment is suggested by the fact that in the preparation of the New Revised Standard Version of the Old Testament, largely done by sub-committee work, the translation of this commandment required a meeting of the full committee for several hours, a meeting that ended with an evenly split vote. The matter was decided by a vote of the Chairman, a New Testament scholar of note, who broke the tie.

[20] On the importance of developing a realistic theology and the potential of Scripture to facilitate that enterprise, see Michael Welker, *God the Spirit* (Minneapolis: Fortress, 1994), 40–49.

[21] See below, 51–67.

Commandments dealing with relationships to God and to neighbor (see below) but only if one understands those relationships as breaking down in various ways into quite extensive and varied relationships and systems. The Commandments have their effect precisely in such complex interactions.

The claim that there is a *coherence* to the Commandments is an insistence that the two previous features, contingency and complexity, do not mean that the Commandments are a kind of moral smorgasbord where everything is up for grabs and so complicated that there is no fundamental direction, no wholeness to the moral life that is shaped by these Commandments. Here are ten directions. Elsewhere in Scripture some have seen a list of twelve, a Dodecalogue, and maybe the ten were originally in groups of threes or fours. A list is a list, and one can always add or subtract or counter with another list. Thus the various cartoons and jokes about adding or taking away a commandment (usually adultery!). But the moral direction of the Commandments depends in large measure on the fact that they present a coherent understanding of what life in relation to God and neighbor is all about. That is best indicated, in my judgment, in the serious attempt to spell out some of the complexity and contingency of the Commandments as fully as possible, but such spelling out is a large enterprise, rarely attempted but perhaps accessible in good ways in the various confessional and catechetical presentations of the Commandments. More simply, one can note the many ways in which interpreters have described the structure and wholeness of the Commandments, their arrangement and movement, from the worship of God to the love of neighbor, through a commandment (Sabbath) that has to do with both worship of God and love of neighbor, the movement of the Decalogue in its second table from the innermost circle of the family out to matters of life, marriage, property, reputation in an order that is quite intelligible and suggests a hierarchy and ordering of values that makes coherent sense.

Even more important, the Commandments give coherence to the varied complex collections of laws. It was precisely this coherence that Calvin sought to show by arranging the laws of the different collections in Exodus, Leviticus, Numbers, and Deuteronomy according to the Decalogue and then discussing them in relation to the particular Commandment that they were to be associated with. The way the story is told in Deuteronomy makes this connection between the complexity of the statutes and ordinances and the coherence of the Commandments quite evident. That is, the Commandments are presented with their order and structure and then the rest of God's teaching is presented as a Mosaic specification of the various and complex instances in which the fundamental stipulations operated. While the presentation suggests that this is further teaching, the sharp dif-

ferentiation between the direct address of the Commandments and the Mosaic teaching suggests they represent a further elaboration of the greater
complexity, and conversely, the reader of this further complex legislation
has a structure in which they may be seen to be coherent and whole.

So it is that in the interpretation of the Commandments in order to be
guided by them in the love of God and the love of neighbor, we are attentive to the contingencies that may be present in their carrying out even as
we are persuaded of their unchanging and enduring appropriateness. We
need to understand the complexity of their application to thinking and acting, to valuing and doing, even as we find their simplicity helpful for comprehending and learning them and holding them close in our minds and
hearts. We assume and find that the whole of these Commandments is sufficient in their being a true whole, a comprehensive and ordered instruction
about how to live that is not fragmented or partial, not chaotic or meaningless, not simply a list of dos and don'ts without structure and intelligibility.

Bottom Up and Top Down

As a third way of viewing the Commandments, and particularly the relation of the Commandments to the other laws and the stories, oracles,
hymns, and other biblical literature, I want to draw on a scientific model
represented specifically in the theological work of the scientist-theologian
John Polkinghorne.[22] Scientists – and others – may talk about working either *top down* or *bottom up*. What this means for Polkinghorne is that one
starts the theological task from phenomena, experience, and particularity.
Out of that one may then generalize and develop theory and larger statement. In terms of Christology, for example, it would mean that one would
start with the human figure of Jesus and then out of that determine that one
is forced to recognize that adequate talk of him is driven to employ the
language of the divine as well.[23] Rather than starting with general principles, one extrapolates toward the general principles from the phenomena
that are experienced.

In some sense, the difference is similar to the difference between deduc-
tive and inductive thinking. But the imagery of top down and bottom up is
a self-consciously metaphorical way of speaking and suggestive for thinking about the commandments. But rather than thinking that the functioning
of the Commandments is *either* top down *or* bottom up, the relation of the

---

[22] See especially his Gifford Lectures, *The Faith of a Physicist: Reflections of a Bottom-
Up Thinker* (Minneapolis: Fortress, 1996), *passim*.

[23] Ibid., 142.

Commandments to the other legislation and other biblical genres may be seen as both top down and bottom up. That is,

1. The ethics of the Commandments is a top-down way of working. They are supremely top down in that they genuinely come from above, that is, from God. They are a given from which other things are to be deduced. Part of the reticence of some ethicists to work within the framework of a divine command ethics is that it seems to suggest that the human person brings nothing to the ethical work of valuing, acting, deciding, etc. That is, they see divine command ethics – most widely exemplified and known in the Decalogue – as too much top-down. Ethics is given or imposed upon the human creature who is seen as having nothing to contribute except to obey.[24]

2. In fact, however, the ethics of the Commandments works also in a bottom up manner. That is reflected in the collections of laws, stories, oracles, proverbs, and the like. The meaning and effect of the prohibition is not simply deduced from the prohibition as if it were a principle but is worked out in various kinds of individual and corporate experiences, cases handled in the courts, instruction from parents, stories told out of the experience of the Israelite people, and the like. The result, then, is the complex picture of the meaning of the commandments that is not really or fully seen in the commandments themselves. Indeed, that meaning can only be determined in a bottom up way as the community lives out its life under the impact and control and guidance of these basic words.

Space

The final metaphors I want to propose for our thinking about the way the commandments work are *spatial* ones. Spatial metaphors have a long standing place in Christian thinking and Christian theology, most prominently in the image of the kingdom of God, a metaphor thoroughly of space and place, unless one reduces it to the "reign" or "kingship" of God, in which case the spatial dimension becomes fuzzy and the concept may become spiritualized in a way that the spatial metaphor, the sense of God's rule manifest in some context, is lost in a vague generality about God's rule. In their various works on theological and philosophical ethics, Charles Taylor and William Schweiker have suggested that every indiviual

---

[24] See William Schweiker, "Divine Command Ethics and the Otherness of God," *Power, Value, and Conviction: Theological Ethics in the Postmodern Age* (Cleveland: Pilgrim, 1998), 155–170.

carves out some kind of *moral space*.[25] By this, they mean that we live in some moral and cultural world "that poses questions about how to live as well as providing sets of value and norms for life – orientation to some idea of good, however defined, precedes our actions."[26] Schweiker goes on to suggest that the basic elements of the moral space of life are "1) human beings as self-interpreting, social agents; 2) patterns of interaction between people and their world(s), including different modes of being in the world(s); and 3) the mediation of self-understanding, and thus the identities of individuals and communities, by values and norms."[27] Taylor would give particular attention to the relation between our orientation in a moral space and our identity, our identity being shaped by our stand on moral and spiritual matters but also by our reference to a defining community.[28]

My argument would be that, in their context, the Commandments serve to answer the questions that are inherent in the definition of moral space and its basic elements that Schweiker and Taylor set forth here and as such serve to overcome the most primordial forms of moral terror that can beset us: tyranny and chaos.[29] Tyranny, through which a "wrongful authority has defined one's moral universe"[30] and removed the possibility of acting in a moral space as persons for whom a sense of self and the search for the good are united in a coherent whole, was overcome in the act of the Exodus, a real and also paradigmatic saving event in which the Lord of Israel put down the tyranny of the Egyptian pharaoh. The character of the other form of moral terror, which is chaos, is evident in the very meaning of the term "chaos," that is, "empty space." Moral terror is either the constriction of the possibility of moral action by authoritarian control or the absence of the possibility of moral action by the empty space that is created by chaos. The fending off of chaos is the meaning of the spatial metaphor of Sinai, the place where moral space was defined for the community, the starting point of an arc of moral understanding that is still folding while already

---

[25] Charles Taylor, *Sources of the Self: The Making of the Modern Identity* (Cambridge: Harvard, 1989); William Schweiker, "Power and the Agency of God," *Theology Today* 52 (1995), 204–224 (reprinted in Schweiker, *Power, Value, and Conviction: Theological Ethics in the Postmodern Age* [Cleveland: Pilgrim, 1998], 33–53).

[26] W. Schweiker, "Consciousness and the Good: Schleiermacher and Contemporary Theological Ethics," *Theology Today* 56 (1999), 181.

[27] Schweiker, "Power and the Agency of God," 34.

[28] Taylor, *Sources of the Self*, 36.

[29] W. Schweiker, "Time as a Moral Space: Moral Cosmologies, Creation and Last Judgment," in *The End of the World and the Ends of God: Science and Theology on Eschatology*, eds. J. Polkinghorne and M. Welker (Harrisburg: Trinity, 2000), 124–138.

[30] Ibid.

definitive.[31] In other words, Sinai is where slaves became moral agents and were given a framework to work out the patterns of interaction between themselves and their world, both near and far, and a coherent structure of values and norms to define themselves as individuals and as a community. The Commandments thus define the space of freedom and create in effect a defining community whose framework by which the questions of value and norms, the patterns of interaction among members and in relation to others, and the fundamental definition of one's self are determined is provided by the Ten Words of God. The Commandments forever characterized the freedom of God as a freedom vis-à-vis the other and self-identity as a part of a defining community. But the very definition of the community and the identity of the individual members is all wrapped up in and shaped by the moral space provided by the Commandments. The identity of this community is an outcome of their escape from the moral terror of tyranny and the chaos of empty space.

What the Commandments do, therefore, is to chart the moral topography of the Christian life, a topography that, because of the other images and metaphors I have called upon is found to be diverse and detailed, a map that takes one in many directions and charts windy paths, straight and highly visible routes, places to settle in, hills to be climbed, home territory and foreign territory, and the like. To be somewhat more architectural as well as geographic in using the image of moral space, the Commandments create a structure in which one is at home, where one can find one's way around because the topography is understandable and the framework familiar. One of the most obvious things about the Commandments is the way in which people all over and from highly varied contexts say, "I know those things." "I am at home with those directions." "They are intelligible and make sense to me, even when I sometimes have a difficult time fitting in with them."

But let me carry this spatial imagery one step further. The moral space of the Commandments can be defined. It does not stay on a generalized or abstract level. The moral space of the Commandments is the good neighborhood. By definition, the moral space in which the Christian community operates is a neighborhood. It is a community and it knows the character of the other members of the neighborhood. They are twofold: God and neighbor. These are not indefinite selves. These are persons who occupy a space in relation to the one whose identity is in this community

---

[31] On Sinai as a metaphor for the continuing process of learning and working out the meaning of the Commandments in a fashion that continues long after the primal event, see Walter Brueggemann, "Justice: The Earthly Form of God's Holiness," in Brueggemann, *The Covenanted Self*, ed. P. D. Miller (Minneapolis: Fortress, 1999), 49.

and who lives by this framework. They are a deity whose words and deeds are sharply and permanently etched in the experience of those who live in this space and this neighborhood. This is why the question, "Who is my neighbor?" is such a definitive one. It defines the community in which we live. It marks out the moral space of our lives. It lets us know the context of our freedom. It identifies the other over against which all of our life is lived. In some sense we do not know what to do or how to act without knowing our neighbor. The Bible's insistent reference to the neighbor and to the brother-sister is because the moral space of human life is marked out and defined by those other selves whom we know as brother-sister or as neighbor and by the self of God.[32] It is in the Commandments that one first encounters the concern for the neighbor as a defining characteristic of this community and as a primary focus of moral obligation. That is made explicit in the final Commandments on false witness and coveting, but it is implicit in the entire second table of the Decalogue and begins in the Deuteronomic form of the Commandments with the Sabbath Commandment and with the neighbor who is enslaved.[33]

---

[32] Part of the coherence and structure of the Commandments is found in the movement from the first words, "I am the Lord your God" to the final words, "everything that is your neighbor's."

[33] For development of the metaphor of the good neighborhood in relation to the Commandments, see below, 51–67.

4. The Good Neighborhood

Identity and Community through the Commandments

One of the contemporary cultural definitions of desire and well-being is the "good neighborhood."[1] Without a lot of analysis or argument, the culture generally presumes that life is best in a good neighborhood and problematic to a high degree in a bad one. In most popular or implicit understandings of what constitutes a good neighborhood, it is clear that there are highly tangible dimensions and many intangibles. One can intuitively recognize a good neighborhood when one sees it; there are physical characteristics that belong to the image of desire and well-being, such as nice and decent houses of varying sizes, attractive gardens and lawns, calm streets, persons getting along with one another, playing, talking, and the like. But there are also less tangible dimensions that have to do with the character of the persons who live there, how they understand themselves, what they are about in their lives, and how they relate to others in the neighborhood. By definition, at least according to the dictionary, a neighborhood customarily involves a permanent gathering of persons in proximity to each other, usually with distinguishing characteristics.

From two directions, "neighborhood" presents itself as an image for rich thinking about moral community in relation to the Commandments. The most obvious is the use of the "neighbor" as a defining moral category in the Commandments. The other impetus for appropriating this image is the way in which *spatial* notions, language, and imagery have come into play for both moral reflection in general and speaking about the Commandments. Acknowledging his indebtedness to Charles Taylor's *Sources of the Self*,[2] William Schweiker has argued that human beings exist in a "moral space" that "confronts us with questions about how to orient our lives and

---

[1] While this term has no particular identifiable source, I am indebted to Walter Brueggemann for prompting my thinking about this as a way of speaking about the moral space in which the Commandments operate. While it is the case that the term "good neighborhood" can be a code word for identifying a racially exclusive neighborhood safe from the encroachments of impoverished or "different" folks, my aim is precisely to counter such misuses of the term by drawing from an understanding of community that has shaped the Judaic and Christian communities of faith from the beginning.

[2] Charles Taylor, *Sources of the Self: The Making of the Modern Identity* (Cambridge: Harvard University Press, 1990).

also provides a background of distinctions of worth that persons use to guide their lives."[3] He suggests: "The place of human existence is always a space defined by questions about how to live and commitments to what is and ought to be valued in human life."[4] In this context, therefore, I am appropriating this insight and image to argue that the Commandments offer an inviting place to live, a locus for human existence that is defined in ways that make the space and existence within its bounds desirable and good. That such a spatial metaphor may be appropriate for speaking about the moral dimensions of the Decalogue is further indicated by the frequent spatial images that have been drawn into interpretation and analysis of the Commandments.[5] Thus one of the books on the Decalogue is titled *Signposts to Freedom*.[6] And when others speak about the Commandments, they may speak about the commandments as marking the "boundaries" of life under God, providing "fenceposts" for direction, marking out the "area" of freedom and responsibility, giving much "latitude" in the moral life. The notion of the "good neighborhood" is a way of claiming such spatial language but giving some *specificity* and *valuation* to the moral space. My contention in this essay, therefore, is that the Commandments, as presented in their context and in view of their continuing force among later generations, serve to define the good neighborhood, the formation of a community that is the desirable locus of well-being, the place to live the good life, a place to call home and feel at home. In other words, the Commandments present themselves as a way of identifying the "distinguishing characteristics" (so the dictionary) or the marks of the good neighborhood.

Identity and Community

This assumption arises out of indications in the text that the giving of the Commandments served as the *constitution* of a community and a definition

---

[3] William Schweiker, *Power, Value, and Conviction: Theological Ethics in the Postmodern Age* (Cleveland: Pilgrim, 1998), 5.

[4] Schweiker, *Power, Value, and Conviction*, 34.

[5] For further discussion of the significance of space as a category for conceptual and moral thinking, see James W. Flanagan, "Space," in *Handbook of Postmodern Biblical Interpretation*, ed. A. K. M. Adam (St. Louis: Chalice, 2000), 232–237; Edward S. Casey, *Getting Back into Place: Toward a Renewed Understanding of the Place-World* (Bloomington: Indiana University Press, 1993); and idem, *The Fate of Place: A Philosophical History* (Berkeley: University of California Press, 1997). See also the review of both books by Robert McCarter in *ThT* 56 (1999), 139–143.

[6] Jan M. Lochman, *Signposts to Freedom: The Ten Commandments and Christian Ethics* (Minneapolis: Augsburg, 1982).

of how it was to live out its life. That the story presents the proclamation of the Commandments at the beginning of the sojourn of the people after their delivery from Egypt and then reiterates them as they are poised to enter the land that will be the space of the good neighborhood suggests the definitive character of the Commandments for this community. The formality of the constitution of the community is marked in the text to a high degree with the gathering of the people at the "mountain of God" (Exod 3:1; 4:27; 18:5; 19:3 [LXX]; 24:13) and the various preparatory acts to get ready for the divine word.

The Decalogue begins with "I am the Lord your God" and closes with "your neighbor." Within those borders, identity is given or made known and a community is formed. This community does not constitute itself, nor does it evolve. It is created in the formality of a covenant agreement between YHWH, the Lord, and the people. In this agreement, each party becomes forever defined in relation to the other. Thus, the Hebrews, the Israelites, the children of Jacob are in effect given a new name, "the people of YHWH." Whatever acts stand in tension with that definition become problematic henceforth. Conversely, this deity is permanently defined as "your God" or our God. The expression "YHWH your/our God" is ubiquitous in the literature, grounded in the Prologue to the Commandments and the Shema (Deut 6:4–9), where the divine declaration of the Commandments is turned into a confessional claim of the people. At times, certainly in the Deuteronomic material, it seems impossible to name this deity without the epithet that connects the deity to the community.[7] In effect, neither community nor deity have separate existences once the covenant is established.[8] Even though both may experience real abandonment on the part of the other for a time, they are forever linked.[9]

---

[7] In Deuteronomy alone, the expression "the Lord our/your God" appears over 300 times.

[8] Such a claim cannot be read so as to exclude the Lord of Israel from having other stories, redemptive or otherwise, with other peoples, for there is inner-biblical testimony to such relationships (e.g., Amos 9:7). The weight of the claim is on the exclusion of Israel from having stories with other deities, as the First Commandment so indicates. Yet the connection is so tight that it is difficult to imagine a way of understanding YHWH that would not always include the relationship to Israel. At least, those who find the biblical story identifying have only that lens through which to view the character of both deity and community. On this issue, see Patrick D. Miller, "God's Other Stories: On the Margins of Deuteronomic Theology," in *Realia Dei: Essays in Archaeology and Biblical Interpretation in Honor of Edward F. Campbell, Jr. at His Retirement*, eds. P. H. Williams, Jr. and T. Hiebert (Atlanta: Scholars Press, 1999), 185–194; repr. in Patrick D. Miller, *Israelite Religion and Biblical Theology: Collected Essays* (JSOTSup 267; Sheffield: JSOT, 2000), 593–602.

[9] The many references to Israel "abandoning" the Lord in Jeremiah and elsewhere do not need enumerating, but there is also a tradition about the Lord abandoning the people (e.g., Isa 54:7–8).

Implications for Community

The implications that the Commandments bear on the moral shape of community are significant and can be briefly delineated.

Formation of a particular community. The texts of Exodus and Deuteronomy do not speak about a *general* understanding of community but of the formation of a *particular* community whose identity as a people is evoked by their relationship to the Lord and is inextricably tied to that relationship. There is a logically prior relationship to those of kinship, geographical proximity, shared experience, and the like – though these are also dimensions of this particular neighborhood as often of others – that constitutes this community. That is the relationship articulated in the initial words of the community-constituting act: "I am the Lord your God, who brought you out of the land of Egypt, out of the house of slavery" (Exod 20:2; Deut 5:6).

Transcendent ground. The community so constituted is "a more than human fellowship."[10] It has a transcendent ground. Whether or not there is any historical connection between the apparently early name for this community, *ʿam yhwh* (e.g., Num 11:29; Judg 5:11, 13; 20:2; 1 Sam 2:24; 2 Sam 1:12), and the Decalogue, that identification or characterization is fully in conformity with the Commandments and the Shema. As such, this community is not self-defining but other-defined. The degree to which that is the case is indicated in the first set of commandments, where the focus is on the relationship to the deity. This is the ground for the rest of the commandments, the neighborly ones.[11] The rules for the neighborhood are not confined to the neighborly relationship; they do not begin there, but they do end up there. The neighborhood or space of the Commandments is thus counter-cultural, at least to the extent that the culture operates as if God did not exist.[12] It is a place where the primary practice is the love of God as

---

[10] I am conscious of the appropriation of a term that was, in effect, the motto of the World Student Christian Federation.

[11] If it is the case that one should read from the prologue into the First Commandment in a causal way, that is, "because I am the Lord your God . . . you shall have no other gods before me," such a syntactical connection carries over implicitly into the other commandments. That is obviously the case for the first three, but there is no reason for assuming the connection is dropped as one moves into the rest of the Commandments.

[12] See Reinhard Hütter, "The Twofold Center of Lutheran Ethics: Christian Freedom and God's Commandments," in *The Promise of Lutheran Ethics*, eds. K. L. Bloomquist and J. R. Stumme (Minneapolis: Fortress, 1998), 44. On the presupposition of God's non-existence or the indifference to the question as a feature of the modern consciousness, see, for example Emmanuel Levinas, *Entre Nous: On Thinking of the Other* (New York: Columbia University Press, 1998), 18–19.

a character-forming enterprise, or, to use both the biblical language and that of Martin Luther, learning "how to trust completely in God as our ultimate good."[13] Even the commandments in behalf of the neighbor's well-being serve this character-forming enterprise, particularly the prohibition of coveting the things that belong to one's neighbor (see below on human desires). The transcendent ground of the community also implies something about the source of moral identity and how it may be possible for the community – both individually and communally – to act morally (see below).

Morally constituted community. The formation of a moral community is not the by-product of the formation of community. This community is *constituted* around the issue of relationships and how it is that members of the community are to live their lives together, their conduct toward one another. The moral character of the community is inherent, constitutive of its being as a community. The way in which and the degree to which the Pentateuch is *tôrâ* and the degree to which the Torah flows out of the Commandments and the giving of the Commandments are indicators that the community formed at Sinai is to be a neighborhood and not only a people. In fact, the giving of the Commandments begins a process of transforming a people into a neighborhood without relinquishing its character as a particular community whose unity is a matter of kinship as well as proximity. One of the clearest indications of this is that while the kinship relationship remains definitive, the instruction about how to live in the neighborhood affects all who live there, all who are neighbors, including the *gēr*, that is, including persons who move into the neighborhood but do not belong to the family, the clan, the ethnic community (e.g., Exod 20:10 [cf. 23:12]; Deut 5:14; Exod 12:49[14]; Lev 24:22; Num 9:14; 15:15–16[15]; 15:29–30; Lev 19:33–34[16]; cf. Exod 12:19; Lev 16:29; 17:8, 10, 12, 13, 15; 18:26;

---

[13] Levinas, *Entre Nous*, 18–19.

[14] "There shall be one law (*tôrâ*) for the native (*ʾezraḥ*) and for the alien (*gēr*) who resides among you."

[15] "You and the alien shall be alike before the Lord."

[16] "The alien who resides with you shall be to you as the citizen among you; you shall love him as yourself." It is not clear whether the terms *ʾaḥ* or *rēaʿ* ever include the *gēr* in their frame of reference. In fact the many references to treating the resident alien and the native/citizen (*ʾezraḥ* in Exodus–Numbers, but *ʾaḥ* in Deuteronomy [e.g., 1:16]) alike suggest that may not be the case. But the very presence of these references indicate that the resident alien is to be treated as a member of the neighborhood, that the rules apply to him/her as well as to the native/citizen/brother. Lev 19:18 and 34, with their calls to "love your neighbor as yourself" and "love the resident alien as yourself," serve to identify the resident alien as the recipient of exactly the same moral treatment as the neighbor (cf. Deut 10:19). The alien is to

Num 35:15). This people have become a moral community, and the prospect of living as a good neighborhood depends henceforth not upon their membership in the family but upon their willingness and ability to be moral. That orientation toward the moral, however, is derivative from their identity and self-knowledge as slaves redeemed by YHWH, who is their God.

Time and space. The community is one that exists in time and space. It assumes a conventional locale, proximate relationships, place to live, and the provisions for life. But the community so defined and constituted by the Commandments is not fixed in a *particular* time and space. It may be constituted at different times and places. It is assumed that the community created by this formal covenantal act and given definition of the character of its life together is a *continuing* community. The assumption of that continuity is tied to kinship relationships, to successive generations, whose instruction in the moral character of the community is a prime concern.[17] Kinship relationship is critical and later shows itself not only within Judaism (and even among those hostile to Judaism) by the question of what de-

---

be regarded as "like yourself," with the same needs and endangerments. [On the meaning of the construction here, particularly the term *kāmôkā*, "like yourself," see the essay by Andreas Schüle, "'Denn er ist wie Du' Zu Übersetzung und Verständnis des alttestamentlichen Liebesgebots Lev 19,18," *ZAW* 113 (2001), 315–334.]

The brother/sister/neighbor and the alien are bound together morally even if they are not the same categories. Both are members of the good neighborhood. The references in Leviticus to "anyone (*ʾîš*) of the people of Israel or any resident alien residing in Israel" (Lev 20:2; cf. Num 19:10; 35:15) and to "anyone of the house of Israel or any resident alien residing in Israel" (22:18) serve to preserve the ethnic differentiation apart from the proximity designation but insist that the proximity relationship works in the same way. That some differentiation is made within the statutes is indicated in Lev 25 where, for example, if a "brother" falls into difficulty, you treat him like a resident alien (v. 35). But the stipulations that follow describing the appropriate treatment indicate how one treats a neighbor/brother in Israel, that is, not taking interest in advance, not lending them money with interest or providing them food at a profit. The most extensive difference is also found in this chapter: slaves may be acquired from the surrounding nations and also from the resident aliens residing with you (vv. 44–46). Deuteronomy makes a single differentiation between the resident aliens and the Israelites as members of the sacral community by indicating that meat that dies of itself may not be eaten by Israelites but may be given to aliens (14:21). At the same time, Deuteronomy is explicit about including the resident aliens in the gathering of the people to hear the terms of the covenant and to be instructed about the rules of the neighborhood in which they are going to live (29:10; 31:12) and accept them by entering into covenant. On the *gēr*, see now Christiana van Houten, *The Alien in Israelite Law* (JSOTSup 107; Sheffield: JSOT, 1991); and Jose E. Ramírez Kidd, *Alterity and Identity in Israel* (BZAW 283; Berlin: Walter de Gruyter, 1999).

[17] That is particular evident in the way that the biblical book most shaped by the Commandments, Deuteronomy, places heavy stress on teaching the next generations the way of the Lord.

termines who is a Jew but also within Christianity, for which it is critical that its messianic figure is a Jew and its earliest leader insists on viewing the church as grafted onto the tree that is Israel (Rom 9–11). In other words, the particularity of this community never disappears. So matters of kinship and election are never off the table, and it is difficult to submerge them, as if the community so defined by this formal covenantal act can transcend its character as a people and its particular election into a community whose very character is dependent upon the relationship to the Lord of Israel and the way that neighborly life is defined in the community-constituting act.[18]

Voluntary association. The moral community constituted in relation to "the Lord your God" and in relation to "your neighbor" is a voluntary association. That is, those who live in this community and by this definition of community do so because they wish to, voluntarily (Exod 19:3–8). But the inherent notion of voluntary association is complex. It is not as if persons wander in off the street and decide to hook up with the persons who are there, with like-minded people, and so on. If the covenantal moment is a constituting moment and one that depends upon the community's agreement, upon the decision of individual members that they choose this neighborhood – as it does – the community has a prior history that is also determinative of its makeup and brings them together. History and kinship, election and deliverance bring this community into being. It is not, however, formally constituted as a neighborhood for living together apart from the willing decision of one and all, of all as one (Exod 19:8), to live by the constituting rules, by the polity set forth in the divine revelation of the Commandments and the Mosaic teaching. That decision is not only voluntary; it is one that is taken up as a *welcome obligation,* as an appropriate response to the experience of deliverance from slavery. Obligation is not imposed (though it is certainly expected by the deity – see next item) but assumed.

The fact that the community readily disobeys the moral obligations it has taken upon itself does not vitiate the voluntary and welcome assumption of the obligation as a mark of the good neighborhood. But it does identify the reality of sin as something that comes into the neighborhood and has to be dealt with. The moral problematic between the willing acceptance (Exod 19) and the immediate disobedience (Exod 32–33) has been examined in a helpful way by Jacqueline Lapsley in a study of the problem

---

[18] For a treatment of the Decalogue in relation to family and kinship issues, see now the two essays by Ron E. Tappy, "Lineage and Law in Pre-Exilic Israel" and "The Code of Kinship in the Ten Commandments,"in *RB* 107 (2000), 175–204, 321–337.

of the moral self in the Book of Ezekiel. She uncovers a conflict between
different moral anthropologies, one of virtuous moral selfhood and another
more deterministic one, suggesting that the people of this neighborhood as
they lived out their lives were "inherently incapable of acting in accord
with the good (they possess a neutral moral self)."[19] Ezekiel offers a solu-
tion: a new moral identity is given in the knowledge of God and the
knowledge of self, so that "character displaces action as the central component of the moral self."[20] Or at least the new moral identity becomes the
source of actions, and the focus of the book in its final chapters is more on
the divinely given identity than on the actions of the community. The move
from virtuous selfhood to the gift of a new being, that is, "a moral identity
formed and sustained by a transcendent God" that makes possible a new
mode of action, is also a dimension of the decalogical tradition, as indicated by the movement in Moses' speeches from the injunction to Israel to
"circumcise the foreskin of your heart, and do not be stubborn any longer"
(Deut 10:16) to Moses' final climactic declaration:

Moreover the LORD your God will circumcise your heart and the heart of your descendants, so that you will love the LORD your God with all your heart and with all your soul,
in order that you may live. . . . Then you shall again obey the LORD, observing all his
commandments that I am commanding you today, and the LORD your God will make you
abundantly prosperous in all your undertakings, in the fruit of your body, in the fruit of
your livestock, and in the fruit of your soil (Deut 30:6, 8).

Deuteronomy reinforces this word with its consequent indication that the
commandment is neither too difficult nor too far away. It is at hand and
accessible (30:11–14). The final Mosaic speech holds the gift of a new
identity, a new character, and the capacity to carry out the right action in a
realistic tension appropriate to the complexity of the moral self as it is actually lived out.

Sanctions and Rationalities. Participation in the moral community is both
sanctioned and rationalized. The motivation clauses of the Decalogue and
their counterparts in the various legal codes serve to do both. Negative
outcomes for failure to conform to the stipulated marks of the neighborhood or, in more traditional language, to keep the Commandments, are
made explicit, but the rationalization is not purely negative. Throughout
the first half of the Decalogue, various reasons are given why the particular
prohibitions or Commandments should be kept and observed. These in-

---

[19] Jacqueline E. Lapsley, *Can These Bones Live? The Problem of the Moral Self in the
Book of Ezekiel* (BZAW 301; Berlin: Walter de Gruyter, 2000), 185–186.
[20] Ibid., 186.

clude not only sanctions for disobedience (as in the prohibition of idolatry and against misuse of the divine name), but also visions of the good (as in the prohibition of idolatry and the commandment to honor parents) and appeals to experience and memory as a way of encouraging conformity to the stipulations laid out in the covenant (the Sabbath commandment). In all of this, one perceives a way of effecting moral community that makes attention to the distinguishing characteristics a highly desirable commitment, the reasonable thing to do.

Obedience to God. Obedience to God rather than to human beings defines this moral community. That is seen not only in the emphasis placed upon loyalty to the Lord of Israel but also in comparison with similar ethnic and national communities contemporary with Israel. This is a point that Eckart Otto has made strongly in recent writings.[21] It is exemplified in the loyalty oath of Deut 13:2–12, a negative reflex of the commandments prohibiting the worship of other gods and the making of images, as well as in the positive reflex of these in the commandment calling for the exclusive love of the Lord of Israel in the Shema.[22] Otto has noted that Deut 13:2–12 is a translated version of Esarhaddon's loyalty oath. In the Assyrian version, any criticism of the king, any suggestion of rebellion or insurrection, whether from prophets, members of one's own family, or members of the royal family, was to be reported to the king, and the one who spoke of rebellion was to be executed. The good neighborhood constituted out of the Commandments knows such loyalty oaths and places them prominently to the fore. But they require loyalty to the redeeming God, not to any member of the neighborhood or any ruling figure. There is no ultimate authoritative[23] claim in this neighborhood except that of the deity. The relationship

---

[21] See for example, E. Otto, "Human Rights: The Influence of the Hebrew Bible," *JNSL* 25 (1999), 1–20.

[22] At this point, the distinction between the prohibition of other gods and the prohibition of images of either YHWH or the other gods does not make a difference. Deut 13 has both in mind. The First Commandment is clearly in view for the issue is going after "other gods" (the language of the First Commandment) versus the worship of "the Lord your God . . . alone" (the Shema). Whether or not idolatry per se is in the picture, the language of the Second Commandment is present also in the double reference to "serving" other gods (vv. 3, 7) and the testing to see whether "you indeed love the Lord your God with all your heart and soul" (v. 4). The language of "loving" God comes in the Second Commandment in the Decalogue (5:10), but it is associated with the First Commandment by its presence in the positive form of the First Commandment, the Shema (6:5).

[23] On the distinction between authoritative and authoritarian, see J. Vining, *The Authoritative and the Authoritarian* (Chicago: University of Chicago Press, 1986). The distinction is between "willing obedience and obedience for its own sake" (77). I am indebted to Jeffries Hamilton's unpublished paper, "How to Read an Abhorrent Text: Deuteronomy 13 and the Nature of Authority," for this reference.

to the neighbor is not ultimate and not one of obedience. The only other relationship in the neighborhood that comes close to this is not a political one. It is a kinship one and has to do with the way that children relate to their parents. The language there is comparable to the way in which the community is to relate to God: honor (see the Fifth Commandment to honor father and mother). The good neighborhood, the moral community defined at Sinai, is a political community (see below on Levinas and *le tiers*), and in its history rulers are present and act. But what the Torah does is to set the king not as equivalent to the parent but as on a par with every other member of the community in that his primary responsibility is to live by the moral definition that is given in the constituting of the community, in the creation of the good neighborhood (Deut 17:18–20). Nothing is said about the members of the community being obedient to the king but only about the king not being other than the members of the community and being under the same moral code as they are.

Human desire. In the movement from the first Commandments, which have to do with the locus of one's ultimate trust, to the final Commandment, which has to do with the control of our desire for the goods of our neighbor, the Commandments inscribe an approach to human desires as an aspect of the good neighborhood. In Reinhard Hütter's succinct appropriation of Luther's conviction as expressed in his *Large Catechism*, "They stubbornly keep our desires directed toward God." To that end, Luther proposed to weave the Ten Commandments into a mode of prayer, serving to form the desires of the members of the community toward God. He saw in the regular study, meditation, and reflection upon the Commandments a combination of instruction, thanksgiving, confession, and petition that can shape human desires toward their true object, which is the starting point of the Commandments (the prohibitions of the worship of other gods and the making and worshiping of idols).[24]

Outside recognition. Persons outside the neighborhood are able to recognize the quality of life within this neighborhood and identify it as desirable. Their grounds for doing so are precisely the norms that have been set

---

[24] See Martha Ellen Stortz, "Practicing Christians: Prayer as Formation," in *The Promise of Lutheran Ethics*, eds. K. L. Bloomquist and J. R. Stumme (Minneapolis: Fortress, 1998), 67. That the inclination toward idols has to do with human desires and is to be connected with the last commandment(s) is well illustrated in the Deuteronomic instruction to the Israelites to burn the idols of the nations around them when they enter the land: "Do not covet the silver or the gold that is on them and take it for yourself, because you could be ensnared by it; for it is abhorrent to the Lord your God" (Deut 7:25).

forth, the constituting rules and polity for the life together (Deut 4:6, 8), as well as the transcendent ground of the community's life (v. 7). This neighborhood is easily recognizable as a good place to live. Both grounds for that recognition – "What nation has a god so near to it as the Lord our God is whenever we call to him? And what other great nation has statutes and ordinances as just as this entire law . . . ?" – are at the center of the constituting covenantal act: the relationship with "the Lord your God," which is defined by the deity's act of compassionate deliverance,[25] and the relationship to the neighbor, whose just character is determined and defined by the Commandments and their elaboration in the statutes and ordinances.

Order and freedom. Both order and freedom are built into the moral community shaped by the Commandments. The Commandments take the community from disorder and slavery (Egypt) to order and freedom (the good neighborhood of the Commandments, a community of time and place). The focus of attention is customarily on effecting an order as the Commandments are understood prescriptively. Whether prescriptively or descriptively interpreted, they clearly function to lay out guidelines, directions, and parameters that give structure to the life of the community formed and directed by them. But as is often noted, the Commandments leave much open; they provide a lot of elbow room, as it were, in the moral space they effect. There are wide realms of human life and conduct left without moral requirement, although it may be possible to infer from what is given how one might act and what the character of community life would be like on other issues. Furthermore, the direction that is given through the Commandments needs much fleshing out and receives it in the statutes and ordinances, which identify the long and often complex trajectory of meaning, action, and effects that extends out of each of the Commandments and the Decalogue as a whole. Indeed, there is much to be spelled out in cases that, even if more time and circumstance controlled, nevertheless, give much direction for the life of the neighborhood, particularly as it tries to unpack the moral formation the Commandments evoke. As the Commandments are indeed unpacked through the statutes and ordinances, the case law and other legal formulations in the Pentateuch, they are revealed to encompass a rich, detailed, and coherent sense of how to

---

[25] See the Exodus story and note the linguistic argument of Norbert Lohfink that the calling to the deity referred to in Deut 4:7 is the cry of the oppressed and the poor. The laws build into the system the compassionate divine response that evoked the divine deliverance, the deity's hearing the cry of distress and coming to deliver. See N. Lohfink, "Poverty in the Laws of the Ancient Near East and of the Bible," *ThS* 52 (1991), 34–50.

live in a structured, free moral space. Freedom has limits and direction; it is not constricted or chaotic.

More specifically, the order and freedom of this moral community are experienced in *time* and *place*. That is, the order of *time*, exemplified particularly in the seven-day cycle, is in behalf of freedom from the oppressive potential of work or labor (the Sabbath commandment). The primary form of freedom is found in the regularity of time, which guarantees release from hard labor. It is no accident that this order in behalf of freedom is undergirded in the Deuteronomic form of the Decalogue by a recollection of the Exodus deliverance (Deut 5:15), for the experience of slavery and non-freedom in Egypt was the experience of unrelenting and oppressive work. This freedom in time is then extended into a sabbatical principle that operates to bring release from all forms of economic bondage (Deut 15).

The order of *place* is the realm of freedom. It is identified only at one point in the Decalogue, specifically the commandment to honor one's parents. But the movement from the giving of the Commandments (Exodus) to the recollection of their giving (Deuteronomy) enhances the way in which the neighborhood is marked out as a space for life. It is in the commandment regarding the honor of parents that the community hears that its life is in a gifted place, "the land that the Lord your God is giving you." This order of space is marked not so much by substantive freedom as it is by substantive goodness.[26] It is a place of blessing, articulated in the provision of life and the provision of good. The neighborhood is marked specifically as a *good* neighborhood in two ways: it is gifted space and it is a place where good can happen ("that your days may be long and that it may go well with you"). But the latter is effected precisely as the community constitutes itself by this covenant and makes its space one that is marked by the distinguishing characteristics embodied in the Commandments as specified, particularized, and exemplified in the statutes and ordinances.

The Other and others. It is not possible to talk about either the order or the freedom without a large sense of the Other and others. The moral community effected by the Commandments is one in which human self-understanding is found in an encounter with the Other. In this sense, they offer an example of the concern for the Other that is accentuated in the eth-

---

[26] In the divine allotment of land for the various members of the community, there is a precise order whose purpose is to provide the freedom for life on the land and access to its productivity without restriction except that restriction that keeps each member/family from undercutting the freedom of the neighbor for life on the land (Josh 13–22).

ics of Emmanuel Levinas.[27] The Other is found not only in the neighbor but in the relationship between God and the community. Each comprehends moral purpose in relation to the Other. That relationality is definitive of human existence and experience but also determinative of who God is. This is not, however, a Buberian "I-Thou" relationship, which is too reductionistic a way of viewing the moral community. Here Levinas is helpful with his insistence that in the moral community there is always "the third party" (*le tiers*). In the Decalogue, the third party is the neighbor. In Frank Yamada's helpful interpretation of Levinas's ethics, he summarizes as follows: "Encountering the Other is the primary experience that makes possible the working out of ethical acting and thinking. The realization of a third party, however, disrupts my bi-symmetrical relation to the Other and thus forms the basis for society. *Le tiers* requires me to think about issues that are larger than my own relation to the Other. It creates the necessity for talking about justice for other human beings and the world."[28] The moral community is a fully social one precisely because it is a neighborhood in which the definitive relationship includes the third party from the start.

Relationships. The structure of order and freedom, therefore, has to do with relationships. Such relational order is not primarily oriented toward a broad hierarchy of human relationships, though some hierarchy is assumed (for example, in the commandment having to do with Sabbath rest and the prohibition of coveting). Alongside certain *assumed* relationships, there are those that are explicitly *effected, nurtured, or protected in the Commandments.* The latter are several:

1. The *sovereign deity and the redeemed community*, a relationship that is both personal/individual and corporate/communal in that, according to the narrative, the community as a whole is explicitly addressed by the Commandments, while the form of address ("you") is regularly cast in the singular. Each individual member of the community is addressed by the obligations and possibilities of the Commandments but only as part of the community as a whole. This is not an individual ethic; it is communal from the start and applies to the community. Yet the ethic is individual insofar as the directions and structure apply to each member of the community. This is one of the many ways in which the ethics of the Bible function to keep a complex but coherent relationship between the part and the whole, between individual and society, the one and the many.

---

[27] E.g., Levinas, *Entre Nous*.
[28] Frank Yamada, "Ethics," in *Handbook of Postmodern Interpretation*, ed. A. K. M. Adam (St.Louis: Chalice, 2000), 81.

The initial encounter with the other is found in the community's call to the worship and service of "the Lord your God," so that the Other with whom it deals first and always is the sovereign and redeeming God, whose actions have made possible the formation of this particular moral community. But it is just as true that the deity also deals first and always with the other who is discerned in the community, both in its corporate expression and in its individual lives. The way in which that relationship constantly slides back and forth between individual and community is evident in large measure in the oracles of the prophets.

2. *Member of the community and neighbor*, a relationship that is made explicit in the last two (or three) commandments with the prohibitions against false witness "against your neighbor" and against coveting the wife of "your neighbor" or the house of "your neighbor," or, for that matter anything that belongs to "your neighbor" (Exod 20:16–17; Deut 5:20-21). There is a structured moral movement from the encounter with the other as deity to the encounter with the other as neighbor.[29]

There is some danger that *the neighbor may disappear* from the picture as the community interprets the moral space of the Commandments. That is, it is possible to turn the moral direction of the Commandments inward so that they have to do with the individual's life apart from the neighborhood and thus no longer become crucial for life in the good neighborhood. They are seen to have to do with personal attitudes and actions that might indirectly affect the neighbor but are not primarily oriented toward the well-being of the compatriot in the neighborhood.

There is little danger that the prohibition against *killing / murder* would be viewed as not having to do first of all, if not only, with the protection of the life of the neighbor. And it is highly likely that the prohibition of *stealing* will regularly be perceived as protecting the property of the neighbor. Even there, however, it is easy to miss the fact that the first protection is not the property of the neighbor but the neighbor herself or himself, that is, protection of the life of the neighbor from being stolen or *kidnapped* for personal gain and profit (see Exod 21:16).[30]

A more common disappearance of the neighbor is found in the commandment against *adultery*. It is easy and commonplace to interpret the prohibition of adultery as restricted to "my" marriage relationship, even though the context clearly indicates that the marriage of "my" neighbor falls under the protection in this Commandment. To be sure, adultery has terrible effects upon the marriage of the one who commits adultery, which

---

[29] On the relation of the resident alien (*gēr*) to the neighbor, see above.

[30] A. Alt, "Das Verbot des Diebstahls im Dekalog," *Kleine Schriften zur Geschichte des Volkes Israels* I (München: C.H. Beck, 1953), 333–340.

merit attention in the moral discussion about adultery. But the Commandment does not have its primary aim at the spouse of the violator (whether
male or female) but at the damage done to the neighbor and the marriage
relationship of the neighbor. Insofar as the neighborhood defined by the
Commandments deals with issues of sexual relationships, the starting point
is the way in which neighbor relations are endangered by violating the
marriage relationship of the other.

Even Commandments with explicit reference to the neighbor may be
interpreted in such a way that the neighbor and his or her well-being disappear as the primary concern of the Commandment. This is evident in the
way in which the commandment against *false witness* is often turned into a
general prohibition against *lying*. It is certainly possible to see deceit in
general as coming into play in this commandment. In the Psalter, no commandment is set more prominently to the fore, often in relation to deceit
broadly understood. But even there, the primary reference and context in
which the concern for lying arises is in the way in which the *neighbor* is
harmed by false witness, whether through gossip, rumor, or the more technical case of judicial perjury (e.g., Amos 5:10). So also the prohibition
against *coveting*, where the neighbor is mentioned *three* times, may be
turned into a resistance to *greed and consumerism*, phenomena that indeed
may belong to the trajectory of the commandment but should not displace
the primary concern of the commandment, which reflects the attitude of a
member of the neighborhood *not as a personal stance* but as it leads to actions *detrimental to the other*. Lodged within the moral space of the last
commandment, greed has to do with its effects against the neighbor, not so
much with a generally inordinate love of things or desire of things as with
a desire for the things of the neighbor that leads to other acts against the
neighbor—killing, adultery, stealing, false witness, etc. To the extent, then,
that broader matters come in view, for example, greed and consumerism,
they do so as neighbor concerns for the good of the neighborhood.

3. *Member of the community and slave*, the starting point in the Decalogue for the relationship with the neighbor as other. The Sabbath Commandment in its Deuteronomic form sets the rest of the male and female
slave as its particular objective. It presumes the capacity of the members of
the community to find and provide for rest and relaxation, but it fixes a
time for such rest specifically so that the members of the community who
are not free – and one presumes that the slave meant in this instance is first
of all a Hebrew, that is, a neighbor who is now in a situation of economic
endangerment and so forced into bonded service – may find the rest that is
necessary for human life. So the neighbor is first encountered in a way that
is problematic, that is, as slave, but the encounter is subversive in that it is
set to provide release for the slave. That such release is meant to be a fore-

taste of ultimate release is clearly indicated by the laws bringing about permanent release of debts and slaves in the seventh year (Deut 15). The relationship to the other as a member of the neighborhood who is economically threatened is opened by creating characteristics that will serve to resist economic oppression and bring about economic restoration.

4. *Member of the community and family*, the primary relationship within the kinship ethos and, more generally, the primary relationship within a neighborhood. It is characteristic of the moral space filled by these guidelines and distinguished by this way of living that the family is undergirded precisely where it is most vulnerable, the breakdown of the care and respect of adult children for their parents. The protection of the parents by ensuring their honor and respect is a protection of the family.

5. *Member of the community and nature*, a subdued but present association in the Commandments as the Sabbath Commandment and the coveting Commandment lift up cattle, the ox, and the ass as being provided rest and protection (cf. Exod 23:12; Lev 25:3–4). The significance of this should not be overlooked. These are work animals, and so there is self-interest in providing for their rest. But the Sabbath Commandment cannot be seen simply as a self-interested statute. It rather seeks to be comprehensive in setting aside the rest time. That includes the natural world. That such a broader relationship to nature is envisioned is underscored when the sabbatical principle is carried over in the statutes to include the land and fields. Again, self-interest may be a part of this because the land that lies fallow is renourished, but the harmonious interface of people and land is evident in the fact that the time of rest is beneficial to both parties in the relationship. A further dimension of the relationship between the community and nature in the Sabbath rest is seen in the indication that such rest for the land envisions accessibility to its produce as available to the *wild animals* as well as to the poor (Exod 23:10).[31]

Memory and experience. Morality is rooted in memory and shared experience. Both the Prologue, which recalls the redemptive work of God that created the possibility of a moral community, and the Deuteronomic Sabbath Commandment, which recalls the experience of slavery and redemption either as the goal of the Sabbath observance or its impetus, mark this community as one whose identity is constitutive of moral possibility. The memory of God's redemptive work on their behalf brings the knowledge of God to life and becomes the ground of the moral life. That this memory is

---

[31] The inclusion of nature in one's definition of community has been especially argued by Wendell Berry in various works, e.g., *Sex, Economy, Freedom, and Community* (New York: Pantheon, 1993).

a shared one means that the neighbors have a common ground for the moral life. It is in the act of remembering that the community discovers its ground and finds the source of the moral life outside itself but rooted in its experience, an experience available in memory. That memory may be actualized by later generations for whom the experience of the Lord's redemption is indirect, that is, available only in the memory as the story is told and retold. In that process, new generations are given a memory (Deut 11:1–7)[32] and the covenant is made afresh with each new generation (5:3). Moral obligation and moral identity, action and character, come together as the community remembers what God has done and places its trust in the redeeming Lord.[33] That such self-understanding erupts in moral action is precisely the point of the Sabbath Commandment, as the provision of rest for bonded slaves is grounded in the experience of God's provision of rest and freedom from slavery for the community. The self receives its identity out of this shared experience that is recalled in memory: the memory of Pharaonic oppression, the Lord's liberating act and its revelation of the character of the source of moral understanding, and the connection to the neighbor who is "like yourself" in memory and in present reality.

---

[32] See Patrick D. Miller, *Deuteronomy* (Louisville: John Knox Press, 1990), loc. cit.

[33] As Jacqueline Lapsley has reminded me, that memory may be a *negative* memory of the people's sinfulness, as in the case of Ezekiel. One may also cite the way in which Pss 105 and 106 preserve the story of God's faithfulness in Israel's history as a character-forming memory (Ps 105) but also the story of Israel's sinfulness in that same history (Ps 106). Both positive and negative memories are crucial to authentic self-understanding and identity, as well as to the shaping and reshaping of community.

5. The Story of the First Commandment[1]

The Book of Exodus

Interpretation of the Commandments in story form and via the biblical stories and books is both an ancient and contemporary practice. In the Midrash on the Ten Commandments, fascinating – and fantasy – stories are told about ways in which Jews through the ages kept or disobeyed the Commandments. In a more recent collection of essays on the Ten Commandments, edited by Rachel Mikva, Jewish writers interpret the Commandments afresh, and virtually every essay engages in some story-telling to interpret the meaning of the Commandment under discussion. Last year, I picked up two books on the Ten Commandments. One is by the law professor and legal writer, Alan Dershowitz. Titled *The Genesis of Justice* and subtitled: *Ten Stories of Biblical Injustice that Led to the Ten Commandments and Modern Law*, Dershowitz's book retells ten stories from Genesis and argues that the Book of Genesis and the first part of Exodus are a narrative prelude to the revelation at Sinai and serve to prepare for the revelation of the Commandments by showing the need for laws and rules. About the same time, the biblical scholar David Noel Freedman brought out his book, titled *The Nine Commandments: Uncovering the Pattern of Crime and Punishment in the Hebrew Bible*. There he argues that from Exodus to Kings the books recount the violation of the first Nine Commandments one by one through each book, with the Tenth Commandment being broken implicitly in each violation of the other Commandments. Another biblical scholar, Calum Carmichael has argued, rather extremely, that the laws in fact originated out of narratives.

Whether or not these particular analyses stand up over the long haul is not so much the issue as the way they point to the possibility of interpreting the Commandments via *story* and *book*. That is certainly the case with the First Commandment, which comes to play in various and significant ways in virtually all of the narrative books of the Old Testament. I will not try to demonstrate that fact, which is not difficult to do, but, within the time lim-

---

[1] This essay was presented as one of the Sprunt Lectures at Union Theological Seminary-PSCE in Richmond, Virginia in 2002 and again later that year as part of the Spring Lectures at Central Baptist Theological Seminary in Kansas City, Kansas.

its before us, turn to the biblical book that is the most immediate context for the First Commandment and ask how the *story* told there and the *book as a whole* inform us about what matters and what is at stake in the primary or foundational obligation of the Commandments.

The Book of Exodus is the specific context for the Ten Commandments. They are repeated in Deuteronomy, but the repetition is a recall of the revelation on Sinai, which stands at the center of the Book of Exodus. As the story and the book develop, we are given several interpretive clues to what is at stake in the First or primary commandment. (And henceforth I will use either the term First Commandment or primary commandment as shorthand for the complex that includes the Prologue, the prohibition of other gods and the prohibition of making images and worshipping other gods or idols.)

I would begin by noting the way in which the story of *Exod 1–15* is told in terms of the *two* parts of the Prologue: the *identification* or self-presentation of the Lord – "I am the Lord" – and the *characterization* of the Lord as redeemer from slavery – "who brought you out...." The two main foci of the Exodus narrative in 1–15 are exactly those two matters. For in Exod 3–4, the account of the call of Moses, the critical moment is the revelation of the name of the God: "When they ask me what is his name, what shall I say to them." "I am who I am/I will be who I will be...the Lord," is the response. Then in Exod 5–15, we hear the detailed and long story of the Lord's bringing the people out of the land of Egypt out of the house of bondage. But already in the call narrative, it is clear that the words and deeds that follow will give an identity to the God who speaks. Again and again we hear in the ensuing narrative the words, "that you may know that I am the Lord." And when the Exodus is completed, it culminates in a song of praise: "I will sing to the *Lord*, for he has triumphed gloriously...this is *my God* and I will praise him... *the Lord is his name*" (Exod 15). One may read Exod 1–15 as entirely and solely an interpretive account of the meaning of the Prologue to the Commandments and the elaborated narrative ground for the claim of the First Commandment.

A further interpretive clue to what is at stake in the primary commandment is also given by the story of the Exodus. It is the largest explicit linguistic connection between the story of the Exodus and the Commandments. That connection is represented in the thematic function of the word "serve" or "worship," the Hebrew verb *ᶜbd* and its derivatives, nouns meaning a) service or labor/work; and b) servant or slave. This word appears twice at the beginning of the Decalogue, once in the Prologue where the Lord's self presentation is as the one who "brought you out of the land of Egypt, out of the house of slavery (*ᶜăbādîm*)" and a second time in the prohibition "You shall not bow down to them or serve (*ᶜbd*) them," the immediate context indicating "them" refers to the manufactured idols, but also includes the "other gods" (which, syntactically, is the only plural antecedent to which the "them" of "you shall not serve them" can refer). This conjoining of a prohibition against the making of idols with an expression that nearly always refers not just to idols but also to "other gods" – you shall not bow down to them or serve them – is one of the primary reasons for seeing the First and Second Commandments as inextricably one directive with two foci: against the worship of other gods and against the making and worshipping of images of any god.

But the language for *serving* and *service* occurs nearly *thirty times* in Exod 1–15, the account of the Exodus. And there it moves back and forth between *two contexts*. One is its frequent usage in reference to the hard labor or hard service imposed by the Egyptians on the Israelites, making them their slaves. So in chapter 1, the story begins right off the bat with the narrative report that because the Israelites have experienced the fulfillment of the creation blessing and have been fruitful and multiplied and filled the land, the Egyptian king enacts what he calls a shrewd policy: Oppress the Israelites with hard service so they will not increase. "They imposed harsh service on the Israelites. They made their life bitter with hard service/labor in mortar and bricks and in every kind of labor/service in the field, all their service that they made them serve with harshness" (Exod 1:13–14).

The policy fails, of course, as does the Egyptian king's effort to eliminate all the boy babies. But the failure of the policy does not mean a withdrawal of it. This harsh service or slavery continues and becomes the ground for Israel's cry to God: "After a long time, the Egyptian king died. The Israelites groaned *from their service/slavery*. And they cried out, and their cry went up to God *from their service/slavery*" (Exod 2:23). It is this plea of oppressed slaves that evokes God's notice and the call of Moses. In the course of the conversation between Moses and the Lord, at the point of Moses' anxiety about his capacity to go in and confront the king of Egypt and then to bring the Israelites out, the Lord promises him two things, one is the promise of Immanuel, foreshadowing the meaning of the *ʾehyeh* name, "I will be," to be revealed in the ensuing conversation: *ʾehyeh immāk* = "I will be with you." The other promise is of a sign: "When you have brought the people out of Egypt, *you shall serve God on this mountain.*" Up to this point, all the words about service have been of an oppressive service and slavery to the Egyptian king. Now we hear a word about a *service of the Lord* that is the ultimate outcome of the Exodus deliverance. This is the second thematic usage of the word "serve."

The significance of this alternative service language is developed and sealed in the repeated *interplay* of and *tension* between the Lord's demand to the king, "Let my people go *that they may serve me*," and the increased burden of hard service placed on the Israelites by the king. The initial request to the king of Egypt is to let the people go that they may celebrate a festival in the wilderness and to let the people go a three days journey in the wilderness to sacrifice to "the Lord our God." But this is met by an even heavier ᶜ*ăbōdâ*, the labor of making the bricks without straw, the essential ingredient. Again and again we continue to hear of the slavery and harsh service, *ten* more times (5:1, 9, 11, 17–18; 6:5–6, 9; 14:5, 12). But now a counterpoint moves through the narrative as again and again we hear also the demand of the Lord to the Egyptian king, no longer to let my people go a three days journey to sacrifice but a direct and simple: "Let my people go that they may serve/worship me." *Thirteen* times that demand of the Lord is the center of the confrontation between Moses and the king of Pharaoh (4:23; 7:16, 26 [=8:1]; 8:16 [=v. 20]; 9:1, 13; 10:3, 7, 8, 11, 24, 26; 12:31). The issue is not finally simply a respite from the labors, though the need for that becomes the grounding for the Sabbath commandment in Deuteronomy. It is the question of whom this people will serve. Will their service be to the king of Egypt or to the king of heaven, the Lord of Israel? That is the issue that arises and is resolved in the deliverance from Egypt. That is the issue behind the primary commandment. One does not have to identify the king of Egypt as a god to realize that the Exodus, with its continuing *other* theme, "That you may know that I am the Lord," is at its heart a story of who is God and who is in control of history. The initial response of the Egyptian king to Moses bringing the word of the Lord to him is: "Who is the Lord that I should heed him and let Israel go? I do not know the Lord, and I will not let Israel go." (Exod 5:2). Whom shall you serve? The gods and their human representatives, whose rule is manifested and experienced in oppressive and tyrannous enslavement or the Lord who hears your cries and knows and sees your suffering and delivers you from the house of slaves. One is not to miss the way in which the Prologue to the Commandments defines the land of Egypt. It is a home for slaves. The alternative is sharply put: the service of the Egyptian king or the service of the Lord. So when Israel hears the initial word that you shall have no other gods and you shall not bow down to and shall not serve or worship other gods, it hears that as a word of grace as well as a word of demand. The service of the one is the worship of a gracious God who hears the cry of the oppressed, whose ears are especially attuned to that wavelength and who moves into that situation. The service of the other is submission to human tyranny. The obligation of the First Commandment begins as an *alternative* and *preferable* service. Henceforth, there will always be the issue of whether the service of the other gods is the rejection of a service in freedom for one that turns service into slavery and is indifferent to the-human need for rest and relief.

In the conjoining of narrative and law, of story and commandment, the community learns how freedom and service are properly held in one. In the process neither freedom nor service is denigrated. The paradigmatic story of God's mighty works is summarized in "I am the one who brought you out of the house of slavery." God wills us free. When Jesus reads from the book of Isaiah in the synagogue at Nazareth "on the *Sabbath* day," he reads from two texts: "The Spirit of the Lord is upon me, because he has anointed me to bring good news to the poor. He has sent me to *proclaim release to the captives and recovery of sight* to the blind, to *let the oppressed go free...*" The two Isaiah texts are brought together around a single Greek catchword, *aphesis*, the word that translates "release" in Isa 61 and "go free" in Isa 56:8. It is the enterprise of setting free, of bringing release that Jesus announces as the heart of his ministry when he says, "Today this scripture is fulfilled in your hearing." That same Greek word is the standard New Testament word for "forgiveness," God still at work to set us free from whatever is our enslavement.

But the community set free knows from the beginning of its Exodus story that its journey out of Egypt keeps going to the mountain. And there they enter into the service of this Lord who has redeemed them. It is in the service of the one who sets free that this community is called into being. Its first rule of life is to serve no other power as ultimate. Its confidence in so doing rests in the knowledge that the one who insists on no other service or worship is the one who is there with them ("I will be with you") and who hears the cries of suffering and will deliver ("I brought you out of the house of slavery).

In such service there is freedom. As Paul Lehmann has put it, the Commandments come to the community of faith with the offer: "Seeing that you are who you are, where you are, and as you are, this is the way ahead, the way of being and living in the truth, the way of freedom!" "In this world," Lehmann says, "the Decalogue is at hand as a primer for learning to spell, and especially to spell out freedom."[2] The freedom of the one who brought you out of the house of slavery is not the freedom of an endless and ultimately meaningless pursuit of all desires but the freedom to pursue the end, the *telos*, of all desire in the service of God.

That is why the community, as it leaves the mountain and continues its journey in the world, always carries the Psalter under its arm, with the

---

[2] P. Lehmann, *The Decalogue and a Human Future: The Meaning of the Commandments for Making and Keeping Human Life Human* (Grand Rapids: Eerdmans, 1995), 85.

words and music to express the praise and trust that are the truest expressions of the service of the Lord of Israel. It cannot sing the psalms of praise and bow down before any other god. It cannot say the Lord is my refuge and give its ultimate service to any other lord, oppressive or alluring.

Unlike the harsh service under tyranny and in slavery, the service of this God is not imposed. There are other options. The alternative is clear, and the meaning of the relationship is laid out in no uncertain terms. And there are consequences. But the story makes very clear that it is up to the people to choose the service of this God. Three times (in chaps. 19 and 24) we hear the people say in response to the divine commands "All that the Lord has spoken we will do." The responsibility to decide and to choose is put even more sharply in Deut 30: "See I have set before you life and death, good and bad. If you obey the commandments of the Lord your God...you shall live....So choose life...loving the Lord your God, obeying him, and holding to him.... The choice is even more open in the covenant renewal ceremony in Josh 24. Joshua says to the gathered tribes: "Now if you are unwilling to serve the Lord, choose this day whom you will serve, whether the gods you ancestors served in the region beyond the River or the gods of the Amorites in whose land you are living; but as for me and my household, we will serve the Lord" (v. 15).

The ultimate freedom is the freedom to say yes or no, but the choice must be made. In freedom, the service alone of the one God who is the Lord of Israel is the only choice. So desire and liberty and possibility, affect and thought, are uni-directional. Or better, they are under control, they are placed in service. In this free service in freedom, all oppressive service is overcome and negated, even when it exists. This is not a created or enacted or fought for political or moral freedom. This freedom, as the theologian Reinhard Hütter has put it, "receives God's commandments as its own proper form, longs to embody these commandments, and regards living joyfully according to them its rightful enactment. The signs of true freedom are first true worship [i.e., service] and second delight in God's commandments by meditating on them unceasingly and following them joyfully. It is, as the story of the Commandments make clear, a gift."[3]

As the story of the Exodus continues out of the Lord's speaking the Commandments to the people, it moves into Moses' teaching of the statutes and ordinances, an occasion that both Exodus and Deuteronomy ascribe to the people's fear of having ever to meet the Lord face to face again, and so they press Moses to be their representative. The teaching is

---

[3] Reinhard Hütter, "What Is So Great about Freedom?" *Pro Ecclesia* 10 (Fall 2001), 458.

not over in the story, but now it continues through Moses' mediation. The ordinances of the Book of the Covenant in Exod 21–23 serve to stipulate, specify, illustrate, and develop the basic directives of the Commandments, to spell out this freedom in service in more detail. I want to call particular attention to the preface and conclusion that bracket this further teaching we have dubbed the Book of the Covenant. These are words of the Lord to Moses, prefatory to the extended collections of statutes and ordinances that follow (Exod 20:22–26).

I would call particular attention to the beginning of this unit. That is, the more detailed spelling out of Israel's freedom in obedience, of the modes of its life together and under the Lord, begins with a reiteration of the basic commandment: "You shall not make alongside me gods of silver and gods of gold you shall not make for yourselves." The command prohibits other gods and it prohibits visible images of a god.[4] That reiteration of the primary commandment in verse 23 is, however, rooted in an assumption stated in the preceding verse and given an implication in the following verse. The presupposition is simple: "You have seen for yourselves that it was from heaven that I spoke with you." The significance of this brief statement is spelled out at some length in Deut 4. Both the Exodus and the Deuteronomy texts provide a ground and an interpretation of the prohibition of images of deities. "You have seen for yourselves that I *spoke with you from heaven.* So you shall not make alongside me gods of silver or gold." "Since you saw no form when the Lord spoke to you at Horeb out of the fire...do not act corruptly by making an idol for yourselves in the form of any figure..." The Lord "spoke from heaven" and "you saw no form" are the grounds for the prohibition of idols. It is thus clear that while all images of gods are prohibited, there is clearly in mind the prohibition of representations in plastic form of the Lord of Israel, who speaks from heaven and out of the fire. Both notions assert the transcendence of this deity and the incapacity of capturing who and what the Lord is in any form of anything on earth. The true service of God resists the attractiveness and the allure of those representations that would seem to let us get at the God who cannot be gotten at. In the images of the God who speaks from heaven and the God who speaks from the fire, both the transcendence and the proper immanence of God are asserted. In the prohibition of images the transcendence and immanence are protected. God is accessible through the word. But it is the word that comes from outside ourselves, from beyond our world. And it is the word that is immediately before us, dazzling, illuminating, but wholly uncontainable, dangerous and consuming, untouchable

---

[4] Walter Brueggemann, "The Book of Exodus" (NIB; Nashville: Abingdon, 1994), 861.

in any fashion, not to be captured – and to try to do so is to risk destruction. The word of the Lord comes from beyond and so is not available in
anything in this world. The word of the Lord is an illumining and revealing
light that is at the same time terribly dangerous and always elusive.

The word from beyond comes as an illumining fire to speak to us. Thus
the prohibition of images not only guards the reality of God from all forms
of reality that are not God but it prepares the way for the incarnation, the
word that comes from beyond into our life as a light that enlightens everything, the word now made flesh, still not something *we* can *produce* and
mistake for the center of all meaning and value, but the word of the Lord
freely among us, addressing us, calling us, instructing us – from heaven,
out of the fire.

There is then a significant further implication of the Commandment
arising out of the prohibition of making "gods of silver and the gods of
gold" and the immediately following command: "You need make for me
only an altar of earth..." It is not simply the making of the image of the
Lord or any other deity that is ruled out of bounds. Something is said about
the character of worship of the Lord of Israel by the explicit reference to
images of gold and silver in contrast to the altar of earth. Elsewhere in relation to this commandment, the community is warned to burn the images
of the gods of the peoples around them with fire and "do not covet the silver or gold that is on them and take it for yourself." (Deut 7:25). And
throughout the prophets, one hears strong denunciations of the idols and
gods made of gold and silver. Images of deities were made of all sorts of
materials–clay, copper, bronze. Few of those recovered in Syria-Palestine
were made of silver and gold or plated in precious metal. But here the Lord
puts strong weight on that form of making images. So the use of extravagant wealth in the service and worship of the Lord is under rejection here
as much as the making of images per se. Over against a worship of wealth
is the simplicity and earthiness of the altar of earth. Even if stone is to be
used, it is not hewn stone but the rock or stone as it is found on the ground.
A tone is set for the worship of the Lord of Israel that is sometimes missed
in the awareness of its aniconic character. At least a dimension of that aniconic character is the rejection of extravagance and affluence as necessary
or even desirable in the worship of the one God. The true worship of the
Lord does not require an affluent community. The proper worship of God
is possible with the simple elements of life, dirt and stone. Not only is a
more elegant worship unnecessary; it is under question. In this story of the
First Commandment, the presence of gold and silver in worship is more
likely to reflect the worship of some one or some thing other than the Lord
of Israel.

The passage thus stands in a *powerful tension* with other moves that are
made in the history of Israel's religion. The Solomonic temple was full of

gold, and gold and silver vessels were part of David's worship of the Lord. Indeed the Book of Exodus tells of the Lord's instruction to build the tabernacle out of offerings of gold, silver, bronze, fine yarns, fine leather, etc. The tension is not easily resolvable. The temple as the place of the Lord's presence was a clear affirmation of its viability in the worship of the Lord. And the prophet Haggai reports at the building of the second temple that the Lord says, "The silver is mine, and the gold is mine." But the ambiguity of that enterprise cannot be missed. The temple was built with forced labor and cost great sums of wealth, drained from the resources of the nation and other nations. The church cannot live in its Solomonic temples and forget the call for an altar of earth instead of gods of silver and gold.

There is a direct line from this instruction to the words of Jesus: You cannot serve God and mammon. You cannot serve God *with* mammon. The simplicity of the Christian life begins in the simplicity of its worship, lest the one who is worshipped disappear in the affluence, and the silver and gold become the gods that are worshipped.

As the book of Exodus continues from this point, it moves directly into the Book of the Covenant in chapter 21: "These are the ordinances that you shall set before them." I want to call attention only to one thing here. That is *how* the Book of the Covenant *begins*. It begins with an extended body of case law on treatment of slaves, but more particularly about provision for the release of slaves in the seventh year. In the Deuteronomic Code, the analogous statutes clearly are connected to the Sabbath Commandment and come at that place in the decalogical ordering of the Deuteronomic Code in chapters 12–26. Now the Book of the Covenant does not betray as much order and logic to its arrangement as the Deuteronomic Code, even though both are explications of the Ten Commandments. Still one may ask why these slave statutes come first here at the book of the Covenant and immediately after the words about not worshipping the gods of silver and gold? That surely has to do with what we have learned already from the story, that humane treatment of those in bondage and the possibility of freedom is central to the worship of the Lord of Israel. That was and still is the first item on the agenda, the resistance to oppressive servitude in behalf of the true service that sets free. Remember that in Deuteronomy, when the children ask in time to come, "What is the meaning of the decrees and the statutes and the ordinances that the Lord our God has commanded you?" The answer is not an interpretation of the details of the teachings. The response you are to make to interpret the laws is: "Slaves, we were Pharaoh's slaves in the land of Egypt, and the Lord freed us from Egypt with a mighty hand."

Then at the end of the Book of the Covenant there is a kind of coda that points to the future and the journey through the wilderness into the land

God is giving (Exod 23:23–25). The Second Commandment and especially the thematic language of serve or worship is reiterated here. We now have it in both negative and positive form: "You shall not bow down to their gods and worship/serve them"; and "You shall worship/serve the Lord your God." How does this repetition of the Commandment carry our understanding forward? The most obvious and immediate answer is to recognize in this bracketing of the Book of the Covenant with reiterations of the principle commandment an emphasis that presses us precisely to recognize that we are in fact before the basic and primary and foundational requirement of life under this God: You shall worship and serve this God alone. But beyond that, one other thing is noticeable. Now we hear what will be echoed again and again in the stories and books that follow, to wit that obedience to this demand to have no other gods besides the Lord and not to make and worship idols is not a foregone conclusion. The temptation to turn to other objects of loyalty, other claims of power and productivity, will be immediately at hand once you are part of a larger culture, once you live alongside other peoples who do not serve the Lord. It is the *cultural temptation* that arises so clearly and so easily that the biblical texts are always enjoining caution. The prohibition of foreign marriages was a guard against the easy way in which one's eyes may be drawn away from the Lord in the face of the cultural alternatives. The text that follows the verses I just read betrays an anticipatory awareness that the people of the land will not be driven out quickly, that Israel will have to live among them. They will offer visible, novel, and tangible objects of attraction that will claim your eyes and your minds and your souls. They will promise affluence and productivity. They will create divided loyalties and divided hearts.

The primary story in the rest of Exodus is the story of the *making of the golden calf*. Occurring shortly after the giving of the Commandments and the instruction of the Book of the Covenant, with only the plans for building the Tabernacle in between, the listening community hears about the significance of the primary commandment and the propensity for Israel to turn away and seek visible gods, to find something tangible that may suffice to protect us, *especially in extremis*. This is a kind of test case. As the story has moved through the six-chapter instruction for building the Tabernacle, which Moses has received alone on the mountain, it has indeed been a long time that Moses has been gone. The people say they do not know what has happened to him. So we need a god to lead us. Aaron, make us a god. You know the story of how Aaron made a calf and said, "These are your gods, O Israel, who brought you up out of the land of Israel." And the people sacrificed to it/them. The slippery line between the worship of another god and the making of an image that can be regarded as an image of the Lord is evident here. Does the golden calf represent other gods or is it a representation of the Lord of Israel? It does not really matter. Because the real issue is that the community has lost faith in its Lord and created its own god. "Now there is something we can see and bow down to and touch. We can make it take us out of the wilderness and do what we want. We now have some control over this situation. This will be our god."

Let me make only a couple of comments about the story. The first is to observe how the calf is made. When the people make their request, Aaron says, "Take off the *gold rings* that are on the ears of your wives, your sons, and your daughters, and bring them to me." And he makes the calf out of the people's gold rings. The first instance we have of explicit breaking of the primary commandment is the making of a golden image. The earlier connection between the iconic tendency and economic extravagance and wealth is underscored. It is in effect a substitute of affluence and wealth as the object of worship for the Lord who sets free and who is free and whose name is not Mammon but "I will be who I will be."

Second, it is here in this story, and indeed already anticipated in an earlier narrative in Exodus, that we learn unequivocally what Martin Luther stressed so vigorously in his Larger Catechism. The issue of the Primary Commandment, both with regard to finding other centers of meaning and value other gods and with regard to fashioning and forming those objects that will receive our ultimate loyalty, the issue is, fundamentally, *where and in whom or in what do we place our ultimate trust.* Luther began his interpretation of the First Commandment in this way: "A 'god' is the term for that to which we are to look for all good and in which we are to find refuge in all need. Therefore to have a god is nothing else than to trust and believe in that one with your whole heart." And the test cases are probably especially in the situations in extremis when circumstances would undo us, as Luther recognized. An earlier Exodus narrative has prepared us for this "test" case. But let me come at it by way of Deut 6:13–16, where we have a positive restatement of the first three Commandments: The Lord your God you shall fear; him you shall serve, and by his name alone you shall swear. Then two prohibitions follow. The first one is a rearticulation of the primary Commandment in its negative form: Do not follow other gods, any of the gods of the peoples who are all around you because the Lord your God *who is present with you* is a jealous God. The *second* prohibition, however, is not formulated as an obvious restatement of the primary Commandment and seems somewhat incongruous with the preceding verses: "Do not put the Lord your God to the test as you tested him at Massah." To understand that reference, however, one needs to recall what happened at Massah. It is recounted in Exod 17. Massah is the place between Egypt and Sinai where the people were thirsty and quarreled with Moses saying, "Why did you bring us out of Egypt to kill us and our children." The Lord told Moses to strike a rock, and water came forth. But the place received its name Massah, "test" because, as the text says, "The Israelites quarreled and tested the Lord, saying, "Is the Lord among us or not?"

In both of these stories, the cry for water and the cry for gods to go before us, the fundamental issue of the First Commandment is at stake. It is there in the *explicit* question of the people in Exod 17, "Is the Lord among us or not?" and in the *implicit* question of the people in Exod 32, "Who will lead us out of the wilderness into the land?" In Deut 9, where Moses recounts the making of the Golden Calf and in summary at the end refers to Massah and other places where the people lost faith, he says, in conclusion, "you rebelled against the command of the Lord your God, *neither trusting him nor obeying him.*" (Deut 9:23). "Do not follow other gods, because the Lord your God *who is present with you* is a jealous God." In all those situations of threat and danger, when the mountains shake in the midst of the earth and the foundations of our existence crumble, we do not have to ask the question "Is the Lord among us or not?" That question has already been answered.

In the last years of her life, after several strokes, my mother made a final visit to our home. She could still talk and draw some, which she loved to do. She would fall asleep at night reading, of all things, Karl Barth's *Göttingen Dogmatics*, which by that time I doubt she could follow very much, though she underlined every line for page after page. Not long after she died, we discovered the yellow legal tablet that she had kept by her bed during those days, ostensibly to take notes. On it was scribbled – I don't know how many times – and now barely legible, three words over and over, "Trust and obey, trust and obey, trust and obey...." It was, for her family, an unintended final witness about how life is to end – there where it is to be lived from the beginning, "Trust and obey."

6. The Story of the First Commandment

The Book of Joshua

More than once, the reader of the Torah is told, either explicitly (Exod 34:28; Deut 4:13; cf. 10:4) or implicitly (e.g., Exod 19:5) that the "covenant" enacted at Sinai is "the ten words." The substance and content of the covenant, the covenantal stipulations and requirements for the community of Israel, has its primary formulation in the Decalogue. There are more detailed specifications and illustrations of what the Commandments mean and how they play out in the daily life of the community, specifications that are laid out in the statutes and ordinances. But those are Moses' teaching of the meaning of the Commandments, so they serve to underscore the way in which the Commandments are the substance of covenant rather than diminishing that claim.

There is a sense in which the whole of the Commandments, and thus the essential covenantal claim and responsibility, is enfolded into the First Commandment, though one may well want to speak rather of the "primary" commandment and recognize the way in which the so-called Prologue and the commandments against having other gods and making idols and images are all held together as a single comprehensive word.[1] The force and meaning of this primary commandment, embodied in its positive form in the Shema (Deut 6:4–5) and elsewhere (e.g., Deut 6:13), is developed in various ways in the biblical literature. These modes of elaboration and interpretation include statute and ordinance, story and narrative, prophetic oracle and proverb, and praise and thanksgiving. The First or Pri-

---

[1] This point is at the heart of Martin Luther's interpretation of the Decalogue in his Catechisms, where each subsequent commandment is seen as in some sense a playing out of the claim of the First Commandment that we are to fear and love only the Lord. He explains the First Commandment as meaning "We are to fear, trust, and love God above all things." Then he goes on to interpret each subsequent commandment as meaning: "We are to fear and love God, so that..." The various numerations of the beginning of the Decalogue, including the Jewish understanding of the Prologue as the First Word and the joining of no other gods and no images, which is characteristic of both Jewish and Lutheran numberings, is indicative of the way in which the opening of the Commandments is a complex directive that can be sorted out but not easily separated into distinct units. For convenience sake, when commandments are identified by number in this essay, the First Commandment refers to the prohibition of other gods and the Second Commandment to the making of images and the serving of gods and images.

mary Commandment, is so fundamental to the covenantal life of Israel that it dominates the books of the Torah and the Former Prophets. One might argue that from Exodus through the Books of Kings, the First Commandment is a sort of touchstone and that much of the narrative and legal materials serves to develop a sense of the force and significance of this primary covenantal stipulation in the life of the community, whether familial, official, cultic, or political. In short, there is a sense in which these books of the Old Testament tell the story of the First Commandment, and, in so doing, teach and instruct the community that lives by these scriptures about what it means to keep the covenant, that is, the commandments. Through the story that is told, as well as through other component parts, each book provides an interpretation of the Primary Commandment.

In this context, it is my intent to look at one of these stories of the First Commandment: the Book of Joshua. For one of its fundamental intentions would seem to be a narrative interpretation of and a plea for conformity to the claim of the First Commandment. Its very location as the next book, the next word, after Deuteronomy sets the reader up to anticipate the play of the First Commandment in the book. Deuteronomy sets the Shema, the positive form of the First Commandment, as the thematic word of Moses' speeches in the land of Moab, on the boundary of the Promised Land. The First Commandment is indeed the primary thing that Moses has had to say. Now the reader begins to see how that claim plays itself out in the story of the entry into the Promised Land.

The connection to Deuteronomy is immediate in the opening divine address to Joshua. It consists of three parts: the assignment to enter and take the land; the exhortation to be resolute and not dismayed; and the requirement to observe all the teaching that Moses has commanded, meditating day and night on the book of the torah, that is, the book of Deuteronomy. All that follows stands under this expectation, that the love of God as Moses has instructed will guide the way of the leader Joshua, day and night.

The opening story of the Book of Joshua is a particular refraction of the claim of the First Commandment. The encounter between the spies and Rahab is set entirely around her confession, and thus her conversion to the worship of the Lord of Israel. There are two facets of her confession in Josh 2:8–13. One is the explicit assertion that "The Lord your God is indeed/the only God in heaven above and on earth below" (2:11). This is not a report on Rahab's part. It is her own confession of faith in YHWH and a positive formulation of the prohibition against having other gods. The story of the taking of the land begins with the conversion of one of the Canaanites to the true worship of the Lord. In other words, the opening to the land is through an act of obedience to the First Commandment. Rahab's confessional speech becomes the single ground for the spies' confidence that the Lord has delivered the land into their power. They were sent out on a mission of reconnaisance. The information gained is the reality uncovered by Rahab's confession: The people of the land are in complete fear of the Israelites. The particular act that manifests Rahab's loyalty to the Lord of Israel is the protection of the spies, and that is remembered when she is spared at the overthrow of Jericho (6:25). That act distinguishes her from her countrypeople, who have also seen the power of the Lord and whose hearts have melted in fear and dread. The service of the Lord enjoined in the First Commandment is not simply a confessional word. It is acted out and acted upon.

There is something further here that is a particular way in which the Book of Joshua seems to interpret and understand the significance of the First Commandment. Beginning with the story of Rahab and continuing on through the rest of the account of the taking of the land, a critical factor in what happens is *the response to the deeds of YHWH*. What happens is very much determined by how people respond to the action of YHWH. In this instance, widespread fear is indicated, a fear of the Lord arising out of the reports of the Israelites' victory. This is at one and the same time a fear of YHWH – "we have heard how the Lord dried up the water of the Red Sea" – and a fear of the Israelites – "what you did to the two kings of the Amorites that were beyond the Jordan, to Sihon and Og, whom you utterly destroyed" (2:10). Ps 28:5 condemns the wicked: "Because they do not regard the works of the Lord or the work of his hands." The work of the Lord, which is sufficient ground for the claim of a total covenantal loyalty, should evoke a full and total commitment to the one whose mighty deeds are extravagantly clear. The Book of Exodus suggests the way in which the power and claim of the Lord to be God alone is unfolded and made visible in the powerful activity of God, in this instance to deliver the Hebrew slaves from the oppressive power of the Egyptians. Again and again, one hears the claim that what is happening is so "that you may know that I am the Lord" (Exod 6:7; 7:5; 8:23 [MT v. 18]). Especially indicative is Exod 9:14–16:

[14]For this time I will send all my plagues upon you yourself, and upon your officials, and upon your people, so that you may know that there is no one like me in all the earth. [15]For by now I could have stretched out my hand and struck you and your people with pestilence, and you would have been cut off from the earth. [16]But this is why I have let you live: to show you my power, and to make my name resound through all the earth.

The deeds of the Lord are to show the Lord's power and thus to evoke praise of the name of the Lord. The name may resound without the praise, but the appropriate response to the recounting of the powerful deeds of the

Lord is precisely the kind of confession that Rahab makes: The Lord your God is indeed God in heaven above and on earth below.[2]

In the story of the meeting of the spies and Rahab, the deeds are seen, but there are two kinds of responses. The people of the land see the terrible deeds of YHWH, but those deeds are not considered or regarded (Ps 28:5 – *bîn*). Fear and dread do not evoke the fear that is worship and service. While we are not really told anything about the response of the people in general to the terrifying news of the drying up of the waters of the Red/Reed Sea, *resistance* to the action of the Lord, despite the terrifying evidence, is specifically embodied in the action of the king of Jericho, who engages in a vigorous pursuit of and search for the Israelite spies. This is consistent with what follows in the rest of the conquest narrative, where the primary response is explicitly that of various kings.

For Rahab, however, the response is quite different. In her case, fear evokes a confession of faith and beyond that a deed of loyalty signaling her clear commitment to the Lord, even at the cost of disloyalty to her own people. Early on in this story of the First Commandment, the seriousness of the choice that is implicit in it is uncovered. It is a total loyalty that brooks no other final commitment and may require the abandonment of loyalties and commitments that had seemed secure; at least, one may assume that such would have been the case for Rahab.[3]

As Lawson Stone has pointed out, the beginning of chapter 5 parallels 2:10–11; only in this instance the powerful act of the Lord is the drying up of the waters of the Jordan.[4] The parallel structure of 2:10–11 and 5:1 in-

---

[2] Compare the statement of the nations in Ps 126:2: "The Lord has done great things for them." The fact that Rahab does not say "our God" is not an indication of some reservation or a formulation that places her outside the fold. She is speaking to the Israelite spies and so identifies YHWH properly as their God. What her statement goes on to indicate, however, is that she knows that this one is God alone.

[3] It should be noted, of course, that Rahab does not give up her loyalty to her family. The family as the primary social context is evident in this story, and one has the impression that the protection of the family has a claim significantly beyond loyalty to the larger urban or social setting. But there is no doubt that her conviction and the actions based upon it are evidence of disloyalty to the king of Jericho as much as they are evidence of her new loyalty to YHWH.

[4] L. Stone, "Ethical and Apologetic Tendencies in the Redaction of the Book of Joshua," *The Catholic Biblical Quarterly* 53 (1991) 25–36. Stone has uncovered a redactional move operative in the accounts of the battles with the inhabitants of the land that he describes as reflective of an apologetic and ethical concern on the part of those responsible for the transmission of the book in its final stages. He argues, "certain ethical dimensions of holy war did concern the tradents of Joshua, to the extent that the holy war traditions in their earliest form represented an unusable past" (36). To over come this past, "moves were made to guide the reader to a nonmilitaristic, nonterritorial actualization of the text..."(ibid). The move that was

dicates that the entrance into Canaan is to be seen as comparable to the event of the Exodus.[5] As the king of Egypt was called to respond to all the demonstrations of YHWH's power "that you may know that I am YHWH," so now the kings of Canaan are called to a similar response. Indeed a similarity between the Egyptian response and that of the kings is suggested in Josh 11:20, where the resistance of the kings of the land is attributed to the Lord's hardening of their hearts.

The alternatives reflected in Josh 1–6 then play themselves out in the rest of the campaign against the Canaanites. As Stone notes: "The verbal parallels between these two texts establish an analogy between Yahweh's action in the exodus and in the presence of Israel in Canaan, and strongly emphasize the contrasting responses of Rahab and the kings of Canaan."[6]

He suggests that Josh 1–5, as signaled by 2:10–11 and 5:1, serves to establish Israel's presence in Canaan as a divine act, a demonstration of the power of YHWH. A response is anticipated, as the very first story indicates: affirm or resist. Then in chapters 6–8, Israel's victory over Jericho and Ai is the act of YHWH in Canaan, comparable to the Exodus event in Egypt. "Once Jericho and Ai fall, the reader who has attended carefully now awaits a response from the Canaanite kings in chapters 9–11. This response is immediately forthcoming."[7] Rather than responding in commitment to YHWH, as did Rahab, the kings resist. The result is, in effect, that the narrative ends up construing "the entire military campaign after Ai as a defensive reaction."[8] Even the Gibeonite cunning treaty with Israel is condemned and becomes the basis for Canaanite action.

While it is difficult to discern exactly at what level the redactional moves identified by Stone came into the story, he goes on to suggest that the Deuteronomistic level of the story clearly turns "the literary structure of act – response in which the *Canaanites* were annihilated for their obduracy into a summons for *Israel* faithfully to obey God's written Torah."[9] This happens by the addition of 1:1–9; 8:30–35; and chapter 23. Such an analysis of the growth of the text may well be the case, but the torah passages of chapters 1 and 8, which serve their own function in eliciting a commitment to the Lord, are not identical to what happens in the narrative

---

made was to effect a redaction that focused on the response to YHWH's powerful action. As Stone puts it, "the conquest first illustrated the necessity of an affirmative response to Yahweh's action, then became a paradigm of obedience to the written Torah" (ibid).

[5] Ibid., 29.
[6] Ibid., 32.
[7] Ibid., 33.
[8] Ibid.
[9] Ibid., 35.

of chapters 2–11. The latter chapters, at least, serve, in very precise terms, to lift up the matter of how one regards and responds to the mighty acts of YHWH as the central concern. The opening story indicates what is expected, a commitment that embodies the full loyalty called for in the First Commandment; the narratives of the conflicts with the kings of the Amorites and of Canaan show the inappropriate response and in that process both turn the rest of the engagements into defensive actions on the part of Israel and provide a kind of apologetic for the holy wars of Israel, which would have been unnecessary if the kings had responded as did Rahab.

A feature of the narratives, especially in Josh 10–11, that is directly tied to the claim of the First Commandment is the presence of the *ḥērem*, the ban or utter destruction of the Canaanites. While the ban is present in Josh 6–7, there it seems to reflect a vow made to secure the help of the deity and a part of the ritual form of holy war present in that story. In Josh 10–11, however, as well as in other places, for example, 2:10 and 8:26, there is little about the things devoted to the Lord for destruction and thus taboo. Rather than the *ḥērem* as a vow to the Lord, what we encounter is the ban as a systematic move carried out against the various towns and cities and under the command of the Lord (10:40) or of the Lord through Moses (11:12, 20). In most of these instances, undoubtedly, we encounter the Deuteronomic or Deuteronomistic understanding of the ban, as the Lord's command conveyed through Moses. In Deut 7, the ban is grounded in the insistence on no accommodation to the religious practices of the inhabitants of the land:

[2][A]nd when the LORD your God gives them over to you and you defeat them, then you must utterly destroy them. Make no covenant with them and show them no mercy.[10] [3]Do not intermarry with them, giving your daughters to their sons or taking their daughters for your sons, for that *would turn away your children from following me, to serve other gods.* [4]Then the anger of the LORD would be kindled against you, and he would destroy you quickly. [5]But this is how you must deal with them: break down their altars, smash their pillars, hew down their sacred poles, and burn their idols with fire.

The ban, therefore, is rooted totally in the First Commandment, and the book of Joshua thus confronts the reader with the threat to the First Commandment that is perceived to be found in easy alliances with those who do not serve the Lord, a point that is underscored in Joshua's final speech

---

[10] It is often suggested that the Israelites violated this Deuteronomic requirement when the spies made a covenant with Rahab. This ignores the critical point that the covenant is made only after she has, in effect, converted to Yahwism, has made her confession of faith as a Yahwist.

to the people when he warns that if they intermarry among any of the survivors, the Lord will not continue to drive the people out before them (Josh
23:12).

Before turning to the conclusion of the book, a more implicit but recognized dimension of the way the Book of Joshua serves to uphold the Primary Commandment and support its influence is in the way that Joshua is
portrayed as an incipient Josiah. King Josiah was the monarch about whom
the Deuteronomistic Historian wrote that he was the only king "who turned
to the Lord with all his heart, with all his soul, and with all his might, according to all the law of Moses" (2 Kgs 23:25). Nowhere else in all of
Scripture is the claim made of such total obedience to the Shema, the Primary Commandment in positive form. The relevance of this datum is that
interpreters have demonstrated that Joshua, as portrayed in the Book of
Joshua, is an anticipatory model for Josiah. His attention to the law book
(Josh 1:7–8; 8:30–35; 23:6) is one of the primary features of the profile of
the Israelite leader in the book of Joshua that leads interpreters to suggest
that he is portrayed as "in many ways a thinly disguised Josianic figure."[11]

Nowhere is Joshua's embodiment as the faithful observer of the First
Commandment more evident than in his speeches at the end of the book.
The Deuteronomistic speech of Joshua in chapter 23:6–13 is a many-
faceted invocation of the Primary Commandment. Following a general injunction to be careful to observe all that is in the Book of the Law, the
leader warns against calling on the name of any of "their gods" and tells
the people not to "swear" or "serve" or "bow down" to them. All of this is
the language of the commandments prohibiting having other gods, serving
or bowing down to these gods or their images, and taking up the name of
God, that is, swearing, emptily. In good Deuteronomic style, these commandments are held together as one whole (e.g., Deut 6:13; cf. vv. 14–15),
the full expression of the Primary Commandment to love and serve the
YHWH alone. The positive form of this commandment is then set alongside the prohibitions: "Only cleave to the Lord your God" (v. 8).

Consistent with the earlier narrative part, Joshua then sets the mighty
and powerful acts of the Lord in driving out the nations as that which
should lead the people to "love the Lord your God" (vv. 9–11), an explicit
echo of the Shema (Deut 6:4–5), the positive form of the First Commandment. Joshua also warns against intermarrying among the survivors on the
implicit assumption that will draw the people away from the true worship
of YHWH (see above). Finally, at the close of the speech, his last word is a
warning that should the people break or "transgress" the covenant, the

---

[11] Richard D. Nelson, "Josiah in the Book of Joshua," *JBL* 100 (1981) 540.

Lord will be angry and they will quickly perish off the land. That transgression of the covenant is explicitly defined. It is when the people "go and serve other gods and bow down to them" (Exod 20:5//Deut 5:9).

The last words of the book are perhaps the clearest elaboration of the Primary Commandment. It is the covenant renewal ceremony at Shechem in chapter 24.[12] The issue of obedience to the Primary Commandment is enjoined at the very beginning with the reference to the fathers of old who "served other gods." There follows then the long historical summary/prologue (vv. 2–13). Unlike the historical summaries in Deut 6:20–25 and 26:5–9, this summary is entirely first person divine speech. It is in effect an elaboration of the Prologue to the Commandments: "I brought you out of the land of Egypt" (see especially vv. 5–6). And with its repeated first person claims – I took, I gave, I sent, I freed, etc. – the divine speech is once again a recounting of the mighty deeds of the Lord that merits a response of full obedience. It also makes the case for the worship of this deity over against other gods by indicating how completely Israel's existence has been dependent upon what the Lord has done for them.

The corollary of all this first person rehearsal of the divine deliverance is then given in verse 14: "Now therefore fear YHWH and serve him," the positive form of the First and Second Commandments. The other side of this requirement is "Put away the gods that your ancestors served beyond the River and in Egypt and serve the Lord" (v. 14b). The critical term is the one that is found in the commandment prohibiting images and their worship: "serve" (*ᶜbd*). The word appears *eight* times in vv. 14–16 with reference to serving the Lord or serving other gods. Then in vv. 18–24, virtually each verse has a reference to "serve the Lord" (one time the reference is to serving other gods).

Joshua's injunction is to "serve him," *bĕtāmîm ûbeʾĕmet*. The language here is not decalogical, but it is a formulation that interprets the obedience of the first commandment in a way reminiscent of the Shema's call for Israel to love the Lord with heart and soul and all that you have. The service of God is to be rendered in a blameless and faithful manner. There is no possibility of divided loyalty. The "Yahweh alone" demand of the Primary Commandment is to be adhered to without reservation and is to be a continuing mode of existence.

A particular nuance of the story of the First Commandment in Joshua is the indication of a prior history of serving other gods, not only by the an-

---

[12] On the critical issues and the dating of this chapter, see now Ed Noort, *Das Buch Josua: Forschungsgeschichte und Problemfelder* (Erträge der Forschung; Darmstadt: Wissenschaftliche Buchgesellschaft, 1998) 205–247.

cestors in Mesopotamia, but even in Egypt. The exclusive worship of
YHWH is a new thing. This is a quite different perspective from what one
finds in Exodus where all the traditions see some direct connection between the worship of the Lord and the prior worship of the ancestors and
the people in Egypt. Indeed, Joshua can still pose the alternatives: service
of the gods of the Amorites or the service of the Lord, a rather surprising
option in the Deuteronomistic History. There is a larger story about Israel's coming to serve the Lord alone. Josh 24 both points to that larger
story and reflects it.

The response of the people in verse 17 draws again on decalogical language and the Primary Commandment: "For it is the Lord our God who
brought us and our ancestors up from the land of Egypt, out of the house of
slavery..." The verb is ^clh, "bring up," instead of the customary decalogical
verb $ys^{\jmath}$, "bring out." But the Primary Commandment is explicit in the
reference to "out of the land of Egypt, the house of slavery." These two
phrases, prefacing each of the Decalogue formulations, occur virtually always with reference to the Commandments and in nearly every instance
are associated with the First Commandment. Furthermore, in the response
of the people, this divine deliverance "from the land of Egypt, the house of
bondage" is the basis for their fervent claim: "Far be it from us that we
should forsake the Lord in order to *serve other gods*" (v. 16). That logic is
precisely the way the Decalogue works, grounding the prohibition of other
gods and the consequent prohibitions in the divine claim, "I am the Lord
your God who brought you out of the land of Egypt, out of the house of
bondage." This vow of obedience to the First Commandment is then underscored or repeated with words that echo both the First Commandment
and its positive formulation in the Shema: "We also will serve the Lord,
for he is our God" (v. 18b; cf. 22:34).

The intensity with which the whole of this book and the climactic covenantal occasion are shaped by the Primary Commandment is seen in
Joshua's words to this apparently decisive word. He expresses a skepti-
cism, again in the words of the Second Commandment: "You will not be
able to *serve the Lord*, for he is a holy God; he is *a jealous God*" (v. 19), to
which the people respond with even more fervor: "No, we will *serve the
Lord!*" (v. 21). Yet, a third time, the people pledge their allegiance in the
language of the Decalogue: "The Lord our God we will serve..." (v. 24).
The community is placed under a tension that will reflect its life henceforth: "You cannot pull it off" versus "Yes, we will." Both claims are
made in emphatic ways. The story will indicate how much the former becomes the case, and the people find themselves under divine judgment and
thus reliant upon the Lord "gracious and merciful, slow to anger." In that
context, it is easy to forget the serious intention of this people to serve

their Lord and the word of this text that the problem they face is in the nature of the God they serve, at least as it is formulated in Joshua's speech.
It is God's nature as holy and jealous rather than the sinfulness of the people that will keep them from serving the Lord. That their sinfulness is implied should not allow one to hear the emphasis of the text in a way that
places the issue entirely in the lap of the people. There is a sense in which
they are caught from the start, and from the start they resist being so determined.

As it opens the Deuteronomistic story of life in the land, the book of
Joshua begins the record of Israel's covenantal life. Deuteronomy sets the
Decalogue as the center of that covenantal existence, and Joshua explains
how that works. It has to do with the centrality of the Primary Commandment, out of which all the rest of Israel's adherence to the words of the
Lord is seen to flow. The service of YHWH as the critical dimension of
Israel's life and faith and as the ground of its enjoyment of the blessings of
the land is first articulated, somewhat surprisingly, by an outsider whose
acknowledgment of the Lord of Israel becomes the "key" to the promised
land. That confession of Rahab sets a tone and sets the stage for the critical
issue for the whole book: Will you respond to the mighty acts of the Lord
with a full and exclusive service? The story is told around that question,
which is set before those in the land as well as Israel itself. The narratives
pose the issue for the *inhabitants*; the covenantal renewal occasion at the
end sets this question as the fundamental issue for *Israel*. In the book of
Joshua, the people fully realize this and know what is at stake. The emphatic character of their response in the covenant renewal at Shechem seals
the issue. As at Sinai, the people have once more made a firm commitment
to serve the Lord alone and no other gods. The stone of witness, a witness
against themselves, is a bridge between the end of this book and the rest of
the Deuteronomistic History. The rest of that story is also about the Primary Commandment; and the stone of witness will be a relentless reminder
when the people turn away and follow after other gods. The less pleasant
but still important word of the book about the full obedience of the Lord is
its warning about becoming at ease with the surrounding culture so that the
people can no longer distinguish between desire and trust, between the attractiveness of the other religious voices and claims and full loyalty to the
God whose power and might, whose activity in Israel's behalf, is manifest
in all the events of deliverance and conquest. The rationale for the ban is
an indication of how serious is this concern about slowly being attracted
toward other loyalties and away from the Lord of Israel. Joshua's words at
the covenant renewal at Shechem indicate how much this was "in their
blood," so to speak, so much a part of their history that the decision could

not be presumed. It would need to be attested and regularly claimed through all the coming generations. Covenantal renewal will always be an appropriation of the fundamental claim of the Primary Commandment.

7. The Psalms as a Meditation on the First Commandment

In the Preface to his *Large Catechism*, Martin Luther makes two broad generalizations about the Ten Commandments. One is to the effect that "those who know the Ten Commandments perfectly know the entire Scriptures." The other is a generalization also but somewhat more specific as well. He said: "Moreover, what is the whole Psalter but meditation and exercises based on the First Commandment?" What follows is an effort to spell out in some detail what one might say in support of Luther's claim in this second generalization. In the process, I am proceeding further along a path that I first sought to open up in an essay on the interaction between Deuteronomy and the Psalms.[1] The centrality of the Commandments in the shaping and theology of Deuteronomy makes it a fairly natural move to focus more specifically on the way in which the Commandments are reflected and refracted in the Psalter.[2]

One may and probably should begin with the first Psalm, not only because starting at the beginning is a natural move but even more because Ps 1 indeed serves an introductory and indicative function with regard to the rest of the Psalms and the Psalter as a whole. It sets at the start a focus on the torah of the LORD, on the instruction or law of the LORD, as the central matter for the blessed life. Such attention is constant (day and night) and is the purpose or delight of the one who walks in the way of the LORD. The "torah" referred to here comprehends more than the Ten Words, but proba-

---

[1] Patrick D. Miller, "Deuteronomy and Psalms: Evoking a Biblical Conversation," *Journal of Biblical Literature* 118 (1998), 3–18; repr. in P. D. Miller, *Israelite Religion and Biblical Theology: Collected Essays* (JSOTSup 267; Sheffield: Sheffield Academic Press, 2000), 318–336.

[2] The paper makes no assumptions about the age and formation history of either the Psalter or the Decalogue. Those are much debated matters. It is clear that both documents come to us in contexts belonging rather late in the history of Israel as reflected in the Old Testament. In the case of the Decalogue, its present forms belong to Deuteronomic and Priestly contexts. In the case of Deut 5, there are solid indications that its present shape is centered around the Sabbath Commandment and so may belong to a post-exilic shaping. The project envisioned here is a literary and theological reading of the respective documents, not an effort to describe the historical shaping or formation of either one. In that sense, I stand with Luther as a reader more than as a redaction critic, though I am conscious of those issues in a way that may have been less the case for the Reformer.

bly less than is often presumed. The most likely reference is to the Book of Deuteronomy.[3] To the extent that is the case, the centrality of the Ten Commandments is immediately to the fore. The Book of Deuteronomy is largely a book of instruction that centers on the Ten Words and the specifics of case law and other instruction that grows out of those words.[4] That such "delight" and "meditation" on God's instruction, embodied particularly in the Commandments, is central to the Psalter, is further indicated by the presence of an interest in "meditation" on the divine instruction in the other two torah psalms (19:15 [*hegyôn*]; 119:15, 23, 48, 78, 97, 99, 148 [*śîḥ*]) and by more specific reference to delight in the "commandments" (=*miṣwôt*) of the LORD in Ps 112:1. This stance of "delighting" is paralleled in this instance by "fearing the LORD," an aspect of the First Commandment that is crucial for the Psalter (see below).[5] The direction suggested by the Psalter's introduction in the first Psalm is accentuated by the role played by Ps 19, with its exaltation of the torah of the LORD in its various forms, as well as by the mountain that rises in the last part of the Psalter and dominates the whole, Ps 119. In that psalm, as well as in any psalm, one may not always be certain if any particular technical term for instruction, word, law, commandment, decree, or whatever specifically has in mind the Ten Words, but they are the framework in which all the rest fits.[6]

What Is the First Commandment?

To this point, I have focused quite generally on the Psalter's encouragement of attention to the divine instruction in general as a central dimension of what it is about. That is to show at the start that attention to the commandments and decrees of the LORD is not a secondary or casual matter in

---

[3] For arguments in support of that claim, see Miller, "Deuteronomy and Psalms."

[4] See in this regard, Dennis Olson, *Deuteronomy and the Death of Moses* (Overtures to Biblical Theology; Minneapolis: Fortress, 1994).

[5] One may note already at this point the inclusion in the list of terms for divine instruction in Ps 19 (*tôrat yhwh, ʿēdût yhwh, piqqûdê yhwh, miṣwat yhwh,* and *mišpĕṭê yhwh*), the expression that seems to be of a different order: *yirʾat yhwh*. The association of this term with the divine instruction embodied especially in the Commandments is a central feature of the Psalter and one that is shared with Deuteronomy (see below and Miller, "Deuteronomy and Psalms," in *Israelite Religion and Biblical Theology*, 333–334).

[6] It may be possible in some instances to see a specific reference to the Decalogue, as Zenger has suggested for the term *ʿēdôt* in Ps 99:7 ["The God of Israel's Reign over the World (Psalms 90–106)," in Norbert Lohfink and Erich Zenger, *The God of Israel and the Nations: Studies in Isaiah and the Psalms* (Collegeville, MI: Liturgical Press, 2000), 170], but it is difficult to be confident in any particular usage that only the Decalogue is in view.

the Psalter. The torah is in view from the start and focused attention to it is presumed and nurtured by the psalms that follow the introduction.

It is particularly the First Commandment, however, that Luther claimed reverberates throughout the Psalter, and so I want to turn specifically to that claim. Let me begin by raising the issue of the delimitation of the First Commandment as a way into the question of how it is that one recognizes the impact of that Commandment in the Psalter. Simply to say the First Commandment is to leave a few things open. Clearly one has in mind the prohibition "You shall have no other gods beside(s)/before me." All the traditional enumerations of the Commandments assume this. Beyond that, however, there are significant differences in ways of numbering the Commandments, all of which are rooted in different features of the text. In some structural analyses, especially present in Jewish tradition, the first Word or Commandment begins with the self-presentation of the deity: "I am the LORD your God who brought you out of the land of Egypt, out of the house of slavery, so you shall have no other gods before me." There are cogent arguments for tying these opening words to the prohibition that immediately follows.[7] In other enumerations – and this would include that of Luther – the First Commandment incorporates the prohibition against the making and worshipping of images, understood by many as a second commandment. While it is possible to distinguish making idols from having more than one god, the rationale for incorporating this prohibition into

---

[7] Such an interpretation does not preclude understanding the Prologue as also introducing *all* of the Commandments. Jeffrey Tigay has argued that it does both things, citing various ancient sources for both understandings. In his argument for seeing the self-presentation formula as "the beginning of the first commandment" he cites both Philo and Josephus. His own analysis makes the argument for the material itself:

"The verse also serves as part of the first commandment, "you shall have no other gods beside Me." This is indicated by other passages in which God likewise identifies Himself as the God who freed Israel from Egypt and prohibits the worship of other gods, and which seem to allude to the present passage (Judg 6:8–10; Ps 81:9–11). In these passages, God stipulates that since He and no other deity freed Israel from Egypt, He alone is Israel's God, and the worship of other gods is prohibited. Seen in this light, verse 6 is an introductory motive clause that grounds the first commandment in moral obligation and good sense. For a similarly positioned motive clause, see 14:1."

Tigay cites other biblical texts where this connection is made (Hos 13:1–5; Josh 24:16–18; 1 Kgs 17:35–39; Deut 13:6, 11) and argues that "the obligation to worship YHVH alone because He alone freed Israel from Egypt is the central doctrine of biblical religion," indicating that the logic here is covenantal logic as modeled in the international treaties that established exclusive relationships. He notes that this understanding is reflected in the NJPS translation of the opening sentence as "I the lord am your God...," implying by the translation that it is the lord and no other. (Tigay, *Deuteronomy* [The JPS Torah Commentary; Philadelphia: The Jewish Publication Society, 1996], 63.)

the first one and seeing it as an elaboration rather than as a second command are multiple. They include:

- repetition of the language *ʾanôkî yhwh ʾĕlōhêkā*, "I the LORD your
  God" from the self-presentation formula,
- confinement of the first person divine speech to the self-presentation
  formula and the two prohibitions that follow,
- the idols and images envisioned in the elaboration of this commandment in Deut 4 probably being images of the LORD,
- the only plural antecedent that can function as the object "them" of the
  expression "bow down and serve/worship them" being the "other gods"
  of the first prohibition,
- the idiom "bow down and serve" (*hištaḥăweh* and *ʿābad*) nearly always
  having as its object "other gods" not idols or images (e.g. Exod 23:24;
  Deut 6:14; 8:19; 11:16; 17:3; 29:25; 30:17; Jos 23:7, 16; Judg 2:12–13,
  19; 1 Kgs 9:6; 2 Kgs 17:35; Jer 13:10; 16:11; 22:9; 25:6).[8]

The reason for elucidating the justifications for these different enumerations is that they all revolve around the question of the extent and character
of the First Commandment and suggest that, in looking at its echoes and
resonances in the Psalter, one may expect to see them in references and
allusions to the self-presentation formula and to the prohibition against images and idols as well as the prohibition against having other gods. It is
necessary therefore, here as elsewhere, to think of the First Commandment
in the broadest sense.

That point may and must be carried still further. John Calvin, among
others, noted that for the Commandments every prohibition has a positive
counterpart and every positive injunction has its counterpart in a prohibition. That, of course, is evident within the Decalogue itself in the positive
and negative forms of the Sabbath observance Commandment. But it is
present also in the various positive forms of the First Commandment, the
most obvious of which is the Shema: "Hear, O Israel, the LORD is your
God, the LORD alone. So you shall love the LORD your God with all your
heart and with all your soul and with all you have" (Deut 6:4-5; cf. 13:4;
30:6; Josh 22:5; 23:11). The exclusivity that is inherent in the prohibition
of the First Commandment is articulated here in positive form in the
phrases at the conclusion: "with all your heart and with all your soul and
with all you have."

---

[8] Either of the verbs by itself can be used for bowing down to or serving idols or images.
Several times the reference to other gods is qualified by "of wood or stone," e.g., Deut 4:28;
28:36, 64.

There are other positive forms of the First Commandment especially in Deuteronomic and Deuteronomistic material.[9] One of the places where the First Commandment is clearly in view in positive form but with different vocabulary is Deut 6:12–13:

> [12]Take care that you do not forget the LORD, who brought you out of the land of Egypt out of the house of slavery. [13] The LORD your God you shall fear; him you shall serve, and by his name you shall swear.

The exhortation to "fear (*yārē'*) the LORD your God" is identified as a positive form of the First Commandment by the language of the self-presentation formula that introduces the Decalogue before that exhortation. It is confirmed as a form of the First Commandment by the presence of the commandments against making and worshipping images and misusing the name of God in sequence after it in the customary decalogical language, but also in positive form: "You shall not bow down to them or serve them" = "him you shall serve"; "you shall not take up the name of the LORD your God in vain" = "by his name you shall swear."[10] For each of these commandments there is thus a positive corollary.

The decalogical character of these verses is underscored by what follows immediately in verses 14–16:

> [14]Do not follow other gods, any of the gods of the peoples who are all around you, [15]because the LORD your God, who is present with you, is a jealous God. The anger of the LORD your God would be kindled against you and he would destroy you from the face of the earth. [16]Do not put the LORD your God to the test, as you tested him at Massah.

The explicit prohibition of going after other gods is joined with the language of the "jealous God" from the Second Commandment.[11] Alongside these familiar expressions are two other dimensions of the First Commandment, one positive, and one negative. The positive one is the reference to the LORD "who is in the midst of you" or "who is present with you" (*běqirbekā*), the force of which is clarified by the seemingly out-of-place prohibition, "Do not put the LORD your God to the test."[12] These are two sides of the same coin pointing to another form of the content of the

---

[9] In addition to passages discussed below, see Deut 10:12.

[10] Cf. Miller, "Deuteronomy and Psalms," 333–334.

[11] This is one of only three places where the expression *'ēl qānā'* appears outside of its occurrence in the Decalogue. The other instances in Exod 34:14 and Deut 4:24 are also explicit discussions of the worship of other gods or of images of the lord or of other gods.

[12] In the Exod 17 account of the episode at Massah and Meribah, the "testing" of the lord is interpreted as the people saying "Is the lord among us or not?" (*běqirbekā*). On this theme, see above, 68–79.

First Commandment – the trust in the presence and power of the LORD your God, a very prominent aspect of the substance of the First Commandment in the Psalms.

In this connection, one may note other positive forms of the First Commandment in Deuteronomy that are echoed in various ways in the Psalter.[13] Twice in Deut 10 a sequence of commands is given that reflects the First Commandment. In verse 12, Moses says:

> So now, O Israel, what does the LORD your God require of you? Only to fear the LORD your God, to walk in all his ways, to love him, to serve the LORD your God with all your heart and with all your soul...

Then, at the end of the chapter, a similar exhortation:

> [20]The LORD your God you shall fear, him you shall serve; to him you shall cling; and by his name you shall swear. [21]He is your praise, and he is your God, who did with you these great and marvelous things that you saw with your own eyes.

An important addition to the positive formulations, particularly with reference to the Psalms, is the inclusion of the sentence: "He is your praise." The context sets the praise of the LORD, and the praise of the LORD alone, as a form of obeying the primary commandment to have no other gods except "the LORD your God." The connection between the fear and praise of the LORD alone and all the wonderful things that the LORD has done is reflective of the sequencing of the self-presentation announcement at the beginning of the Decalogue and the prohibition against having other gods. One grows out of the other. The response to the wonderful deeds of the LORD is a primary manifestation – or betrayal – of adherence to the First Commandment.

In the passages just cited, the exhortation to "fear the LORD your God" is at the center of things, as it is in Deut 13:4–5:

> [4]Do not heed the words of that prophet or that dream-diviner. For the LORD your God is testing you to find out whether you really love the LORD your God with all your heart and with all your soul. [5]Follow none but the LORD your God, and fear none but him; keep his commandments alone, and heed only his voice; worship none but him, and hold fast to him alone.

---

[13] While the reflections of the First Commandment in the Psalter are not exclusively in reference to Deuteronomic formulations, the language and concerns of Deuteronomy are present, whether or not Deuteronomy is the explicit source of them. On the strong connections between Deuteronomy and Psalms, see Miller, "Deuteronomy and Psalms."

Verse 4 sets the matter explicitly as a test of Israel's adherence to the command of the Shema and the next verse underscores that with various positive expressions for keeping the First Commandment: following, fearing, keeping the LORD's commandments, obeying, serving, and holding fast.

In all of these instances, there is some emphatic or other dimension, pointing to the exclusiveness of the people's worship and service of the LORD. That may be done by the inclusion of "with all your heart and with all your soul" or by the syntactical emphasis that is given by placing the objects of the verbs, the LORD's name and pronouns referring to the LORD, at the beginning of the sentence. Such constructions may be translated in different ways, as is done above, but all of them are modes of signaling that it is to the LORD alone that one clings, the LORD alone that one follows, serves, fears, listens.[14]

The "fear of the LORD" as a positive form of the First Commandment is found in other Deuteronomistic material, specifically 2 Kgs 17:32–39:

[32]They also *feared*[15] the LORD and appointed from among themselves all sorts of people as priests of the high places, who sacrificed for them in the shrines of the high places. [33]So they *feared* the LORD but also served their own gods, after the manner of the nations from among whom they had been carried away.
[34] To this day they continue to practice their former customs. They do not *fear* the LORD and they do not follow the statutes or the ordinances or the law or the commandments that the LORD commanded the children of Jacob, whom he named Israel. [35]The LORD had made a covenant with them and commanded them, "You shall not *fear* other gods or bow yourselves to them or serve them or sacrifice to them, [36]but you shall *fear* the LORD, who brought you out of the land of Egypt with great power and with an outstretched arm; you shall bow yourselves to him, and to him you shall sacrifice. [37]The statutes and the ordinances and the law and the commandment that he wrote for you, you shall always be careful to observe. You shall not *fear* other gods; [38]you shall not forget the covenant that I have made with you. You shall not *fear* other gods, [39]but you shall *fear* the LORD your God; he will deliver you out of the hand of all your enemies.

These verses are part of an elaborate explanation of why the worship of the gods of the nations existed alongside the worship of the LORD in the former territory of Israel that had been made into an Assyrian province after the fall of Samaria. The important thing in this context is the extended use

---

[14] Similar formulations may be found also in Deut 11:13 and 22. The latter verse shows that it is possible to formulate the exhortation without using emphatic construction or the addition of "with all your heart and with all your soul." But the Deuteronomic positive forms of the First Commandment most often include them.

[15] A number of translations translate the repeated forms of the verb *yārēʾ* by the term "worship." This is very appropriate, for that is what is meant. I have kept the language of "fear," so there can be no doubt what word is in view.

of the word "fear" for the attitude toward the LORD embodied in the First Commandment. The covenant is to be understood as what was embodied in the Ten Words (cf. Exod 34:28; Deut 4:13). The language of the First and Second Commandment is present with reference to "other gods" several times as well as the equation of "fear" with "bow down and serve."[16]

What this means for the investigation of the First Commandment in the Psalter is that one is looking for reflections of any or all of the three parts here described: language or sentiments that express what is represented in the divine self-presentation, the prohibition against having other gods besides the LORD, and the making and worshipping of either idols or other gods. One may expect often some indication of the exclusivity of worshiping, the LORD that is, expressions that indicate no other, the LORD alone, and the like. Further, one may expect to encounter positive forms of the First Commandment and its claims, starting with the reverberations of the Shema but including other formulations and language as well.

The Decalogue Psalms

It may be appropriate then to begin with some negative data. That is, one does not find reference to "other gods" in the Psalter, except obliquely (Ps 16:4). The word *pesel*, the primary decalogical term for the images occurs only two times in the Psalter, though there are other words for idols or images in important contexts. The terminology for "strange god" (*ʾēl zār*) occurs only two times (Pss 44:21; 81:10) and "foreign god" (*ʾēl nēkār*) only once (Ps 81:10). There are not a lot of expressions about "God alone/only" though again there are some important instances.[17]

Some of these texts, however, are important instances of the impact of the First Commandment on the psalmody of the Old Testament even if they are not extensive. The two psalms most often cited as referring to the Decalogue are Pss 50 and 81. The former is more reflective of the second

---

[16] One may discern here what is not generally the case that it is possible to speak of "fearing" the lord while "fearing" other gods. There is a tension in the text, indicative of the way in which an explanatory argument is being made about the practices of non-Yahwists. The latter part of the text, verses 34b to 40, is an emphatic effort to set "fear" of Yahweh as precluding "fear" of the other gods.

[17] In his treatment of the First Commandment as a kind of center of the Old Testament and thematic throughout, Werner Schmidt puts most of the weight on this dimension with regard to the Psalter. He identifies places where the exclusivity is expressed in such terms, but they are not many and some of them are rather tangential (*Das erste Gebot: Seine Bedeutung für das Alte Testament* [Theologische Existenz heute Nr. 165; München: Kaiser Verlag, 1969], 40–43).

table of the Decalogue, especially in verses 18–20, where there are echoes of the prohibitions against stealing, adultery, and false witness. Even in this psalm, however, the indictment of the people begins with the divine announcement of an intention to testify against the people, and that begins with the claim "I am God, your God" (v. 7), which, in light of the psalm's context in the Elohistic Psalter, should be understood as a reflection of the beginning of the Decalogue, "I am the LORD your God."[18] This is accentuated as the divine speech begins with the imperative *šimʿâ ʿammî*, "Hear, O my people, that I may speak to you" paralleled in the next colon with the clause, "O Israel, that I may testify against you." As Erich Zenger has noted, the frequency of this imperative call to Israel to hear or to give heed in the Deuteronomic Mosaic speeches around the giving of the Commandments, specifically Deut 4:1; 5:1; and 9:1, but especially the Shema in 6:4, together with the theophanic character of the psalm itself suggests a conscious reflection of the Sinai/Horeb theophany.[19]

In Ps 81, one encounters perhaps the most explicit reference to the First Commandment in the entire Psalter. Not surprisingly, it has many affinities with Ps 50 as well as with Ps 95, three psalms that probably share a common cultic setting around covenant renewal and in that context reflect the centrality of the First Commandment.[20] It begins with a call to praise God with various instruments. Then an oracle is heard, the voice of God recalling the deliverance from slavery and then moving to a strong admonishment to Israel to listen. It is at this point – that is, what it is the people are supposed to listen to or to have listened to, that the First Commandment comes into view:

[9]Hear, O my people, while I admonish you;
　O Israel, if you would but listen to me!
[10]There shall be no strange god among you;
　you shall not bow down to a foreign god.

---

[18] The opening words of the psalm – *ʾēl ʾĕlōhîm yhwh* – may also be an anticipation of the divine self-presentation in verse 7. The warning against forgetting God in verse 22 may be a more distant reflection of the First Commandment inasmuch as that language appears in some of the historical psalms as well as in the prophets.

[19] "Das Redekorpus beginnt mit der invertierten Selbstvorstellungsformel, wobei die elohistische Bearbeitung den Eigennamen JHWH durch den Gattungsnamen ersetzte. Sowohl der Sprachgebrauch (Nähe zum Dtn) wie die Parallele im Festpsalm 81 [9–11] und der eigene Kontext (Theophanie) machen in [7] eine bewusste Anspielung an die Sinai-bzw. Horebtheophanie mit Dekalogverkündigung wahrscheinlich." (F.-L. Hossfeld and E. Zenger, *Die Psalmen I: Psalm 1–50* (NechB Altes Testament 40; Würzberg: Echter Verlag, 1993), 313.

[20] For the commonalities among these three psalms suggesting a common cultic and, more specifically, festival setting, see Zenger, *Die Psalmen I*, 309–310. The specifics of that cultic setting are difficult to determine and have been the subject of much discussion.

¹¹I am the LORD your God;
   who brought you up out of the land of Egypt.
   Open your mouth wide and I will fill it.

The First Commandment is reflected in four ways. One is the explicit quotation of much of the self-presentation formula "I am the LORD your God
who brought you up out of the land of Egypt." The prohibition of the First
Commandment against having other gods is present in the language "not
shall there be" a strange god among you, and the language of the commandment against making and worshipping images is there in the expression "you shall not bow down to a foreign god." There is yet a further
manifestation of the First Commandment in these verses. It is the echo of
the Shema in the parallel sentences "Hear, O my people"// O Israel." That
echo continues and carries this focus on the First Commandment further
into the indictment of Israel. One may presume from this extensive reference to the First Commandment and the lack of any other commandment,
statute, or divine instruction that the indictment that follows in the rest of
the Psalm is precisely because of the failure of the people to live under the
claim of that commandment as expressed from the self-presentation formulation through the worshipping of strange gods. But nothing specific is said
in the indictment except the repeated claim that Israel did not or would not
"listen" (*šāma*^c). Reference to Israel's need to listen or heed occurs three
times between verses 9 and 14 (9, 12, 14). As in Ps 50, the Shema is very
much in the background of the divine speech and judgment. The criterion
for Israel's faithfulness as a people is measured by this commitment alone
to the God who brought them out of the land of Egypt with no turning to
some god who was strange to them.

The elaboration of the self-presentation formula as a ground for sole
worship of "the LORD your God" in the preceding verses of Ps 81 (7–8) is
the freeing of Israel from its burden. More specifically, it is the fact that
the LORD answered the call of distress of the people. There is a direct connection between the hearing of the cry of distress and responding to it and
the claim of this god to be Israel's god alone. The reference to strange god
and foreign god is quite important. The concern is not so much about images as it is about who is Israel's god and why and thus the reason why
"my people" are to pay no attention to gods who are strange and foreign to
them and their experience.

Erich Zenger has called attention, along with others, to the way in
which Ps 81 leads into Ps 82. The connection is indicated not so much by
lexical and other such resonances but in the way in which both are marked
by divine speech, mediated through the prophetically influenced Asaphite
speaker. Both psalms, he notes, are held together by their focus on the
binding validity of the primary or first commandment. In Ps 81, that focus

is rooted in the Exodus experience and the claim that arises out of it for Israel's devotion only to the God who heard the distress and delivered them. In Ps 82, the First Commandment is played out in a drama in which all the other gods are placed under the judgment of mortality, so that the LORD alone can claim the worship and homage, not just of Israel but also of all the nations (v. 8). The claim of the self-presentation formula and the First Commandment is universalized and made applicable to all the nations. There is a further significant tie to Ps 81, however, that particularly reflects the way in which the Psalter focuses upon and becomes a meditation on the First Commandment. A parallel may be discerned between the insistence in Ps 81 on Israel's exclusive worship of the LORD because of the people's experience of having their cries of distress heard and of being delivered from oppression and the rationale for the death of all the gods in Ps 82. The latter happens for one reason alone, and that is the failure of the gods to do what the LORD has done as recalled in Ps 81 – deliver from oppression and injustice. Even as Ps 72 tells of the subjection of all the kings of the earth to the LORD's anointed because he delivers the needy when they call, so Ps 82 says that the rule of the peoples of the earth is dependent upon divine attention to the cry of the needy for help. There is thus a direct tie again between the claim of the First Commandment and the experience of suffering, outcry, and deliverance. Therein is the only basis for having a god. The God who so acts is the only god you have.

The Asaphite Psalter comes to an end with the conclusion of Ps 83, a communal lament that is a prayer for God's help against the surrounding hostile nations, a number of whom are named in the psalm. The prayer calls on the Lord to destroy these nations just as the LORD did to Sisera and to the nobles Oreb and Zeeb and the princes Zebah and Zalmunna (Judg 7:25; 8:1–21). The prayer and the psalm concludes with the plea:

[19]Let them know that you, whose name is the LORD,
   are alone most high over all the earth.[21]

The move that is made from the exclusive claim of the LORD over Israel to the universalizing of that claim by the de-deifying of all the other gods and the LORD's replacement of all the other deities in ruling the nations is now extended to the nations themselves in the prayer that they may know that it is the LORD alone who rules over the earth.

---

[21] The absence of verbs in the verse after "Let them know" creates some ambiguity reflected in the differences in the various translations, e.g., JPS Tanak translation: "May they know/ that Your name, Yours alone, is the lord/ supreme over all the earth."

The Enthronement Psalms

While the focus of attention so far has been upon the Elohistic, but more specifically the Asaphite Psalter at its end – because of explicit and implicit references to the First or Primary Commandment in several of its psalms – one should not assume that this thematic is peculiar to that particular group of psalms. Indeed in the present redaction of the Psalter, one may say that the Asaph Psalms provide an entrée into the climax of the Psalter in Book IV and the Enthronement Psalms, an important connecting link being provided first by Ps 95 and then by the historical psalms 78, 105, and 106 (see below).[22] While there are motifs within the initial psalms of Book IV that are important reflections of the First Commandment, I want to start with the Enthronement Psalms proper and their fundamental claims. The major assertion is there at the very beginning of Ps 93: the LORD is king.[23] The claim in this instance is cosmic and universal in scope, reflected in the LORD's creation of the world and the LORD's rule from the very beginning. There is little elaboration, simply exultation of the LORD.

Then in Pss 95–99, the claim that the LORD is king or the LORD rules is repeated in each psalm. The first of these has been associated with the Asaphite Pss 50 and 81 as a psalm for a festival celebration in which divine anger against a faithless Israel is uttered through a prophetic oracle. It also shares with those psalms the claim of the First Commandment, here asserted primarily in the initial claim of the psalm after the call to praise and thanksgiving in verses 1–2. The praise is due:

[3]Because the LORD is a great God,
    and a great King above all gods.

The ground for this claim is again the creative work of the LORD (vv. 4–5), but the claim is elaborated now in a way beyond that of Ps 93. The rule of the LORD is above all gods. The drama worked out in Ps 82 is here as-

---

[22] On Book IV and the Enthronement Psalms as a climax of the Psalter, see Gerald H. Wilson, *The Editing of the Hebrew Psalter* (Society of Biblical Literature Dissertation Series; Chico, CA: 1985), as well as Zenger, "The God of Israel's Reign over the World (Psalms 90–106)," and the literature cited there in note 1.

[23] It is not necessary in this context to rehearse or even to insist upon a particular point of view about how best to translate and understand the phrase *yhwh mālāk* in these psalms. In any translation, it is a claim about the exclusive rule of the lord over the gods and the peoples as well as over Israel. While Wilson and others view this repeated claim in Book IV as over against the failure of human kingship, a perspective that is quite legitimate and arguable, the interest in this context is the claim of the lord's rule over against the rule of other gods and nations, not only over against Israel's human rulers.

sumed. The gods are there but only as subjects and subordinates of the king above all gods – the LORD. The psalm goes on, however, beyond this assertion to articulate the force of the First Commandment in a positive way:

[6]O come, let us worship and bow down,
    let us kneel before the LORD our Maker!
[7]For he is our God,
    and we are the people of his pasture,
    and the sheep of his hand.

In these verses, the people embody the requirement of the First Commandment and assert what both it and the self-presentation formula introducing it claim as they affirm that the LORD "is our God." The phrase "our God," which is the community's response to the First Commandment, is heard more often in the Enthronement Psalms than any other body of psalms, in most instances in the phrase *yhwh ʾĕlōhênû*, "the LORD our God" (Pss 90:17 (*ʾădōnai ʾĕlōhênû*); 92:14; [94:23]; 95:7; 98:3; 99:5, 8, 9). The claim that the LORD is king is set alongside the claim that the LORD is our God.

The argument of Ps 93, developed further in Ps 95, is picked up and elaborated even more in Ps 96. The call to sing to the LORD that begins Ps 95 echoes once more but is carried further into a call to "declare his glory among the nations, his marvelous works among all the peoples." This latter exhortation is an important aspect of the way in which the First Commandment is kept in Israel and among the nations, but we shall come back to that. Once again the ground for the assertion that the LORD is king is that "the LORD made the heavens." As in Ps 95, but even more explicitly in Ps 96, the LORD's work of creation is a claim made over against all the other gods. Because the LORD is great and because the LORD made the heavens, "he is to be feared above all gods, for all the gods of the peoples are idols (*ʾĕlîlîm*)" (vv. 4–5).[24] The further implication of all this is that, as Ps 82 asserts in its conclusion, the LORD will come to judge the peoples in righteousness and justice, a righteousness and justice that, by inference from Ps 82, the gods of the nations have failed to enact.

In Ps 97, the cry that the LORD is king opens the psalm and leads into a theophanic description of the LORD's coming and the announcement that "the heavens proclaim his righteousness and all the peoples behold his glory" (v. 6). The conclusion of Ps 83 that the LORD alone is Most High

---

[24] For the rootage of this contrast between the humanly made idols and the heavens made by the lord and the lord's abode in one of the first interpretations of the First Commandment in Exod 20 after the giving of the Decalogue, see the discussion of Ps 115 below.

over all the earth is repeated in verse 9, but the "alone" dimension is spelled out in the parallel colon: "you are exalted far above all gods." That all of this is explicitly an interpretation of the claim of the First Commandment is made very clear in verse 7, which stands in the middle of this section. Over against the peoples beholding the glory of the LORD, the Psalm announces that:

[7]All worshipers of images (*ʿōḇĕḏê pesel*) are put to shame,
   those who make their boast in worthless idols (*ʾĕlîlîm*);
   all gods bow down (*hištaḥăwû*) before him.

The language of the Second Commandment is explicit here. Indeed, this is the only instance of the use of the word *pesel* in the Psalter. The verbs *hištaḥăweh* and *ʿāḇaḏ*, which are the verbs for bowing down and worshiping/serving in the Second Commandment, are present here though in reverse order. And the corollary of Israel's not "bowing down" before the other gods or before the images or idols is that the other gods shall bow down before the LORD.

Ps 98 reiterates the themes of the preceding psalms and concludes with the same word as Ps 82: the LORD is coming to judge the earth and that judging/ruling activity shall be couched in justice and righteousness. Finally the Enthronement Psalms conclude with the declaration once more at the beginning of Ps 99 that "the LORD is king." Again that assertion is made vis-à-vis the peoples and the manifestation of that rule is in justice and righteousness. Nothing is said explicitly about the gods or the idols. That point has been made in the previous psalms. But it is worth noting that there are more repetitions of the expression "the LORD our God" here than in any other psalm (4 times), so that whatever claims are being laid out in these Enthronement Psalms they are about the one that Israel knows and worships as "our God." Ps 100 sounds a coda to these psalms with its further call to the worship of the LORD and to

[3]Know that the LORD is God.
   It is he that made us, and we are his;
we are his people, and the sheep of his pasture.

The Historical Psalms

The so-called historical psalms – 78, 105, and 106 – make a quite particular contribution to the Psalter's meditation on the First Commandment. I would suggest that what the historical psalms do is tell the story of the Israelites as the story of the First or Primary Commandment understood in the fullest sense. That is, these psalms recount in poetic fashion the people's deliverance and their failure to respond to that deliverance by giving themselves totally in worship and service to the God who redeemed them, which is what the self-presentation formula and the First and Second Commandments are about. With reference to Ps 78, which is separated from the other two as a part of the Asaphite Psalter, the indictment of the people for their sin in verses 56–58 is because "they provoked him to anger with their high places, they moved him to jealousy with their idols." Making God "jealous" (*qānāʾ*) with images (*pĕsîlîm*) is a clear reference to the Second Commandment with its motivation clause, "I the LORD your God am a jealous God (*ʾēl qannāʾ*). That accusation, however, is placed under the heading: "Yet they tested and rebelled against the Most High God" (v. 56). That note of the people *testing* God is thematic for the psalm. As the story of Israel is told, it is reported three times that they tested God (vv. 18, 41, and 56). In this last instance it is by their high places and idols, their worshipping of idols and other gods. In the first instance, it is said that:

[18]They tested God in their heart
    by demanding the food they craved.
[19]They spoke against God, saying,
    "Can God spread a table in the wilderness?
[20]True, he struck the rock
    and water gushed out
    and torrents overflowed;
but can he also give bread
    or provide meat for his people?"

Then in verse 41 and following, the accusation of testing God is made against the people another time and this time more emphatically:

[41]They tested God *again and again*,
    and provoked the Holy One of Israel
[42]They did not remember his power,
    or the day when he redeemed them from the foe;
[43]When he displayed his signs in Egypt,
    and his miracles in the fields of Zoan.

The psalm goes on at that point to recount those signs and miracles at great length, including leading the people out, guiding them in the wilderness, and driving out nations before them (vv. 44–55). The outcome of all that, however, is what is recounted in verses 56–58: They tested the Most High, did not keep his decrees, and turned away, moving the LORD to jealousy because of their images.

The story of Israel as recounted in the psalm is a story of repeated sin and rebellion. Its particular character in this recounting is a constant *test-*

ing of God. Putting God to the test has a dual character to it. The people do not respond to the powerful and mighty acts that the LORD has done in their behalf – marvels in the land of Egypt, dividing the sea and letting them pass through it, leading them with a cloud, splitting the rocks open to provide water (vv. 12–16). This was the critical distinction between Rahab and the other Canaanites in Josh 2. She heard of the LORD's mighty acts and feared; the others heard and disregarded.[25] In Ps 78, it is the Israelites themselves who hear and see and disregard. What that means is articulated then in verse 22: "... they did not put their faith (*he'ĕmînû*) in God and did not trust (*bāṭaḥ*) his saving power (*yĕšûʿātô*)." The theme of the psalm is that the people did not trust the LORD to be able to care for them despite all the signs of that power used in their behalf in the past. They turned to images and idols.

In the story of the Exodus, the critical episodes in the failure of the people to live by the First Commandment are the account of the Golden Calf when the people asked Aaron for gods to lead them out because Moses had left and the episode at Massah/Meribah when the people tested the LORD and said, "Is the LORD among us or not?"[26] It is not surprising, therefore, to find in Ps 95, where the claim of the First Commandment is prominent, that when the LORD indicts the people through prophetic oracle, it is because they hardened their hearts at Meribah/Massah:

[9]When your ancestors tested me,
And put me to the proof, *though they had seen my work.*

And in the related Ps 81, again a psalm in which the First Commandment in its full form is to the fore, that incident is referred to once more, as it is in Ps 106 (see below), though in this instance it is described as God testing the people.[27]

In all of these cases, the First Commandment is seen to have at its heart what Martin Luther suggested was indeed the fundamental issue of the Commandment: Having a God "is nothing else than to trust and believe in that one with your whole heart."[28] These psalms, which uncover this issue

---

[25] Patrick D. Miller, "The Story of the First Commandment: The Book of Joshua," *Covenant as Context*, eds. Andrew Mayes and Robert B. Salters (Oxford: Oxford University Press, 2003),   (see above, 80–90).

[26] Patrick D. Miller, "The Story of the First Commandment: The Book of Exodus" (see above, 68–79).

[27] These are the only three places in the Psalms where the incident at Meribah/Massah is mentioned.

[28] One can see how thoroughly Luther interprets the commandment in these terms by the opening paragraphs of his instruction on the First Commandment in "The Large Catechism":

so thoroughly, make two points. The crucial one is that the expectation of complete trust that is in the First Commandment and is its most positive formulation is not an expectation out of nothing but one that is rooted in an ongoing experience of the trustworthiness of this God. The other point is that the disobedience of the First Commandment by the failure of the people to put their trust in the LORD and the LORD's power is a pervasive and continuing problem in the history of Israel. One may, in effect, tell that story as a narrative of Israel's failure to keep and live by this Commandment.

Nowhere is that more evident than in Pss 105 and 106, the other two historical psalms, and the psalms that conclude Book IV of the Psalter. Ps 105 does not seem immediately relevant to the point because it is about the LORD's many acts in behalf of Israel, while it is Ps 106 that recounts the people's failure. But that is just the point. Ps 105 tells the story that provides the ground for an expected trust and obedience. Ps 106 tells what happened contrary to what was expected.[29]

As Ps 106 tells Israel's story, there are two ways in which that history is a history of sin:

1) The people turned to idols and the gods of the nations. This happens three times in the recounting of the history:

"You are to have no other gods."

That is, you are to regard me alone as your God. What does this mean, and how is it to be understood? What does "to have a god" mean, or what is God?

Answer: A "god" is the term for that to which we are to look for all good and in which we are to find refuge in all need. Therefore, to have a god is nothing else than to trust and believe in that one with your whole heart. As I have often said, it is the trust and faith of the heart alone that make both God and an idol. If your faith and trust are right, then your God is the true one. Conversely, where your trust is false and wrong, there you do not have the true God. For these two belong together, faith and God. Anything on which your heart relies and depends, I say, that is really your God.

The intention of this commandment, therefore, is to require true faith and confidence of the heart, which fly straight to the one true God and cling to him alone. What this means is: "See to it that you let me alone be your God, and never search for another." In other words: "Whatever good thing you lack, look to me for it and seek it from me, and whenever you suffer misfortune and distress crawl to me and cling to me. I, I myself, will give you what you need and help you out of every danger. Only do not let your heart cling to or rest in anyone else."

(*The Book of Concord: The Confessions of the Evangelical Lutheran Church*, eds. Robert Kolb and Timothy J. Wengert [Minneapolis: Fortress, 2000], 386–387). The reverberations in the psalms of such a reading of the First Commandment are evident in what follows.

[29] On the historical psalms generally, see Walter Brueggemann, *Abiding Astonishment: Psalms, Modernity, and the Making of History* (Louisville: Westminster John Knox Press, 1991).

Verses 19–23: They made a calf and worshipped an image (*massēkā*)

Verses 28–31: They attached themselves to the Baal of Peor

Verses 34–39: They did not destroy the nations as commanded but mingled and learned to do as they did, which means "they served (*ᶜābad*) their idols" (v. 36) and "prostituted themselves in their doings" (v. 39).

2) The people did not trust the Lord and did not respond to the Lord's wonderful works. Virtually the rest the psalm is an account of their sin.

Verse 7: They did not consider the wonderful works of the LORD but rebelled against the Most High.

Verses 13–15: They soon forgot his works and put God to the test in the wilderness.

Verses 24–25: They despised the pleasant land, having no faith in his promise.

Verses 32–33: They angered the LORD at the waters of Meribah.

The psalm is thus a recounting of the fundamental ways in which the community did not live out the requirement and expectation of the First Commandment: They turned to other gods in visible ways, and they did not trust the LORD, "having no faith in his promise," as verse 24 puts it.

Trust in the Lord

The centrality of trust in the LORD as the fundamental requirement of covenant obedience and of life in the community of those redeemed by the LORD is not peculiar to these psalms or even to the Psalter. I have already pointed to the issue arising in the Book of Exodus when the people tested Moses. When Job recounts the ways in which he has lived by the law and, more specifically the Commandments (Job 31),[30] his testimony relative to his following the First Commandment is couched in these terms:

[24]If I have made gold my trust,
  Or called fine gold my confidence.

---

[30] For the way in which Job 31 is set in relation to the Decalogue, see Manfred Oehming, "Hiob 31 und der Dekalog," in *The Book of Job*, ed. W.A.M. Beuken (BETL CXIV; Leuven: University Press, 1994), 362–368; and *idem*, "Ethik in der Spätzeit des Alten Testaments am Beispiel von Hiob 31 und Tobit 4," in *Altes Testament: Forschung und Wirkung: Festschrift für Henning Graf Reventlow*, eds. Peter Mommer and Winfried Thiel (Frankfurt: Peter Lang, 1995), 159–173.

The issue is not the worship of other gods in the more specific sense of the named deities of the nations, but it is most assuredly the question of where Job has put his ultimate trust.

Job's point is echoed in Ps 52:8–9, where fearing, trusting, and taking refuge (see below) all come together in the psalmist's distinction between the righteous and the evildoer:[31]

⁸The righteous will see and fear,
    and will laugh at him [the evildoer], saying:
⁹"See the one who would not make God his refuge,
but trusted in the greatness of his riches,
    and sought refuge in wealth."

Over against the trust in riches of the evil-doer, the psalmist then declares his or her "trust in the steadfast love of God for ever and ever" (v. 10b). That affirmation is then paralleled by the promise "I will thank you for ever because you have acted" (v. 11a), and the reader is led to hear the interaction between placing one's trust in the LORD alone and giving thanks, a thanks that is evoked by the things the trusted one, the LORD, has done. Unlike what happened in the story of Israel's disobedience, this psalmist responds in trust and thanksgiving and praise to the LORD's great deeds.

In a totally different context, the initial summary of Hezekiah's reign says: "He trusted only in the LORD the God of Israel…He clung to the LORD; he did not turn away from following him, but kept the commandments that the LORD had given to Moses" (2 Kgs 18:5a, 6). Immediately prior to the conclusion that Hezekiah trusted in the LORD only, we are given the grounds for this conclusion: He did what was right; he removed the high places, broke down the pillars and cut down the sacred pole (or asherah), and he broke into pieces the bronze serpent because the people of Israel had made offerings to it. In other words, the two dimensions of the First Commandment are brought together again and they are seen as a sin-

---

[31] The testimony of Job and the psalmist is an indication that the tendency in modern interpretation of the force of the First Commandment to set money and wealth as an alternative god is anything but a simplistic modern analogy to the ancient reality. Money and wealth were as clearly an alternative object of trust then as now, as well indicated by Jesus' words about not being able to serve both God and Mammon. His very use of the Aramaic term is an indication that he wants his audience to be aware of the equivalency. This is a god.

Luther makes money the first illustration of what is at stake in the First Commandment:

    There are some who think that they have God and everything they need when they have money and property; they trust in them and boast in them so stubbornly and securely that they care for no one else. They, too, have a god – mammon by name, that is, money and property – on which they set their whole heart (*The Book of Concord*, 387).

gle reality. Hezekiah's trust in the LORD alone is reflected in the abolition of all competing cults. Or, vice versa, Hezekiah's elimination of the worship of the cults that were not part of the worship of the LORD was an act of trust in the LORD alone. Even the expression "he clung to" (*wayyidbaq*) is a positive expression of obedience to the First Commandment (see Deut 10:20; 13:5).[32]

Coming back to the Psalter, one is aware of the pervasiveness of this theme of trust in the LORD alone. To the extent that the Psalter is a meditation on the First Commandment, it centers in the many ways in which the issue of trust is raised and the many ways in which trust in the LORD is seen to have its basis in the wonderful and saving deeds of the LORD and its outflow in how people respond to those marvelous deeds. A cardinal example is Ps 111. It begins with the Hallelujah call to praise and parallels that with the declaration "I will give thanks to the LORD *with all (my) heart,* in the company of the upright, in the congregation. " This phrase clearly echoes the Shema with its call for a total commitment to the LORD, that is, a love of the LORD "with all your heart." In this case, the totality of commitment is manifest in thanksgiving and praise. From that announcement, the psalmist proceeds to declare, "Great are the works of the LORD" and then enumerates them at length. In other words, the psalm responds to the wonderful deeds of the LORD by recital of them as the grounds for praise, a note that returns at the end with the final sentence: "His praise endures forever."

Ps 9 begins in the same fashion: "I will give thanks to the LORD with all my heart" and sets as a parallel to that intention: "I will tell of all your wonderful deeds" (v. 2).[33] The recounting in this instance is a report of the LORD's mighty power over the enemies of the psalmist, who may be the king, though the text does not make that clear. While Ps 111 sets the wonderful works of the LORD very broadly, encompassing creative and redemptive acts having to do with the people, Ps 9 celebrates the same kind of marvelous power as manifest in behalf of the one who now prays and calls again for the LORD's deliverance. When, in verse 12, the psalmist calls on others to sing the praises of the LORD and declare his deeds among the peoples, the specific deed or type of act that is lifted up is: "He does not forget the cry of the afflicted." Immediately prior to this verse, the

---

[32] Note Luther's appropriation of this same language for interpreting the First Commandment.

[33] This sentence occurs also at the beginning of Ps 138, which works very much in the manner of Pss 9 and 111.

psalmist says: "Those who know your name trust (*baṭaḥ*) in you/ for you do not abandon those who seek you" (v. 11).[34]

The Promise in the First Commandment

At this point, we are brought before one of the significant manifestations of what it means to live under the First Commandment. It is customary to see in the Decalogue a list of instructions for the people and to presume that all the implications of obedience have to do with those who are so instructed and the way they live their lives and respond to the God who has so instructed them. Whatever obligation is there on the part of the LORD is presumed as already fulfilled by the claim of the self-presentation formula "…who brought you out of the land of Egypt, out of the house of slavery." It is particularly in the psalms that we hear most sharply that insofar as the people live by the First Commandment there is a continuing implication *for the LORD*. That is, the First Commandment is both the ground of the cry for help and also comes to expression, to manifestation, in the cry for help. Turning to this God in trust rather than to other sources is an act of obedience to the First Commandment. Because that trust is reliable, as the self-presentation formula has indicated, living according to the First Commandment means that one can know or trust God's powerful presence. Loyalty to the LORD is thus reciprocal (Ps 115:13; 145:20). Further, the love of the LORD can be enhanced and under girded by the experience of God's delivering presence (Ps 116:1).

This means that it is precisely in the worst of circumstances, those situations signaled by the laments, that the First Commandment comes strongly into play. In the face of disaster, one turns to this deity for refuge and not to any other. The introduction to the Psalter makes this point in a way that then carries throughout the collection. It concludes at the end of Ps 2 with the words: "Blessed are those who take refuge in him" (v. 11).[35] It is not simply that God is by definition a refuge, and so one can see here one of the attributes or images of God, but that whoever takes and finds refuge

---

[34] One may see reflected here not only the self-presentation formula where the name is set forth at the beginning of the Decalogue – "I am the LORD" – but also the Third Commandment lifting up the name of God for careful use and protection against misuse. Here in Ps 9 is an illustration of the positive form of that commandment, the devotion to the name of God and the recognition of what the name means in the experience and hope of the people.

[35] On the pervasive and structural role of the motif of the lord as refuge in the Psalter, see now Jerome Creach, *Yahweh as Refuge and the Editing of the Hebrew Psalter* (JSOTSup; Sheffield: Sheffield Academic Press, 1996).

only in this one – no other gods – whoever chooses to make the LORD the place of refuge as over against something else, some other god, will find that to be a good state, will be blessed, that is, in a position that others will envy.[36] Two psalms later, as the Psalter begins its first series of laments or cries for help, Ps 4 concludes with the expression of confidence that arises out of trusting in the LORD alone:

[9]In peace I will lie down and sleep
    For you alone, O the LORD, will make me dwell in safety.

One may presume that the many psalms that cry out for help and the various psalms of trust are all articulations of this setting of one's life in conformity to the First Commandment and finding that the safe and secure way to live. They do not all show as explicitly as the ones under discussion here how much they are reflective of the First Commandment, but the instances in which that commandment is echoed in more explicit ways leads one to assume that it is always under girding the voice of the psalmist in trouble.

Luther's articulation of the First Commandment sounds as if he has the Psalms very much to the fore when he defines what is meant by "having a god": "A 'god' is the term for that to which we are to look for all good and in which we are to find refuge in all need."[37] So Ps 16 begins:

[1]Keep me, O God, for I take refuge in you.
[2]I say to the LORD, "You are my the LORD;
    I have no good apart from you."[38]
3   [39]
...
[4]Those who choose another [god][40] multiply their sorrows.[41]
    I will not pour out their drink offerings of blood,

---

[36] On the meaning of the word *ʾašrê*, see Waldemar Janzen, "*ʾašrê* in the Old Testament," *Harvard Theological Review* 58 (Ap 1965), 215–226.

[37] *The Book of Concord*, 386.

[38] The Hebrew of this colon is difficult and uncertain. The NJPS version is an alternative that can be defended: "I say to the lord, "You are my Lord, my benefactor; there is none above you." The note to this verse acknowledges that others translate as is done above. For discussion of some of the issues, see Bernd Janowski, *Konfliktgespräche mit Gott: Eine Anthropologie der Psalmen* (Neukirchen: Neukirchener Verlag, 2003), 313.

[39] The translation of verse 3 is very uncertain. The term "holy ones" may have in mind human beings, but it could also refer to divine beings (so NJPS translation). Whether the statement about them is positive or negative is not clear.

[40] The word *ʾĕlōhîm* is not in the text, but there is little doubt that "other god" is what is meant in this instance.

[41] The NJPS translation maintains the specificity of the marital imagery that is present in the verb *māhar*: "those who espouse another [god] may have many sorrows."

nor will I lift up their names on my lips.
5 the LORD is my chosen portion and my cup;
   you hold my lot.

The psalm begins with the claim that the LORD is the refuge of the Psalmist. Reinforcing this, the one praying affirms that the LORD is the one who
is the lord for him or her, thus making a positive affirmation of the instruction of the First Commandment. The meaning of these claims is then seen
to be that this is the one from whom the psalmist, in Luther's phrase, is "to
expect all good." That the point here is also the insistence that refuge and
good are to be found only in the LORD and not in any other god is then
made explicit in the text as the psalmist rejects the possibility of having
anything to do with other gods and their practices. Beginning in verse 5
and continuing through the rest of the psalm, the implication of all this for
the good of the psalmist is spelled out at some length. The assertion that
"the LORD is my chosen portion and my cup" is a way of laying out the
blessing of living by the First Commandment. That is why those who look
at the one who takes refuge in the LORD will say, "Blessed" (Ps 2:12) or, in
the vernacular, "How good it is!" Such a one has learned something of the
character and quality of life that comes from a strict adherence to the First
Commandment. What begins in obligation becomes gift and good, the possibility of life. The psalm describes the life that flows out of what is prescribed. It is in this fashion that the First Commandment is to be understood descriptively as well as prescriptively.

In some of the psalms around Ps 16, one hears similar notes. The royal
Ps 18 begins with elaborate and heaped-up poetic articulation of the LORD
as the refuge of the psalmist:

2 The LORD is my rock, my fortress, and my deliverer
   my God, my rock in whom I take refuge,
   my shield, and the horn of my salvation, my stronghold.
3I call upon the LORD, who is worthy to be praised,
   so I shall be saved from my enemies.

The psalmist tells how in distress he cried out to the LORD and then goes
on to lay out all that the LORD has done for him, returning in verse 31 to
the starting point: "He is a shield for all who take refuge in him." At that
point, the psalmist becomes even more explicit about the way in which all
of this is a reflection consistent with the claim of the First Commandment:

[31]Who is God except the LORD?
and who is a rock besides our God?–[42]
[32]The God who girded me with strength
and made my way safe (or perfect).

The psalmist asserts an experiential understanding of what is involved in the First Commandment and the reciprocality inherent within it. There is only one God and one rock of refuge.[43] It is "the LORD our God" as the parallelism of verse 31 confirms, echoing the language of the Shema.

One hears a similar word in Ps 21, another royal psalm:

[7]For the king trusts in the LORD,
and through the steadfast love of the Most High he shall not be moved.

It is significant for the Psalter as a meditation and exercises on the First Commandment that the king be seen as representative of such obedience, as the royal Pss 18 and 21 attest.

It is in Ps 22, that one encounters the strongest equation of the cry of the sufferer for help with trusting in the LORD alone. After the initial terrible cry of despair – but one that is addressed to "My God, my God," an explicit personal appropriation of the relational language of the Shema and the Commandments – the psalmist remembers the story of his or her ancestors in the following way:

[5]In you our ancestors *trusted*;
they *trusted*, and you delivered them.
[6]To you they *cried*, and were saved;
in you they *trusted*, and were not put to shame.

The parallelism of the lines equates the crying out with the threefold reference to trusting, even as it also says that such crying out in trust was met with divine deliverance.[44]

---

[42] The image of God as rock is at the center of Deut 32 and is the distinctive character of the lord over against all other gods as, for example, in verse 37: "Where are their gods, the rock in which they took refuge... Let them rise up and help you, let them be your protection." So also the expression "I, even I, am he; there is no god besides/with me" in verse 39 may be understood as "an emphatic affirmation that THE LORD is a rock, in contrast to other gods who have proved powerless" (Nathan MacDonald, *Deuteronomy and the Meaning of Monotheism* [Forschungen zum Alten Testament 2. Reihe, 1; Tübingen: Mohr Siebeck, 2003], 89).

[43] On the imagery of God as rock, see Dieter Eichhorn, *Gott als Fels, Burg und Zuflucht: eine Untersuchung zum Gebet des Mittlers in den Psalmen* (Bern: H. Lang, 1972).

[44] Werner Schmidt, along with others, has argued that the opening word of verse 30 is to be read as ʾāk lô, "only to him" rather than ʾākĕlû, "they shall eat," as is found in the Masoretic Text. He cites this as an example of the Yahweh alone dimension of the Psalter,

While it is not possible or necessary to cite all the texts that speak in various ways of trusting in the LORD, Ps 31 is one of the explicit instances in which trust in the LORD is set specifically over against other alternatives:

> ⁷I⁴⁵ hate those who pay regard to worthless idols,
>   but I trust in the LORD.

The expression translated here as "pay regard to worthless idols" (*haššōmĕrîm hablê šāwᵓ*) is ambiguous in meaning. NJPS translates as "rely on empty folly." The expression itself appears one other time in Jonah 2:9, but its meaning there is not any clearer than it is in Ps 31. The term *hablîm*, however, occurs elsewhere where it seems to refer to idols (Deut 32:21; Jer 8:19; 10:8; 14:22; 1 Kgs 16:13, 26). Jer 2:5, when looked at alongside verse 8, points in the same direction. In this instance, the rejection of the idols/gods as reliable is set over against the psalmist's trust in the LORD.

Even more forthrightly and unambiguously does Ps 115 reject the idols in favor of trusting in the LORD:

> ²Why should the nations say,
>   "Where is their God?"
> ³Our God is in the heavens;
>   He does whatever he pleases.
> ⁴Their idols are silver and gold,
>   the work of human hands.
> ⁵They have mouths but do not speak;
>   eyes, but do not see.
> ⁶They have ears but do not hear;
>   noses but do not smell.
> ⁷They have hands, but do not feel;
>   feet, but do not walk;
> they make no sound in their throats.
> ⁸Those who make them are like them;
>   so are all who trust in them.

---

expressing in this instance a universal hope, which includes even the dead who shall bow before the lord: "Only before him shall fall down all who sleep in the earth." It is the confession of the exclusivity of the power of God, which is not taken away from the realm of the dead (*Das erste Gebot*, 43). While this is a widely accepted text correction, it is sufficiently uncertain that one can not put much weight upon it.

[45] There is significant textual basis in both Greek and Hebrew witnesses for reading this as second person ("you hate"), as does the NRSV. The point being made here is operative whether the reference is to the lord's rejection of persons like this or to the psalmist's rejection.

While many of the reflections of the First Commandment in the Psalter
echo Deuteronomic language and concerns, this sequence reflects the first
reference to the First Commandment in Exod 20, immediately after the
giving of the Decalogue. When the people draw back in fear after the
LORD has spoken the Ten Words, the LORD speaks a second time, this time
to Moses:

²²Thus you shall say to the Israelites: "You have seen for yourselves that I spoke with
you from heaven. ²³You shall not make gods of silver alongside/with me (*ʾittô*), nor shall
you make for yourselves gods of gold.

The formulation is peculiar to this text, but the *ʾittô* of the first clause
functions analogously to the *ʿal pānay* of the First Commandment while
the prohibition "you shall not make for yourselves" is a plural form of the
beginning of the commandment prohibiting the making of images.[46] The
making of idols is clearly what is being talked about, but the language
"*gods* of silver" and "*gods* of gold" is language again of the prohibition
against having other gods. So the Exodus text blends the First and Second
Commandment into one, affirming the reading of those two commandments as a single commandment. Ps 115 reflects the Exodus text in two
ways: One is, of course, the focus on the made gods, on the idols. The
other is in its beginning the denunciation of the idols with the reference to
"our God" being in heaven. The reference to the heavenly abode of "our
God" is a way of distinguishing between "the LORD our God" and all the
made objects that people set up as gods and treat as gods, by putting their
trust in them.

The psalm is a powerful assertion of the power of the God of Israel over
against the idols and human works of the nations, whose impotence is a
reflection of their idol-gods. The psalm thus confesses what the First
Commandment requires, and flatly identifies the issue at stake as the question: "Whom do you trust?" The psalm not only derides those who trust in
human creations that can do nothing. It also makes repeated calls to Israel
(perhaps to differentiate elements within the religious congregation)[47] to
"trust in the LORD":

⁹O Israel, trust in the LORD!
    He is their help and their shield.
¹⁰O house of Aaron, trust in the LORD!

---

[46] Cf. the analogous expression in Deut 32:39: "There is no god with me" (*ʾên ʾĕlōhîm
ʿimmadî*).

[47] The three addressees in these verses may represent the laity (Israel), the priests (Aaron),
and proselytes (God-fearers).

He is their help and their shield.
¹¹You who fear the LORD, trust in the LORD!
   He is their help and their shield.

The same argument in much the same words, at least with regard to the in-
capability of the idols, is made again in Ps 135, the psalm that flows out of
Ps 134 and opens up the triad of psalms between the Psalms of Ascents
and the final group of David psalms. The echoes of Ps 134 are so complete
that one can describe Ps 135 as being formed out of pieces of Ps 134. The
call to "bless the LORD" that is the theme of Ps 134 (vv. 1–2) becomes the
climactic call of Ps 135 at its conclusion (vv. 19–20). The address to
"those who stand by night in the house of the LORD" in Ps 134:1 is repeated at the beginning of Ps 135 (v 2), and the prayer for the LORD to
bless you "from Zion" at the end of Ps 134 (v 3) is matched by the doxology at the end of Ps 135: "Blessed be the LORD from Zion." One may,
therefore, connect the descriptive clause "maker of heaven and earth" in Ps
134 to the way in which Ps 135 portrays the ways of the LORD:

⁶Whatever the LORD pleases he does,
   in heaven and on earth,
   in the seas an all deeps.

The one who is maker of heaven and earth is the one who does whatever is
pleasing in heaven and earth. In this instance, however, that point is specifically made in reference to and over against all the other gods:

⁵For I know that the LORD is great;
   our Lord is above all gods.

Like many of the other psalms observed to this point, this one goes on then
to describe the wonderful deeds of the LORD in creation and in behalf of
Israel (vv. 7–12). That leads to both the praise of the LORD and the ridicul-
ing of the idols of the nations and those who trust in them, here in virtually
the same language as one finds in Ps 115. The final call to Israel, Aaron,
and those who fear the LORD is to "bless" (*bērek*) the LORD, in distinction
from the call to "trust" the LORD in Ps 115. The difference, however, is a
reminder of the way in which the act of thanksgiving, which is what is implied in "blessing the LORD," is an aspect of worshipping the LORD alone.

Ps 40 makes a similar point, albeit more briefly and somewhat more
cryptically. The psalm begins with the testimony of the psalmist that the
LORD heard his cry and delivered him, a testimony that will evoke from
those who have witnessed it the fear of the LORD and trust in the LORD (vv.
2–4). Here again one finds that note sounded that is so common to the
Psalter and reflects its bringing to life of the demands and outcomes of the

First Commandment. The one who fears the LORD and puts her trust in God by waiting patiently for the LORD to hear her cry – that is, lives by the demand of the First Commandment – now bears witness to the benefits of such living and the reciprocal loyalty that is inherent in the First Commandment but not as visible in its primary literary context in Exodus and Deuteronomy as it is in the Psalms. Such devotion and trust in the worst of circumstances evokes a divine response that, in turn, creates a story or witness powerful enough to elicit a broadening circle of those who trust in the LORD alone: "Many will see and fear and put their trust in the LORD" (Ps 40:4). The blessed state of those who so respond, who "see and fear and put their trust," is contrasted with those who go after false gods:

⁵Blessed is the one who makes the LORD his trust,
    who does not turn to the proud,
        to those who go astray after falsehood.

While one cannot be absolutely sure that the word *kāzab* at the end of the verse refers to false gods, that is the most likely interpretation, especially in light of the use of the expression "turn to" (*pānâ ʾel*), which is often used for turning to other gods, idols, and their cultic functionaries (cf. Lev 19:4, 31; 20:6; Deut 31:18, 20; Hos 3:1). The term "falsehood" (*kāzab*) is like *hablê šāw* in Ps 31:6. It is a surrogate for the false and worthless gods.[48] The way of the LORD is contrasted in its beneficial effects with the way of the false gods and idols.

The cry of the suffering one for help in Ps 86 is rooted in such claims as: "You are my God" and "[I am] the one trusting in you (*habbōṭēaḥ ʾēleykā*)."[49] The assumption that is expressed there in personal terms – that the LORD of Israel is alone the one in whom the psalmist trusts – is then turned into an elaborate confession:

⁸There is none like you among the gods, O the LORD,
    nor are there any works like yours.
⁹All the nations you have made shall come
    and bow down before you, O the LORD.
¹⁰For you are great and do wondrous things;
    you alone are God.

---

    [48] See in this connection E. Zenger on Ps 40 in Zenger and Hossfeld, *Die Psalmen: Psalm 1–50*, 255.
    [49] Note how this claim grows out of the conclusion of Ps 84: "Blessed is the human being who trusts in you" (*bōṭēaḥ bāk* – v. 13).

Once more the psalmist gives voice to one of the powerful positive expressions of the First Commandment, to wit, that this God, "the LORD our God," is "my God" and this God alone is truly God, not only for the one who sings this psalm but for all the nations, who will bow down before the LORD of Israel and not before the gods of human hands.

Returning, then, to Book IV and the movement from the Asaphite Psalter into Book IV, where there is so much explicit reflection of the First Commandment, one finds the theme of God as refuge and ground of trust is not as prominent here, but it is the starting point of a series of psalms that center in the claim inherent in the First Commandment, that the LORD rules over all the cosmos and over all other powers. If Ps 83 concludes with its call for the peoples to know that the LORD alone is Most High over all the earth (v. 19), Ps 91 repeats the identification of the LORD with the Most High (vv. 1–2 and 9)[50] on the way to its assertion that the one who makes the LORD /Most High his or her refuge, fortress, and dwelling place will find protection from the most terrible of dangers. The way of the First Commandment is a safe way:

[14]The one who loves[51] me, I will deliver;
   I will protect the one who knows my name
[15]When he calls to me, I will answer him;
   I will be with him in trouble;
   I will deliver him and honor him.[52]

This divine promise is uttered in regard to the one who says to the LORD: "My refuge and my fortress, my God in whom I trust" (v. 2). Ps 92, then continues the identification of the LORD alone with the Most High (v. 2) and proceeds to declare the greatness of the LORD's works as the basis for praise (v. 5). From there on, the Enthronement Psalms express the congregation's praise of the one who is sovereign over all.

In a rather different fashion, the First Commandment is to the fore in one of the communal laments as an aspect of the claims of innocence on the part of the community in its cry for help. Ps 44 first recounts all the marvelous deeds of the LORD in behalf of Israel but then goes on to describe the new situation in which terrible things that have happened to the people, which can only be understood as brought about by this same God

---

[50] Cf. Ps 97:9 where the identification of the lord as "Most High over all the earth" is paralleled by the sentence, "You are exalted far above all gods."

[51] The word for "love" here is not the customary verb *ʾāhab* but the rarer verb *ḥāšaq*, occurring in Deuteronomy with reference to the lord's strong love and desire for Israel (Deut 7:7; 10:15).

[52] Cf. Pss 81:8; 99:6.

who in the past so often delivered them. In verses 17–21, the community asserts that all this bad has happened to them even though they have behaved properly:

¹⁷All this has come upon us,
   yet we have not forgotten you,
   or been false to your covenant.
¹⁸Our heart has not turned back,
   nor have our steps departed from your way,
¹⁹yet you have crushed us in the place of jackals
   and covered us with deep darkness.
²⁰If we had forgotten the name of our God,
   or spread out our hands to a foreign god,
²¹would not God search it out,
   for he knows the secrets of the heart.

All the expressions in this plea of innocence make it clear that their claim is precisely faithfulness to the First Commandment. In the words of Richard Clifford:

> The sin of which the community claims to be innocent is reducible to one: violation of the first commandment. All the phrases of human failure in the poem – being false to the covenant, the heart turning back, allowing one's steps to depart from the way (vv. 17–18), forgetting, worshiping other deities – describe apostasy.[53]

The psalm thus stands in a powerful tension with the historical psalms 78, 105, and 106, discussed above, as the argument of those psalms that Israel's judgment arose from its failure to live by the First Commandment is here explicitly rejected by the community as grounds for the present experience of suffering at the LORD's hands. The abrasive and uneasy existence of the communal lament psalms alongside the other psalms is further underscored in this tension.[54]

---

[53] Richard Clifford, *Psalms 1–72* (Abingdon Old Testament Commentary; Nashville: Abingdon, 2002), Zenger has suggested that the reference to God knowing the secrets of the heart is a reflection of the command to love God "with all your heart" (*Die Psalmen: Psalm 1–50*, 277).

[54] On this particular genre of psalms and the many interpretive and theological issues they pose, see Murray Haar, "The God – Israel Relationship in the Community Lament Psalms (Diss. Union Theological Seminary in Virginia, 1985); Paul Wayne Ferris, Jr., *The Genre of Communal Lament in the bible and the Ancient Near East* (SBLDS 127; Atlanta: Scholars Press, 1992); Frederick W. Dobbs-Allsopp, *Weep, O Daugher of Zion; A Study of the City-Lament Genre in the Hebrew Bible* (Biblica et orientalia, 44; Rome: Pontifical Biblical Institute, 1993); and Walter C. Bouzard, Jr. *We Have Heard with Our Ears, O God: A Sources of the Communal Laments in the Psalms* (SBLDS, 159; Atlanta: Scholars Press, 1997).

The Fear of the Lord

The earlier discussion of positive forms of the First Commandment compels us to note one of the most pervasive echoes of that injunction. It is in the Psalms' exaltation of *the fear of the LORD*. It is possible to fear the LORD and serve other gods as well, as the discussion of 2 Kgs 17:32–39 above has revealed. The Deuteronomic modes of referring to the fear of the LORD as a way of conforming to the First Commandment generally manifest some sort of emphasis that represents the exclusivity of this fearing. Such formulations are less common in the Psalms, which more often speak of or instruct about fearing the LORD without reference to other gods and without formulations that include an element of exclusivity. One may presume, however, that the numerous instances in which the fear of the LORD is claimed, urged, and presumed are indeed exercises on the First Commandment. Fear of the LORD is reflected or manifest in trust (e.g., Ps 40:4–5; 52:8–9; 115:11). As Ps 34 invites its hearers to "Come, O children, listen to me; I will teach you the fear of the LORD," it describes one of the primary ends that is reached as the psalms are prayed, sung, and taught. They teach the fear of the LORD even as they express it in new songs and old. The testimony of the psalmists is uttered in the congregation of those who fear the LORD (Ps 22:26; 66:16), and the Psalter is full of meditations on the benefits that accrue to those who fear the LORD. They lack no good thing (Ps 34:9); they are continual recipients of the steadfast love of the LORD (Ps 103:11, 13, 17); they receive food at the hands of the LORD (Ps 111:5) as well as God's promise (Ps 119:38); and blessing continually is theirs (Pss 112:1; 128:1, 4). The LORD hears the cry of those who fear God (Ps 145:19) and takes pleasure in them (Ps 147:1). The reciprocality inherent in the relationship created by an existence shaped by the First Commandment in its full expression is nowhere more attested than in the Psalms.

Finally what Deuteronomy signals only briefly comes to its fullest expression in the Psalter. The fear of the LORD coalesces with the Hallelujahs as the praise of the LORD is a vivid testimony to the community's living under the First Commandment. That praise permeates the Psalter, but it grows louder as one moves through the whole, climaxing first in Book IV and the Enthronement Psalms but reaching its final crescendo in the conclusion to the Psalter, the coda that is found in Pss 145 to 150. At the end, there are no subjects left to praise other gods, no instruments left to sing to other the lords. The whole cosmos and all the choirs of heaven and earth bear testimony to the LORD your God. The positive meaning of the commandment against the misuse of the name of God is brought directly into view as Ps 148 calls for praise from the heavens on high, the hosts of an-

gels, sun and moon, stars and highest heavens – all to praise the name of
the LORD:

[13]Let them praise the name of the LORD,
   for his name alone is exalted.

8. The Commandments in the Reformed Perspective

The Commandments and the Law

The Commandments present a special case when it comes to asking how the Reformed tradition interprets Scripture. The Decalogue is one of two biblical texts that have been incorporated into the theological tradition as well as into the exegetical, the other being the Lord's Prayer. It is taken up and interpreted within both systematic doctrinal formulations, as, for example, Calvin's *Institutes*, and also within a number of the Catechisms of the Reformed tradition, for example, Geneva, Heidelberg, and the Westminster Larger and Shorter Catechisms. While the Commandments are not explicated in some of the Confessions, the Second Helvetic makes it clear that catechizing the young and making sure they learn the rudiments of the faith involves learning the Ten Commandments as well as the Lord's Prayer and the Creed. The Westminster Confession identifies "the Law of God" with the Commandments, and the Scots Confession takes up the Commandments implicitly in its treatment of the works that are counted good before God (Chap. XIV). My impression is that this tradition of focusing attention upon the Commandments, particularly in relation to sin and the law or those good works one ought to do, is less common in more recent confessions and catechisms.[1]

It should not be presumed that this theological inclusion of the Commandments is peculiar to the Reformed tradition or begins there. Catechetical instruction in the Commandments was introduced into the church's life by Augustine, and he himself began a theological analysis of the Decalogue about A.D. 400 in one of his treatises against the Manichaeans

---

[1] For example, the two recent Presbyterian confessions of the Presbyterian Church in the United States of America ("Confession of 67" and "A Declaration of Faith"). When the Presbyterian Church US created a contemporary confession of faith ("A Declaration of Faith") in the 60s and 70s, one of the strongest criticisms it received when it sent a draft out to the church for response was its lack of explicit focus upon the Commandments. While there is a paragraph that speaks of the law as restored to us as gift and delight through Christ, there is no special reference to the Commandments in the final form of this confession. Cf. Lukas Vischer, ed. *Reformed Witness Today: A Collection of Confessions and Statements of Faith Issued by Reformed Churches* (Bern: Evangelische Arbeitsstelle Oekumene Schweiz, 1982). Consistent with the tradition, the recent Study Catechism of the Presbyterian Church USA includes sections on the Creed, the Commandments, and the Lord's Prayer.

("Contra Faustum") and returned to it in various ways.[2] During the Middle
Ages, the Decalogue came increasingly into the confessional practice, but
Luther gradually moved away from that, proposing that the setting in life
of the instruction in the Commandments belonged rather to the living room
and family instruction than to the confessional.[3]

All of this means that in some fashion the Decalogue functions as *doctrine* in its wholeness and in its special place, whether that is to be understood as teaching about the law or the elaboration of good works. As Edward Dowey has shown, in Calvin, who provides both a starting point and
a foundation for our understanding, the law is a part of the knowledge of
God the Creator and of God the Redeemer, but that relationship is dialecti-
cal in that "the law belongs to God's orderly, eternal, revealed will for his
creatures and is the background and goal of redemption, but is not truly
known or obeyed except in the special, gratuitous work of Christ..."[4] What
is sometimes missed in the treatment of Calvin's understanding of the law
and more particularly the Decalogue is that he places it distinctly in the
context of the *history of salvation*, so that not only is it not abrogated but it
is a part of the story that leads to Christ (*Institutes*, II. vii). He makes it
clear that by law he means not only the Decalogue but the form of religion
delivered from God by the hands of Moses, which includes "shadows and
figures corresponding to the truth." And this includes the family or poster-
ity of David. There is a kind of history of salvation movement in Books I
and II that has the law very much as an ingredient as the doctrinal explication moves from the interpretation of God the Creator and Provider to the
fall of Adam and to God the Redeemer in Jesus Christ. The intrusion of sin
and the inability to keep the law of God has made it necessary for God's

---

[2] B. Reicke, *Die zehn Worte in Geschichte und Gegenwart* (Beiträge zur Geschichte der
biblischen Exegese, 13; Tübingen: J.C.B. Mohr, 1973), 10; J. P. Christopher, *St. Augustine:
The First Catechetical Instruction [De Catechizandis Rudibus]* (Ancient Christian Writers, 2;
Westminster, Maryland: The Newman Bookshop, 1946), 5–6. The more extensive treatment
of Augustine's Decalogue catechesis is to be found in Paul Rentschka, *Die Dekalogkatechese
des hl. Augustinus: Ein Beitrag zur Geschichte des Dekalogs* (Kempten: Verlag der Jos.
Kösel'schen Buchhandlung, 1905). Rentschka shows how prior to Augustine there was some
attention given to the Decalogue but it played no central dominant role. The Two Ways topos
and tractate dominate in the earlier works, as, for example, in the *Didache*. In a number of
instances, again as for instance in the *Didache* or the *Shepherd of Hermas*, the Decalogue is
brought into place as a way of defining sins and transgressions.

[3] Ibid., 13.

[4] Edward A. Dowey, Jr., *The Knowledge of God in Calvin's Theology*, 2nd rev. ed. (Grand
Rapids: Eerdmans, 1994), 239. On Calvin's understanding of the law in general and his interpretation of the Decalogue in particular, see I. John Hesselink, *Calvin's Concept of the Law*
(Princeton Theological Monograph Series, 30; Allison Park, Pennsylvania: Pickwick Publications, 1992).

mercy to be manifest in redemption, that is in God's saving work in Jesus Christ. This movement, however, is often skewed in ways that betray Calvin's true perspective on the law. For example, in one of the most widely used compendia of Calvin's theology, the law is entirely under the rubric of sin and the excerpted discussion has to do completely with the problem of human inability to keep the law and the condemnation that the law brings forcing us on the mercy of God.[5] In that summary, chapter 7 of Book II is omitted altogether even though this is the introductory discussion of the law and the setting or context for Calvin's discussion of the law and more specifically his elaboration of the Commandments. In fact, Calvin understands the law as one of the modes by which Christ has been manifest to the elect. The giving of the law was "not done to lead the chosen people away from Christ, but rather to hold their minds in readiness until his coming; even to kindle desire for him and to strengthen their expectation, in order that they might not grow faint by too long delay." (II. vii). As the Psalms indicate, David shows that in the law he discovered the Mediator (II. vii. 12).

So it is in this *Heilsgeschichtliche* context that Calvin can identify and elaborate the third use of the law, and here he means specifically the moral law that is spelled out in the Decalogue. Acknowledging that the first use of the law is as a mirror that "warns, informs, convicts, and lastly condemns every man of his own unrighteousness" (II. vii. 6) and that the law also serves to restrain the unregenerate, Calvin insists that there is "a third and *principal* [italics mine] use, which pertains more closely to the *proper* purpose [italics mine] of the law...." This use "finds its place among believers in whose hearts the Spirit of God already lives and reigns" (II. vii. 12). But the faithful are not those of a particular time, either saints of Israel or those of the church. "For this reason we are not to refer solely to one age David's statement that the life of a righteous man is a continual meditation upon the law [Ps 1:2], for it is just as applicable to every age, even to the end of the world" (II. vii. 13).[6] Such an understanding of the law as "the best instrument for them [the faithful], to learn more thoroughly each day, the nature of the Lord's will to which they aspire, and to confirm them in the understanding of it" naturally leads into a detailed explanation

---

[5] Hugh T. Kerr, ed. *Calvin's Institutes: A New Compend* (Louisville: Westminster John Knox Press, 1989).

[6] All quotations of the Institutes are taken from the translation of Ford Lewis Battles in *The Library of Christian Classics*, ed. J. T. McNeill (Philadelphia: Westminster, 1960).

of the Decalogue (II. vii. 12). For whatever helps one better understand God's will merits a careful discussion.[7]

It is at this point that one notes some difference from Luther's interpretation, at least in its theological understanding of the law. While both Luther and Calvin share basic understandings of the law, Luther saw no way in which the law *as law* could function in this third sense, which Calvin saw as the primary one. What was for Calvin the pedagogical use, the law as showing our unrighteousness and thus condemning us, was for Luther the primary function of the law.[8] As such, this use was not simply pedagogical but *theological* and central to the very character of redemption and justification by faith. Indeed for Luther, the law is whatever serves to unmask our sin and our idolatry, whatever opens us up to the gift of the gospel by exposing our sinfulness and our inability to live under demand without the gift. Various kinds of things can do this and not simply what we customarily think of as "law." It is clear that Luther's conviction of the power of grace matched only by the incapacity of human righteousness and his own experience of justification by faith so shaped him that a fundamental difference between Lutheran and Reformed interpretations of the law, theologically and practically, opened up. Dowey has described the differences as follows:

For Luther and Lutheranism, the Calvinistic version of the third use of the law is a failure to perceive the radicality of Luther's first use, and it risks a new form of legalism in the doctrine of salvation. For Calvin and Calvinism, Luther's view elevates the accidental,

---

[7] Calvin also includes a brief discussion of the uses of the law at the end of his long commentary on the law in the Pentateuch. His commentary structures the discussion of the various laws in relation to the Commandments and concludes with a brief presentation of the sum of the law (love of God and of neighbor) as found in Deut 10:12–13; 6:5; and Lev 19:18) and finally of the uses of the law. Although Calvin's focus is more on the theological or pedagogical use of the law to convict the unregenerate, his commentary discussion does not differ in any significant way from the treatment of the uses of the law in the *Institutes*, Book II, and at the end of his commentary discussion Calvin refers the reader to that part of the *Institutes* for further discussion.

[8] Luther called the theological use "the true office and the chief and proper use of the law" [cited in John E. Witte, Jr. and Thomas C. Arthur, "The Three Uses of the Law: A Protestant Source of the Purposes of Criminal Punishment?" *Journal of Law and Religion* 10 (1992), 436, n. 8.] In the *Smalcald Articles* (1537), Luther's section "Concerning the Law" treats both the civil and theological uses of the law: "Here we maintain that the law was given by God, in the first place, to curb sin by means of the threat and terror of punishment and also by means of the promise and offer of grace and favor... The foremost office or power of the law is that it reveals inherited sin and its fruits. It shows human beings into what utter depths their nature has fallen and how completely corrupt it is." (*The Book of Concord: The Confessions of the Evangelical Lutheran Church*, eds. R. Kolb and T. Wengert [Minneapolis: Fortress, 2000], 311).

sin-caused function of the law into its all-inclusive role at the expense of what God meant to be the law's proper function both in creation and in redemption.... Law for Luther raises images of a theology of self-salvation and a devilish perversion of the divine promise; and for Calvin, law raises images of order and structure, indeed the very structure of God's love in both creation and redemption.[9]

This difference is real and reflected in various ways in the history of Lutheranism and Calvinism and their attitudes toward law and ethics. But the difference should not be overemphasized.[10] For the different understandings of law conceal important points of contact exemplified precisely in the place they give to the Decalogue.[11] Luther gives as much attention to the Decalogue in his catechetical and theological discussion as do Calvin and the Reformed theologians.[12] Three things are to be noted about Luther's interpretation. One is that, like the Scots Confession, Luther offers extended treatment of the Decalogue as the theological framework and definition of what are the works that are counted good before God.[13] Second – and this is the ground for the first point – the Decalogue has every bit as dominant a place with Luther as it does with Calvin, but Luther un-

---

[9] Dowey, "Law in Luther and Calvin," *Theology Today* 41 (1984), 146–153.

[10] This point is underscored by Witte and Arthur: "For our purposes, the differences between the Lutheran and Calvinist formulations of the uses doctrine should not be exaggerated. The influential Lutheran writer Philip Melanchthon stressed the educational use of the law from 1535 onward, and his formulations appear in several authoritative Lutheran confessions and theological tracts of the sixteenth and seventeenth centuries." (436, n. 8). They call attention to the summary of the Lutheran position on the three uses of the law in the *Formula of Concord*, where the third use of the law is specifically and extensively affirmed. It is worth noting, however, that in that context the third use is taken up precisely because of its controversial character in Lutheranism. That "controversy" is indicative of the fact that Lutheran theologians and historians of doctrine have not been of a single mind on the validity and place of the third use of the law.

[11] "Their approach to the law differs considerably in emphasis, but they are in complete accord concerning the worth and significance of the decalog." (Hesselink, *Calvin's Concept of the Law*, 101).

[12] On Luther's interpretation of the Decalogue in relation to contemporary interpretations and valuations, see Timo Veijola, "Der Dekalog bei Luther und in der heutigen Wissenschaft," in *The Law in the Bible and in its Environment*, ed. T. Veijola (Publications of the Finnish Exegetical Society, 51; Göttingen: Vandenhoeck & Ruprecht, 1990), 63–90 [Reprinted in T. Veijola, *Moses Erben: Studien zum Dekalog, zum Deuteronomismus und zum Schriftgelehrtentum* (Beiträge zur Wissenschaft vom Alten und Neuen Testament, 149; Stuttgart: Kohlhammer, 2000), 29–47]. For a powerful appropriation of Luther's treatment of the Ten Commandments in the *Larger Catechism* by a contemporary ethicist, see Paul Lehmann, *The Decalogue and a Human Future: The Meaning of the Commandments for Making and Keeping Life Human* (Grand Rapids: Eerdmans, 1995).

[13] One of Luther's most extensive interpretations of the Commandments is in his "Treatise on Good Works."

derstands the Decalogue as *doctrine* rather than law.[14] That is with reference to the Decalogue for the believer, that is, for faith, as over against the Decalogue for the unbeliever, for those who do not have faith.[15] For the former, for the baptized believer, the Decalogue functions as gospel or doctrine, not as law. That is why it is in the *Large Catechism*: "anyone who knows the Ten Commandments perfectly knows the entire Scriptures." (*LC*, Preface). The Decalogue belongs, as has traditionally been the case, with the Creed (and the Lord's Prayer) as teaching. For faith, the Decalogue is not that law that exposes our unrighteousness, though it does that for the unbeliever, who is prepared by the Decalogue *as* law, to receive the gospel. The Commandments continue to be crucial to Christian life and faith as teaching about the will of God, not as law that undoes us. In this respect, Luther is not far from Calvin, who, in his discussion of the third and principal use of the law, frequently speaks of it as "instruction" or teaching. And, as with Luther, what he has in mind is precisely the Commandments.

The third significant feature of Luther's handling of the Decalogue is the way in which the First Commandment, the worship of God alone, dominates and in fact incorporates all the other commandments. As Luther treats the Commandments in this fashion, he manifests a thoroughly evangelical understanding of them. This is evident, for example, in his *Small Catechism* where the interpretation of each commandment begins with the words "We are to fear and love God...," thus placing each of the commandments in complete dependence on the first one, whose total definition or interpretation is: "We are to fear, love, and trust God above all things."[16] Obedience of each commandment is a specific manifestation of the faith of the believer.

It is to be noted in this connection that Luther did not place much weight on the Preface or Prologue to the Commandments, while Calvin gave prominent place to it, not only in his exposition in the *Institutes* but in an extended section on "The Preface to the Law" in his Harmony of the

---

[14] William Lazereth notes that "Ps 1,19,119 are cited by *both* to defend the parenetic use of the gospel (Luther) and the third use of the Law (Calvin)" (private communication).

[15] See in this regard the citation from Luther's *Against Latomus*:

"I say, therefore, that just as the law of the Decalogue is good if it is observed – that is, if you have faith, which is the fullness of the law and righteousness – so also it is death, and wrath, and no good to you if you do not observe it – that is, if you do not have faith. This is so, no matter how many good works you do – for the righteousness of the law, that is, of the Ten Commandments is unclean and abolished by Christ even more than is the righteousness of ceremonies." (Cited in William Lazareth, *Christians in Society: Luther, the Bible, and Social Ethics* (Minneapolis: Fortress, 2001), 127.

[16] Ibid., 226.

Pentateuch. The evangelical ground of the Decalogue was for Calvin rooted in the claim of the Preface and the story it told, while for Luther that ground was in the First Commandment proper.

An important point of connection between Calvin and Luther that is not always recognized is their perception of what the First Commandment was all about. Luther put it pointedly when he said: "Moreover, what is the whole Psalter but meditation and exercises based on the First Commandment?"[17] While Calvin did not make the connection to the Psalter explicit, he interpreted the duties implied in the First Commandment under the four general heads: adoration, trust, invocation, and thanksgiving. When this happens, "our minds" are directed to the living God: "Thus steeped in the knowledge of God, they may aspire to contemplate, fear, and worship his majesty; to participate in his blessings; to seek his help at all times; to recognize, and by praises to celebrate, the greatness of his works—as the only goal of all the activities of this life" (II. viii. 16). Such an understanding leads directly into the Psalms as the paradigmatic articulation of true obedience to the First Commandment.

The Division, Numeration, and Order of the Commandments

The division of the Commandments into the two tablets is a matter of moment in the Reformed tradition, something that is noted by Calvin and the Catechisms. The fact that the tablets were carved in stone is for Calvin a clear indication of their permanence, that they are not "something transient" like the ceremonies.[18] For Calvin, the division into two tablets was a part of God's simplifying of the law and teaching us, God's accommodation to us, so that we would be reminded of our duty to God (the first four commandments) and to our neighbor (the six remaining commandments), a reflection of the two part Great Commandment. The number ten was also a part of this simplification, the law of God so succinctly presented that we could count its various directives on our fingers. Calvin and other Reformed theologians attended to the way in which the ten was worked out and regarded this as a matter of significance and not simply a reflection of different traditions. Calvin argued *for* the separation of the prohibition against other gods and the prohibition of images and their worship and *against* the separation of the coveting commandment into two command-

---

[17] In Luther's Preface to the *Large Catechism*.
[18] B. W. Farley, ed. *John Calvin's Sermons on the Ten Commandments* (Grand Rapids: Baker, 1980), 249.

ments. This was in part because the tradition supported it, both in the Jewish interpreters and in such greats of the church as Origen and Augustine. The Catholic and Lutheran traditions had incorporated the prohibition against images in the First Commandment and, in fact, Augustine had seen that prohibition as more pedagogical than a separate commandment. He viewed the two tables of the law as consisting of three and seven, the love of God being elaborated in three commandments (against false gods, misuse of the name and Sabbath observance) reflecting a Trinitarian impulse.[19] The separate standing of the prohibition of idols has had large impact on the Reformed tradition, where idolatry became a major issue and specifically the representation of God in any other form than is allowed for in Scripture. It would be a mistake, however, to read this correlation between the lifting up of the prohibition of images in the Commandments and the resistance to images (of God, saints, whatever) as a one-directional movement. The shift in that direction in no small measure grew out of the conflict over images in the Swiss church. The initial moves to isolate the prohibition of images in the Decalogue did not involve citations of the earlier church fathers on this or reference to Philo and Josephus. That came only later.[20] But the ordering of the Decalogue reinforced the resistance to images and idols and helped to make this resistance a mark of the Reformed tradition. Luther's incorporation of the images into the prohibition of other gods was consonant with his lighter concern about the images in the churches.[21]

David Willis has underscored the evangelical context in which this emphasis on the Second Commandment is to be understood in Calvin. It is not simply a matter of obedience to the Commandment but that the freedom of the Christian resists being drawn back into "the servitude that sets in to the extent that we are diverted from what has been completely offered and extended by the gracious God whose glory shines forth in the face of Jesus

---

[19] For the way in which Augustine laid out these three commandments in relation to the three persons of the Trinity, see Rentschka, *Die Dekalogkatechese des hl. Augustinus*, 142–144. Calvin regarded this numeration on Trinitarian grounds as "a most trivial reason" (Book II. viii. 12)

[20] For discussion of these matters, see Reicke, *Die zehn Worte*, 27 and *passim*.

[21] On the history of the prohibition of images in the church's tradition, see R. H. Charles, *The Decalogue* (Edinburgh: T. & T. Clark, 1923), 14–88. While his tone betrays his indignation at the way in which the prohibition has been handled, Charles' account fairly elaborates the procedures by which this prohibition was subverted in the Middle Ages and even much later as it was often omitted, or confined to the notes or explained away in notes. The Eastern Church did not omit the prohibition of images but insisted it applied only to stone images and not to painted wooden images (E. Nielsen, *The Ten Commandments in New Perspective* (Studies in Biblical Theology. Second Series, 7; London: SCM Press, 1968), 11, n. 1.

Christ."[22] That is, indeed, true of all the Commandments. This particular one, which flows out of the fact that our reliance is entirely upon the Word that has come to us and that God is the sole witness and proper witness of himself, leads to a continuing emphasis upon the Word and the lifting up of the verbal over against the visual as well as the heavy emphasis upon preaching and the concerns for simplicity and order in worship.[23]

A further issue in the order and numeration of the Commandments is the question of how Exod 20:2 (Deut 5:6) is to be understood. For Calvin it was a matter of indifference whether this verse was understood as a preface or as part of the First Commandment. But its significance was clear. In the preface we are given guidance as to whether adherence to the Commandments is to be understood as duty and obligation or as an expression of gratitude. The answer for Calvin and his followers is both.[24] The Geneva Catechism, Question #139 puts the matter succinctly with reference to the preface:

M. Why does He mention this at the beginning of His law?
C. To remind us how much we are bound to obey His good pleasure, and what ingratitude it would be on our part if we do the contrary.[25]

The Heidelberg Catechism places the Decalogue and its interpretation under the rubric of "Thankfulness" and sees in it an explanation of "what gratitude I owe to God for such redemption." (Question #1).[26]

---

[22] David Willis-Watkins, *The Second Commandment and Church Reform: The Colloquy of St. Germain-en-Laye* (Studies in Reformed Theology and History, 2/2; Princeton: Princeton Theological Seminary, 1994).

[23] See the discussion of John H. Leith, "John Calvin's Polemic Against Idolatry," in *Soli Deo Gloria: New Testament Studies in Honor of William Childs Robinson*, ed. J. McDowell Richards (Richmond: John Knox Press, 1968), 111–124. Leith has noted that Calvin's polemic against idolatry focused on several key areas: the use of images in worship and education, the tendency to divinize the church in the Catholic notions of church and sacraments, and the liturgy, where simplicity, sincerity, intelligibility, and conformity to God's word are criteria of proper worship, something that is always in danger of being idolatrous.

[24] See e.g., Calvin's *Institutes*, II. viii. and his First Catechism (sometimes called *Instruction in Faith*).

[25] Here, as elsewhere, the note of thanks is present primarily in its negative form, that is, in speaking of ingratitude reflected in not keeping the Commandments rather than thanks as the motive for keeping them.

[26] For various places in his commentary and sermons on Deuteronomy where Calvin reiterates the sense of gratitude that undergirds and effects obedience, see Hesselink, *Concept of the Law*, 107.

Principles of Interpretation

At the beginning of his treatment of the Decalogue in the *Institutes* (Book
II. viii), Calvin identifies *three premises* that in a broad sense reflect a
mode of interpretation or serve to identify some of the assumptions belonging to the interpretation of individual commandments.

    1. The Commandments have to do not only with "outward honesty" but
with "*inward and spiritual righteousness*" (Book II. viii. 6 – italics mine).
The Commandments are thus a *spiritual* matter and involve not only outward obedience but also an internal conformity, that is, in heart and mind
as well as in act. This is quite different from human laws where only the
external act can be determined and dealt with. Consistent with the direction suggested in the Tenth Commandment as well as in Jesus' interpretation of the Commandments, Calvin says:

> But God, whose eye nothing escapes, and who is concerned not so much with outward
> appearance as with purity of heart, under the prohibition of fornication, murder, and
> theft, forbids lust, anger, hatred, coveting a neighbor's possessions, deceit, and the like.
> For, since he is a spiritual lawgiver, he no less addresses himself to the soul than to the
> body. (II. viii. 6)

Already in this move, Calvin opens up a wider meaning to the individual
precepts, in this case toward a governing not only of sinful *actions* but of
those *thoughts* that can be sin and lead to sin. Lust, wrath, and hatred are
not explicitly forbidden by the Commandments, but their spiritual meaning
makes that the case. In his Commentary on the Heidelberg Catechism,
Ursinus follows this direction by claiming that the Decalogue "demands in
every commandment internal and external obedience in the understanding,
will, heart and actions of the life..."[27] So in the Heidelberg Catechism, the
question is asked with regard to the prohibition of killing: "But does this
commandment speak only of killing?" And the answer is given: "In for-
bidding murder God means to teach us that he abhors the root of murder,
which is envy, hatred, anger, and desire for revenge, and that he regards all
these as *hidden* [italics mine] murder." The idea of hiddenness has to do
with the internal and spiritual dimension of the Commandment. So with
regard to the commandment against adultery, the Heidelberg Catechism
expands on the sin of adultery "since both our body *and soul* [italics mine]
are a temple of the Holy Spirit."

---

[27] *The Commentary of Dr. Zacharias Ursinus on the Heidelberg Catechism* (Phillipsburg,
New Jersey: Presbyterian and Reformed Publishing Company, n.d.), 502.

2. A second premise set forth by Calvin is of crucial importance in interpreting the Commandments. In his biblical interpretation generally, Calvin claimed that recognition of the presence of figurative language was necessary to understand God's accommodation to human need. With regard to the Decalogue, the figure or trope that was all-important was *synecdoche* (Book II. viii. 8).[28] He noted, accurately, that this figure of thought occurs frequently in Scripture but found it most extensively in the Decalogue: "Obviously, in almost all the commandments, there are such synecdoches, that he who would confine his understanding of the law within the narrowness of the words deserves to be laughed at." In a somewhat paradoxical way, synecdoche, that is, figurative thought, is for Calvin, a "way to lead us with straight and firm steps to the will of God." This is the way by which a *fulsome* and *extended* interpretation may be seen to be a proper discernment of what God wills in the Commandments:

We must, I say, inquire how far interpretation ought to overstep the limits of the words themselves so that it may be seen to be, not an appendix added to the divine law from men's glosses, but the Lawgiver's pure and authentic meaning faithfully rendered. (Book II. viii. 8)

The truthfulness of the interpretation is accounted for by synecdoche. That Calvin saw this as getting at the heart of matters rather than moving away from a literal sense into figurative flights is indicated by his judgment that such figurative interpretation was a way of getting at the *purpose* or *end* of the Commandment:

Therefore, plainly a sober interpretation of the law goes beyond the words but just how far remains obscure unless some measure be set. Now, I think this would be the best rule, if attention be directed to the reason of the commandment; that is, in each commandment to ponder *why* [italics mine] it was given to us. (II. viii. 8)

Out of this understanding, Calvin derived a three part approach to the interpretation of each commandment: a) First is to examine the *subject* of the Commandment, that is, what is it talking about; b) second is to inquire after the *end* of the Commandment in order to see what it lets us know is either pleasing or displeasing to the Giver of the law; and c) third, to develop an argument from the commandment to its *opposite*. This last move is what especially opened the interpretation of the Commandments to a wider scope. Calvin described what he meant as follows: "[I]f this pleases God,

---

[28] For an extended treatment of Calvin's use of figurative language, including his use of synecdoche, see Roland M. Frye, "Calvin's Theological Use of Figurative Language," *Calvin Studies IV*, ed. J. H. Leith and W. Stacy Johnson (Davidson, NC, 1988), 73–94.

the opposite displeases him; if this displeases, the opposite pleases him; if he commands this, he forbids the opposite; if he forbids this, he enjoins the opposite…. [W]hen a good thing is commanded, the evil thing that conflicts with it is forbidden… the opposite duties are enjoined when evil things are forbidden." The common working assumption would have been that the virtue that is opposite to any vice was the abstinence from the vice. Calvin said the virtue went much further than that, "to contrary duties and deeds" (Book II. viii. 9).

The specific example Calvin cites in this methodological or hermeneutical discussion is the prohibition of *killing* and his summary statement shows the operation of both this second premise, the presence of synecdoche, and the first premise, the spiritual or internal understanding of the Commandments:

Therefore, in this commandment, 'You shall not kill,' man's common sense will see only that we must abstain from wronging anyone or desiring to do so. Besides this, it contains, I say, the requirement that we give our neighbor's life all the help we can. (Book II. viii. 9)[29]

By means of synecdoche, simply stated in this prefatory way, Calvin begins to open up the trajectory of meaning of the Commandment in two ways. First of all, the Commandment directs us against "wronging anyone," that is, against *any* physical endangerment of the neighbor, not just killing, much less just murder. And second, every prohibition in the Commandments is seen to have a positive implication. This is a major move – though not confined to Reformed interpretation – for the Commandments are often interpreted with particular attention to the *restricted* character of the *negative* formulation. That is, they are seen to be limited to certain areas and leaving a wide area of moral freedom. Much that has to do with the moral life is thus seen as left unaddressed by the Commandments. Such a contemporary understanding is quite foreign to the Reformed mode of interpretation, enunciated by Calvin and followed by many others. On the

---

[29] This way of understanding and interpreting the Sixth Commandment is central to the study paper of the Presbyterian Church US, titled "The Nature and Value of Human Life," which set the commandment against killing as the biblical basis for the whole theological and ethical analysis of abortion, euthanasia, suicide, capital punishment, and war. Contrast the approach of Richard Hays, *The Moral Vision of the New Testament: A Contemporary Introduction to New Testament Ethics* (San Francisco: Harper Collins, 1996), whose only reference to the Decalogue is a citation of this Commandment as of no use in thinking about abortion because the Commandment only has to do with murder, which everyone is against (446).

basis of the synecdoche, the part tells about the whole and helps us discern what the Commandment is after in a large sense.[30]

3. The third premise for Calvin was the division of the Decalogue into its two parts, one having to do with religion or pure worship and the other with charity, one with love of God and the other with neighbor. This point has already been discussed. Here one may simply add the interpretation given to this third premise by Dowey. He argues that Calvin's point here is that in these Commandments we find a brief form of all that God requires of human beings and thus a *universalizing* of the Commandments. This concept of the Decalogue regards it as a "specially accommodated expression of universal, eternal law."[31] It is not as clear in the *Institutes* that Calvin's point is the universalizing one, but the whole thrust of his interpretation makes that claim. Further, Dowey argues that this universalizing move is evident in his Harmony of the Pentateuch where the Commandments are the general category under which are put the other laws as ceremonial, political, and judicial supplements. These supplements are temporally and locally conditioned and so are transient and passing. "[The moral law is] the true and eternal rule of righteousness, prescribed to men of all ages and nations who wish to conform their lives to the will of God."[32]

In all of this – spiritualizing, figurative, and universalizing moves – a way of reading and interpreting the Commandments is laid out that provides a rich and expansive moral trajectory of the Commandments, one that requires some serious moral thinking and acting, the specifics of which are already well developed in the catechisms of the Reformed community.[33]

---

[30] In his comment on the individual commandments, Calvin often develops a synecdochic interpretation.

[31] Dowey, *The Knowledge of God*, 226.

[32] Ibid., 227.

[33] E. Domergue has summarized these three moves as indicating that the commandments "are at the same time particular and general, negative and positive, material and spiritual." (Cited by Hesselink, *Concept of the Law*, 146, n. 147). I am indebted to several persons who have helped me understand some of the complexities of Luther's understanding of the law and the Decalogue and its relation to Calvin's thinking on these same matters, but I would like to acknowledge particularly the assistance of Reinhard Hütter, Cynthia Rigby, and William Lazareth.

9. "That It May Go Well with You"

The Commandments and the Common Good

The centrality of the Decalogue for marking the contours of trust in God and life with our neighbor is an assumption that both guides the discussion that follows and is further undergirded within it. In this essay, it is my intention to uncover the various ways in which the Commandments, particularly within the context of their presentation in the Book of Deuteronomy, provide a way of thinking about the common good for the community of faith that receives the Commandments as the way to live for those redeemed and ruled by the living God, the Lord of Israel and the Lord of the church. Identity is given and community is formed by the word of God to ancient Israel in the Commandments, a word that continues to tell us who we are and how we are to live. Because Christians discover that what they receive as God's word for life resonates with the experiences and stories of others who may not identify with the story of God's way with Israel and the church, it is appropriate also to explore what possibilities there may be for a wider conversation about the common good in light of the Commandments.

The Commandments in the Context of Deuteronomy

A. While the giving of the Commandments occurs in the Sinai pericope in Exod 19–24 and is thus set as a part of and response to the Lord's delivery of the Israelites from Egyptian slavery, it is the Book of Deuteronomy that is framed from beginning to end as an elaboration of the Commandments as the covenant that orders Israel's life.[1] As the context for the Command-

---

[1] I am assuming here the various studies of the Book of Deuteronomy that have pointed to signs that the Deuteronomic Code (chaps. 12–26) is ordered or structured along the lines of the Decalogue and so is to be understood as a development, specification, and illustration of the meaning and force of the Commandments. See, for example, Dennis Olson, *Deuteronomy and the Death of Moses: A Theological Reading* (Overtures to Biblical Theology; Minneapolis: Fortress, 1994). That this is not a modern construct is evident in Luther's lectures on Deuteronomy, where he begins his commentary on each chapter by relating its subject matter to one of the Commandments. Indeed he comments at the beginning: "If you want to give this book a name suitable for our use, you will correctly call it a most ample and excellent expla-

ments, Deuteronomy presents itself as a combination of *teaching* and *constitution*, of *instruction* and *polity* for the people of God about how they are to live as the Lord's people and as a community of brothers/sisters/neighbors.[2]

1. The *instruction* is developed in relation to the way in which the community's good, defined often as life, is something to be taught and learned and in that process also rationalized and urged. This teaching is to be written down, read again and again, repeated and talked about (Deut 6:4–9). Specifically in the context of Moses' retelling the story of the Lord's giving of the Commandments, Deuteronomy sets to the fore the need to learn and teach these words:

[10]"Assemble the people for me, and I will let them hear my words, so that they may learn to fear me as long as they live on the earth, and may teach their children so...."
[14]And the LORD charged me at that time to teach you statutes and ordinances for you to observe in the land that you are about to cross into and occupy. (Deut 4:10b, 14)

Behavior in conformity to this mode of existence, however, is something that needs exhortation and explanation, reasons for obedience and motivations indicating the attractiveness of the way described therein.[3] That is a

---

nation of the Decalog. After you know it, you could want nothing more that is needful for understanding the Ten Commandments. For it teaches this people to live well [a theological definition of the common good?] according to the Ten Commandments in both spirit and body." *Lectures on Deuteronomy*, in *Luther's Works*, eds. J. Pelikan and D. Poellot (Saint Louis: Concordia Publishing House, 1960), 9:14.

[2] For a more extended development of this dual purpose for the Book of Deuteronomy, see below, "Constitution or Instruction? The Purpose of Deuteronomy;" repr. from *Constituting the Community: Studies on the Polity of Ancient Israel in Honor of S. Dean McBride, Jr.* (eds. S. Tuell and J. Strong; Winona Lake, Indiana: Eisenbrauns, 2003). The case for Deuteronomy as a form of polity has been set forth in convincing fashion by S. Dean McBride, "Polity of the Covenant People," *Interpretation* 41 (1987), 229–244. The character of Deuteronomy as teaching and instruction has been noted often. For a recent defense of this way of perceiving the book, one that is in conversation with McBride, see Olson, *Deuteronomy and the Death of Moses*.

[3] Here, therefore, Deuteronomic understanding of the law, and indeed the formulation of the moral good in the directives of the Commandments, anticipate Aquinas' emphasis on the character of the law not only as orienting one toward the common good but also as a norm of reason. In every instance of the inclusion of an explanatory or hortatory clause, the rationality of the Commandments and the law is asserted. See in this respect, Jean Porter, "The Common Good in Aquinas" in this volume. On the importance of a public discourse about the common good, see, also in this volume, Robin W. Lovin, "Public Discourse and Common Good." While his concern is for a discourse that brings various elements into conversation about the common good, Deuteronomy points to another kind of rationality that centers in education and persuasion of a good already conceived. [References in this essay to "in this volume" refer to the original publication and other essays contained therein.]

part of the learning and appropriation. Further, a strong emphasis is placed upon the need for *future generations* to be taught the Commandments and to learn them and their specific implications. So the teaching has to do with inculcating a way that is open to the future and can guide the future.

2. The *polity* and *constitutional* dimension is developed in relation to the character of the community as a socio-political entity that organizes its life in all its dimensions and understands its covenantal shape as having to do with all facets of its life. The constitution or polity has to do with the sacral/cultic, the political, and the social. The polity envisioned transcends the distinction between religious and political community and thus provides an opportunity for thinking about and conceiving the common good in a way that incorporates both.[4] The Deuteronomic vision, embodied constitutionally and foundationally in the Commandments, is a complex pluralistic system where the political, the theological/religious, the educational, and the moral can be identified, but they coalesce in such a way that it is not possible to identify the good of the whole in any one category or social system apart from the other spheres. And while interpersonal relationships are at the center of the moral space in which the Commandments provide an orienting perspective, the body as a whole, the political entity of Israel, is the addressee or recipient of the Commandments, and the consensual response is a response of that entity. So while one may speak of "community," "people," and the like, one does so in cognizance of the fact that this is also a political order, traditionally described as a state.[5] The nature of the community whose common good is sought, protected, and enhanced via the Commandments is complex rather than simple. It ranges from cultic to socio-ethnic, from kin to polity.[6]

---

[4] This assertion carries with it the recognition that there are more complex manifestations of contemporary, social, political, and religious communities than envisioned by Deuteronomy and that it is precisely when these communities are differentiated from one another in some fashion that the difficulties often arise. Nor does Deuteronomy have a sense of a global community, though it does address questions of relation to other political entities.

[5] The self-presentation of the Book of Deuteronomy is, of course, that of a community without official political structures, wandering in the wilderness and about to enter the promised land. But the actual context of the book is fully in the monarchical and state period, and there are all sorts of clues within the book that point to such, not least being chapters 16:18 through 18:22, which provide for various courts and authority figures and how they are to operate in the community, as well as the system of officers set up by Moses in Deut 1, which is probably a reflection of a judicial reform in the ninth century or later (2 Chron 19:4–11. For a more precise history of the notion of "state," see William T. Cavanaugh, "Killing for the Telephone Company: Why the Nation-State is Not the Keeper of the Common Good," in this volume.

[6] On issues of definition and character of the "community," the significance of identity and participation, see now Eric Mount, "It Takes a Community – Or At Least an Association"

The Book of Deuteronomy presents itself further as a constitutional document that is *appropriate for changing situations*. Its instruction guides the community, but its application to changing circumstances, including changes to the shape and character of the social and political order, invites the community to keep asking how the fundamental directions suggested here are to be worked out in new situations.[7] There is an assumption that the common good of the community is discernible and can be formulated. It is also assumed that the community will have to keep seeking to discern that common good, while continuing to be directed by the foundational instruction. The community has torah and no longer needs a Moses, but it will have to keep asking what the specifics of the instruction are in each new time.

3. The coming together of instruction and polity is in the conception of "this torah" as "covenantal law, the divinely authorized social order that Israel must implement to secure its collective political existence as the people of God."[8] A covenantal structure for the life of the people is presumed and implemented in both the Decalogue and the Deuteronomic instruction. Thus the good of the community's life is framed in a sociopolitical structure involving voluntary commitment and obligatory actions. While one may use such terms as guidelines, basic principles, foundations, and the like, the Decalogue is not presented as such. It is not set forth as an abstraction from the specific context that defines the Decalogue or is defined by the Decalogue, that is, the covenant. What we find in the Decalogue is, therefore, covenantal stipulations (familiar from analogous forms in the ancient Near East). These stipulations serve to "constitute" a community of relationships – the relationship between God and the people and the inner-working relationship among the people. The covenantal ethos is a

---

in this volume and his earlier work, *Covenant, Community, and the Common Good: An Interpretation of Christian Ethics* (Cleveland: Pilgrim, 1999).

[7] The necessity of developing ways in which the constitutional and normative directives of the Commandments are played out in the life of individuals and the community is indicated by the differences between the Book of the Covenant in Exod 21–23 and the Deuteronomic law in Deut 12–26, both of which are to be understood as a specifying and illustrating of the way in which the Commandments are to guide in particular cases. At least some of the differences seem to reflect a changing social and economic setting behind the two bodies of statutes and ordinances.

[8] McBride, "Polity of the Covenant People," 233. Cf. the comment of Norbert Lohfink growing out of his study of the term "assembly" (קהל=*qāhāl*) in Deuteronomy and its place in the narrative setting of the giving of the Commandments in Deuteronomy: "...Israel as such was perfectly constituted only through the Horeb [Sinai] covenant. Only by this event did it *become* a קהל *in the exact sense of the word*" ("Reading Deuteronomy 5 as Narrative," in *A God So Near*, ed. Brent A. Strawn and Nancy R. Bowen (Winona Lake, IN: Eisenbrauns, 2003), 274.

community ethos.[9] And the stipulations are not primarily to give general principles but to effect a community of harmonious relationship, a community of peace and blessing, doers of the good and the right and thus recipients of the good and blessing (see below).

B. Both the Commandments and the Book of Deuteronomy assume and depend upon an intimate connection between the community as a whole and its individual members and thus an interaction between thinking about the *community* and the *individual.*

1. One of the ways this interaction is evident in the text is a feature usually relegated to stylistic or source critical functions, that is, the constant interchange between second person singular and second person plural in Deuteronomy. Moses' address to the people, therefore, moves back and forth between plural and singular address in a way that defies easy explanation. One thing that happens is the reader/listener hears a "you" and a "you all," fully interchangeable and thus is constantly being addressed both as part of the larger whole and as individual recipient of the divine/Mosaic instruction. This interchange between personal and communal modes of address is intrinsic to the Commandments, which are singular in form and so address the community as individuals. But the Commandments in their narrative context are addressed to the *assembled community.* A further implication of this dual mode of address is that the singular mode, which clearly is a way of setting the covenantal stipulations upon each member of the community, may also be received as a singular address to the community as a whole. That is, Israel hears itself addressed as "you" and thus faces the responsibility of continuing to decide about who is its neighbor, *as a community.*[10]

2. The Commandments offer a definition of the community that seeks a common good. It is individuals existing in a complex of various relationships. The beginning and ending of that complex is the relationship to God and the relationship to the neighbor. Thus the first four commandments explicitly have to do with the fear and worship of "*the Lord* (= YHWH) *your God*" (but with significant social, legal, and political implications – see below),[11] and the last two-three (dependent upon the numbering) make

---

[9] See Mount, "It Takes a Community – Or At Least an Association."

[10] It is not surprising, therefore, that ethnic issues arise in the question of "Who is my neighbor" as posed to Jesus. While the Deuteronomic Code distinguishes between the way of treating the neighbor and the resident alien from relations with the foreigner, the Commandments open the issue for the community as a whole vis-a-vis others outside the community and do not let the question of the neighbor remain a purely intra-community definition.

[11] This specifying of the name of the deity is not to be skimmed over lightly. The one who

explicit reference to *"neighbor"* (4x). In between, there is a transition from the relationship to the Lord to the relationship with others, ultimately the neighbor, but not only the neighbor. That is, covenantal obedience and its outcome in the good of the community also involves familial relationships (honoring parents), responsibilities falling upon those who have oversight of others and relationships to those who are in some sort of dependence or service that does not leave them free to act on their own (the Sabbath Commandment). The complex of relationships also includes the world of nature and specifically the animal world. In the reflexes of the Sabbath commandment in the Book of the Covenant, the release and rest include the agricultural realm as well (Exod 23:10–12).[12]

3. The moral space effected by the Commandments and specified in the Deuteronomic Code (chaps. 12–26) thus incorporates a variety of complex relationships and systems: power relationships (e.g., king and subject, master and bonded servant, husband and wife, employer and employee, priest and lay person, lender and borrower, judge and plaintiffs, land-owner/property owner and landless, etc.), family relationships, communal relationships, property definition, systems of loans, systems of welfare, accessibility to economic goods, management of agricultural systems and animal needs, judicial structures, and the like.

4. While it is not necessary to argue the issue of whether or not rights theories focus excessively upon the individual or to challenge the legitimacy of rights arguments in seeking the common good in its moral dimension, it is important in this context to note that the way in which the Commandments provide a structure and space for the moral life is not in terms of *rights* but in terms of *responsibilities*. One may use other terms, such as, "duties" or "obligations," in this respect, but the term "responsibility" better connotes what takes place in the Decalogue. Several primary spheres of human good – work and rest, family and household, marriage, reputation and truth, the administration of justice, goods and property (economics in a broad sense), life and freedom, and human desire – are areas in which hu-

---

claims the allegiance, obedience, and worship of the people *this way*, that is, by the keeping of the Commandments is the Lord (YHWH), the one attested by the words and deeds recounted in the story. In the reception of the Commandments, one does not have to do with a general notion of deity but with the one who led the Hebrew slaves to freedom and showed them how to live in freedom *this way* (see below).

[12] Note that the issue is not posed in terms of crop rotation in the modern sense but a provision of rest for the land as well as for its occupants and also, once again, a rest for the land so that those without means of productivity may avail themselves of its volunteer crops. Note in Job 31:38, one of Job's claims of innocence and obedience to the law is that his land has not cried out against him and its furrows have not wept. (See W. Janzen, *Exodus* [Scottdale: Herald Press, 2000], 312–313).

man flourishing, and so the good of the community as a whole, are protected by the assumption of responsibility for the good of the other, for the good of the neighbor. The orientation of the Commandments is always toward the other, whether the other is the God whose proper worship is the ground of all other acts or the other is the neighbor/brother/sister.[13] The rights of the individual are presumed, but the way into those rights is always by way of responsibility for the neighbor. "My" rights, "my" well-being, and the like are insured and protected not by any claims or actions of my own but by my being a neighbor to others who stand under the same responsibilities toward me that I have toward them.[14] There is thus a reciprocal responsibility operative.[15] The implicit reciprocality is what enables the Commandments to chart the moral space for a *common* good. One may indeed derive from the Decalogue an implicit set of rights that belong to being and staying human, but they are inferential and as such do not define the moral space of the Commandments at its primary level.[16] In this respect, Paul Lehmann's formulation is appropriate, not being and staying human but making and keeping human. Precisely out of *orientation toward the other*, the Commandments open up *the natural world* as a full part of the realm of responsibility, something that is readily apparent in the way in which the illustrative cases spell out the particularities and force of the

---

[13] The Commandments are where the category of "neighbor" is introduced into the biblical story. With the Commandments, the reality of "your neighbor" becomes controlling for the moral life of the community. Its continuing significance as a moral category is indicated by its reappearance as a major issue in the parable of the Good Samaritan in the New Testament.

[14] A recent advertisement by Liberty Press for the publication of the writings of the Scottish philosopher Gershom Carmichael speaks of "the manner in which he justified the natural rights of individuals. Those rights included the natural right to defend oneself, the natural right to own the property on which one has labored, and the natural right to services contracted with others." From the perspective of the Commandments, those "rights" are "natural" and safeguarded only by being and having a neighbor. On the place of responsibility in and for community, see also Mount, "It Takes a Community – Or At Least an Association."

[15] On the notion of reciprocal responsibility, see P. Lehmann, *The Decalogue and a Human Future: The Meaning of the Commandments for Making and Keeping Human Life Human* (Grand Rapids: Eerdmans, 1995). Lehmann speaks of rights being transformed as responsibilities, which is intrinsic to the ethical perspective of the Commandments.

[16] A recent formulation of this reciprocality is that of John Witte Jr.:

> Protestants have thus long translated the moral duties set out in the Decalogue into reciprocal rights…. Each person's duties towards a neighbor…can be cast as a neighbor's right to have that duty discharged. One person's duties not to kill, to commit adultery, to steal or to bear false witness thus give rise to another person's rights to life, property, fidelity and reputation.

"Between Sanctity and Depravity: Law and Human nature in Martin Luther's Two Kingdoms," *Villanova Law Review* 48 (2003), 762.

Commandments in the legal codes (see above) but is already evident in the inclusion of the animal world in the Commandments themselves (Deut 5:14, 21). Intrinsic to the Decalogue, therefore, is a way of thinking and acting that is toward the common good, that assumes a shared understanding and actions that shape human life in terms of responsibility for the well-being of others and not simply as a general good (Love your neighbor) but articulated and worked out in the primary spheres of human existence and common life. The preference for responsibility over rights is intrinsic to the vision of the common good of the Commandments. That has large implications for the way in which the community develops law, juridical procedures, welfare systems, and modes of protection in all spheres.

C. The Book of Deuteronomy sets "the good" as a primary topic of conversation and understands it as *way*, *gift*, and *goal* for the community's life.[17] In all these respects the good is something that comes from outside. As a conformity to the covenantal stipulations, the Commandments, by definition, assume a kind of moral realism, a claim that the goods belonging to or defining this living space are independent and outside of the ones who orient themselves thereby even if manifest only in the acting and doing of the community.[18] But the good comes from outside in another sense and that is as *blessing*[19] and *gift*.[20] At the same time, the good is also brought into reality and experienced by the actions of the people. Go the good way "so that it may go well with you" (Deut 5:16). The common good, therefore, is not simply *achieved*; it is both *sought* and *received*. The characteristic modes of the community in its pursuit of and enjoyment of the com-

---

[17] See in this respect Victor Furnish's essay in this volume identifying the good that is found in an uncommon love as both a gift and a claim ("Uncommon Love and the Common Good: Christians as Citizens in the Letters of Paul"). Relative to Deuteronomy and the Commandments, it is important to see how the good is that path along which one walks and also the goal of all one's actions.

[18] Such an understanding is presumably inherent in a theistic approach, but it is confirmed in this case by the way in which the Commandments are received by the community as a theophanic word. On the varying kinds of moral realism, see the helpful discussion of Ruth Abbey, *Charles Taylor* (Philosophy Now; Princeton: Princeton University Press, 2000), 26–31.

[19] Note Deut 8:10 "When you have eaten and are satisfied, then be sure to thank the Lord for the good land that he has given you." The text also includes a warning against thinking "My hand and my power have gotten me this" (v. 17).

[20] The "good land" is often spoken of as "given" by the Lord (1:25, 35; 4:21; 6:18; 8:10; 9:6; 11:17). See also the Mosaic instruction to "rejoice in all the good the Lord is giving to you" (26:11).

mon good are thanksgiving and obedience. The flourishing of the community is both gift and goal, but it is found by choosing to walk the way.

Along with the *good* as a gift and way, Deuteronomy sets *life* as the goal, reward, and outcome of proper conformity to the responsibilities defined by the covenantal relationship and indeed suggests an implicit correlation of the good and life. In this regard, attention should be drawn to the decisive and climactic moment of the book in the enactment of the covenant at Moab after Moses has reminded the community of the Decalogue and further instructed them about its implications in the specifics of the law when Moses sets the decision before the people:

[15]See I have set before you life and good, death and disaster... [19]Choose life, so that you and your descendants may live, [20]loving the LORD your God, obeying him, and holding fast to him; for that means life to you and length of days, so that you may live in the land that the LORD swore to give to your ancestors, to Abraham, to Isaac, and to Jacob. (Deut 30:15–20)

D. In Deuteronomy, the good of others is not something that is enjoined as a separate act apart from the regular activities of life. It is something that is achieved within them. Two cardinal examples can be cited. One is the way in which the enjoyment and celebration of God's gift in and through the regular celebratory festivals is something that is inclusive of all the community so that all are provided for. *Rejoicing* in the good that God has given *includes within it* the *doing* of the good, that is, including everyone in the celebration of the good gifts, providing for the whole of the community.[21] Within the context of this community, the centrality of an inclusive and celebratory meal "before the Lord" is unavoidably a eucharistic anticipation. Second, the laws do not so much instruct one on how to add good to the life of the neighbor as they indicate how each member of the community is to carry on his or her life so that he or she does not inhibit the good for all that is inherent in the life of the community that lives by this instruction and constitution. The good of the neighbor is not "in addition to" but worked out in the everyday activities of human life. The laws do not set forth a lot of good things to do. The good is found in making sure – in one's enjoyment of the good gifts, God's good and "the work of your hands" – that others are not cut off from the good.[22]

Michael Welker has suggested that one begin to see the laws not simply as requirements to be done but as provisions for securing expectations. A

---

[21] See, for example, the festival laws of Deuteronomy in 14:22–28 and 16:1–17; cf. 12:17–19.

[22] See below on the purpose of the Sabbath commandment to provide rest for male and female bond servants.

culture of expectations is secured in the community's attention to the covenantal stipulations and the particulars of living this way. That security of expectations, arising out of a structure of responsibility to the other identified as both "the Lord your God" and "your neighbor," is another way of speaking about the common good.[23]

Securing the Common Good through the Commandments

Relative to the *substantive* character of the common good, the Commandments help to mark out a sphere of moral space and action in behalf of the common good. Such delineation is evident as one examines the particular commandments.

A. The first four commandments explicitly have to do with the fear and worship of God. Several implications may be drawn from that fundamental fact:[24]

1. The good of the individual and of the community, the possibility of their flourishing, is directly related to their recognition of the Lord of Israel as determining their life and receiving their full obedience and worship. This means that there is no other possible ultimate concern, no other center of meaning or value on which those who live by this word can rely.

2. In the Jewish tradition, the first of the Commandments, or, more literally, of the Ten Words, is what others call the Prologue, the self-presentation of the deity as redeemer of an enslaved people and the one who comes to them as "your God." The Commandments are before the people not simply as a good way to go but as a claim on their lives. They do not stand outside the ground of the Lord's liberation of the people from oppression. They are received as directives for living, but living as those who have been freed from political and social servitude in order to be the servants of the Lord.

3. All other facets of life in community, for the good and for the other, flow out of the worship of the Lord alone. The double-sidedness of this is implicit in the First Commandment and explicit in the Shema (Deut 6:4–5), the positive form of the First Commandment: a) The love and service of the Lord as God. There is a positive obligation to commit oneself fully

---

[23] M. Welker, "Security of Expectations: Reformulating the Theology of Law and Gospel," *The Journal of Religion* 66 (1986), 237–260.

[24] The numbering of the Commandments in this essay is according to the Reformed tradition, which separates the prohibition of the worship of other gods (the First Commandment) from the making and worship of images or idols (the Second Commandment).

(heart, soul, and everything) to the Lord. And b) The exclusion of any other possible ultimate loyalties. The commandment's prohibitive form is critical for its resistance to the transformation of penultimate claims to ultimate ones.

B. The commandments of the first table of the Decalogue have significant social, legal, and political implications:

1. The First Commandment has to do with the one in whom we trust and the locus of our ultimate obedience. It is a *political* claim and often has played out quite specifically in the political realm. Both praise and prayer are basic manifestations of living by the First Commandment. They are political acts that signify where one's ultimate obedience lies and one's judgment about what power is finally operative in the world.[25] Obedience is a form of discipleship, and the language of discipleship begins with the First Commandment. The *economic* dimension of the worship of other gods is widely evident in the biblical story. Violation of the First Commandment centered heavily on systemic and communal devotion to the economic gods (for example, Baal in Hos 1–3; the Queen of Heaven in Jer 44; and Mammon in Matt 6:24 // Luke 16:13).[26]

2. The prohibition of the making and worshiping of images has political and economic implications as well, if some of the contemporary investigation is on target. Because of the close relation to the image of the god and the image of the king, the resistance to divine images may be an early manifestation of Israel's resistance to human kingship in light of its covenantal polity under the rule of the sovereign Lord of Israel. In addition, a number of texts indicate that the prohibition has some connection with the character of idols and images as being cast in silver and gold. Thus the Israelites are warned against coveting the silver and gold of the idols, both because one may be drawn away from the worship of God and because the silver and gold are themselves tempting. There is an economic danger in the worship of the idols, whether they are images of the Lord or of other gods (See Exod 20:23; Deut 7:25; Josh 7; Judg 8:24–27; and chapter 17).[27]

---

[25] Note in this connection, Karl Barth's insistence that the resistance indicated in the Barmen Declaration was a manifestation of obedience to the First Commandment, not simply a resistance to tyranny. Note also the significant role that the First Commandment played in forming a basic ground for resistance to the Vietnam War in the 60s.

[26] On the connections between political and economic power in the nation state, see Cavanaugh, "Killing for the Telephone Company," in this volume.

[27] For further discussion and references to the secondary literature, see P. D. Miller *The Religion of Ancient Israel* (Louisville: Westminster Press, 2000), 21–23.

3. The misuse of the name operates especially in the law court, that is, in the judicial sphere. See the "swear falsely" in Deut 6:13, which is a positive formulation of this commandment, and note that the Jewish Publication Society Tanakh translates the Commandment: "You shall not swear falsely by the name of the Lord your God." In Deuteronomy, the term "in vain" is the same word used for "false" in the Ninth Commandment that forbids "false" witness. The social dimension of the commandment has to do with *truth in the courts* and the possibility of a *proper administration of justice*. That is seen to be a matter of the relationship with God (third commandment) as much as with the neighbor (ninth commandment). The political and religious dimensions of this commandment, however, are not to be overlooked, for it sets a resistance to the light or empty invocation of the deity's name or the appropriation of the name of God as a ground for one's own agenda in full awareness that such a move is in fact to turn the ultimate into the penultimate and the holy into the profane. Even the invocation or promulgation of the Commandments to serve one's own political and cultural ends can be a violation of the name of God. The same is true for the easy and common tendency to trivialize the Commandments in jokes, cartoons, or simplistic and reductionistic dismissal of their pertinence for life. That discernment between appropriate and inappropriate invocation of the divine name is not always an easy task does not release the community from engaging in just such discernment (see Part V below).

4. The Sabbath rest is rooted in both the creative work of God, as a rest after labor that imitates the divine order (so the Exod 20 grounding), and in the work of God to liberate the oppressed and give freedom to those in bondage (so the Deut 5 grounding). The work-rest cycle belongs both to an acknowledgement of the ground of life in the work of God and to what is needful to make and to keep human life human. In its non-utilitarian purposelessness, Sabbath rest, therefore, is clearly a part of devotion to the Lord. At the same time it is given a purpose that is both humanitarian and socio-economic and the first specific instance of protection of the good of the neighbor, in this case, the economically dependent neighbor "your male and female slave" (Deut 5:14). The Sabbath is set to protect or provide for regular rest for those who are in one's service or economic control and incapable of getting the rest unless it is structured into the system.

As the Deuteronomic Code interprets the Sabbath commandment of the Decalogue and applies it specifically to cases, it makes clear that this has to do with both *money* and *labor* as *commodities* or as means of becoming economically endangered. That is evident in Deut 15, the first part of which has to do with loans and the remission of loans and pledges every seventh year and the second part of which has to do with bonded service because of debts, a labor that is not to continue past the seventh year and is to be rewarded by provision of the means for the formerly indebted or bonded person to begin life with sufficient economic resources not to be endangered again. The cases and specifics growing out of the commandment against *stealing* incorporate all sorts of ways in which economic endangerment is addressed and economic support is protected. To the extent that the Commandments chart the moral space in which the community may find a shared good, that enterprise is heavily oriented around the safeguarding of economic sufficiency against its undoing.[28] In the Commandments, the common good is effected largely by the protection and provision of economic goods.

C. The preceding discussion indicates that the distinction between the right and left tables of the Commandments is a blurred one. Nevertheless, the "other" envisioned as the direction toward which life and thought are directed is more specifically the focus in the second table of the Commandments.

1. The orientation in moral space (see below) that is provided by the Commandments and the sense of the common good that they encourage rests in no small measure upon the way in which the Sabbath commandment and the commandment to honor parents serve as bridges between the love of God and the love of neighbor. That is especially the case with regard to their effecting a starting point for the relationship with the neighbor. There is a logical starting point and an illogical one. The *illogical* one is already indicated in the discussion of the Sabbath commandment above. The purpose of the Sabbath rest in the Deuteronomic form of the Decalogue is so that your male and female slave may have rest such as you have, that those whose work and labor are under your control may be released. This illogical starting point is rooted in the fundamental *theological* logic of Israel's story, evident not only in the grounding of the Commandments in the story of God's liberation of this people from slavery but articulated precisely as the meaning of the Commandments and the statutes and ordinances. When in future generations, the children ask their parents, "What is the meaning of the decrees and the statutes and the ordinances that the Lord our God has commanded you?" the mothers and fathers are to answer: "We were Pharaoh's slaves in Egypt, but the Lord brought us out of Egypt with a mighty hand"(Deut 6:20–21). The redemption from slavery has set a different kind of logic at work: The initial and special concern

---

[28] For a more detailed exploration of this claim, see P. D. Miller, "The Economics of the Straying Ox: Property and Possessions in the Light of the Commandments" in *Having Property and Possession in Social and Religious Life*, ed. W. Schweiker (Grand Rapids, MI: Eerdmans, 2004).

is for the oppressed, dependent, vulnerable, and non-free members of the community. It is only after that point is made and insured in the Sabbath commandment and the sabbatical principle growing out of it that one can then move on to the neighbor who is met in the other relationships of communal life. Here, as elsewhere in the Commandments, the orientation is toward responsibility. One may indeed infer a *right* to rest from hard labor. But the Commandments do not make such a claim. They assume the human need and see the common good not in assertion of that right but in making sure that it is protected for those who cannot assume it for themselves.

The *logical* starting point for protecting the good of the neighbor, already implicit in the Sabbath commandment is the *family*.[29] That starting point is provided in the commandment to honor parents. As such, the family is opened up as an important part of the moral framework provided by the Commandments. The reciprocal responsibility inherent within the neighbor commandments would seem, at first glance, to be inoperative in this commandment. Thus it suggests a hierarchy of human relationship that insures the good of the ones at the top of the hierarchy. There is, however, an implicit reciprocality operative within this commandment. That reciprocality is made explicit in the development of the trajectory of this commandment in Ephesians, where the commandment is quoted as the ground for the "Pauline" injunction: "Children, obey your parents in the Lord" (Eph 6:1). That injunction, however, is followed directly by its corollary, thus achieving reciprocity even in this hierarchical situation: "Fathers, do not provoke your children to anger." The reciprocal enhancement of the good is further indicated in the setting of the Commandment in a *generational* pattern. There is an implicit awareness that while the young are to honor the old, the children their parents, it is inevitably the case that the

---

[29] The way in which this commandment serves as the starting point for thinking about life with the neighbor and responsibility of the other is demonstrated in Lev 19, the text most closely connected to the Decalogue. Sam Balentine has pointed to a chiasm in the structure of the chapter that "reverses the order of the Commandments in the Decalogue, elevating Commandment number five, reverence for father and mother, to the position of first importance.... The lead commandment to revere father and mother (v. 3a), who represent the most intimate union in the family structure, is amplified with further commandments (vv. 9–35) that extend the requirement for ethical relationships to the broader "community" of all God's creation. The land must be harvested with a compassion that does not ignore the needs of the poor (vv. 9–10; see also vv. 23–25), and plants and animals must be protected against mixed breeding that weakens the species God has created (v. 19). The welfare of the human community must not be jeopardized by dishonesty (vv. 11–12), oppression (vv. 13–14), economic injustice (vv. 15–16, 35–36), hate and vengeance (vv. 17–18), abusive sexual practices (vv. 20–22, 29), or disrespect for elders or aliens (vv. 32–33)...." (*Leviticus* [Interpretation Commentary; Louisville: Westminster John Knox, 2002], 161–162).

young grow old and the children become parents so that their good is protected by the establishment of a pattern that begins with their insuring the
good of their parents but will carry through for their own well-being as the
pattern carries over to the next generation.

There are two other things to be observed in the commandment that
structures family relationships. One is that it is here that the Decalogue explicitly identifies the "good" as the goal of living according to this pattern,
that is, the description of life under God embodied in the Commandments.
The motivation clause "that it may go well with you" is explicitly underscored in the Ephesians text, reminding the community that this is the one
commandment with a promise, a promise of the good as an outcome of the
mode of behavior and life prescribed in the commandment(s).

The second significant dimension of the Commandment is its opening
up a larger sphere of good, specifically the way in which persons in the
community relate to authorities and leaders. Paul Lehmann's comment on
this is worth quoting in full:

> The crux of Luther's interpretation of the fourth commandment is its insistence that   the
> relations between parents and children are paradigmatic of human wholeness.[30] This is
> the case because the relations between parents and children are pivotal to the nurture of a
> humanizing apperception that converts the otherwise dehumanizing polarization between
> inequality and equality, and between authority and freedom, into a creative and fulfilling
> congruence. The secret of this conversion is the reciprocal responsibility in, with, and
> under which inequality and equality, authority and freedom are joined.[31]

The filial responsibility to honor and treat well one's parents and the reciprocality inherent in that responsibility is an appropriate starting point for
thinking about necessary assymetrical and hierarchical relationships of all
sorts: employer-employee, teacher-student, judge-petitioner, ruler-subject,
and the like.

2. The family as a social unit of reciprocal responsibility for the good
across generations and the parent-child relationship as the starting point for
discerning the good in relation to the other is then given further direction

---

[30] This reading of the trajectory of the commandment to honor parents is not, of course,
peculiar to Luther. It is widespread in the history of interpretation of the Commandment and
has clear rootage in the Deuteronomic polity. Deuteronomy orders the Deuteronomic Code in
chapters 12–26 roughly according to the outline or order of the Decalogue and thus underscores the character of the Code as a specifying and illustrating of the force of the Commandments in various specific instances and cases. Immediately after Deut 15, which deals
with the sabbatical principle releasing debts and slaves in the seventh year, comes a section in
chapters 16–18 dealing with the leaders or "authorities" in the community, explicitly judges
and elders, prophet and priest. This is a spelling out of the force of the family commandment.

[31] Lehmann, *The Decalogue and a Human Future*, 152.

and support as a sphere of the common good by the prohibition against *adultery*. The orientation of the commandment is toward the neighbor, not towards one's own marital relation. That is, what is being protected in the commandment is the marital relation, the husband-wife relation, of one's neighbor. So both aspects of the family relationship – the husband-wife relation and the parent-child relation – are nurtured and undergirded, in one case by encouraging an esteem and respect across the generations and in the other by securing the basic relationship from encroachment by any other that would effect a breach in the marriage.

Once again, the character of the Commandments as effecting responsibility toward the neighbor's good has the concomitant outcome of securing one's own marital relation from violation and harm, both by my not having violated my own marriage in committing adultery with the wife of another but also by my neighbor's care in protecting my marital relationship by not committing adultery with my wife. Thus, a major feature of the common good secured by a community that lives under this direction and instruction is that each member is concerned for protecting the good of his neighbor(s) rather than focused on securing her own good.

3. It is appropriate at this point to recognize an important feature of the long history of interpretation of the Commandments that is central to the prohibitions of the second table of the Decalogue but is not confined to it. The meaning of the Commandments and the way in which they provide direction for faith and life is to be found in recognizing that every prohibition contains within itself a positive responsibility as every positive command contains within itself a negative warning (keep the Sabbath – do not do any work on the seventh day; honor your father and mother – fathers, do not provoke your children to anger). While not confined to a single strand of tradition, such an understanding of the Commandments has been central to their interpretation in the Reformed tradition. For John Calvin, there was always a three-part approach to the interpretation of each commandment. One sought after the subject of the commandment, the end of the Commandment, and its *opposite*, that is the injunction to good in the prohibition and the warning against the bad in the command. His classic example was the commandment against killing, which, in light of its subject and its end, clearly meant not simply a prohibition of killing or murdering somebody else but a warning against harming one's neighbor in any way. Further, the opposite was inherent in the commandment in its full sense, to wit, the one is enjoined to do all one can for the neighbor's good, or as Calvin put it: "...we give our neighbor's life all the help we can."[32]

---

[32] *Calvin: Institutes of the Christian Religion*, edited and translated by John T. McNeill and Ford Lewis Battles (The Library of Christian Classics; Louisville: Westminster John

4. A further aspect of securing the common good through the appropriation of modes of conduct identified in the Commandments is the recognition of the strong connection between *thought* and *deed*, between *intention* and *act*. This is the critical point of the final commandment(s) that prohibits coveting anything that belongs to one's neighbor and in various ways intensifies the nature of responsibility opened up in the second table by recognizing that what is guarded there is vulnerable first of all through the inner workings of envy, greed, and desire that can lead to acts that are prohibited by the other commandments.[33] That *acting* is the mode of endangerment of the neighbor's good is clear because the language for coveting most often occurs in biblical stories and prophetic sayings that go on to describe the act that erupts out of the envy and greed. Indeed, it is the connection between envy and greed that is at stake here, greed being the acquisitive move against the neighbor to enhance one's own well-being at the expense of another member of the community.[34]

It is this dimension of the working of the Commandments that is accentuated in Jesus' teaching of them. His antitheses in the Sermon on the Mount do not represent a critique of the Commandments or another and different or better teaching. Rather Jesus here uncovers and unpacks the force of the commandment against coveting and focuses much of his teaching on the close re-

---

Knox, 1960), Book II. viii.9. Consistent with this understanding of the Commandments, the former Presbyterian Church in the United States, before its reunion with the United Presbyterian Church, prepared an extensive statement on "The Nature and Value of Human Life," dealing with such issues as war, suicide, euthanasia, abortion, and capital punishment on the basis of an understanding of the commandment against killing in both its negative and positive dimensions.

[33] "If the Decalogue devotes its final commandment to prohibiting desire for whatever belongs to the neighbor, it is because it lucidly recognizes in that desire the key to the violence prohibited in the four commandments that precede it. If we ceased to desire the goods of our neighbor, we would never commit murder or adultery or theft or false witness. If we respected the tenth commandment, the four commandments that precede it would be superfluous." (René Girard, *I See Satan Fall Like Lightning*, trans. James G. Williams [Maryknoll: Orbis, 2002], 11–12). Girard sees in the Tenth Commandment a perception of the centrality of mimetic desire in human nature, which, while good in itself, turns constantly to violence. The commandment signals a "revolution" in the handling of mimetic desire that is carried through in Jesus' call for an imitation or mimesis of himself that thus sets human desire away from self love and the violence of rivalry against the neighbor and towards the imitation of God.

[34] As Girard recognizes, the term that is used in the Tenth Commandment is simply the word for "desire," which can often be an appropriate or acceptable feeling. The problem is the mimetic desire that becomes rivalry, that is, the desire for what belongs to one's neighbor. The deep problematic and danger of desire is, of course, signaled very early in the biblical story in the decision of the first woman to eat of the fruit of the forbidden tree because it was "desirable." The term that is used there is the same as the term in the Commandment (*ḥāmad*). Without the control of desire, there is no chance for a *common* good.

lationship between what goes on in the heart and how one acts. Rather than going beyond the Commandments, Jesus takes them further and gets to the "heart" of the matter (pun intended). He also continues the tradition that began in the Old Testament and continues on in Paul of seeing in the whole and the particularity of the Commandments a fundamental principle: Love your neighbor. So the Commandments provide both complex and simple ways of seeking the good of the whole. The complexity is in the particular working out of what the Commandments are after, a development that begins in Scripture with the stories, the prophetic sayings, the wisdom literature, and all the many pieces of case law in the Torah. That working out continues in the teaching of the church beginning with Jesus and Paul and continuing through the history of the church to the present, exemplified in but not confined to the centrality of the Commandments in the church's catechesis.[35] The simplicity is in the accurate reduction of the pursuit of the good of all to the continuing enactment of the love of God and neighbor-love.

The Commandments as Moral Framework

Precisely because the present discussion is about the common good and because that "common" is open and not finally determined, it is appropriate now to ask about the possibility that the community whose identity is worked out and whose life is defined by these words from the Lord, that is, by the Commandments, may find some companionship, some commonality with others who may not share the same identity or story. On the way to that question, and as a bridge between the community whose identity and direction are given at Sinai and other communities, I would like to propose two metaphors for thinking about how life is lived, two metaphors for the moral, that are appropriate for thinking about the function of the Commandments but may and do have wider applicability.

Both for the self and for the community, however limited or widely the "community" is defined, the need for some moral *framework* or *structure* belongs to the character of being human and to the possibility of being

---

[35] Note how the catechisms not only include the Commandments but go on to offer extensive development of the trajectory of meaning that arises out of each commandment. Obvious examples may be seen in Luther's Shorter and Larger Catechisms and the Westminster Larger Catechism, but there are many more. For the central role that Augustine played in setting the Commandments within the catechesis of the church as well as developments before and after Augustine, see Paul Rentschka, *Die Dekalogkatechese des hl. Augustinus: Ein Beitrag zur Geschichte des Dekalogs* (Kempten: Jos. Kösel'schen Buchhandlung, 1905). Cf. Bo Reicke, *Die zehn Worte in Geschichte und Gegenwart* (Beiträge zur Geschichte der biblischen Exegese, 13; Tübingen: Mohr [Siebeck]), 8–50.

human or of making and keeping human life human (Lehmann's powerful cliché). Such a moral framework may be understood by some to be autonomous, by others as heteronomous, and by still others as theonomous. Some such frames of reference may be more grounded in story and shared communal experience (family, political, sacral communities, and the like) while others are rooted more in some rationality or inferred system of virtue. However such structures are erected, it is difficult to avoid some moral framework, at least within a communal life of even the most minimal sort.

At the same time, it is clear that in the modern world moral frameworks are problematic precisely at the point of assuming there is a *single* moral framework, for no moral framework can be taken for granted as *the* moral framework, universally applicable to all.[36] The result may be a demittal to a moral pluralism, at least in principle. Different structures, providing varying senses of identity and orientation or of identity and the good coexist alongside each other within single communities or among and across different communities.[37] Or persons identify with a particular moral framework to a high degree while others come at the same framework more tentatively, appropriating some aspects and reticent about others. Still others may stand within a framework while understanding it as only one among other possibilities. And even in this case, one may be more or less positive about other possibilities.

Such a moral framework would seem to be a presupposition of a common good. At a minimum, the very terminology of "common good" builds in assumptions about some moral framework undergirding or supporting it or providing a moral space in which one may live out, search for, discover, and experience the common good. And here one may put forth the second metaphor for the moral. To the extent that the common good presupposes a *commons*, then it is appropriate also to speak of a moral *space* in which the self and others determine and share a common good, in which the self and others find a shared identity and a common orientation about how to live. That is, the structural and spatial concepts of moral *framework* and moral *space* provide metaphors for development of a multi-dimensional and complex depiction of the moral life as a central dimension of the common good. The danger of such concepts also becoming static and fixed[38] is off-

---

[36] Charles Taylor, *Sources of the Self: The Making of the Modern Identity* (Cambridge: Harvard, 1989), 17. For discussion of some common examples of moral frameworks, such as the honor ethic, the rule of reason, transformation of the will, and the like, see pages 20–24.

[37] Ibid., 25–40.

[38] The terms "static" and "fixed" are not inherently pejorative. Stasis may be life-saving; foundations keep things from falling down. But stasis that is not attentive to changing conditions may create obsolescence; and some structures need to be mobile or capable of moving if there is an earthquake.

set if both *structure* and *space* are set in a temporal and spatial *arc of understanding*, a trajectory of meanings, acts, and effects that receive their grounding in the moral framework and their orientation in the moral space but attend to ever changing contexts of varying sorts (personal, communal, historical, geographical, economic, etc.).

The Commandments create, in effect, a defining community whose structure by which the questions of value and norms, the patterns of interaction among members and in relation to others, and the fundamental definition of one's self are determined is provided by the Ten Words of God. The very definition of the community and the identity of its individual members are all wrapped in and shaped by the moral space provided by the Commandments.[39]

The Openness of the Commandments

The question that remains, however, is whether there is any possibility that the shape and space for life that is defined and laid out, constructed and landscaped by the Commandments has any connection with the moral framework and moral space that others perceive and by which they live. It is not essential that that be the case. Dialogue may go on from utterly different vantage points and out of quite different stories. At the same time, there may be fruitful interchange precisely when one discovers some common ground.[40] In what follows, various reasons are given *from within the tradition itself* that suggest the possibility of the Commandments contributing to a more broadly shared understanding of the common good.

1. Within the literary and theological context in which the Commandments are given as divine word, they are seen to be *foundational* and *perduring*, not restricted to times and places. They are foundational in that they open up a way of living in freedom and in covenant with the redeeming God that is worked out in various ways in different contexts and new situations. The relationship between the Commandments and the other legal collections in the Torah is such that while the collections are specific cases and illustrations of the force and bearing of the Commandments in the land and through time, the Commandments continue as the unchanging constitutional directives. The presence of collections of case law (Exod 20:22–23:33; Deut 12–26 following each account of the revelation of the

---

[39] For a more extensive elaboration of this point than is possible within the confines of this essay or as a supplement to the points being made here, see above, 51–67.

[40] See, for example, the essay in this volume by Milner Ball on Black Elk.

Commandments (Exod 20 and Deut 5) as the direct word of God, explicitly separated from them by narrative device (Deut 5:22–33; cf. Exod 20:18–20), and varying significantly from one another even as they deal with much common subject matter points to the difference between the legal collections and the Commandments. They are perduring both by the narrative, which does not set them as belonging to a particular time and place,[41] that is, "the land you are about to occupy," and by their continuing force and character as starting point in the divine instruction about the good and the right, about life in community with God and neighbor, exemplified in both the prophets and the Sermon on the Mount. In itself, this dimension of the Commandments does not take one outside the community that receives them in covenantal obedience, but it indicates their openness in time and space.

2. The Book of Deuteronomy explicitly identifies the "statutes and ordinances," as kept by Israel as evidence to the other peoples of what a wise and discerning nation Israel is:

[6]You must observe them [the statutes and ordinances] diligently, for this will show your wisdom and discernment to the peoples, who, when they hear all these statutes, will say, 'surely this great nation is a wise and discerning people!'....[8]And what other great nation has statutes and ordinances as just as this entire law that I am setting before you today? (Deut 4:6,8).

The wisdom and justice of the statutes and ordinances Moses teaches as trajectories of meaning and action flowing out of the Commandments are recognizable by other peoples, and there is an implicit suggestion that they are desirable to others, that there is an envy of Israel on the part of the other nations because of their wise and discerning laws. Jon Levenson comments with regard to this text:

[T]he commandments in question are the unique heritage of Israel granted her at a particular moment in her sacred history. But the desirability of these laws is presented as something universally recognized....[T]hey are the universal, undeniable proof of the intellectual acuity of Israel....Deut 4:5–8 views observance of the commandments as the

---

[41] Sinai, while a specific locus at a moment in the story of Israel, moves beyond that to become a kind of metaphor for the moral space of the community. New teaching of the meaning and force, of the particularity and ramifications of the Commandments goes on, starting with Sinai, but, whereas Moses teaches the meaning of the Commandments afresh on the plains of Moab (Deuteronomy), there is no second or new revelation of the Commandments or an equivalent covenantal structure. Moses refers *back* to Sinai in remembering the revelation of the Ten Words but teaches the community afresh at the border of the Promised Land what these words are all about, what is the meaning of covenantal existence in the new territory, now far from the wilderness of Sinai.

fruit of both faith and reason, of Israel's unparalleled *Heilsgeschichte* and universal human perceptivity. Torah is the intersection and consummation of the particular and the universal.[42]

One may add to these considerations the recognition, precisely within Deuteronomy – though not alone there – that the Lord has other stories with the other nations.[43] The gods whom Israel is not to worship have been "allotted to all the peoples everywhere under heaven" (Deut 4:19; cf. 29:26; 32:8–9). There is an implicit assumption that the worship of the other nations, identified in relation to other deities and other religious systems is, in fact, a provision and work of the Lord of Israel. One may set alongside this Deuteronomic hint the indication of exodus stories among other nations in Amos' oracle:

Are you not like the Ethiopians to me,
    O people of Israel? says the LORD.
Did I not bring up Israel from the land of Egypt,
    And the Philistines from Caphtor and the Arameans from Kir? (Amos 9:7)

The notion of shared moral structures is not explicit in these texts but it may be inferred.

3. In their original socio-historical setting, the world of the ancient Near East, certain of the concerns of the Commandments were shared by other religious and political communities. In his articulation of the foundations of a moral code operative in Israel and Mesopotamia, Karel van der Toorn finds them in the second table of the Decalogue and documents this with extensive reference to all sorts of Mesopotamian texts. He goes on to show that respect for the gods and particularly avoidance of lighthearted use of the divine name in frivolous oaths and blasphemy was characteristic of both Akkadian texts and the Bible.[44] Further, one may note that whereas

---

[42] Jon Levenson, "The Theologies of Commandment in Biblical Times," *Harvard Theological Review* 73 (1980), 26.

[43] Patrick D. Miller, "God's Other Stories: On the Margins of Deuteronomic Theology," in *Realia Dei: Essays in Archaeology and Biblical Interpretation in Honor of Edward F. Campbell, Jr. at his Retirement*, ed. P. Williams Jr. and T. Hiebert (Atlanta: Scholars Press, 1999), 185–194; repr. in P. D. Miller, *Israelite Religion and Biblical Theology: Collected Essays* (JSOTSup 267; Sheffield: Sheffield Academic Press, 2000), 593–602.

[44] Karel van der Toorn, *Sin and Sanction in Israel and Mesopotamia: A comparative study* (studia semitica neerlandica; Assen/Maastricht: Van Gorcum, 1985), chap. 2. The same point is made by J.J.M. Roberts when he writes: "Even the Ten Commandments, delivered to the Israelites at Mount Sinai/Horeb by the voice of Yahweh, contain little that would not have been acknowledged everywhere else in the Near East." Then, however, he adds an important caveat that continues to have significant relevance for the appropriation of the Commandments: "Apart from the limitation of worship to the one God, the prohibition of images, and

the Sabbath per se is not a shared religious practice in the world of the Bible, the provision for release of slaves and debts that is at the heart of the Deuteronomic understanding of the purpose of the Sabbath commandment was significantly a part of Mesopotamian practice in the royal proclamations of release of debts and taxes as well as other procedures that released slaves from their labor.[45]

4. There is a long association of the Decalogue with the natural law.[46] From the patristic period onward, both the Golden Rule and the Decalogue are seen as providing the substance of the natural law, which is to be understood as of universal validity, to be recognized by persons. Jean Porter comments: "...it makes sense to take these precepts [of the Decalogue] as statements of fundamental moral norms that are both generally known and foundational in the sense that other norms can be derived from them."[47] On inner-scriptural grounds the same thing can be argued, as I have noted above.[48] The theological grounding of the natural law is that it is contained in the divine law, as Porter argues for the scholastic tradition. Scripture provides a normative formulation of the natural law (Golden Rule) and "offers the paradigmatic statement of the immediate moral implications of the natural law, in the form of the Decalogue." [49]

While Porter's argument is an analysis of the tradition, it is in behalf of reclaiming such an understanding for contemporary Christian ethics, as her subtitle indicates. Others have sought to do the same in different ways. Reinhard Hütter has argued for a close association of the Decalogue with the natural law in contemporary ethical discussion. His suggestion is that

---

perhaps the observance of the Sabbath, these commands simply embody in a very pithy formulation the ethical standards common in the region." ("The Bible and the Literature of the Ancient Near East," in J.J.M. Roberts, *The Bible and the Ancient Near East: Collected Essays* [Winona Lake, IN: Eisenbrauns, 2002], 45). A significant tension is inherent in this mix of commonality and differentiation that continues to be an issue in the openness of the Commandments to their wider appropriation. As van der Toorn notes, however, even in the first table there are correspondences within the wider world of the Commandments appearing that may be of significance for the conversation.

[45] For the evidence and discussion of relation to biblical practices, see J. M. Hamilton, *Social Justice and Deuteronomy: The Case of Deuteronomy 15* (SBL Dissertation Series, 136; Atlanta: Scholars Press, 1992), 45–72; and Moshe Weinfeld, *Social Justice in Ancient Israel and in the Ancient Near East* (Jerusalem and Minneapolis: Magnes and Fortress, 1995), 75–96.

[46] See especially J. Porter, *Natural Law and Divine Law: Reclaiming the Tradition for Christian Ethics* (Saint Paul University series in ethics; Grand Rapids: Eerdmans, 1999), esp. chap. 3.

[47] Ibid., 168.

[48] See above, 3–16.

[49] Porter, *Natural Law*, 132.

the Decalogue helps us "remember" the natural law more fully in various contexts that all human beings share:

Christians individually and the church corporately do not have any privileged knowledge in detailed practical moral matters. They, however, find themselves bound by the perspectives and insights of a path that God has willed for all humanity. The commandments as the way of human freedom in communion with God are the basis for re(dis)covering the "natural law."…. Natural law is not "something out there" that we eventually "bump" into if we search long enough. Neither is it to be found "written" in our genes or in the stars…While some principles of practical reason are accessible to all of us, the natural law in its fullness is not simply inscribed in our minds. Instead diverse practices and traditions that structure human society display a matrix of contingent and unpredictable resonances with God's purpose for humankind as articulated in the narratives of Israel and Jesus. In particular structures of responsibility (their vocations), Christians have to discern and judge the resonances and dissonances in light of God's commandments.[50]

Robert Jenson has seen in the negative formulations of the Commandments (as well as in their substance) something of a kind of natural law:

In their bare negative formulation…the commandments of the second table apply to all polities, including those that do not belong to the narrative in which the commandments appear and that must therefore substitute joint pursuit of self-interest [a secular definition of the common good?] for love of God. In this role the commandments state minimum conditions: no society can subsist in which the generations turn against each other; in which vendetta has not been replaced by public organs of judgment and punishment….
Whether or not we wish to call the commandments in this negative abstraction natural law is perhaps mostly a matter of conceptual taste. The commandments are explicitly given by God to Israel and the church, but any people must know them in their negative mode if it is indeed to be a people even by less stringent definition. And existing peoples show that they do know them.[51]

It is possible also to see the incipient application of the norms of the Commandments already in the biblical narrative prior to their utterance by the Lord at Sinai, as James Skillen notes in his essay in this volume, where he argues for "the creational origin and foundation of these responsibilities."[52] The presence of unacceptable desire in Genesis has already been noted above, but one may add to that the judgment of Cain because of the

---

[50] Reinhard Hütter, "The Twofold Center of Lutheran Ethics: Christian Freedom and God's Commandments," in *The Promise of Lutheran Ethics*, eds. K. L. Bloomquist and J. R. Stumme (Minneapolis: Fortress Press, 1998), 50–51.

[51] R. Jenson, *Systematic Theology*, Vol. 2, *The Works of God* (New York: Oxford University Press, 1999), 86. Cf. the concluding sentence of his essay in this volume, "The Triunity of Common Good": "As for the ground of such judgments [that is, of earthly polities], the church need look no further than the ten commandments; if there is natural law, they republish it, if not, they are all we have or need."

[52] "'The Common Good' as *Political* Norm."

murder of his brother (Gen 4:1–16; cf. 9:5–6), the emphasis on the Sabbath in the Priestly creation account, which is then drawn into the Sabbath Commandment in Exod 20:11, and Ham's dishonoring of his father Noah (Gen 9:18–27).

The Endangerment of the Commandments

It thus should not be a matter of surprise that the Commandments belong to a larger realm of moral space than is represented by Sinai. The tradition itself so indicates and, in fact, we find evidence of them in other polities. Furthermore, Christian ethics has always overlapped in various ways with more general ethical modes.[53] In the case of the Commandments, one indication of this is the way in which they have become a kind of cultural code for the common good. That is, there is a sense that the culture needs these commands to order its life, whether or not they are firmly rooted in a religious tradition. Or it may be that the religious tradition is acknowledged but is not perceived as critical for the cultural appropriation. It is perceived that the common good is enhanced as all live by these directives, whether or not they associate themselves with the communities of faith out of which the Commandments and their keeping originate or in any way with the religious grounds that may be inherent in them.

Precisely at the point of the broader cultural use of the Commandments, however, one can perceive special dangers to their proper appropriation, dangers found precisely in their capacity for openness. Like any icon they can be genuine windows to the Holy One or they can be superficial and idolatrous covers for the proper worship of the Lord. Indeed, they may be both at the same time. There are probably several ways in which the open-

---

[53] See, e.g., the comment of Gilbert Meilander: "Even if Christian moral knowledge is built upon no foundation other than the biblical narrative of God's dealings with his world, that story itself authorizes us to seek and expect some common moral ground with those whose vision is not shaped by Christian belief. Thus, although the Christian way of life is itself a particular one sustained within particular communities, it has within it more universal elements. And the understanding of life which faith seeks, if it is truly understanding, will to some extent admit of 'translation' into the language of public life – which life it both affirms and seeks to transform. Moreover, biblical faith calls for trust in the free God, whose grace alone can ultimately sustain the life of discipleship in the world. For all these reasons it seems best to describe Christian ethics as a two-tier ethic – in part general and able to be defended on grounds not peculiarly Christian: in part singular, making sense only within the shared life of the faithful community" (*Faith and Faithfulness* [Notre Dame: University of Notre Dame Press, 1991], 19–20). Meilander's more extended discussion of this issue in his chapter on "The Singularity of Christian Ethics" is helpful in this regard.

ness of the Commandments also endangers them, but I shall mention only three:

1. Perhaps the largest endangerment of the Commandments is the one already mentioned and that is the use of the Commandments against the Commandments, specifically the way in which cultural uses of the Commandments may become incipient violations of the Second and Third Commandments. Perhaps that is nowhere more vividly exemplified than in the actual turning of the Commandments again into tablets of stone, bronze, etc. as they are set up in front of governmental buildings, hung on the walls of court houses, and the like. There may be good motives behind such moves, but the outcome is often a civil or cultural manipulation of the Commandments that ignores their context and gives only lip service – if even that – to the first table of the Decalogue. The divine authority is assumed as a ground for enforcing the second table, but the fear and love of God that is embodied in the first table is not really at stake. The Commandments have become an end in themselves. As the icon becomes an object of devotion and the God who speaks through it disappears, not only have the tablets become an idol but the name of God has been co-opted for secular and political ends, valid as those ends may be. So the community that engages in such practices is in danger of violating the commandment that safeguards the use of the divine name. Paul Lehmann's translation of Luther accurately catches up what is at stake and what is violated in the casual appropriation of the Commandments: "You shall not go about with the name of God as though it makes no difference."[54]

2. Overlapping with the danger of idolatry and empty use of the divine name is the tendency to trivialize the Commandments. That happens immediately, of course, when the first table is ignored. It is dismissed as of little account other than to provide a stamp of approval on the prohibitions that really matter. The trivialization is most apparent, however, in the way that the Commandments have become a kind of slogan, one that is tossed about in an unsubstantial way. The Commandments become either a joke, the subject of cartoons and actual jokes, or they become a catchall category for all sorts of things that have nothing to do with the Commandments. Thus we have web sites on "The Ten Commandments of Golf" and books

---

[54] *The Decalogue and a Human Future*, 101. I heard recently of a hotel that has in its elevators posters of the American flag with the Beatitudes inscribed across it and on the breakfast serving table a stone replica of the Commandments with a cross on them. Thus the sacred is treated casually, the Christian tradition is appropriated for political ends, and the Ten Words of God are placed on a par with sausage and eggs, though the food surely gets more serious attention.

on *Thou Shall*(sic) *Prosper: Ten Commandments for Making Money* (by a rabbi, no less!). The word of the Lord has become a cultural cliché.

3. Finally, one cannot ignore the reductionistic and simplistic handling of the Commandments that arises out of their familiarity. They are seen as simple and obvious rules whose sphere of significance is self-evident and quite narrow. The ubiquity of the Commandments leads many to dismiss them as a negative and simplistic approach to morality. They are as helpful and useful as the next self-help book. Indeed, the next self-help book will probably confirm that as it uses the rubric trivially: "The Ten Commandments of...."

Having cautioned against the endangerment of the Commandments that is incipient in their openness and familiarity, one must go on to warn also against an understanding of the Commandments in context that implicitly seems to forbid their appropriation by those who do not share that context, that is, the story and experience in which the Commandments come to us, or do not take that context seriously. Fighting against the endangerment and misuse of the Commandments needs to take place in a way that does not close off their serious appropriation by others who see in them – or even in some of them – a way to a larger good.

All of this is to suggest that in the Commandments, which Christians receive out of the story of God's redemptive purposes for Israel and the whole human race, there is at least some significant theoretical and actual common ground for thinking with others who do not share that story about what constitutes community, the moral, and the good of each and all. That this potential and actual common ground may be muddy at times and that the Commandments may become more cultural icon than actualized modes of living by trust in the living God and in responsibility for the good of the neighbor does not mean that one should give up the effort to identify in these modes directions that many in various communities find conducive for the common good. Christians and Jews bring these "ten words" to the table for conversation about how we find, enjoy, and live the good. We may find that our partners in the conversation will already understand.

The Eschatological Trajectory of the Commandments

Finally, it is important to note that to the extent the Commandments point us to God's intended good, they reflect another kind of openness. Insofar as the Commandments are descriptive as well as prescriptive, they give us some picture of the Kingdom of God and so they speak not only about the life we live but the life to come. Surely that is what is intended when Jesus draws the Commandments prominently into his Sermon on the Mount, the intention of which is to instruct his disciples in the kingdom of heaven or the kingdom of God. The mix of the ethical and the eschatological in the Sermon is true of the Commandments, which are a part of the Sermon. One Christian theologian has put it this way:

We are promised the day when God's intentions for us will be done. The ultimate purpose of the Decalogue is to tell us how things then will be. When we teach them to ourselves and our children, this is the last and best thing we are to say: "God is making a world of love to God and one another. See how fine that world will be. We will be faithful to God. We will be passionate for one another. We will be truthful for one another. We will...."[55]

The Rabbis made the same point in one of their own stories:

At the same time when God was giving the Torah to Israel, he said to them, "My children, if you accept the Torah, and observe my commandments, I will give you for all eternity a thing most precious that I have in my possession." "And what," asked Israel, "is that precious thing which thou wilt give us if we obey the Torah?" The world to come – the world to come," said the Lord. "Show us in this world an example of the world to come," says Israel. "The Sabbath – the Sabbath is an example of the world to come."[56]

As Christians keep the Sabbath on Sunday, the day of Jesus' resurrection, and – synecdochally – in their keeping of all the Commandments, they anticipate the coming of the Kingdom and receive a glimpse into the world to come.[57]

---

[55] Robert W. Jenson, *A Large Catechism* (Delhi, NY: ALPB, 1999), 12.

[56] Abraham J. Heschel, *The Sabbath* (New York: Farrar, Straus and Young, 1951), 74.

[57] On the importance of synecdoche, the whole found in a part, for interpretation of the Commandments, see John Calvin, *Institutes of the Christian Religion*, 1 (The Library of Christian Classics, 20; Louisville: Westminster John Knox Press, 1960), Book II, 8/8. Note his own comment on the Sabbath commandment:

"It would seem, therefore, that the Lord through the seventh day has sketched for his people the coming perfection of his Sabbath in the Last Day, to make them aspire to this perfection by unceasing meditation upon the Sabbath throughout life" (Book II, 8, 30).

The Psalms

10. The Ruler in Zion and the Hope of the Poor

Psalms 9–10 in the Context of the Psalter

In the recent investigation of the Psalter as a book, a strong case has been made for seeing its center and climax in its declaration of the rule of the Lord, explicitly articulated in a number of places in the expression "the Lord is king" (*yhwh melek* e.g., Pss 29:10) and variants (e.g., Pss 24:10; 95:3; 98:6; 99:4; 149:2) or "the Lord reigns" (*yhwh/ˀělōhîm mālak*, e.g., Pss 47:9; 93:1; 96:10; 97:1; 99:1) but evident in many other ways throughout the Psalter, including the personal reference "my king" (e.g., Pss 5:3; 44:5; 68:25; 74:12; 84:4).[1] In three significant ways this centering on God's rule of the world, including Israel, the nations, and the whole of creation, is strongly connected to David and his successors as the human rulers charged with representing the rule of God in the human community.

One is the presence of a number of psalms that seem to focus on the human ruler, that is, the so-called *Royal Psalms*, some of which are strategically placed within the Psalter to help make the connection between the divine rule and human rule.[2] That the Psalter has this conjoining of divine and human rule at its center is reinforced by the presence of the first Royal Psalm as part of the introduction to the Psalter, that is, Ps 2, appropriately included in the introduction because it, more than any other psalm, explic-

---

[1] Gerald Wilson has presented a cogent and persuasive argument that the climax of the Psalter is in the Enthronement Psalms in Book IV, announcing the enduring rule of the Lord of Israel in the face of the failure of the monarchy (*The Editing of the Hebrew Psalter* [SBLDS 76; Chico, CA: Scholars Press, 1985]). James L. Mays has suggested that "The Lord Reigns" is the center of the Psalms, its root metaphor (*The Lord Reigns: A Theological Handbook to the Psalms* [Louisville: Westminster John Knox, 1994]).

[2] Wilson, *The Editing of the Hebrew Psalter*, 207–208. Cf. the summary discussion and further reflections of J. Clinton McCann, Jr., "Books I–III and the Editorial Purpose of the Hebrew Psalter," in *The Shape and Shaping of the Psalter*, ed. J. C. McCann, Jr. (JSOT Supplement Series, 159; Sheffield: JSOT Press, 1993), 93–107. There may be other Royal Psalms than those traditionally so designated (2, 18, 20, 21, 45, 72, 89, 101, 110, 132, 144:1–11) in that there are clearly other psalms that refer to the human king and there seem to be some others that express the voice of the king, a point to be argued here with reference to Pss 9 and 10. For a strong effort to identify a more expanded role for the king in the Psalter, see John H. Eaton, *Kingship and the Psalms* (Studies in Biblical Theology, Second Series, 32; London: SCM Press, 1976).

itly lays out the connection between God's rule and the rule of the king.[3] A second way the connection is emphasized is in the attribution of a large number of the psalms to David, Israel's king par excellence, in the super-scriptions that precede many of the psalms. Third is the shared association of the rule of the Lord and of the king with Zion, a point that is made at the beginning of the Psalter (Ps 2:6) and constantly reaffirmed.

The introduction to the Psalter, however, is not simply a pointer to the rule of the Lord over the nations and kings as exercised through David and his line. Ps 1, which makes up the first part of the two-part introduction to the Psalter, says nothing about the king or about human and divine rule. It is rather about the Lord's way as the way of the righteous and the contrast of that way with the way of the wicked, a way that will end in judgment and destruction.

Two notes are sounded, therefore, in the introduction, notes that rever-berate throughout the rest of the Psalter. The contrast between the right-eous and the wicked and the conflict between them occupies much atten-tion in the psalms that follow. This is especially evident in the many psalms of lament, in which those who are righteous or innocent cry out for God's help against their enemies, against the wicked, against evil doers.[4] So also, God's rule and its exercise by and through the anointed of the Lord pervade the psalms that follow. By and large these two themes are articulated in different genres and different psalms (prayers for help or la-ments versus Royal Psalms, and Enthronement Psalms), though this is not always the case, especially inasmuch as the Royal Psalms are not really a distinctive genre but a thematic category comprising various genres. Where they come together first in the Psalter is in Pss 9 and 10, a psalm combination that is probably quite late in its composition and apparently artfully constructed and intentionally set within its context. It may be ar-gued that no other psalm so fully joins the basic themes of the Psalter – the rule of God, the representative rule of the king, the plea for help in time of trouble, the ways of the wicked and the righteous, and the justice of God

---

[3] For the place of Ps 2 as formally a part of the introduction to the Psalter, see, e.g., Pat-rick D. Miller, "The Beginning of the Psalter," in McCann, ed., *The Shape and Shaping of the Psalter*, 83–92; repr. in *Israelite Religion and Biblical Theology* (JSOT Supplement Series, 267; Sheffield: Sheffield Academic Press, 2000), 269–278.

[4] Some of the laments or cries for help do acknowledge some sin and consequent guilt and see what has happened to the one(s) praying as reflective of divine anger, punishment, or judgment (e.g., the so-called Penitential Psalms). But such psalms are in a minority and bal-anced by those that assert an innocence before God (e.g., Pss 7, 17, 139, etc.). Even among the Penitential Psalms, while a sense of sin and guilt may dominate a psalm like Ps 51, it is more muted in other psalms, e.g., Ps 6.

on behalf of the weak and the poor. It is likely that the psalm was created precisely to bring all these notes into a single and powerful chord.[5]

That Pss 9 and 10 represent a single psalm originally that has been split into two psalms in the Hebrew tradition is widely acknowledged. Some of the indicators of the unity of these two psalms are obvious.[6] They are developed around an acrostic pattern that sets up the first word of each verse according to the sequence of the Hebrew alphabet and continues through both psalms; there is no superscription at the beginning of Ps 10, a feature uncommon to Book I of the Psalter except with regard to Pss 1 and 2 and Pss 32 and 33, where also one is to read these pairs as a conjoined set and not as discrete and individual psalms;[7] and the Greek translation treats the two psalms as a single psalm.

There are still other indicators of the fact that the two psalms are to be read together. Thematically, the Lord's rule holds the psalms together. It is the starting point and assumption of Ps 9 (vv. 5, 8),[8] and it is the conclusion and hope of Ps 10 (v. 16). The call to the Lord, "Rise up!" which occurs ten times in the Psalter, is the dominant petition in both psalms (9:20 and 10:12). The expression "in times of trouble" (*lĕ'ittôt baṣṣārâ*), a somewhat peculiar Hebrew expression, occurs only here, and it appears in both psalms (9:10; 10:1). Its occurrence in Ps 9 in the midst of the declaration that "the Lord is a stronghold for the oppressed[9] // a stronghold in times of trouble" is the grounds for the complaint/question at the beginning

---

[5] Hossfeld has suggested that these two psalms provide a kind of "small theology of the rule of YHWH" (Frank-Lothar Hossfeld and Erich Zenger, *Die Psalmen I: Psalm 1–50* (Die Neue Echter Bibel; Würzburg: Echter, 1993), 82. For other treatments of these two psalms, see in addition to the commentaries: Walter Brueggemann, "Psalms 9–10: A Counter to Conventional Social Reality," in *The Bible and the Politics of Exegesis: Essays in Honor of Norman Gottwald*, ed. David Jobling et al. (New York: Pilgrim Press, 1991); repr. in Brueggemann, *The Psalms and the Life of Faith*, ed. P. D. Miller (Minneapolis: Fortress, 1995), 217–234; Notker Füglister, "'Die Hoffnung der Armen ist nicht für immer verloren.' Psalm 9/10 und die sozio-religiöse Situation der nachexilischen Gemeinde," in *Biblische Theologie und gesellschaftlicher Wandel: Festschrift für Norbert Lohfink S.J. zum 65 Geburtstag*, ed. Georg Braulik, Walter Gross, and Sean McEvenue (Freiburg: Herder, 1993), 101–123; Robert Gordis, "Psalm 9–10 – A Textual and Exegetic Study," *Jewish Quarterly Review* 48 (1957), 104–22; Klaus Koenen, "Völkervernichtung und Völkermission. Die theologische Bedeutung der Textgeschichte erläutert am Beispiel von Ps 9, 21," *Biblische Notizen* 54 (1900), 22–27.

[6] See the brief but helpful discussion of Wilson, *The Editing of the Hebrew Psalter*, 173–174.

[7] Compare Pss 42 and 43, which are also to be read as a single psalm.

[8] The versification used here for Ps 9 is according to the Hebrew Bible.

[9] As is often the case in the Psalms, it is difficult to be sure what aspect of time is implied in the verbs. The presence of *wayhî* at the beginning of this sentence has led Hans-Joachim Kraus to read this as a past action sentence: "Then Yahweh *became* a fortress for the oppressed." [*The Psalms* (Minneapolis: Augsburg, 1988), vol. 1, 189].

of the lament in Ps 10: "Why, O Lord, do you stand afar off? // Hide your-self in times of trouble?" Further, one notes that while Ps 9 seems to focus upon "the nations" (*gôyīm*) as the enemy and Ps 10 on "the wicked" as the ones doing in the petitioner, both psalms identify the wicked and the na-tions with one another (9:6, 16–17, 18; 10:15–16). And those who are be-ing done in by whatever group are regularly called the "afflicted" (*ʿānî/ʿānāw*) in both psalms and more specifically identified as "op-pressed" (*dak*) and "poor" (*ʾebyôn*) in Ps 9 and as "oppressed" (*dak*), "in-nocent" (*nāqî*), "hapless"/"helpless" (*ḥēlĕkâ/ḥelkāʾîm*),[10] and "orphan" (*yātôm*) in Ps 10.

The unity of the two psalms is an important factor in their interpretation and to be firmly maintained in light of all these signals, precisely because the two psalms are not easy to read together and do not flow smoothly into one another or create a single entity that looks like any other psalm or even represents, as a whole, any typical genre. Ps 9 begins in song of thanksgiv-ing and moves then to a prayer for help, a move that is heightened in Ps 10, a reverse of the cultic movement from lament to thanksgiving.[11] If in-deed the two psalms have been constructed carefully as a unit, and possi-bly in the latest stages of the formation of the Psalter, then one must make a serious effort to read them as a whole.[12] While there are many issues on the way to working out a full and complex interpretation of these psalms, the focus here is on the speaker of the psalms and the implications for thinking about the psalm's meaning in the light of who it is that speaks and how the psalm fits into the Psalter as a whole.

The identity of the one who sings and prays in this psalm would seem to be the human ruler, the king.[13] There are two obvious pointers to this con-clusion. One is the superscription that ascribes these psalms, along with the

---

[10] On this unusual word, see Füglister, "'Die Hoffnung der Armen ist nicht für immer ver-loren'," 122, n. 59.

[11] See Walter. Beyerlin, "Die *toda* der Heilsvergegenwärtigung in den Klageliedern des Einzelnen," *ZAW* 79 (1967), 208–224; and Patrick D. Miller, *They Cried to the Lord: The Form and Theology of Biblical Prayer* (Minneapolis: Fortress, 1994), chap. 5. There is a similar reversal of the customary and logical order in Ps 40.

[12] The date of Pss 9–10 is no more to be determined precisely than is the case for most psalms. The usual assumption, in light of terminology, e.g., the frequent reference to the *ʿani*, the use of the acrostic form, and the like, is that the psalm belongs to the post-exilic period and may even be Hellenistic. See, for example, Klaus Seybold, *Die Psalmen* (Handbuch zum Alten Testament I/15; Tübingen: J.C.B. Mohr, 1996), 55; and Hossfeld in Hossfeld and Zen-ger, *Die Psalmen I*, 82.

[13] See the comment of Peter Craigie, "The substance of the psalms lends itself to a royal interpretation, at least in the initial stage of their history." (*Psalms 1–50* (Word Biblical Commentary; Waco, Tex.: Word Books, 1983), 117. John Eaton argues also for a royal inter-pretation of the speaker in Ps 9–10 (*Kingship and the Psalms*, 32–33).

other psalms in Book I of the Psalter, to David. The second basis for assuming that we hear in these psalms the voice of the king is the prominent
place that the nations and peoples have in the two psalms, especially in Ps
9 but also in Ps 10, as noted above.[14] The psalm is couched in first person
singular style with the nations identified as both the enemies of the one
who prays and also the wicked before God. In the context of the Psalter
and more immediately Book I, this opposition is especially to be heard as
reflective of conflict between the Lord's appointed ruler and the nations of
the earth.[15]

There has been resistance to seeing the king as the speaker because the
nations as enemy seems to be a theme confined to Ps 9, and Ps 10 seems to
be more of a cry for help from one of the oppressed or poor.[16] It is this
shift in subject matter as well as the reverse order of the genres of thanksgiving and lament that have led interpreters to treat the psalms separately
and to hear in their words different voices. But if the psalm is a constructed and intentional unity, then one would expect to encounter a single,
common voice throughout unless there were explicit indicators to the contrary. Such indicators, however, are not present.[17] A single "I" speaks
throughout the psalm, one whose personality and specifics are carefully
hidden but whose place and stature are indicated directly by the criteria
mentioned above. There is nothing in Ps 10 to counter this assumption.
Certainly it is not the case that the increased focus on the poor or the af-

---

[14] In an excursus in his dissertation, Gert Kwakkel takes up the question of the possible
royal reading of psalms not traditionally assigned to the genre of Royal Psalms, particularly
the ones with which he is dealing in his study of the theme of upright behavior as grounds for
deliverance (e.g., Pss. 7, 17, and 26). He does not think that a strong case can be made for
regarding these and other psalms as royal, as some have suggested. In his discussion, however, he says: "The arguments taken from the nature of the enemies are most convincing in
those cases in which foreign peoples are responsible for the hostilities (as in Ps. 9 and Ps.
118)..." (Gert Kwakkel, *"According to My Righteousness": Upright Behaviour as Grounds
for Deliverance in Psalms 7, 17, 18, 26, and 44* [Groningen: Rijksuniversiteit Gronigen,
2001], 290.

[15] This is especially the case in the light of Ps 2, where the *gôyim* and the *lĕʾummîm* stand
in opposition to the Lord's anointed, as is the case in Pss 9–10.

[16] See, e.g., Seybold, *Die Psalmen*, 56.

[17] In his investigation of the possibility of Royal Psalms outside the generally accepted
number, Kwakkel argues that a royal interpretation is appropriate for parts of a psalm in
which there seem to be no elements indicating the involvement of a king if there are other
places in the psalm in which the king is involved. That is, the editors assume that all of the
psalm could be read and used as parts of a Royal Psalm even if the king is absent from large
parts of the psalm. The particular example Kwakkel uses to illustrate this is Ps 18, which has
large sections that do not explicitly or by implication assume the involvement of the king, but
is regularly regarded as a Royal Psalm because of its conclusion, which clearly points to the
king as the speaking voice (Kwakkel, *"According to My Righteousness,"* 287).

flicted, which begins already in Ps 9 and continues throughout the whole, suggests that the psalm has to be by an individual member of the community who has suffered assaults of some sort at the hands of wicked brothers and sisters. A deep concern for the poor and the oppressed, for the needy and the orphan, was a cardinal responsibility of the ruler of ancient Israel. Throughout the royal Ps 72, the king's responsibility for the maintenance of the cause of the poor and needy and oppressed is central. And Jeremiah essentially defines kingship in terms of whether or not the king attends to the needs of the poor. Pss 9 and 10 are a cardinal example of the incorporation of the poor into the king's prayer and his identification with their need.

If the royal character of these psalms is most evident in the first one and the cry for help on the part of or on behalf of the oppressed and the needy is most evident in the second one, neither element is missing from the other psalm. The accomplishment of this psalm in its artful composition is precisely the joining of these themes, indeed of the major themes of the Psalter in one whole. Ps(s) 9–10 is the psalm that most fully joins the two primary features of the Psalter in one: the lament dimension – the fate of the righteous and the wicked at the center of a cry for help by one in trouble – and the theme of the Lord's rule (and the king) and the fate of the nations. These are generally treated as separate psalmic themes, though they come together more often than recognized. Here their joining in one is in a large way. The psalm(s) are almost a cardinal example of an Enthronement Psalm with the declaration of the Lord's kingship and the call for the Lord to rise up in judgment against the nations and peoples of the earth to manifest a righteous rule in the whole of the universe, as evidenced especially in the protection of the poor and needy from their oppressors, whoever they may be. At the same time, there is hardly any psalm that better embodies the typical lament prayer for help, with its complaint against God (e.g., 10:1ff.), its complaint against the wicked who threaten to do in the righteous, the poor/needy/helpless/afflicted (e.g., 10:2–11), and its petitions to the Lord to rise up against the wicked/enemies/nations (9:20–21; 10:12, 15). Only in Ps 14 do we hear anything equivalent to the challenge to the Lord's power and presence in the midst of a wicked and oppressive world as is heard in the various quotations of the wicked in Ps 10:

"God will not seek" (10:4)

"There is no God" (10:4)

"I will not be moved from generation to generation" (10:6)

"God has forgotten. He has hidden his face. He will not see forever" (10:11)

"You [God] will not seek it out" (10:13)

The quotations of the wicked are an implicit complaint on the part of the faithful ruler, who prays and who has asked the questions himself first (10:1). The continued capability of the wicked to oppress and do in the afflicted and helpless is seen as a reflection of a godless spirit, but the evidence is visible to the psalmist/king who prays. So the hidden thoughts of the wicked expressed by the psalmist become the psalmist's own fears, his own complaint against God.

As in all the prayers for help (except Ps 88), there are words of trust that express the confidence of the ruler in the midst of the cry for help (e.g., 9:16–19; 10:14, 16–18). Indeed the psalm begins with a song of thanksgiving that sets all that follows in the context of the experience of divine deliverance already known and experienced (9:1–7).

The complex joining of powerful complaint and cry for help with assertions of the Lord's rule means that these different kinds of voices, these different kinds of claims, are not to be heard apart from one another. One may talk about distinctive themes in this regard and recognize that one theme dominates a particular psalm while the other theme is prominent in other psalms. But the affirmation of the Lord's kingship is articulated in the context of and in the face of precisely all the human questions and fears that come to expression in the psalms of complaint and lament. Here lament and complaint are encompassed in praise and thanksgiving at the beginning (9:1–13) and the declaration of the eternal reign of God over the nations of the earth (10:16) and in behalf of the weak (10:17–18) at the end. As Ps 72 asserts that the claim of the king to rule over the nations and the kings of the earth is found in his deliverance of the needy and the afflicted (Ps 72:1–4, 8–14), so Ps(s) 9–10 answers the cry of the poor for help with the conviction that the Lord is ruler and as ruler will hear and answer. Theodicy and sovereignty are not at odds with each other but are two sides of the same coin.

Divine sovereignty, therefore, is the weighty word of the psalm, on which depend the hopes and fears of the afflicted, the poor, the weak, and the king as one of these or as representative in their behalf. Three powerful images or metaphors convey its force. The most prominent one is the picture of God as *king*. The rule of the Lord is directly affirmed in language that speaks of the rule as eternal (10:16a), over the nations and peoples (9:12; 10:16b), effected from the divine throne in Zion (9:12; cf. v. 15). What is most critical and at the heart of the joining of the two themes is the fact that the Lord's rule is particularly manifest in power to deliver the weak and the afflicted from their oppressors, from the wicked and the evil one (9:12–13;10:16–18). Divine rule is always an exercise in power, but that is not a neutral power. It always has a moral content to it. According to this psalm, divine rule and power are most evident in God's attention to those who cry out in pain, shame, hurt, and affliction.

The moral character of the divine rule is further indicated with the metaphor of the Lord as *judge*. This is not distinct from the royal image. On the contrary, twice the judging activity of the Lord is specifically identified as a royal activity:

You have sat on the throne giving righteous judgment (9:5)

He has established his throne for judgment (9:8)

But it is specifically as judge that the Lord recognizes and adjudicates the right of the weak and the afflicted. The image dominates the psalm as much as the picture of God as ruler (9:5,8–9, 17, 20; 10:5). Because the Lord is a righteous judge, the just cause of the one who is oppressed by the wicked/nations will be upheld (9:5). The one who "judges the world with righteousness" and "judges the peoples with equity" (9:9) is the hope of the lowly and the afflicted (9:8–11), an assumption one can take up in confidence and against all the assumptions of the wicked (whether nation or evil person) that they can get away with their evil deeds because the psalmist king has experienced God's deliverance and just judgment as redemptive in the past.

The power of this divine ruler to effect justice for the afflicted is indicated with the imagery of the *warrior* God. This is evident especially in 9:6–7:

⁶You have rebuked (*gāᶜar*)[18] the nations,
   you have destroyed the wicked;
   you have blotted out their name forever and ever.
⁷The enemies have vanished in everlasting ruins;
   their cities you have rooted out;
   the very memory of them has perished.

---

[18] The verb *gāᶜar* "to rebuke, blast" has strong mythopoeic overtones of the divine battle against the chaotic enemies. For discussion of texts from Ugarit as well as the Old Testament, see the treatment of André Caquot in his essay on the root in *TDOT* 3.49–53. Note his summary comments: "The derivatives of *gaᶜar* frequently appear in poetic references to the victory that God won over the waters…" (p. 51) and: "When the etymology and secular use of *gaᶜar* ('to utter a cry') are taken into account, it seems that the central point in the religious use of *gaᶜar* and *geᶜarah* lies in the fearful and threatening voice of Yahweh, which he utters in the thunder, and which functions as a battle cry when he puts various enemies to flight" (53).

So the king can call on the Lord to rise up and strike fear into the nations (9:20–21). The one who decides in behalf of justice also exercises a just power to carry out the judgment and thus to undo the wicked and destroy them and their power over the weak and the lowly.[19]

The mediator of the Lord's deliverance is in some way the king, whose rule over the nations is affirmed here. Zion is the throne of the king and judge of the nations of the earth and the throne of the one through whose actions this rule is carried out. The king is recipient of this powerful deliverance as much as the dispenser of it. No explicit word is said about the king's role in the psalm. For that, one must read Pss 2 and 72 and other psalms. It is important, however, that the rule of the Lord is not apart from its manifestation through the human ruler. The point set forth in Ps 2 is underscored here where we find the first reference to Zion, and specifically to God's rule from Zion, after the introductory reference to Zion as the throne of God's human ruler in Ps 2. Whereas Ps 2 focused more on the human ruler, Pss 9–10 focus on the divine ruler enthroned in Zion.

The ultimate aim of Ps(s) 9–10, therefore, is to declare the rule of the Lord as enduring, powerful over all, and the hope of the afflicted whose deliverance from the wicked is evidence of the Lord's rule. All the references to the divine throne, the abode of the Lord in Zion, and the depiction of the Lord as king, judge, and warrior indicate this psalm is an early anticipation of the psalms that make up the center of Book IV and the climax of the Psalter. When it is heard much later in the Psalter, the claim that "the Lord is king" or "the Lord reigns" and the character of that claim as grounding all the hope of the afflicted, and specifically of the human ruler as afflicted and protector of the afflicted, is not a new thing in the Psalter. It has been prepared for at the beginning.

While no single psalm or set of psalms in Book I of the Psalter can be said to mark an unequivocal center or controlling point, this powerful combination of cry for help and affirmation of divine power and rule flows directly out of the introductory psalms and stands very much at the center of the first collection of psalms in Book I, that is, Pss 3–14. The ways of righteousness and wickedness and the ultimate vindication of the former and perishing of the latter are what Ps 1 sets forth as the subject matter of the Psalter. It is in this combination psalm that those motifs, already anticipated in Ps 7, come to strong prominence with both the words about

---

[19] For further elaboration of the way in which these three metaphors are central to the Old Testament depiction of Israel's God, see Patrick D. Miller, *The Religion of Ancient Israel* (The Library of Ancient Israel; Louisville: Westminster John Knox Press, 2000), 6–12; and *idem*, "The Sovereignty of God," in *Israelite Religion and Biblical Theology*, 406–421.

God's vindication of the just cause of the righteous and the several references to the wicked/enemies perishing (*ʾābad*, 9:4, 6, 7; 10:16; cf. 9:19).

So also the protection and support of the poor and needy, of the orphan and the oppressed that is so much at the heart of the torah in which the righteous one delights (Ps 1:1–3) arises first here as a strong theme that will continue throughout the Psalter. Indeed Ps(s) 9–10 contains one of the largest cluster of terms for the poor and needy of any psalm in the Psalter, including the following words: *dak* ("oppressed" – 9:10; 10:18), *ʿānî/ʿānāw* ("afflicted/affliction" – 9:13, 14, 19; 10:2, 9[2x], 12, 17), *ḥēlĕkâ* ("helpless" – 10:8, 10, 14), *nāqî* ("innocent" – 10:8), *yātôm* ("orphan" – 10:14, 18), and *ʾebyôn* ("poor" – 9:19).[20] Furthermore, *all* of these terms make their *first* appearance in the Psalter in Ps(s) 9–10. That is, it is with this psalm that the "Armentheologie" of the Psalter begins.[21] The prayer for the poor, the weak, the needy, and the oppressed first arises in Ps(s) 9–10, and that happens with such vigor that it places *the protection and support of the poor and the needy* as the fundamental content of the *sovereignty of God*.

That justice and the help of the poor and afflicted is also fundamental to the rule of the human king is evident in the way in which some of these same terms, specifically *ʿanî* (72:1, 4, 12) and *ʾebyôn* (72:4, 12, 13[2x]), cluster in Ps 72 as that psalm sets the king's protection and justice for the poor and the weak as the basis of his claim to rule the nations, a protection manifest by the king's just judgment, a reflection of the judging activity of the Lord. The first occurrence of the divine epithet "helper" (*ʿôzēr*) occurs

---

[20] On these terms for the poor as they are present in Pss 9–10, see the summary comment of F. Hossfeld:

Der Psalm fällt auf durch ein reiches und verstreutes Vokabular zum Thema "Armut". Leitwort ist *ʿānī* "der Arme" ($9^{13.19}$ $10^{2.9.12.17}$), einmal in 9^{19} begleitet vom Synonymbegriff *ʾaebyōn* "der Elende"; daneben tauchen fast singuläre Austauschbegriffe auf wie *dak* "der Bedrückte" (9^{10} 10^{18}) und *helᵉkāh* "der Schwache" ($10^{8.10.14}$). Dadurch weist sich der Psalm aus als einer der typischen Armenpsalmen (9/10 25 34 37 69 72 109), die im ersten Davidpsalter zugleich identisch sind mit der Reihe der akrostischischen Psalmen (9/10 25 34 37). Der Psalm wechselt mühlos zwischen dem Blick auf den einzelnen Armen ($9^{10;.14.19}$ $10^{2.8.9.14.18}$) und dem Blick auf das Kollectiv der Armen ($9^{13.19}$ $10^{10.12.17}$). Die Armut hat viele Facetten: soziale Not und Ausbeutung ($9^{10.13}$), Verfolgung (10^2) Rechtsnot ($10^{7.8}$) und Ausgeliefertsein an die hinterhältige feindliche Übermacht (10^{9f}). Der Beter bedenkt die Armut in all ihren Dimensionen und schildert die eigene wie die der Gruppe der Armen. Er überschaut Vergangenheit, Gegenwart und Zukunft und sieht die Armut sowohl unter sozialem als auch religiösem Aspekt. (*Die Psalmen I*, 81–82).

[21] On the theology of the poor in the Psalter, see Hossfeld and Zenger, *Die Psalmen I*, passim and the earlier classic work of Albert Gelin (1953) translated into English as *The Poor of Yahweh* (Collegeville, Minn.: Liturgical Press, 1964).

in Ps 10:14, where the Lord is the helper of the orphan.[22] The same epithet is then applied to the king in Ps 72 with reference to the king's support of the "afflicted" (*ʿānî*), "who has no helper."

The rule of the Lord's anointed over the nations of the earth is set as a theme of the Psalter in Ps 2, which, like Ps(s) 9–10, understands the rule of the human king from Zion as a manifestation of the eternal rule of the one enthroned in Zion and heaven.[23] If the focus of Ps 2 is on the human ruler, the derivative character of that rule is clear. If Ps(s) 9–10 focus on the Lord as king, the working out of that rule is implicit in the voice of the king as the one who prays and whose rule is defined in the same way as the rule of the Lord – the help and deliverance of the poor, the afflicted, and the oppressed.

The central subject matter of the Psalter is thus fully underway in this lately but carefully crafted psalm. At the beginning of the Psalter, its climax is already anticipated. In the first group of psalms, the juxtaposition of human cries for help and shouts of praise because the Lord reigns lets the reader know that these cannot be separated. The one receives its answer in the other. But the questions of the one are always a test of the other. The sovereignty of God is seen to be nothing other than a protection of the just cause of the afflicted, for whom God's judgment is a safe haven and refuge (9:10). The human ruler will be – in this book as in human experience – both the one who voices the cry for help and the one who brings the power of God on behalf of the weak.

---

[22] On this word and its possible association with a second *ʿzr* root, from an original *ġzr*, preserved in Ugaritic and meaning "hero," "warrior," "protector," or the like, see Jerome Creach, *Yahweh as Refuge and the Editing of the Hebrew Psalter* (JSOT Supplement Series, 217; Sheffield: Sheffield Academic Press, 1996), 35, and the references in n. 34.

[23] See Miller, "The Beginning of the Psalter," 276–277.

11. The Poetry of Creation

Psalm 104

Theological interpretation of creation as a work of God has taken its primary biblical cues from the first chapters of Genesis, recognizing that there are other places where God's creative activity is also spoken of or alluded to (e.g., Isa 40–55 and Job 38–41). The Psalms also include various expressions of praise of the creator (e.g., Pss 8, 19, and 33). In each of those instances, the praise of God's creative power is a feature of a larger whole that encompasses other concerns, so that the focus on creation and what God did and does in the act of creation and its maintenance is only a particular and not very large part of the whole. There is one psalm, however, that not only speaks wholly about God's creation of the world but does so extensively, namely, Ps 104. As the most extended explication of God's work of creation outside of Genesis, it deserves a central place in any attempt to think about God as creator or about the doctrine of creation.[1]

The Structure and Movement of Psalm 104

The psalm begins and ends in praise, thus presenting itself to us as a hymn that is meant to exalt the Lord of Israel and evoke the praises of the people of God. The repeated participles describing the Lord's creative activities (e.g., vv. 2–4, et al.) further serve to define the genre of the psalm as a hymn of descriptive praise.[2] The movement of the psalm is not straightforward. As poetry, the psalm reflects the kind of freedom to repeat, return, and move in different directions even if such freedom is exercised under tight controls in the mind and imagination of the poet. This poem

---

[1] There are clear reasons for seeing connections between this psalm and the hymn of Amenhotep IV to Aten, but such comparative analysis is not the aim of this essay, so those intertextual connections are not pursued here.

[2] On this genre, see among others, Claus Westermann, *Praise and Lament in the Psalms* (Atlanta: John Knox, 1981), 81–151; Patrick D. Miller, *Interpreting the Psalms* (Philadelphia: Fortress, 1986), chapter 5; and Frank Crüsemann, *Studien zur Formgeschichte von Hymnus und Danklied in Israel* (Wissenschaftliche Monographien zum Alten und Neuen Testament, 32; Neukirchen-Vluyn: Neukirchener Verlag, 1969), esp. 81–154.

betrays just such a mixture of freedom and control. The psalm stakes out certain areas of the creative work of God and develops them, but it does so in a way that creates echoes of earlier parts, repeats critical language, and marks pauses of exuberance and astonishment. What follows is a proposal about that movement.

I. Beginning with God and the Creation of Heaven (1–4)

After the opening self-command of the psalmist – "Bless the Lord, O my soul," a call to thanksgiving that forms an *inclusio* around the whole psalm and ties it to the preceding psalm – God is addressed in two formulations: "You are very great" and "You clothe yourself with honor and majesty." Here the praise of God begins by focusing directly upon the object, or better, the subject of praise with language that points the hearers of the psalm to the grandeur and greatness of God. No reference is made to God's activity or work. Only the sovereign and majestic "Lord my God" is in view. Praise begins with its eyes focused solely and fully on God known in greatness and majesty, characteristics whose implications are laid out immediately in the rest of the psalm.[3]

The second of these two formulations leads into the series of doxological participles that are characteristic of the descriptive praise of God: "the one clothing self with light like a garment" (v. 2a). This clause clearly parallels the preceding one, "you clothe yourself with honor and majesty," and so continues the exaltation of God as great and majestic. But in form and content, v. 2a is also parallel to the clause that follows and begins to speak of God as the creator. The function of this descriptive clause as a hinge between the exaltation of the deity and the enumeration of God's creative acts is evident in the following *identification of God with light* and the *light as the first creation of God.*

The equation of God with light is familiar in Scripture in several ways. There are texts that explicitly identify God and light, as, for example, Isa 60:19: "Your Lord will be your everlasting light, and your God will be your glory." In the New Testament, the equation is carried further as "God is light" becomes a part of the church's message and proclamation on a par with "God is love" in the First Letter of John (1:5; cf. 4:8) and the final visions of the Revelation to John envision a time when there will be no

---

[3] Readers of the Psalter may hear in these words echoes of Ps 8, where the creative works of God are also in view and where the definition of the human creature as "a little less than God" is found in the Lord's crowning humankind with "glory and honor," thus reflecting the honor and majesty of God.

need of sun or light and no darkness because "the glory of God is its light" (Rev 21:23) and "the Lord God will be their light" (22:5). The equation of "light" and "glory" is appropriate in that the *kābôd*, which in the priestly tradition and elsewhere is a symbol of God's presence, is itself an image of light and radiance. Thus, this first participial phrase in Ps 104 continues the description of the deity – great and shrouded with honor, majesty, and light.

But light is also the first of God's creations in Gen 1. The one wrapping self in light is also the creator of the light. Light refers both to the beginning of creation and to the wondrous and mysterious nature of God. Note that the initial creative act is not the creation of light and darkness. It is only light, which is part of the very being of God. Darkness comes much later as part of the provisioning work of God and for a particular purpose (see below). There is something significant in seeing the first creative work of God as also characteristic of the being and nature of God. God and the world begin in light, and the light is both God and God's creation.

A series of five participial clauses in vv. 2b–4 sets out the first of three major movements in the poetry of creation (cf. Ps 146:6): the creation of heaven. As in Gen 1, heaven is the first creative work after light. It is no small moment that heaven is created. There is a vital tension in the viewing of heaven as both God's creation and God's abode. From heaven come the decrees that determine all that happens on earth. But heaven is not something other than earth at the point that they are both parts of the created order of God. Solomon attests to the paradox of heaven as the divine locus and the divine creation when he prays to God in heaven and says, "Even heaven and the highest heaven cannot contain you..." (1 Kgs 8:27). The priority of heaven over earth is hinted at in the ordering of creation here and in Gen 1, but it is not a different order than that of earth. Heaven and earth are linked by a common maker.

II. The Creation of Earth (5–23)

Creation of Earth and Water (5–9). The creation of heaven is followed by the creation of earth, but the poetry does not seek to set the sequencing of the acts of creation as a matter of any consequence. The fundamental fact about the earth is its stability.[4] Just as the one who keeps *tôrâ* and is kept

---

[4] The MT begins this section with a third person verb – "he set the earth on its foundations." While that may be the more difficult reading, it makes little sense in the context. More likely is a participial form (*yōsēd*), that is, "the one setting the earth on its foundations." Most of the acts of creation here begin with participial expressions and then may move to finite

by the Lord is not shaken (e.g., Pss 15:5; 16:8; 17:5), so the earth created by the Lord does not shake or totter. The intimation of chaos is found in the reference to the watery deep, the *těhôm* that represents the pre-creation chaotic waters of Gen 1 and even of the Babylonian creation epic. That "deep," however, is here demythologized and turned into a piece of clothing. Its potential for enveloping the earth and thus turning back the creation is hinted at in the description of the deep as a garment with which the Lord covered the earth. But the deep is not pre-existent. Its presence is not mysterious in any way.

The focus on water in the creation of the earth does, however, point to God's ordering and control of what might potentially be chaos. While the covering of the earth with water is the Lord's doing, that relation between the deep and the earth is not God's final intention for the ordering and stability of earth. That comes when the Lord's rebuke, that is, the form of thunder, sends the waters scurrying like animals to their appropriate place, the place that the Lord has set for them.[5] The creation of earth thus occurs in two stages, both of which are the Lord's doing: the covering of earth with the deep and the movement of these waters to places where they may function in a constructive way (see vv. 10–13). Reference to "earth" (*ʾereṣ*) forms a kind of *inclusio* around the section (vv. 5 and 9).

Provision of Water for the Fertility and Life of the Earth (10–13). Again the section opens with a descriptive participle: "the one sending springs in the valleys." It closes with a summary statement that joins two of the key

---

verbal forms, as in the case of these verses. In this instance, the finite verbal forms are especially appropriate as a way of referring to the creation as a past act. The perfect and imperfect tenses that dominate this section of the psalm are probably all to be understood as referring to past events in creation. The parallelism of *qtl* and *yqtl* forms in verse 6 and the return to the *qtl* at the end of this section in verse 9 point to a reading of the *yqtl* verbs in the past tense despite the NRSV move to translate them with present tense. There is a tendency to use *yqtl* verbs to speak of the activity of the creatures and participles and perfect tenses to speak of God's activity.

The participial form of *yāsad* is reflected in some of the Greek witnesses as well as in one of the Psalms manuscripts from Cave 4 at Qumran. For the latter, see Peter W. Flint, *The Dead Sea Psalms Scrolls and the Book of Psalms* (Studies on the Texts of the Desert of Judah, 17; Leiden: Brill, 1997), 97.

[5] Some would see in this poetic rendition of the creation mythological or mythopoeic antecedents having to do with the victory of the high god and the establishment of his palace after the victory is won. That reading seems to assume a great deal that is not explicit in the text and so does not commend itself as a governing metaphor. But the reference to the rebuke of the deep waters by the Lord is an explicit motif reflecting the activity of the warrior or storm god. It recurs in the New Testament when Jesus "rebukes" the wind and sea in the midst of a storm (Matt. 8:26 //Mark 4:39 // Luke 8:24).

verbs of the passage: "The earth is *satisfied* (*śābaᶜ*) with the fruit of your *works* (*maᶜaśeykā*)." The creation of water as a flood control, which was the subject of the preceding section, shifts now to God's provision of water as a source of refreshment and nourishment and life. Verse 13 is clearly transitional: the first half looks back to the preceding verses about watering the earth (cf. v. 3); the second half looks forward to the following verses about providing what is necessary to satisfy the needs of God's creatures.[6] The whole is a marvelous picture of springs and rivers and animals drinking from them. But the rivers are also there as the place where trees grow so that birds have a place to nest and sing. As in the preceding section, the passage concludes with a reference to the chief subject of these verses, earth (*ʾereṣ*). The focus of verses 5–23 is on the earth as the landmass on which the animals and human beings live. The poet turns to the sea later.

Provision of Food (14–16) and Home (17–18) for the Creatures. The passage moves further into God's provisioning for life. As in the previous sections, a doxological participle begins this section and describes the basic divine creative act that characterizes it: "the one making the grass to sprout for the cattle and plants for the service of humankind." This is followed by an explicit series of purpose constructions with two infinitives (*lĕhôṣîʾ* and *lĕhaṣhîl*). The first two verses clearly have to do with the provision of food: plants for animals, bread and wine for human beings. The last two verses, however, building on the reference to the trees of the Lord, describe the provision of place or home for the creatures of earth: the trees as the place for birds (cf. v. 12) and the hills for the animals.

Provision of Time for the Creatures (19–23). Paralleling the description of appropriate food and place, the exaltation of God's creative work moves now to speak of the provision of appropriate times for the different creatures to work for their food, that is, to satisfy their basic needs. This section probably also begins with a doxological participle (*ᶜōśeh* instead of *ᶜāśâ*). The sun and moon and the darkness and light are not simply part of a sequence of creative acts. They are created for a purpose, to provide time for animals to hunt (darkness and night) and for people to do their labors (day). This function of the heavenly elements to provide time is underscored as the section closes with the words "and to their labor *until evening*" (v. 23).

---

[6] On this transitional technique, see H. Van Dyke Parunak, "Transitional Techniques in the Bible," *JBL* 102 (1983), 525–548.

III. Interlude (24)

The poet's movement through the creative and providing work of God is interrupted by a burst of praise and a summary affirmation in verse 24. The whole point of the psalm is expressed in the first colon of the verse: "How marvelous are your works, O Lord!" The rest of the verse continues that exultant praise in a way that brings to conclusion and summarizes the creative work of God. The "all of them you have made" rounds off the extended description. The focus on earth and its creatures is reiterated in the final colon: "The earth is full of your creatures." The pronominal suffix "your" is not surprising here but important because the text has not really spoken about the creation of the creatures. It is all about providing the context for the creatures. Here, however, the point is made explicitly that "all of them" – sensate and insensate things – are "your creatures."

IV. The Creation of Sea (25–26)

The focus of the psalmist's praise hitherto has been entirely upon God's marvelous creation of the earth, of the landmasses, and of the waters that fertilize the land. Even where the "deep" appears in the preceding verses, it is as a garment, a skirt for the earth (*hā'āreṣ*). Now the poet turns to the great waters, the seas, and makes two observations about them, each introduced by a directive "there" (*šām*):[7]

1. The sea is the container for another whole group of creatures, the creeping or gliding things of the ocean. Like the earth, the sea was created as a habitat, specifically as the appropriate place for the manifold sea creatures, of whom Leviathan is the greatest of all.

2. The sea is a means of transportation. As with *hā'āreṣ*, the earth, the sea is a place for both animals and human beings.

IV. A Concluding Coda (27–35)

A series of mostly two-line strophes brings things to a close in different ways, wrapping up the account of God's creation and echoing earlier sounds of the poem.

---

[7] As with all the descriptive elements here, "the great sea" can be connected specifically with the geography with which a resident of Palestine would have been familiar. The Great Sea elsewhere in Scripture is the Mediterranean.

The Providing Hand of God (27–28). The whole of the poem is pulled together in terms of God's provision of what is good and needful for life. The concluding and summary character of these lines is suggested immediately by the *kullām* ("these all") at the beginning and by the "filled/satisfied with good things" at the end (cf. v. 13).

The Creation of Life (29–30). While the creation of sensate creatures comes at the end of this description of God's creative work – as also in Gen 1 – this poetic rendition of the creation has already talked extensively about the living creatures. The key to these verses is the order: death and then life and renewal. The creation of living beings is not reported as another step, or series of steps, in the creation. Like many other aspects of creation the breath of life is part of the providence of God, the provision of continuity, so that each new birth is an act of creation, renewing the earth. Death is on the way to renewal.

A Doxological Benediction (31–32). Now the psalm comes to its end in praise. The qualitative judgment that God makes in Gen 1 that the creation is good is here turned into a wish for the Lord's joyful celebration over "his works." The use of this term "works" triggers a kind of final creation doxology, consisting of participial clauses that have appeared before to refer to the creative acts of God, including the creation of earthquakes and volcanoes.

Ascription of Praise (33–34). The psalmist who sought the Lord's rejoicing and celebration (*śāmaḥ*) in all "his works" now declares that he or she will rejoice and celebrate (*śāmaḥ*) in the Lord.

The Fate of the Wicked (35a). While this note seems an intrusion in the context of the praise of the Creator, one who has read the Psalter from the beginning should not be surprised that a reference is made to the sinners and the wicked. The first psalm introduces the Psalter as an account of the way of the righteous and the wicked. That the psalmist has turned in praise for God's great creative power and imagination does not mean that the reality of the wicked and their presence in this created order is forgotten. The psalmist calls for what Ps 1 says will happen: the disappearance of the way of the wicked.

The Inclusio-Conclusion (35b). The psalm returns to its beginning with the framing self-command: "Bless the Lord, O my soul." This concluding note of praise is reinforced by the hallelujah at the end, though this expression is fluid in the tradition, being set at the beginning of Ps 105 in the Septuagint.[8]

Theological Reflections on Psalm 104

The richness of this psalm cannot be fully developed in any single study. Several observations may be made to suggest something of the contribution of the psalm to our understanding of theology, anthropology, and creation.

1. To begin, Ps 104 offers itself to the community of faith as *one of the most powerful interpretations of the first article of the Creed*: "I believe in God the Father Almighty, Maker of heaven and earth." While that formulation is not exhausted by Ps 104, it elaborates a picture of the "maker of heaven and earth" in detail. The wholeness of heaven and earth as the created works of God and, conversely, the testimony of heaven and earth to the imagination and power of God are the subject of this psalm from beginning to end. Ps 104 fleshes out the making in a way that is reminiscent of Gen 1 while in various respects more fully developed and in other respects more spartan (e.g., the distinctiveness of male and female).

2. The two words that stand out in the psalm are "work(s)/made" (*ma^{c}āśeh/^{c}āśâ*; vv. 13, 19, 24, 31) and "satisfy/fill" (*śāba^c*; vv. 13, 16, 28, and 11 in the Syriac). This is no accident, for they suggest that the psalm's chief subject matter is *the "works" or creation of God and God's "satisfying" or providing for the creation*. That is what this psalm talks about, and, when those are subjects in theological discussion, Ps 104 is a primary text for our engagement.

3. Ps 104 makes us aware how much *poetry is the proper language of creation*. The poetic images of the psalm are many and rich. For example:

- The heavens as a great tent over us all and sheltering the earth. What if it gets holes in it? The earth like a giant oil-rig set up in the midst of the oceans, which, like the doer of *tôrâ*, is not "shaken."
- Clouds as chariots, the Lord's "dune-buggy" on which the Almighty God rides through the skies.
- Thunder scares off the waters, so that they scurry away to their proper homes like frightened animals.
- The deep waters are locked up and held back like a dam.
- The ocean is a giant playpen for sea animals.

---

[8] See Bruce Waltke, "Superscripts, Postscripts, or Both," *JBL* 110 (1991), 577–582.

- Earth quakes when the deity looks and volcanoes erupt at the touch of God's finger.
- The Lord is architect, contractor, and respirator.

Surely no text of scripture speaks more directly and in detail about the creation and about what God did and does in creation and in the sustaining of creation than does this psalm. But here we are not in the genealogical and liturgical style of Gen 1 or the narrative account of Gen 2, both of which have been constantly misinterpreted by the community of faith, who are unable to resist literality, technicality, scientific interpretation, and oversimplification. The beauty of Ps 104 is that it is all about creation as God's act, an act that is complex and beautiful, whose manifestation in the created order is such that difference, complexity, and mutual interdependence are constantly evident.

Here, however, there is no external report vulnerable to literal and scientific analysis. One cannot analyze Ps 104 that way. It is poetry, and we know not to interpret poetry literally. It stirs our imaginations and speaks about God's creative work in the only language that can really incorporate the reality of God in the creative process, thus enabling us to speak of "creation" and not simply "cosmos" or "nature." Ps 104 is not an account, scientific or mythological; it is praise to the "Lord my God." God's creation may indeed be studied, but in the scriptures it is the cause for grand praise. Theologians, therefore, and the community of faith may well be instructed to turn to this text as much as to Gen 1 and 2, if for no other reason than to avoid misreading what the Bible tells us about creation and the creative work of God.

4. Perhaps more than any other formulation, Ps 104 conveys the *centrality of order and purpose in the creation*. From the sending of the waters to their appropriate locales to the setting of night and day for animals and human beings, the *orderliness* of God's creation is underscored. The notion of harnessing the forces of nature is familiar to us as a human activity, from building dams to the splitting of the atom. Here, such harnessing characterizes divine activity. The picture of the chaotic waters bounded and turned into useable water corresponds to the image of dam-building. That feat of engineering is often done precisely for flood control, as in verses 5–9, or as a way of harnessing the power of the water for electricity. And there is surely nothing more devastating or evocative of the return of creation to chaos than the power of a flood of water let loose when a dam breaks.

In this text, however, it is especially the *purposefulness* of God's creative acts that is underscored. Thus, for example, the darkness is created to give time for animals to hunt their prey, and the springs of water come forth to provide water for them. Moreover, water is provided to make the

trees grow so that the birds can nest and sing! A whole sequence of creative acts has bird songs as its goal!

The purposefulness of all that God did and does in creation is implicit in
the celebration of the creation of sea. It is there to enable ships to sail and
sea animals to play. This sense of the purpose of creation is quite explicit,
however, in many other places. The high mountains are "for" the wild
goats, and the rocks are created as a refuge "for" the coneys. The Lord
causes grass to grow "for" cattle and plants "for" the use of human beings.
Especially in the provision of bread and wine, the purposive character of
the divine creative activity is underscored with two infinitives: "to bring
forth food from the earth...to make the face shine with oil" (vv. 14–15).

Thus creation is to be understood as not simply occurring. It is a process
of past and present. Indeed, the poetry does not set neat distinctions between these temporal dimensions or between creation and providence. The
creative process is also complex and filled with significant interactions
among its various elements or facets. This portrayal of an orderly and pur-
poseful creation may be related to the exclamation of the psalmist in verse
24: "*In wisdom* you have made them all." Although the text never raises
the question of "why" creation, it makes clear that creation reflects the
wisdom of God. There is a sensibility to the creation, an intelligibility that
can only come from divine wisdom. This psalm joins with such passages
as Prov 8:22–31 and Job 38–41 to make explicit connection between theological reflection on the creation and the wisdom of the sages. But while
Job 38–41 *argues* for the wisdom of God, Ps 104 discovers it in a *burst of
praise*. It all makes such sense that one cannot but extol the amazing wisdom that has worked it all out.

5. The order and purpose of creation uncover also its *beauty* and the
pleasure it brings. The order of creation is a part of its aesthetics, the beau-
tifully crafted universe of heaven, earth, and sea brought into complex and
pleasurable shape by the artistry of God. The praise of verse 24 is like the
exclamation a viewer makes before a magnificent painting. There is also a
sense of playfulness, joy, and pleasure in this world God made. The word
śāmaḥ, "joy," "celebrate," "take pleasure in," is one of the most common
words of the psalm. This is not an austere portrait of the "works" of God.
There is delight in the world God made and in contemplating it. As a specific instance of the pleasure of creation, wine is to make the heart happy
(*śāmaḥ*). But the psalmist makes this judgment more generally about the
creation with the blessing-wish, "May the Lord take pleasure in (*śāmaḥ*)
his works" (v. 31), and follows that with the personal declaration, "I take
pleasure in (*śāmaḥ*) the Lord" (v. 34b). The goal of creation, in its details
and in its whole, is to provide pleasure and delight.

There are two specific ways in which the creation as a place of pleasure is signaled. One is in the repeated identification of the trees as the locale for birds. Indeed, the ultimate purpose of fresh water is to nurture the birds so that they may sing! The singing of the birds is one of the more obvious pleasures of the created order available to all and irresistible to the human senses. One of the answers to the why of creation is so that birds can sing and, by inference, that other creatures can enjoy their song.

A second way in which this point is made is in the portrayal of Leviathan as God's rubber duck in the great ocean bathtub, as it were.[9] Elsewhere, Leviathan is a terrible, fierce, and intimidating sea creature (e.g., Job 41). But the world God made, whether earth or sea, is not Jurassic Park. It is a place where birds can sing and monsters can play in the great sea. With all that water, God needed something to enjoy it, literally to "play" (*śāḥaq*) in it. The text conjures up in our minds an image of Loch Ness, which everyone hopes really does contain a Leviathan playing in its depths!

One cannot romanticize this picture of a playful world, however. Nature is also there, red in tooth and claw. Indeed, the psalm understands the "preying" of the lion as a kind of "praying" (v. 21). The lions' roar for their prey is paralleled by a line that speaks of their seeking their food from God. The lion's kill is an answer to prayer in this portrayal of God's created order. The chain of nature, dependent upon other animals for their food, is assumed. God's provision of food is extended throughout the natural world, but it incorporates the understanding of a food chain that pits animal against animal (cf. Job 38:39–41).

6. The natural world is to be understood as *a home for the sensate beings God created*, creatures who *share the world together*. Adam, human being, is referred to in the midst of the other animals. There is a clear distinction between humankind and the different animals, but they are talked about in parallel ways as creatures of the world God has made. Humankind assumes not a central or special place but an integral part of the whole. Human and beast are paralleled in God's provision of sustenance (v. 14). God's creating of light and darkness, sun and moon, provides times for the animals to prowl for food (night) and human beings to work for theirs (day). Even in verses 27–30, there is an inclusiveness to the created order that transcends the distinctions and joins all the sensate beings in a shared experience. "*All*" (human and beast) look to God for their food (v. 27). That "all" is the plural subject of every verb that follows. All are dismayed

---

[9] I am indebted to Jon Levenson for this marvelous contemporary translation of the picture of Leviathan sporting in the ocean.

when God's face is hidden. All return to dust. All are created by the spirit of God.

There is thus no language of domination, no *imago dei* that sets human beings apart from or puts them in rule over the other beasts. This rich, beautiful, and orderly world includes both kinds of living beings. They belong together and their provision is God's work, which is as fully there for the one category as for the other. Further, one is conscious of the plants, mountains, and rivers as necessary habitats for the sensate beings. They have their place, their purpose in God's order precisely to provide homes for God's creatures. While bypassing all the complex issues of the interrelationships among these "creatures," the psalm assumes a world in which they are all present, all in their place, all doing their work, and all provided for by God's goodness.

7. The text begs for some reflection on *bread and wine*. It understands both elements as provisions of God in the creation, bread for our strength and our life and wine for our joy and relaxation. Here and elsewhere wine and beer are considered God's good gifts for our enjoyment of life. Noah is identified as the one who brought us "relief from our work and from the toil of our hands" (Gen 5:21). How did he do that? Gen 9:20 states he was the first to plant a vineyard and so provided wine that "gladdens the heart." Noah then gets drunk in the very next verse, and we have the messy little story of his son's disrespect. The Bible knows about this outcome of beer and wine and warns about the way in which God's good gifts can create havoc in their misuse (e.g., Prov 31:4–5).

This text, therefore, reminds us of something very fundamental about God's provision of both our *sustenance* and our *enjoyment*. It is surely no accident that bread and wine, which are the elements of life in this text, are also the "elements" of the church in its sacramental life.

8. Finally, one must recognize that if there are significant resonances and differences between this psalm and Gen 1–2, it seems that Gen 3 is also lurking in the background as the psalm comes to a close with the prayer: "Let sinners be consumed from the earth, and let the wicked be no more" (v. 35a).

We know now that what Gen 3 speaks about is real, and one cannot speak about the creation without a realization that there is a blemish on this wonderful world God has made. It has nothing to do with the way God created it. It has everything to do with the way the human creature responds to it. The "sinners" and the "wicked" can be any who sin, who disobey the divine commands. The context, however, makes us think of any who violate the creation, who take human life, who interfere with God's good provision for each creature, who tear down the trees in which the birds sing, who destroy Leviathan playing in the ocean, who poke holes in the heavenly tent, who let loose the forces of nature that God has brought under control in the very creation of a world. None of that is explicit in this brief concluding imprecation, but the total character of the psalm cautions us against defining the categories of "sinner" and "wicked" too narrowly when we confine ourselves to their apparent reference in the laments of the Psalter.

The Psalm in its Literary and Theological Context

One should not conclude an examination of Ps 104 without some attention to its context. There are explicit indicators that this psalm is to be read in direct connection to the psalms that surround it. The most obvious of these are the *inclusio* "Bless the Lord, O my soul," which occurs not only at the beginning and ending of Ps 104 but also in identical positions in Ps 103. Such a duplication of beginning and conclusion can hardly be accidental or insignificant. That point is underscored, however, when one realizes that this sentence appears nowhere in scripture except as a bracket around each of these psalms. The strong tie of Ps 104 to the psalm that precedes it is further suggested by the presence of a superscription *lĕdāwîd*, "for David," at the beginning of Ps 103 and by the lack of superscription at the beginning of Ps 104 to separate it from the preceding psalm.[10] Furthermore, Ps 103 incorporates the thematic note of Ps 104 ("who satisfies you with good as long as you live," v. 5; cf. 104:28 and other verses) and concludes with a call to "all his works" to bless the Lord, "works" whose detailed description then follows in Ps 104.[11]

The intertextual connections extend to the psalms that follow Ps 104. The "hallelujah" at the end of Ps 104 serves to link it with the psalms that follow, which either begin or end with the same word, at least through Ps 107. The absence of any superscription between Ps 104 and the ones that follow through Ps 107 further links these psalms together. The conclusion to Book IV obviously creates a kind of break between Pss 106 and 107, but

---

[10] In the Psalms Scroll from Qumran Cave 11, fragment E has the beginning of Ps 104 and, like the LXX, includes a superscription *ldwd*. Among other fragments containing the beginning of Ps 104, one seems to have this superscription while another does not. The tradition, therefore, is not unanimous on the continuous reading of Pss 103 and 104. See Flint, *The Dead Sea Psalms Scrolls and the Book of Psalms*, 96.

[11] For further discussion of some of the linguistic connections between Pss 103 and 104 see Norbert Lohfink and Erich Zenger, *Der Gott Israels und die Völker: Untersuchungen zum Jesajabuch und zu den Psalmen* (Stuttgarter Bibelstudien, 154; Stuttgart: Verlag Katholisches Bibelwerk GmbH, 1994), 172–173. They note, for example, that only near the end of Ps 103 and near the beginning of Ps 104 do we have the expression "his ministers" (*mĕšārĕtāw*).

it has often been noted that the connections between these two psalms are strong enough to bridge the separation effected by the benediction.[12]

There are also quite specific vocabulary links between the conclusion of Ps 104 and Ps 105.[13] At the end of Ps 104, the psalmist says, "May my *meditation* (*śîḥî*) be pleasing to him" (v. 34). Then, at the beginning of Ps 105, the psalmist calls for the community to "meditate on (*śîḥû*) all his wonderful works" (v. 2). The act referred to probably involves speaking out loud. I would suggest that the meditation of which Ps 104 speaks is the poem itself, the praise of God that is sung in the psalm. So also the meditation of Ps 105 is the praise of God's wonderful works. The term "wonderful works" (*niplā᾿ôt*) looks backward and forward, backward into God's wonderful works of creation in Ps 104 and forward into the wonderful works and acts for Israel in Ps 105. Further, at the end of Ps 104, there is the sequence of verbs "sing" (*śîr*), "sing praise" (*zāmar*), "meditate" or "tell" (*śîḥ*), and "rejoice" (*śāmaḥ*) to express the psalmist's intention to praise (vv. 33–34). The verbs then follow the same sequence in Ps 105:2-3 with the verb *hithallēl* inserted before the last one. This is the only time in the Psalter or anywhere else in the Bible where this combination appears.

What then is the meaning of these associations? They are several. Most important is the creation of one of several pairs of "twin psalms." The poetic praise of God as creator and sustainer of the world, consequently, must be read and heard with the preceding thanksgiving to God for compassion, mercy, and forgiveness. If the works of God are celebrated in Ps 104, it is the steadfast love of the Lord that is celebrated in Ps 103. One cannot be sung without the other. Similarly, in Ps 145 praise of God for and by "your works" (vv. 4, 10) is joined with thanksgiving that "the Lord is gracious and merciful, slow to anger and abounding in steadfast love" (v. 8; cf. 103:8). Moreover, the declaration that the Lord is "good to all" (v. 9; cf. 104:28) is set alongside the claim that "his compassion is over all *his works*" (v. 9; cf. 103:4, 8, 13; 104:13, 24, 31). In similar fashion, Ps 33:4–7 joins the creative works of the Lord with the works of righteousness and justice. As "the earth is full of your creatures" (Ps 104:24), so also "the earth is full of the steadfast love of the Lord" (Ps 33:5).

---

[12] That is particularly suggested by the way Ps 107 begins with the same formulaic sentence as Ps 106, part of which also begins Ps 105: "O give thanks to the Lord for he is good; for his steadfast love endures forever." But the next verses of Ps 107 (vv. 2–3) also serve to answer the cry that concludes Ps 106 (v. 47). The cry to the Lord to save and gather the people from among the nations is responded to in Ps 107 by reference to those who have been redeemed and gathered from the lands.

[13] For a detailed analysis of possible structural and linguistic connections between Pss 104 and 105, see Pierre Auffret, *Essai sur la Structure Litterarie du Psaume 105* (Biblische Notizen Beihefte, 3; München, 1985), 109–127.

In each of these instances, the community praises the Lord for the works of creation and the works of redemption, for satisfying the earth with good and filling it with steadfast love. The "works" of the Lord are manifold and complex: creating, sustaining, providing, redeeming, forgiving, righteous, and just. One may not escape in any kind of retreat to a cosmic praise removed from the realia of individual and communal history from the realities, the hurts and wounds, the sins and injustices of this life. But the one who redeems and heals the sufferer, whether one or many, is also the one who stretched out the heavens and provides the continuities of the universe's existence. This joining of creation and history, of the universal and the particular, in God's "works" is then underscored as Ps 104 leads on into the "national" hymns of Pss 105 and 106. The wonderful works of the Lord that fill the earth with its creatures also bring salvation to and judgment on the chosen community of Israel. Ps 104 in its literary context evokes a sustained "meditation" upon the God who is all in all, whose works encompass all of history and creation, and whose care of the wounds of the faithful is comparable to God's care of the animals of earth and sea. Such meditation can only end in praise: "Bless the Lord, O my soul! Hallelujah!"

12. The Hermeneutics of Imprecation

The testing place of theology is in its dealing with difficult issues. When tragedy and trouble strike or when things do not make sense in one's life or in the world generally, even those who have not bothered to think about the faith find themselves forced to become theologians, or to call upon theologians – often in the proper garb of the pastor. One way, therefore, in which theology serves the church is by taking up difficult matters of faith and life, to illumine both by thinking critically, historically, faithfully, and prayerfully about scripture.[1] Some of these "hard" matters that confront Christian faith arise from the Bible itself. One of the most obvious is the *hostile and harsh attitude expressed toward one's enemies*, especially in some of the Old Testament texts,[2] notably the stories of the conquest of Canaan and the imprecatory, or curse, psalms. The second of these two genres, *prayers of imprecation*, is the case I am taking up here to see what possibilities lie before us for dealing with this difficult issue.[3] As an entree to the subject, I propose to take up one of the most familiar and most terrifying psalms of the Old Testament: Ps 137.[4]

[1]By the waters of Babylon,
   there we sat down, yea we wept
   when we remembered Zion.

---

[1] Exemplary of this fact is the way in which denominations set up councils and committees of theologians to deal with difficult issues, such as sexuality, abortion, the authority of Scripture, and the like.

[2] One must be careful about assuming that this is only an Old Testament issue. The New Testament also has its expressions of hostility and curse toward opponents who are seen as the enemy, as one sees in some of the epistles and Revelation.

[3] For a helpful effort to show how the "morality" of the conquest of Canaan may already have been an apologetic issue in the redaction of the book of Joshua, see now Lawson Stone, "Ethical and Apologetic Tendencies in the Redaction of the Book of Joshua," *CBQ* 53 (1991), 25–36.

[4] The most recent extended treatment of the imprecatory psalms is Erich Zenger, *A God of Vengeance? Understanding the Psalms of Divine Wrath* (Louisville: Westminster John Knox Press, 1996). This book includes a brief treatment of Ps 137 and some broader hermeneutical reflections. A full treatment of imprecation in the Psalter would need to look at a number of other psalms, as Zenger does. In the more limited confines of this essay, I have chosen what may be the most difficult and disturbing of all the imprecatory psalms.

²On the willows⁵ in its midst
    we hung up our lyres.

³For there our captors demanded
    of us songs
    and our tormentors mirth,
    "Sing for us one of the songs of Zion!"
⁴How could we sing the LORD's song
    on foreign soil.
⁵If I forget you, O Jerusalem,
    may my right hand ...⁶
⁶May my tongue cling to the roof of my mouth,
    if I do not remember you,
    if I do not set Jerusalem
    as the peak of my joy.
⁷Remember, O LORD, against the Edomites
    the day of Jerusalem,
    how they said, "Tear it down! Tear it down!
    Down to its foundations"
⁸O daughter Babylon, you devastator!⁷
    Blessed shall be the one who pays you back
    what you have done to us.
⁹Blessed shall be the one who seizes and dashes
    your children against the rocks.

The very familiarity of this psalm is somewhat surprising in that most of the psalms containing curses against the enemy – whether in large or small part – are not generally held in mind or get much attention in the teaching, preaching, and liturgy of the church, precisely because they are troublesome, a dimension of the Bible that we wish were not there. The *problem* of the curses is kept before us, or at least held in the back of our minds, but not the particular psalms. Ps 137, therefore, is something of an exception.

This is an exceptional psalm for at least two reasons. The first is the power and poignancy of the first two-thirds of the psalm. The plaintive, despairing cry, "How can we sing the Lord's song in a strange land?" tugs at the heart strings and places this psalm in the life and death reality of ex-

---

⁵ The tree may be a poplar that looks like a willow.

⁶ The text is doubtful at this point. The Massoretic Text has *tiškaḥ,* which would appear to mean "may you forget". This is dubious, and the versions have passive forms and the like. Other proposals, including transposing the last two letters of the root have led to a reading that is fairly common in the translations: "wither." Klaus Seybold has candidly, and accurately acknowledged that it is unclear what happens to the right hand (*Die Psalmen,* "Handbuch zum Alten Testament" I/15 [Tübingen: J.C.B. Mohr, 1996], 510).

⁷ The form in the Hebrew is passive, but the active is more likely and is attested in some textual witnesses, though it may be *lectio facilior* in this case. See the discussion in Leslie C. Allen, "Psalms 101–150," *Word Biblical Commentary* (Waco: Word Books, 1983), 237.

ile.[8] Most of the psalms are difficult to locate in a particular historical moment. While referential openness offers rich opportunities for the hermeneutics of the Psalms,[9] this exception to that historical openness, where the voices of the oppressed singers of the psalm cry out from a particular situation of oppression well known to us, evokes a sense of understanding and empathy because we "know" what this psalm is about. In many other cases, we puzzle over the references of the imagery and the petitions. Here, however, the concrete situation is evident. We are drawn into solidarity with those who wept by the rivers of Babylon. The imagery of the willows on which were hung the harps and the picture of Babylonian tormentors taunting the Judean captives reinforce the emotional pull of the song. The reader is drawn into the story with all the sympathies on the side of the "we" who pray this lament.

Even the zealous response of the psalmists to the taunt strikes a chord in the reader-listener. The tenacious commitment not to let go of the memory of home is something known to many who are caught far from home and unable to return. The singing voice may be silenced in tears, but there is no forgetting. Not to be able to sing Zion's songs does not mean that Zion is ever forgotten. Memories of home keep this community going while it is in exile. The reader of the psalm knows that Zion is a *topos* for home, and every reader comprehends and joins with the community that is cut off from home but determined that as long as breath shall last, the particular memories of what it is like back there will be kept to the fore, held on to as the only treasure possible in a foreign land.

The second reason this particular curse psalm is so familiar to us when others are not is the powerful and terrible image of the babies being dashed against the rocks. It is a disturbing image in every way, a picture of violence at its worst: *killing, brutal killing of the most innocent and defenseless*. The repulsiveness of the image paradoxically makes it stick in our mind. But this subject matter is not exceptional in scripture. Brutal killing of babies and ripping open pregnant women appear not infrequently in scripture (2 Kgs 8:12; Isa 13:16; Hos 10:14; 14:1; [Eng. 13:16]; Nah 3:10; and cf. Jesus in Luke 19:44). Indeed, several times, this is an act or threat of *God*, and in Luke 19 Jesus announces the future crushing of Jerusalem

---

[8] This essay focuses on hermeneutical issues posed by Ps 137. The reader is invited to consult the standard commentaries for exegetical details. The psalm may well come from the exile, but the very form of verses 1–3 and the repeated and emphatic "there" (*šām*) of verses 1 and 3 suggest that the speaker is looking back on captivity in Babylon from a later vantage point.

[9] On the hermeneutical possibilities inherent in the historical openness of the Psalms, see Patrick D. Miller, *Interpreting the Psalms* (Philadelphia: Fortress, 1986), chap. 2.

and its children. Such texts, when encountered, also repel us, but they are not generally known and thus have not posed the problem that Ps 137 does. So the hermeneutical problem with Ps 137 is not confined to the subject matter even though such subject matter will always pose hermeneutical problems.[10] One must go further, therefore, with this text and explore other features of the psalm and our reading of it that pose the hermeneutical problem of this text.

For one thing, this is *poetry* in all its *power and evocative possibility*. Few accounts of the exile in Scripture are better known than this and none are able to resonate with a distant audience as well as this one. But one needs to be on guard at this point. The poetry of Ps 137 sucks in the reader inescapably, and it may not be possible to get back out. The second part of the psalm, with its familiar question at the beginning of verse 4 – How could we sing the Lord's song on foreign soil? – leads into verses that we may applaud. But we should not do that without realizing that they are also imprecatory, that is, a *self-imprecation*. The beginning of the curse form is already present in verses 5–6. These verses are an apostrophe to Jerusalem. The zeal and love for Jerusalem is what we hear. But the poet seems to be saying, in effect, "If I should forget you for a moment, let me be like a person with a stroke, unable to speak or move one side of my body." Empathy with the "we" and the "I" of the psalm means a kind of identity with its vehemence that is disturbing, to say the least.

Another feature of the hermeneutical problematic of Ps 137 lies in the combination of our *familiarity* with the text and the *incongruity* effected by the presence of the repulsive violence theme alongside other more compelling and attracting words of anguish in the face of oppression. The same happens in the reading and hearing of Ps 139.[11] Unfamiliar and unused texts may have similar words, but their unfamiliarity means they do not pose the same kind of hermeneutical problem – for example, Pss 10 and 109. Pss 137 and 139, as we begin to read them, draw us in. At one and the same time, we are attracted and repelled. Only certain texts do that for us. Many of the violence texts of the Old Testament and other imprecatory psalms are simply objectionable and have little "play" for us. In the case of Ps 137, however, a unified text engages our horizon in very contradictory

---

[10] As, for example, when we encounter texts that speak of the *ḥērem* or ban, the utter destruction of the seven nations of Canaan, in some instances at the command of the Lord (e.g., Deut 20:17) or the Lord's servant Moses (Deut 7:1–6).

[11] I have suggested a way of interpreting Ps 139 and its imprecations in *Interpreting the Psalms*, 144–153. The remarks there about how the hatred of enemies and the imprecation against them is to be understood theologically supplement the hermeneutical suggestions made here

ways. What is happening in that contradiction and how does this clash of attraction and revulsion happen? Is there any possibility that the unity of the text needs to be carried forward in our appropriation of it so that we also read the whole thing in some meaningful fashion? Or is it that the unity of the ancient text and the contradiction in our reaction are simply incompatible realities, and we have to explore the abrasiveness and friction between them? These are two quite different hermeneutical outcomes. The following observations seek to explore both of them.

We start with the recognition that the Old Testament itself seems to identify this as violence at its worst. The reader of this text – and others like it – cannot read it simply as one more example of a violence-ridden tribal society. The text itself lifts up this kind of act as the extreme form of the destruction of a community. (This is not individual violence; it is community violence.) Here, therefore, there is a sense in which the Scriptures serve not to perpetuate violence, as might seem to be the case by a surface reading and a surface hermeneutic. Rather, they contribute to the exposure and unmasking of violence.[12] The text mirrors the violence that is universal and exposes the violence that is a part of the society and of its God in the context of the announcement of a counter-society and a counter-God.[13] The discernment of such subtle but real exposure is, at least in part, the significance of Rene Girard's work, his identification of the violence that is so prevalent in the Old Testament and the implicit criticism that comes from its counter-voices and from the gospel.[14]

What I am suggesting is that within scripture itself there are explicit and implicit criticisms of the inclination to violence expressed by the "I" of Ps 137 that force a strong hermeneutic of criticism upon us, a critical hermeneutic that comes not from an external source but from the canon itself.

---

[12] For an elaboration of the way the Old Testament works to unmask the human propensity to violence, see Norbert Lohfink, "Der gewalttätige Gott des Alten Testaments und die Suche nach einer gewaltfreien Gesellschaft," in *Jahrbuch für Biblische Theologie*, 2 (1987): 106–136. Cf. among other works by the same author, "Gewaltlosigkeit nach dem Evangelium angesichts der gesellschaftlichen Verankerung der Gewalt," in *Probleme des Friedens* (Frankfurt am Main: Pax-Christi-Bewegung. Deutsches Sekretariat, 1986); "Der 'heilige Krieg' und der 'Bann' in der Bibel," *Internationale katholische Zeitschrift COMMUNIO*, 18 (1989): 104–112; and ",Gewalt' als Thema alttestamentlicher Forschung," in *Gewalt und Gewaltlosigkeit im Alten Testament*, "Questiones Disputatae," 96, ed. N. Lohfink (Freiburg: Herder, 1983), 15–50.

[13] Lohfink, "Der gewalttätige Gott."

[14] The most famous of Girard's works is *Violence and the Sacred* (Baltimore: The Johns Hopkins University Press, 1979). Among those works that have looked most closely at the Scriptures in the light of Girard's work, one may cite especially Raymund Schwager, S.J., *Must There Be Scapegoats? Violence and Redemption in the Bible* (San Francisco: Harper & Row, 1987).

That hermeneutic of suspicion is so strong that we have to ask if it is not the dominant outcome of the reading of the whole of these texts we call scripture. That is, such a text as this is read in the light of other *texts* and of *the whole*. Those *other texts* include some that are similar to Ps 137 in their disclosure of violence wished, announced, and enacted. As such texts – including some from the New Testament – mount up before us, they can expose the violence and make us uncomfortable with it.[15] Still other texts speak against the violence – including, prominently, some from the Old Testament, such as the Isaianic visions of peace and the absence of war and hostility (Isa 2:2–5 // Mic 4:1-5; 11:1–9 [but note v. 4c]), the Psalmic vision of the Lord's destruction of the implements of war (Ps 46:8–9 [Heb. 9–10]), the prayer for the peace of Jerusalem (Ps 122) and wisdom's pragmatic approach to the enemy (Prov 25:21–22).[16] The *whole* of the canon presents the larger picture of God's way and God's purpose from the beginning to the end.[17] That whole, however, cannot be read simply in a linear development or progression. In the midst of the literature associated with the Second Isaiah, for example, where the way of the Suffering Servant who fulfills God's purpose as the one who bears the violence of humanity on behalf of humanity, we encounter Isa 34 and its account of the bloody sword of the Lord. And one of the texts that resonates most with Isa 34 is the Book of Revelation at the end of the New Testament.

In Ps 137, we are drawn to the lament over human and communal suffering, the depiction of oppression, of persons exiled and tormented, of the loss of everything dear and meaningful. What the rest of the psalm does, at a minimum, is to ask if the clash or contradiction we experience in reading the psalm is the result of a sentimental appropriation of the first part so that we do not really know the depth of the psalmist's torment. To find the psalm as a whole both intelligible and meaningful requires that our romantic and sentimental appropriation of the first part be abandoned. These words have their power and truthfulness only within the devastating experience to which they point.

---

[15] Alternatively, the history of the church's use of such texts has also demonstrated the possibility that they may inure the community to violence. There is no guarantee that the hermeneutic being described at this point will operate automatically anymore than is the case with any hermeneutical proposal.

[16] It is worth remembering that Paul's famous words against vengeance in Rom 12:19–20 are built around quotations from the Old Testament that he appropriates for his teaching on the subject (Deut 32:35; Prov 25:21–22; cf. Prov 20:22; 24:29).

[17] For a contemporary presentation of such an understanding of scripture, see Kendall Soulen, *The God of Israel and Christian Theology* (Minneapolis: Fortress, 1996).

I have referred to the *memory* theme in the psalm (vv. 1, 5, 7) and particularly the memory of home, Jerusalem (vv. 1, 3, 5, 6, 7). It is especially in regard to that theme that one risks sentimentalizing and missing the force of that memory, so tenacious that it can evoke a self-curse against its ever being diminished (v. 5). It is indeed memory that keeps this community going, but it is one that also asks God to remember in judgment. And even though the terrible blessing/curse of the final verses is not an explicit invocation of divine action, it is borne on the waves of memory, the memory of what was done to Jerusalem and of Babylonians who are remembered only in the categories experience has provided: captor, tormentor, and devastator. That is the memory of rage, and the reader does not suddenly encounter it in the last verses. It is there from the beginning. The depth of that rage is even greater if, as is likely, this prayer was first articulated *after* the captivity in Babylon was over and is thus a "look back in anger."[18]

At the same time, one is free to ask – if not forced to do so – if even in awareness of the unity of the psalm and the way the end arises out of the beginning, one ought still to experience a contradiction, to ask if there is not a perduring abrasiveness between the two parts of the psalm so that once again criticism rather than retrieval is the last hermeneutical word. There are all sorts of things in scripture, Christology, and the experience of the Christian community – Jesus' words about enemies and those who persecute you, Paul's words about vengeance in Rom 12, the meaning of the death of Christ, the experience of Christian martyrdom, the prayer of Stephen (Acts 7:60), and the like – that will not easily permit our dissolution of the contradiction effected by the psalm.

The hermeneutical problem posed by this text is in no small measure because it is a *prayer*. That is a large part of why Pss 137 and 139 create a visceral reaction beyond that of other texts. Such horrendous prayer for the brutal killing of the children of one's enemies seems to defile the character of prayer itself.[19] But the *form* of the text, however, much that form creates

---

[18] The phrase is taken from the title of John Osborne's play.

[19] In a seminary class on prayer in scripture, I asked the members of the class to prepare their own imprecatory prayers. Three things happened most noticeably when the group met to discuss what they had written:

a) Many simply could not bring themselves to write such prayers.

b) The effort to do so and the effort to talk about or share the prayers they had prepared was an extremely emotional occasion.

c) Virtually everyone who attempted the task did not present a prayer of imprecation against his or her own enemies but offered prayers of rage and solidarity with others who had suffered, for example, women raped or abused. They were not personal supplications but intercessions in community and shared anger at the assaults that somebody had made on another person or persons. In this respect, I would regard their efforts as appropriate outcomes

problems, may also be the only way in which the text can have any possibility *for us*, that is, is in any way capable of being appropriated. We can
read reports of violence all through the Old Testament and be relatively
unmoved by them. But here is a text that speaks in the first person (singular and plural), one that belongs to the prayer book and hymnbook of the
church and thus invites our joining in. By its form the text blocks our dis-
tancing of ourselves from it. We may pass by other texts relatively easily.
Here we are either drawn in to say these words or we have to make a decision to reject them. It is comparable to a congregation standing to recite
the Creed. One has to do something with the text at that point. The partici-
pant is drawn into the community of recitation or must decide consciously
to drop out of it. Such a sharp alternative does not confront us with every
reading of scripture in worship. But that is exactly why this text creates
problems for the contemporary community. We are repelled by and wish to
dissociate ourselves from an expression – blessings on a baby-killer – in a
text to which we cannot otherwise sit loose and from which we cannot easily dissociate ourselves because to read it is to join in with the original
speakers. The only simple way to respond is to cut that Gordian knot, as
some hymnbook Psalters have done, and excise the final three verses of the
psalm, allowing the congregation to appropriate the attracting and attractive part without having to face its outcome in a rage that already boils under the surface of the first part of the psalm.

Paradoxically it may also be the form of the psalm, that is, its character
as prayer, that opens it to the contemporary reader of faith. For one can
turn the whole matter around. Rather than asking if we could ever justifia-
bly pray such a prayer as this, assuming that the issue is simply a matter of
choice, of rational decision, we might better ask whether such *thoughts* as
expressed here have any other permissible context than *conversation with
God*, from whom no secrets are hid, from whom no rage or anger can be
concealed. The unrestrained, justifiable but not justifiable, thoughts are let
loose – but within a particular framework. In this sense, the rage and bru-
tality are not allowed to go public.[20] They are real in this psalm, and there
are terrible moments when they are real in human life. To pray such rage is
at one and the same time to let it go and to hold it back. It is not now a part
of our dealing with our neighbor-enemy. It is a part of our life with God.[21]

---

of their praying as Christians, that is, as those whose prayers for help are now primarily inter-
cessory prayers for others in trouble and distress.

[20] Compare the rage of many of the victims of the Oklahoma City bombing, who shouted
and wept for joy at the conviction of Timothy McVeigh and testified in detail about the bru-
tality of their children's deaths in order to try to convince the jury to sentence him to death.

[21] Jeremiah's laments are a classic example of such letting go of the rage and holding it
back in imprecatory prayer that restricts the anger to the interior life with God.

The prayer thus may become a vehicle for the inner fury of the oppressed, a way – to use the modern expression – of dealing with one's anger. There are other ways, as the Bible well knows (Gen 4:7). But one should recognize that this is a fairly narrow range of hermeneutical possibility. It is precisely not a matter of universal applicability but of limited use, as the ferocity of the psalm gives voice to and channels the ferocity of the soul, turning the fallen countenance that has retaliation and murder in its eyes – or calls for execution – into a raging prayer that finally leaves the matter where Moses (Deut 32:35) and Paul (Rom 12:18–21) both tell us it belongs – in the hands of God.

Finally, I would suggest three things about the place of such a prayer as Ps 137 in the worship life of the community, where our hermeneutical decisions come to life and expression:

1. The liturgical and musical expression of these thoughts can have its place in those traditions and practices where there is a *lectio continua* use of the Psalms. In such a regular on-going reading of the whole Psalter, or at least large portions of it, the imprecations of Ps 137 – and prayers like it – are placed in a larger context and not simply read or sung by themselves. They are abrasive pieces of a larger whole and not lifted up to a special place or made a point of focus by reading them by themselves. The rage is clear, but it is set in the context of all the psalms and the constant listening of the congregation to the images, the deep emotions, the hyperbole – to all the strong and intense language of the Psalms. Such a liturgical context appropriately relativizes the ferocity of the speaker and sets the contradictory responses of the contemporary hearer alongside other experiences of ambiguity, abrasive language, and unexpected or jarring movements of thought. The rest of the psalms give the reader a handle on the white heat of the psalm so that it neither burns unexpectedly nor is it suddenly dropped.

2. It is also possible that the *musical setting* of such a psalm can let the rage come forth and deal with it musically – hearing it, venting it, restraining it, and letting counter tones have their say. One thinks, for example, of Leonard Bernstein's musical rendition of the raging of the nations against the Lord's anointed (Ps 2) in the "Chichester Psalms." The rage is given full expression in the rapid repetition of *lāmmâ rāgĕšû*, "Why do they throng tumultuously?" (Ps 2:1) by the male voices, but they are finally overcome, controlled, and muted by the single melodic counter tenor's repeated *yhwh rōʾî lōʾ ʾeḥsār*, "The Lord is my shepherd, I shall not want" (Ps 23:1). When the Psalms are set to music, the imprecatory elements are given a context – in music and lyrics – for hearing and appropriating them. That is what happens, for example, with Ps 137 in the *Psalter Hymnal* of

the Christian Reformed Church. The final line of the hymn makes just the theological move suggested above by drawing in from elsewhere in scripture the words "Vengeance shall come from God our Lord." That is, the prayer for the destruction of Babylon and the brutal slaughter of its babies is placed under the recognition that such judgment belongs in the context of the loving and just purposes of God, albeit in this case with the emphasis on justice but knowing and assuming the proclivity of God, the leaning of God toward a loving mercy (Exod 34:6–7; Ps 30:5 [Heb. v. 6]; Isa 54:7–8). Vengeance is to be manifest only in God's vindication of God's purpose, not in our revenge against those who have hurt us.

3. When all is said and done, however, we still have difficulty singing "Babylon great, your seed be smashed" (*Psalter Hymnal*). The hymn's euphemistic rendition of the verse, "Happy shall be the one who takes your little ones and dashes them against the rocks" does not help much. At this point, I remember that the Psalms are to be read as critically as any other part of the scripture. The worshiping congregation receives these psalms from its Lord and in the context of his instruction and way. It cannot draw back from that. The words of rage in the psalms do not easily mellow into pleasant and uplifting hymns. So let them stay words of rage in the dialogue of the angry sufferer with God or in our angry suffering with others. Let us not easily baptize them into Christian prayer in those regular acts of worship through which the congregation expresses its faith in God and listens for a word from the Lord.

13. Prayer and Worship[1]

The contemporary study of the Psalter has had as one of its major emphases the rediscovery of the lament psalms and their pastoral relevance. The importance of that is hardly to be overestimated and stands at the center of my own study of the psalms and more broadly of the prayers of scripture. Yet, there remains a kind of tension between prayer and worship. The prayer for help or the lament has its primary focus outside of worship while the hymns of praise are a central part of the community's public worship of God. One frequently hears it suggested or recommended that the lament, as a cry of distress of one in trouble, be brought into the heart of our worship. That, in fact, rarely happens. I want to explore some of the reasons that was, and largely remains, the case as a way of thinking about the liturgical and communal dimensions of prayer, on the one hand, and the pastoral and individual dimensions of prayer, on the other.

Let me, then, set forth a thesis for exploration and development and offer a text by which to explore and develop it:

> The prayer for help, or the lament prayer, is not a feature of Christian worship to be heard by others. It is a feature of human existence to be heard by God. The Lord is addressed; the pastor may listen in. The community is not there. It is part of the problem. The prayer for help is spontaneous, unplanned, wrenched from the experience of pain, but it is not formless. Its aim is to secure help. Its resolution is in words and deeds that transform the situation.

That is the thesis. It does not fit all the data, but it is sufficiently evident to merit further exploration.

The laments of scripture are the preeminent petitionary prayer of the Old Testament. They have their setting in life not in the service of worship of the congregation but in the exigencies of the human condition. One has only to survey the many prayers of persons in the stories of scripture to realize how clearly the prayer for help is a cry of distress that arises out of human pain and not out of liturgical movement. They take place not *in* the community but because there *is no* community. They bear testimony to the

---

[1] This essay is presented in the same form as in its oral presentation. The only documentation included is where specific reference is made to particular scholars.

breakdown of human relationships. Their context is not the gathering of the people but the isolation from others of the one in pain. The voices of the community are heard in the prayers of pain and hurt, but they are not the voices of those who pray. They are rather the voices of mockery and taunt, of rejection and challenge. They do not address God in behalf of the one undone. Rather they ask in taunting voice, "Where is your God?" (Ps 42:3, NRSV). Whether such voices truly speak such words, the one who prays in pain hears such questions as clearly implicitly as explicitly. When the many voices say to the psalmist, "There is no help for you in God"[2] (Ps 3:2, NRSV), they speak the deepest fear of the one who prays, a fear that the prayer for help is itself designed to attack and hold at bay.

The story of Hannah in 1 Sam 1 is instructive in this regard. Her situation is exemplary of those individuals who cry out to God in great hurt and need. Barren in a marriage with a husband who loves her but is also married to another woman who is richly fertile, Hannah experiences the shame of barrenness in a world where the birth of a child was a woman's defining moment. The story places her at the occasion of the family's participation in an annual festival at the sanctuary at Shiloh. However, for her this is not a festive moment. It is an occasion of shame and isolation and loneliness. We are told that whenever the family went up for this celebration, El-kanah's other wife Peninnah would taunt Hannah about her barrenness. The narrative paints a picture of a woman shamed and depressed, crying and refusing – or unable – to eat. Finally, she goes into the sanctuary, and we are told in v. 10, "she was deeply distressed [lit. "her soul was bitter"] and prayed to the Lord and wept bitterly" (NRSV).

Her trouble is personal, social, and theological, as Claus Westermann has reminded us is so often the case in these prayers for help.[3] The symptomatology of the hurt is not simple but complex. She is in deep personal distress, crying, not eating, depressed, and ashamed. That distress also has external causation. Twice the narrative says that the Lord had closed her womb (1 Sam 1:5–6). It does not comment on that, but it lets us know that the distress this woman has experienced was in some fashion God's doing, and we wonder why as much as she would have. If one interpreter of the text (1 Sam 1:6) is correct, it reads at this point: "Moreover her rival [and the term there is the same one that the psalms of lament use to speak of the lamenter's adversary] used to provoke her to anger, so that she would

---

[2] Syriac: Hebrew, "him."

[3] Claus Westermann, *The Psalms: Structure, Content, and Message* (Minneapolis: Augsburg, 1980), 56–61; idem, *Praise and Lament in the Psalms* (Richmond: John Knox, 1981), 169–194, 267–269.

complain aloud that Yahweh had closed her womb."[4] In that translation, we come to comprehend her sense of being beset by God and by the other wife in the family.

One could say much about how the Hannah situation shows us the complexity of suffering, how it helps us see in specific and concrete ways what it is that the prayers of the Psalter are doing when they give expression to laments of sickness and divine abandonment and the attacks of enemies.

In this context, however, I want to pay particular attention to where Hannah is and what happens when she prays. Her prayer is "before the Lord"[5] (v. 9, NRSV). To utter her prayer, she has gone to the sanctuary, that is, specifically to the place where the Lord may be found. Hannah's coming before the Lord, however, is not necessarily an occasion of formal worship by the congregation. Indeed, it would seem most clearly not to be that if one pays attention to the locale and response of the priest, Eli. For the priest is sitting on a chair or bench by the door of the sanctuary. He is not involved in the leadership of worship. Indeed he is outside the context of worship. Four things are evident when we look at the priest-pastor in this regard.

First, his involvement with this woman in pain and distress and his involvement with her prayer are not in the context of the community's worship. That involvement is in the context of the pastoral office. Prayer and worship, not prayer and ministry, are here separate.

Second, the priest-pastor listens in and overhears the prayer. In this case, Hannah has not come to the pastor, but the pastor is there and listens in when the sufferer comes before the Lord to cry out for help. The pastor is not here a therapist or counselor in his office scheduling appointments with persons in trouble. Like a Catholic priest, he is there at the door of the sanctuary. This person, however, does not come to the priest for confession. Hannah comes to the Lord, and the priest-pastor overhears and is drawn into the human plight in prayer.

Third, the priest-pastor misunderstands what is going on. He mistakes true suffering and distress for misconduct. Misdiagnosis is the priestly response. He pays attention only to the surface symptoms and does not see the deeper anguish. The initial response of the priest-pastor is moral reprimand.

Fourth, when this priest-pastor comes to realize what is really happening here when Hannah tells him she is in trouble, he knows that the appro-

---

[4] P. Kyle McCarter, *I Samuel*, The Anchor Bible (Garden City, NY: Doubleday, 1980), 49 and 52–53.

[5] Greek; Hebrew lacks, "and presented herself before the Lord."

priate response is not moral exhortation but the good news of the gospel: "Go in peace, the God of Israel will grant your petition" (1 Sam 1:17).

In sum, the prayer of the troubled, the cry for help that is at the heart of biblical prayer, is not in this instance an act of worship in the congregation. It is an act of the one who is cut off from community, who is alone and isolated. Do not misunderstand; she has been to church. That is the point of the narrative. However, she is alone in a crowd. Even the one who loves her, her husband Elkanah, is distanced from her, despite his efforts to be a good husband, to boost her spirits, to be supportive.

The pastor is both in place and lucky. Ministry happens indirectly. Suffering and prayer are overheard. This is not planned. The opportunity is almost missed. The pastor is both incompetent and yet agent of God's redeeming word. He totally misunderstands and misreads the situation. His first words, if reported in a verbatim, would be torn to pieces by any teacher of pastoral care and counseling. He blows it utterly, as every pastor has done. The priesthood is not a ministry of perfection. (It was not in Eli's case – and we have not heard the last of his imperfections. Wait until the next chapter where we hear about how successful a parent and model he was for his priestly sons!) Nevertheless, the blown opportunity is capable of being redeemed, for this minister of the Lord does indeed know the only word that matters when the troubled soul cries out to God. It is the assuring word of peace, the daring claim that the prayer is heard and not ignored.

Both parts of Eli's response are important – the word of peace and the word about the petition. But there is an ambiguity in the Hebrew of the text (1 Sam 1:17) that is quite important. Traditionally translated as "*May* the God of Israel grant to you the petition you have made to him," it may also be translated as, "The God of Israel *will* grant to you the petition you have made to him." That is, the word of the priest is either his own pastoral prayer for the troubled Hannah or it is his declaration of the good news that God has heard and will respond. It is difficult to say in this instance, but the clearest clue is in the effect his words have upon Hannah. The text reads that when she heard these words, "the woman went to her quarters,[6] ate and drank with her husband, and her countenance was sad no longer"[7] (v. 18, NRSV).

The *outcome* of the prayer and the ministry of the pastor-priest is quite important. It is twofold, the first part contained in the verse I have just cited and the second part in the song of thanksgiving Hannah sings when

---

[6] Greek: Hebrew, "went her way."
[7] Greek: meaning of Hebrew uncertain.

she dedicates the child Samuel to the Lord. We will turn to that in a moment, but for now, I want to pay close attention to the first part of that response, the *word* of the priest-pastor and its *effect* on the petitioner.

Hannah's initial response is an indication of the confidence and trust of this barren and vexed woman, this depressed and bitter person, that God has heard her prayer and will deal with her plight. This time the pastoral words of the priest are neither misunderstanding nor efforts at insight, not even a rehearing or restating of the trouble of the woman. They are words of gospel, convictional language that serves to transform the situation, to turn sadness and depression into joy and gladness, to restore the isolated and lonely one to participation in the family. She eats and drinks with her family and her expression is no longer downcast. She has heard in the words of the pastor the certainty that her prayer has not disappeared into the darkness and that God will grant her petition. Nothing has happened yet. We will have to read further to hear of her pregnancy. But everything has happened. The cry of the depressed and troubled woman has been heard. Her pastor has dared to give her the assuring word of peace and that her prayer is heard and help will be received.

The words of the priest-pastor Eli to Hannah are, in effect, what we have come to call an *oracle of salvation*, a word from the Lord that announces or promises deliverance. That word from the Lord occurs in fairly standard form. On some occasions, it is exactly what Eli says to Hannah: "Shalom, Go in peace." In the eighty-fifth Psalm, the psalmist says: "Let me hear what God the Lord will speak, for he will speak peace to his people" (v. 8, NRSV). Such benedictional words as these have the power to bring divine comfort and support. It is no small matter when, in the liturgy, members of the congregation say to one another, or the pastor says to the congregation: "Peace be with you." We say that too much as a cliché. It is, in fact, what the human heart in anxiety and trouble wants to hear.

The other form of the oracle of salvation is the word that we hear again and again in Scripture: "Do not be afraid, for I am with you; I will help you." One of the clearest formulations of that is in the oracle of salvation in Isa 41:8–13, addressed to anxious and weary exiles in response to their prayers for help. It goes:

[8]But you, Israel, my servant,
    Jacob, whom I have chosen,
    the offspring of Abraham, my friend;
[9]you whom I took from the ends of the earth,
    and called from its farthest corners,
saying to you, "You are my servant,
    I have chosen you and not cast you off";
[10]do not fear, for I am with you,
    do not be afraid, for I am your God;

I will strengthen you, I will help you,
  I will uphold you with my victorious right hand (NRSV).

Such words are, as truly as one can find them, both the answer to prayer – it is always the same word, either "peace be with you" or "Do not be afraid" or both (e.g., Judg 6:23) – and the good news of the gospel. They were the words said to the poor of the earth at the coming of the Christ into the world (Luke 2:10). If we listen to Scripture, there is little doubt what it is that the world needs to hear or what it is that we have to say as ministers of Jesus Christ to those who cry out in pain.

We speak of the ministry of the gospel, but I think, in our minds, that is too much confined to the proclamation of the gospel in the formal act of preaching. There may be a failure of nerve or of conviction if that proclamation is so restricted, and we do not find in the midst of the people's lives those occasions when we can declare with confidence that the Lord has heard their prayers and is there with them to help them. Even if it is less a declaration and more a shared prayer, "May the Lord grant your request," that may have the power to effect a transforming moment and be a piece of the work of God. The passage in 1 Sam 1, upon which I have focused really tests the issue. Eli does not make a feel-better response. This is a claim that what is impossible will become possible. I think that is why we are unwilling to risk a translation of Eli's pastoral response as a declaration and can only speak of it as a hope. But what is not to be missed is that the one who receives this word of peace and the hope or claim of God's positive response is now a changed person. The one who was in distress is at peace. The one who was depressed is now joyous.

Further, the one who was cut off from the community, even when ostensibly very much a part of it; that is, surrounded by family, supported by husband, and the like but feeling absolutely alone in despair because her community can not deal with her problem and taunts her because of it – that lonely and cut off person is now restored to community. If the Hebrew is correct, she not only moves from despair to joy, but she eats and drinks with her husband. In that simple statement, one hears about the restoration of community, about a woman who left the family table in tears of depression and despair and returns in joy to be with her husband. Rehabilitation and restoration of community are important effects of this prayer and the pastoral act that happens ineffectively but truly to bring the word of the gospel.

My suggestion that human supplication or the prayer for help, at least as it is particularly known in the prayers of scripture, is to be distinguished from the public worship of the community is not, therefore, to eliminate prayer from worship. It is, rather, to recognize that the human prayer for help that we see in the prayers of scripture is often those ad hoc cries of people in distress when they are outside community, when they are in the deepest trouble. They are more features of being human than being in worship. The pastor, too, is not far from this struggle of the soul with God, and in some fashion is the bearer of the gospel, the vehicle for the declaration of God's grace in the face of the deepest pain. So, the prayers of supplication that are a part of being human, for all of us cry out in pain, find their place in the pastoral care of souls. The cure is not a therapy removed from the gospel. It is indeed the gospel. In our time, as in every time, the critical issue for ministry is precisely the proclamation of the Good News that in a world where things constantly threaten to undo us, and all too often accomplish that feat, we do not have to be afraid.

Like you, I worry about false words of hope, daring to say what God will do, when I do not seem to know myself. So I am being very clear at this point. I have no inside dope, much less a better therapy; no mode of ministry that is a sure cure for the maladies of soul, mind, and body; nor a program to undo the oppressive structures and acts that we impose and inflict on one another. I have only these clues from scripture that I think are worth listening to, and every now and then a voice from someone who has heard them that tells me they are reliable. I think if we who proclaim this gospel trusted it more, we would risk declaring it more. And maybe our best way is to do it indirectly, through the words of scripture, to say, in effect, that all we have is a word from the Lord, not of instruction or direction about some difficult problem, simply the basic assurance that whatever it is, God is with you and God will help you. You do not have to be afraid.

Hannah's further response to the priest-pastor's assurance of God's peace comes in 1 Sam 2:1–10 in her song of thanksgiving that accompanies her offerings and dedication of the child Samuel. That prayer-song takes us into the service of worship. If the cry for help is uttered in loneliness, the prayer of thanksgiving is sung in community. If separation from the family, from friends, or from the congregation is the common context of human lament and complaint to God, when one hears a glad good news in response to that prayer, the community of family and congregation is precisely the common context of one's joy and thanksgiving. If my first thesis was that the prayer for help is not primarily a feature of Christian worship to be heard by others but a feature of human existence that is heard by God and overheard by the pastor, now I want to argue a second claim or thesis, to wit, that *praise and thanksgiving are not features of human existence to be heard primarily by God but features of Christian worship to be heard by God but especially by others.*

The song of thanksgiving that Hannah sings is set in the house of the Lord at Shiloh, one of the central sanctuaries. It is sung in the context of

Hannah's paying of vows in acts of sacrifice. There is no mistaking what is going on now. Eli is not that obtuse. Hannah comes to Eli, the priest, and now offers both the sacrifice that she had vowed, that is, the gift of her child, and the unvowed but expected offerings of sacrifice.

I now make three generalizations on the basis of this song of thanksgiving in comparison with others that appear in the psalms and elsewhere.

The first is that *the prayer of worship is preeminently the song of thanksgiving and praise.* Hannah's thanksgiving is an act of worship, anticipated from the start, under the leadership of the priest in the sanctuary. The prayer for help we heard in chapter 1 is linked in its very wording to the thanksgiving act that follows the birth of the child. The vow that is the heart of her prayer lets us know that the prayer for help can never be an end in itself. It has a trajectory that reaches from the isolation, the loneliness and despair of the prayer for help, to the joy and worship and gift giving of the song of thanksgiving. Indeed in the songs of thanksgiving in the Psalter, the prayer for help that has preceded it is often quoted as a part of the story of God's help ("To you, O Lord, I cried...'What profit is there in my death'...?" [Ps 30:8–9, NRSV]). When the congregation gathers, its prayer is the particular prayers of thanksgiving and the general songs of praise. We do better with the general than we do with the particular. We provide time for silent confession of each individual's particular and personal sins and often particularize them in the public confession. What we are less prone to do is provide for public expression of thanks. In scripture, it is precisely in an act of worship before God and others that the one who has prayed in trouble gives thanks in joy, declaring what God has done, making clear to the world that God has been at work in her life, that the Lord has done marvelous deeds.

What I am arguing is that in a real sense it is the experience of God's delivering help, of God's companioning presence in the midst of the worst kinds of trouble, that triggers the return to the sanctuary, that effects the gathering of the people in worship. Worship thus begins in the reality of thanksgiving and its expression in prayer and song.

That leads into my second inference from the story of Hannah and from the experience of thanksgiving in scripture. It is simply, but quite importantly, that *in thanksgiving and praise the community is constituted and restored.* The community both utters and hears the call to praise, that imperative exhortation: "Hallelujah, Praise the Lord," that begins the hymn of praise or the call to give thanks to the Lord. Those calls are virtually always in the plural. It is only together that we praise the Lord. I do not mean that we cannot praise God individually. It is in the act of praise that the community is constituted as a community of the people of God – as we call upon each other to lift our voices in song and praise of God, and as we call upon all others, the human community and the cosmic community, to sing the praises of God.

If the community that finally matters is *constituted* in praise, that same community is *restored* in thanksgiving. That is, the act of thanksgiving in scripture is the specific point where the one who has been separated in various ways from other members of the community rejoins and becomes a part of that community in public fashion. The brokenness in relationship that is so evident in the prayers for help is overcome in the gathering of the community to hear the prayer of thanksgiving and to participate in the thanksgiving meal. We do not hear much about the meal, but the *tôdāh* or thanksgiving of scripture seems to have been a sacrificial meal. On several occasions, the people give thanks to God in the context of a sacrificial meal in the presence of God. In the great song of thanksgiving that concludes Ps 22, the psalmist who had been so utterly abandoned, taunted, and beset now declares:

[25]From you comes my praise in the great congregation;
  My vows I will pay before those who fear him.
[26]The poor will eat and be satisfied (NRSV).

The sacrifice, therefore, is not simply the fulfillment of a vow. It is an offering that is shared in that act that most vividly represents the reality of community life – the sharing of a meal.

It is surely no accident that the meal of the Christian community came to be known as the Eucharist, the thanksgiving, for it is pre-eminently that occasion of worship when everyone gives thanks to God for the marvelous deliverance that God has wrought in Jesus Christ. The Eucharist and its thanksgiving prayer catch up all those experiences of members of the community of God's help and of God's presence. If the assuring ground of God's comforting word is that we do not have to be afraid because "I am with you," the thanksgiving meal that we call the Lord's Supper and Communion is the enduring testimony that that promise is real and operative in our life and in our world. So, the community is restored around the table in the knowledge of its redemption and in thanksgiving to God. Those who were afar off have been brought near. Those who were estranged are together again. The community of mangled and broken relationships finds its life together around the table and in the act of thanksgiving.

My third and final generalization is this: Thanksgiving as a dimension of worship is *fundamentally an act of daring testimony.* In Hannah's song of thanksgiving, the Lord is entirely the *subject matter* of all the sentences, eighteen times no less. However, God is rarely the one *addressed* in her song. Sometimes, as in Ps 30, the thanks is predominantly addressed to the

Lord.[8] But in Ps 116, and more often than not, God is as much the one spoken about as the one spoken to. What this tells us is that thanksgiving and praise are features of Christian worship that are to be heard by God but especially by others. Contrary to everything we would expect, the congregation and the human community are the primary addressees, and the Lord listens in. The character of thanksgiving as testimony is explicitly indicated frequently in the Psalms. So in Ps 40, the psalmist testifies: "I have told the glad news of deliverance in the great congregation" (v. 9a, NRSV). In addition, in Ps 66: "Come and hear, all you who fear God, I will tell you what he has done for me" (v. 16, NRSV).

The prayers of thanksgiving are the primary Old Testament form of testimony. They are declarations to others of what God has done. Reformed Christians have tended to leave "testimony" more to the Baptists and other more free-church traditions that seem to focus heavily on the personal dimensions of worship and personal experience as the focus of worship. To the extent that we have abandoned that personal testimony, we have forgotten the very character of thanksgiving as a liturgical act in Scripture. It is in the most profound sort of way a testimony to one person's experience of the power of God to deliver, to be present, to transform from death to life, to lift up from the depths to the heights.

That is where the *audacity* comes in. This is something that needs to be underscored. In our time, we have rediscovered the laments and their significance for our understanding of the nature and character of prayer. However, the daring act of worship in our time is not the lament with its questions to and about God. They are all over the place. The really daring act of worship in our day is the prayer of thanksgiving.

For one thing, the prayer of thanksgiving makes *huge claims on a very narrow base*. Nowhere is that more clear than in Hannah's song of thanksgiving, where she dares to claim that what has happened to her in the Lord's answering her prayer by giving her a child is a demonstration of the power and intent of God to turn the whole world upside down. Power and honor are nullified. Lowliness and neediness are exalted and enriched. Contemporary Christians nearly always pull back from this text because we are bound to the status quo. We do not really want it to happen because of where *we* would end up in the reversal.

Thus, the thanksgiving of the one whose prayer has been answered is audacious, if not scandalous. It dares to suggest that God really does something, that we really do experience the help of the Creator of the universe and can point to that, speak about it, and that our lives are in various ways

---

[8] Vv. 5–6 are addressed to the worshiping community.

transformed by what God has done. Prayer and praise are among the most visible and unambiguous testimonies to the reality of God that we can make, and that in a world where the reality of God is a matter largely of indifference or hostility. Doxology and prayer make no sense in a world where God is not present and trusted. In our thanksgiving and in prayer, we bear clear testimony to the claim that the secular ability to live in a world without taking account of God is neither the last word nor the right one.

Praise and thanksgiving, therefore, turn prayer into proclamation. The very heart of the act of giving thanks and praise is a declaration of what I, or we, believe and have come to know about the Lord of life. It is a declaration that thus calls others to a response to that reality, to see, fear, and trust in the Lord who has taken away my fears and helped me. Ps 103 begins: "Bless the Lord, O my soul, and all that is within me bless his holy name." When it reaches its climax and conclusion, declaring the universal sovereignty of the Lord, then its call becomes equally comprehensive and universal:

[20]Bless the LORD, O you his angels,
>   you mighty ones who do his bidding,
>   obedient to his spoken word.
[21]Bless the LORD, all his hosts,
>   his ministers that do his will.
[22]Bless the LORD, all his works,
>   in all places of his dominion.
> Bless the LORD, O my soul.

14. The Psalter as a Book of Theology

In various ways the assumptions in the title above may seem to be immediately in question, both the claim to think of the Psalter as a book and, secondly, to think of it as a work of theology. The first claim comes into question in light of the character of the Psalter as a collection of many different and separate pieces that do not seem to reflect any particular order, much less continuity of subject matter. One may call a hymnbook a "book," but one does not approach it with the customary expectations one brings to a work of fiction or nonfiction that deals with a particular subject matter or develops an account or tells a story. Inasmuch as the Psalter has as its Hebrew title "Tehillim," that is, "hymns," it may be dubious to make much of a case for its book character. Is it simply a collection of individual psalms, each standing alone with its own integrity, unrelated to other psalms except by various similarities owing to genre?[1] Or can it be read in any sense as a continuous text, whose message is more than the sum of its parts.

That last question raises the issue of reading the Psalms not simply as a book but as a theological book, a systematic-theological work in the sense of a comprehensive presentation of divine revelation, of theology proper, that is, words about God. Inasmuch as the psalms are notable for their character as human words to God rather than the word of God to human beings, as a collection of prayers and hymns rather than comprehensive theological argument, the characterization of this collection as a book of theology seems problematic. When that is accented by the collection character of the Psalter, by the spasmodic movement from one complete psalm to another – and to a psalm that may have nothing to do with the preceding one – then the case for reading the Psalter as a book of theology appears thin.

Despite those formidable problems for reading the psalms as an intelligible and coherent book that is in fact more than a collection, and for reading it as a comprehensive theological work, a number of interpreters are arguing just that claim about the Psalter. That some coherence has been brought to the book at the editing or redactional level is evident in a number of ways:

---

[1] See Norbert Lohfink, "Psalmen in Neuen Testament: Die Lieder in der Kindheitsgeschichte bei Lukas," in *Neue Wege der Psalmenforschung*, eds. K. Seybold and E. Zenger (Herders Biblische Studien, 1; Freiburg: Herder, 1994), 105–125.

1. The presence of an introduction (Pss 1–2) and a conclusion (Ps 150 and, in more elaborated form, Pss 145–150). These psalms that function so as to introduce the Psalter and what it is about and to bring it to an end in a conclusive way that leads the reader to say, "It is ended," "Enough said," "Amen" – or as the Psalter itself puts it, "Hallelujah." Furthermore, the introductory psalm – with its exaltation of a continuous meditation on the instruction of the Lord – suggests that what is before us in the psalms that follow is instruction about the Lord and the Lord's way.

2. The sense of movement that is discernible at the simplest level as one moves through the book and experiences the gradual lessening or muting of the loud and constant voices of lament in favor of the increasing, equally loud voices of praise and thanksgiving.[2]

3. The division of the whole into five separate collections or books, as they are called (Pss 3–41; 42–72; 73–89; 90–106; 107–145 [or 107–150]), identified as such by doxological conclusions (Ps 41:13; 72:18–20; 89:40; 106:48).[3] The purpose of this division is not altogether clear, but many have noted its parallel with the five books of the Torah, itself a collection that is to be read as also in some sense a coherent whole. As the Midrash Tehillim says: "As Moses gave five books of laws to Israel, so David gave five books of Psalms to Israel...as Moses blessed Israel with the words 'Blessed art thou, O Israel' (Deut 33:29), so David blessed Israel with the words 'Blessed is the man'."[4] The Psalter thus presents the reader with a Torah of David alongside the Torah of Moses.[5] Furthermore, the books and their doxologies have been seen to represent theologically prominent stages in the history of Israel: the first two doxologies at the end of Pss 41 and 72 have to do with and reflect on the monarchical time under David and Solomon; the third book brings the downfall of the monarchy into view, as indicated by the conclusion of the final Ps 89; the fourth book, with its echoes of the prayer of repentance of the people at the end of Ps 106, and the concluding verses describing the scattering of the peoples among the nations, has in mind the exile of Israel among the nations. A

---

[2] Claus Westermann, "The Formation of the Psalter," in *Praise and Lament in the Psalms* (trans. K. R. Crim and R. N. Soulen; Atlanta: John Knox, 1981), 250–258.

[3] Erich Zenger has suggested that the doxologies, even though they go back to different hands, provide a complete Psalter hermeneutic. See Erich Zenger, "Der Psalter als Buch: Beobachtungen zu seiner Enstehung, Komposition und Funktion," in *Der Psalter in Judentum und Christentum*, ed. E. Zenger (Herders Biblische Studien, 18; Freiburg, 1998), 1–57.

[4] William Braude, *The Midrash on Psalms*, vol 1, trans. 1959 (Yale Judaica Series 13; New Haven: Yale University Press, 1959), 5.

[5] Bernd Janowski, "Die 'Kleine Biblia': Zur Bedeutung der Psalmen für eine Theologie des Alten Testaments," in Zenger, *Psalter in Judentum und Christentum*, 403.

final transition in Ps 107 leads, with the final book of the Psalter, into the period of restoration.[6]

4. The many subcollections within the whole and within the individual books. In the past these have usually been identified by their superscriptions ("David psalms" or "Korah psalms" or "Asaph psalms") or by the way the divine name is used (thus reference is made to the "Elohistic Psalter" for those psalms in the middle of the Psalter that have a preference for the use of the divine name *Elohim* in the A or first colon of the poetic line). Contemporary investigation of the Psalter, however, has recognized that the coherence of many groups of psalms has to do with their present placing. This is reflected in concatenation of words across two or more psalms, in beginnings and endings that link psalms, in thematic resonances, and in even larger groupings under very general but intelligible notions.[7] Once the reader begins to think about the possibility of a more continuous thematic reading of psalms, it is difficult, for example, to read Ps 22 – the paradigmatic lament of the Psalter and the chief New Testament hermeneutical key to the passion of Jesus – without being aware of its adjacency to a series of royal psalms (Pss 18, 20, 21). This brings the possibility of reading Ps 22 as the voice of the royal Messiah as well as a consciousness of the way it moves from lament into thanksgiving for divine deliverance and onward by means of the words of Ps 23 to a powerful expression of trust in the Lord on the part of one who has been through the valley of the shadow of death but has received the divine word of deliverance, "Fear not, I am with you, I will comfort you with my rod and staff," and who now professes an enduring confidence in the Lord.

---

[6] Ibid., 403–404. See Reinhard Gregor Kratz, "Die Tora Davids. Psalm 1 und die doxologisch Fünf-teilung des Psalters," *Zeitschrift für Theologie und Kirche* (1996), 1–34, esp. 21–24; Rolf Rendtorff, *Theologie des Alten Testaments, Band 1: Kanonische Grundlegung* (Neukirchen-Vluyn: Neukirchener Verlag, 1999), 99.

[7] See, e.g., Frank-Lothar Hossfeld and Erich Zenger, *Die Psalmen 1–50* in *Die Neue Echter Bibel: Kommentar zum Alten Testament mit der Einheits Übersetzung* (Würzburg: Echter Verlag, 1993), 11–14. They suggest that Book I of the Psalter (Pss 3–41) is comprised of the following groups: Pss 3–14 (the suffering existence of the poor and the righteous); 15–24 (the Lord delivers the righteous); 25–34 (the Lord delivers the poor); 35–41 (the suffering existence of the poor and the righteous). To characterize these psalms or even group them in another way may be possible, and it cannot be proven that the editing or redacting had the thematic order above clearly in mind; however, the proposal is a sensible one when the psalms are read together and with these rubrics in mind. For an independent identification of the literary and theological coherence of Psalms 15–24, see Patrick D. Miller, "Kingship, Torah Obedience, and Prayer: The Theology of Psalms 15–24," in Seybold and Zenger, *Neue Wege der Psalmenforschung*, 127–142; repr. in Patrick D. Miller, *Israelite Religion and Biblical Theology: Collected Essays* (JSOTSup 267; Sheffield: Sheffield Academic Press, 2000), 279–297.

Theological Message of the Psalter

I want to suggest, then, that the Psalter can be seen as a theological work, in the full sense of that term, in two ways. One manifestation of its character as a work of theology is the theological presentation of the Psalter as a whole. That is, a reading of the book from beginning to end confronts the reader with a point of view about God and humankind and the purpose and work of God in and through Israel as well as in relation to the larger community of humankind. It is at one and the same time historical and theological. One might naturally expect that for a book as disparate in its contents, and as evidently a collection of individual pieces as is the Psalter, this would be a difficult case to make. As a matter of fact, a good bit of consensus about the theological presentation of the book does exist in the current discussion. I would articulate it this way, drawing upon the work of a number of other scholars, especially the Yale dissertation of Gerald Wilson.[8] Primary ingredients or vehicles of the theological message of the book are the introduction in Pss 1–2 and the conclusion in Pss 145–150, the division into five books, and the royal psalms scattered throughout the book. These are often in strategic places, specifically at the seams of the first three books, but also at one of the climactic points of the Psalter in Ps 101.

The introduction to the Psalter in Pss 1 and 2 first of all identifies two ways that lie before each person: the way of righteousness and the way of wickedness. The determining factor is the degree to which individuals ally themselves to and devote themselves to God's instruction or law. The text is not more explicit about what comprises that instruction, but one's wholehearted appropriation of it is what defines a way of life that is rich, productive, durable, and watched over by the Lord. The second part of the introduction, Ps 2, sets before the reader a quite different agenda, the rule of God over the nations as mediated through the anointed one, the chosen Messiah of the Lord. The conclusion to the whole of the introduction – "Blessed are all who take refuge in him" – alerts the reader both to the dangers that lie along the way of the righteous and to the positive possibilities for those who walk that way in confident trust in the Lord.[9]

---

[8] Gerald Wilson, *The Editing of the Hebrew Psalter* (SBLDS 76; Chico, CA: Scholars Press, 1985).

[9] For a reading of the Psalter as a whole and the editing process that sees it as setting forth thematically the virtue of seeking refuge in the Lord, see Jerome F. D. Creach, *Yahweh as Refuge and the Editing of the Hebrew Psalter* (JSOTSup 217; Sheffield, 1996).

In this double introduction, therefore, both an individual's walk and its outcome – a way that often involves a conflict between righteousness and wickedness, between the good and the bad, and the larger realm of politics, the affairs of rulers and nations, are seen to be the concern of God's rule and the focus of God's attention. The psalms that follow spell out the way of the righteous, often in the face of terrible deeds done by the wicked, as testified again and again in the lament psalms, and lift up the representation of God's rule through the human ruler. The one about whom these psalms speak is at one and the same time the ruler anointed by God and the individual man or woman, whose royal status is well indicated in the words of Ps 8, "You have crowned him with glory and honor...you have put all things under his feet..."[10] The attribution of the psalms that follow to David makes us think of the king as the one who cries out for help and gives praise and thanksgiving. However, as the representative Israelite, David also evokes the experience of every human being. Thus the subject matter of the book is simultaneously the devotion to God's instruction of the individual who is also ruler and the rule of God through the human ruler, whose responsibility is to be a model Israelite, fully attentive to and obedient to the instruction or law of God.[11]

Midway in book 1 this combination of devotion to God's instruction as the way of life and the establishment of the rule of God through the human ruler is lifted up in the chiastically arranged sequence of Pss 15–24. These begin and end with the so-called torah liturgies that identify the way of righteousness expected of any who would stand in the presence of the Lord and then place at their center two things: the victories of the king and the king's righteous conduct (reflected in the royal psalms 18, 20, and 21), and the great value and reward of the law (Ps 19). The anointed person as one who lives by the law and the community as those whose presence before God is a testimony to their devotion to God's way in the law lead climactically to the declaration of God's kingship at the end of Ps 24: "Who is this king of glory? The Lord of hosts, he is the king of glory." In various ways

---

[10] See Patrick D. Miller, "The Beginning of the Psalter," in *The Shape and Shaping of the Psalter*, ed. J. C. McCann (JSOTSup 159; Sheffield, 1993), 83–92; repr. in Miller, *Israelite Religion and Biblical Theology: Collected Essays*, 269–278.

[11] See the summary comment of James L. Mays (*The Lord Reigns: A Theological Handbook to the Psalms* [Louisville: Westminster John Knox, 1994], 132–133): "This intricate pairing as introduction says that all the psalms dealing with the living of life under the Lord must be understood and recited in the light of the reign of the Lord, and all psalms concerned with the kingship of the Lord are to be understood and recited with the torah in mind." Cf. the summary comment of Jerome Creach (*Yahweh as Refuge*, 16): "Within this matrix of meditation on *tôrâ* and submission to Yahweh's rule the whole Psalter is to be read and understood."

these notes are sounded in the rest of book 1, and in book 2, until, as the ending of book 2 says, "the prayers of David are ended."[12]

With book 3, there is a change, reflected in several ways. The opening of the third book raises in the starkest terms the experience of wicked persons at ease and the righteous constantly afflicted (Ps 73). The claim of Ps 1 would seem to be undone by experience, as attested now by the Psalter. However, the psalm goes on to say that all this is incomprehensible until the psalmist comes into the sanctuary and there sees "their end," "their fate" – that is, the ultimate doing-in of the wicked, a reality only clarified in the presence of the one whose rule is over all and will not be undone. The rest of the third book bears significant witness to the doing-in of the people and ultimately of their human ruler. The largest number of communal laments is laid out here, and the conclusion of the book, Ps 89, acknowledges the downfall of the human ruler. Having articulated the Lord's promise not to take away "my steadfast love" from the anointed one or to "violate my covenant," the psalmist now declares, in light of the defeat and overthrow of God's anointed ruler, "you have renounced the covenant with your servant," and asks at the end: "Lord, where is your steadfast love of old, which by your faithfulness you swore to David" (Ps 89:49 [MT 50]).[13]

In book 4 the climax of the Psalter's theology is reached. In this book, the voices of both Moses (Ps 90) and David (Pss 101; 103) are heard. The anointed of the Lord is still in view, but the larger picture of God's rule and of God's work in creation and history is to the fore. That is indicated in several ways. These include the placing of the other great leader of the people, Moses, as the opening voice;[14] the presence of two extended recapitulations of Israel's history at the end of the book, one recounting the Lord's acts of deliverance (Ps 105) and one recounting the many deeds of rebellion that brought the people of Israel under judgment but not to full abandonment (Ps 106); and especially the sustained and repeated exaltation of the rule of Yahweh over the whole world. That rule over Israel and all the nations is declared again and again in the enthronement psalms at the center of book 4, Pss 93–99, with their ringing cry: "The Lord is king!";

---

[12] Ps 72:20. Technically, of course, that is not the case because, as the Psalter grew, other David psalms were added, particularly near the end, to keep the David model before the reader.

[13] For suggestions about how books 1–3 begin to address the problem of defeat and exile, as well as identifying it, see J. Clinton McCann, "Books I–III and the Editorial Purpose of the Psalter," in McCann, *The Shape and Shaping of the Psalter*, 93–107.

[14] For further indications of allusions to Mosaic speeches, see Erich Zenger, "The God of Israel's Reign over the World (Psalms 90–106)," in *The God of Israel and the Nations: Studies in Isaiah and the Psalms*, (ed. N. Lohfink and E. Zenger; Collegeville, MN: Liturgical Press, 2000), 161–190.

"The Lord rules."[15] The book concludes with a response to the claims and queries at the end of book 3, declaring that "for their sake he *remembered his covenant*, and showed compassion according to the abundance of his *steadfast love*." (Ps 106:45), notes that have been sounded again and again in different ways in book 4 (e.g., 92:2; 94:18; 98:3; 100:5; 103:4, 8, 11, 17; 105:8–10, 42; 106:2, 7).

In this declaration of the universal rule of the Lord of Israel the king does not disappear. On the contrary, Ps 101 follows immediately with a pledge on the part of the king to study and walk in the blameless way. The failure of the human king does not mean that this way has been abandoned by the Lord who is king over all. As the beginning of the Psalter (Pss 1–2) and the collection of Psalms in Pss 15–24 bring together the centrality of the torah and the rule of the Lord through the Lord's anointed, so at its end this shared way of the Lord is evident again. At the center of book 5, standing massively over the whole, is Ps 119, the full-hearted expression of commitment to and delight in the Lord's instruction. However, the king's voice is there also, as the book includes three royal psalms. The first, Ps 110, declares (echoing Ps 2), that the Lord will indeed establish his rule through the Messiah, the anointed king; the second, Ps 132, confirms the oath sworn to David but, in the light of all that has gone before, makes that covenant dependent upon the obedience to the Lord's covenant of the kings who follow; the last, Ps 144, is set in the final collection of David prayers, joining with them in reminding the community that this representative of the Lord's rule will yet be beset by others and in need of the Lord's deliverance.[16]

The way of torah is the way to go. It is the way that the Lord's anointed will walk, and as such, in good Deuteronomic style, that ruler will model the way that every individual should go. There is finally only one way, and its outcome is clear and predictable. The joy of the torah, the declarations of God's universal rule, and the experience of God's response to all the outcries and laments of the king and others end up in total and extravagant praise. As it comes to an end, the Psalter becomes a theological ground for what one of the Reformed confessions of faith has called the chief end of

---

[15] The climactic character of the Enthronement Psalms, and of book 4 in relation to the whole of the Psalter, has been observed by a number of scholars, e.g., Wilson, *Editing of the Psalter*, 214–215; Mays, "The Center of the Psalms: 'The Lord Reigns' As Root Metaphor," in idem, *Lord Reigns*, 12–22.

[16] That the reading proposed here, while not specifically christological, is capable of being interpreted eschatologically, or in relation to Christian convictions about the Messiah whom Christians see in Jesus Christ, is surely evident and not to be denied, even if not intended or a necessary interpretive outcome of the reading.

human existence: to glorify God and enjoy him forever. The Psalter does that in all its words and evokes that glorification and joy as the last word of all: the sound of all the voices in the cosmos and all the instruments in the universe joined together in incessant praise of God, one never-ending Hallelujah, the true music of the spheres.

A Doctrine of God

One way, therefore, of perceiving the Psalter as a book of theology is in the exploration of its comprehensive and coherent testimony to the Lord's way, as a theological interpreter of what is going on and what it means for those who live in trust of this God. However, that is not the only way that the Psalter is a book of theology. As I have indicated earlier, there are smaller segments, psalms that resonate with one another or are joined together in specific ways that become in some fashion authentic theological voices, bearing witness to the God of Israel. As one example of many, I would cite the pairing of Pss 103 and 104 in book 4, a significant elaboration of the doctrine of God that underlies the praises of the enthronement psalms.

The two psalms are inescapably linked by their shared inclusions. Each begins and ends with an expression that appears only here in the Psalter: "Bless the Lord, O my soul." In the first of these two psalms, the Lord's rule (103:19) – the thematic claim of book 4 and ultimately the center of the Psalter as a whole – is elaborated specifically in terms of the character of God in relation to human life.[17] In traditional theological categories, the psalm speaks of the attributes of God. However, it speaks of what are commonly called the relative attributes, those that have to do with God's relation to the world and humanity – mercy, love, holiness, and the like – rather than the absolute attributes that have to do more with God *a se* – eternity, omnipotence, immutability, and the like.[18]

---

[17] See Mays, "Center of the Psalms."

[18] The latter attributes are hardly dealt with in the psalms in quite the absolute way that they are often and popularly conceived. In Ps 139, for example, God's omniscience is not an abstract attribute of deity. It is an experienced reality: the psalmist realizes, "God knows all about me!" Ps 139 attests to the omnipresence of God not as an inherent divine attribute but as the psalmist's often-troubling experience of God's being behind and before, everywhere he is, whether he wants that or not. This way of thinking about an absolute attribute belongs to the Psalter's way of resisting abstract theology on behalf of a realistic theology that is directly related to human experience of the divine.

In Ps 103, the focus is upon the character of God as demonstrated in the interaction with individuals and communities. It is, in effect, a psalmic elaboration upon the ancient confessional formula: The Lord is compassionate and gracious, slow to anger and abounding in steadfast love (see Exod 34:6–7). The fundamental attributes are *ḥesed*, ("steadfast love," "lovingkindness,") and *raḥămîm*, ("compassion"). This is manifest in the particular experience of individuals ("my soul," is addressed in the first part of the psalm) through forgiveness, healing, deliverance from death, and the provision of good in life. However, the character of God as compassionate and faithful to the relationship is also an experience of the community, revealed through justice for the oppressed and forgiveness for the sins of a community that often turns from the ways of the Lord. God's compassion is comparable only to that of a parent for a child, but its breadth is wider than the widest breadth imaginable, its duration longer than any experience of durability human life can know.

Ps 104, now inextricably linked to Ps 103 in its beginning and end and in many concatenations, says that more can be said about this God. It turns to speak in an equally poetic voice about this same God in relation to the world as creator and provider.[19] The most repeated words in the psalm are "works/made" and "satisfy/fill." The God who is experienced in compassion and love is the one who made the universe and sustains it – particularly its inhabitants, both human and animal. Creation and providence can be talked about separately in Hebrew as well as in theological discourse, but in the poetry of creation they are a continuous reality. Creation does not simply occur but is a process of past and present. It is as much the providing of food for and places for refuge as it is the creation of the heavens, of light and darkness. Indeed, even light and darkness are provided by God as the context in which human beings and animals go forth for their labor and their food (104:20-23). If Gen 1 puts the stamp of goodness on the creation, Ps 104 does that equally with God's provision and sustenance: "These all look to you.... When you open your hand, they are filled with good things" (104:27–28).

The psalm artfully depicts a highly interdependent creation and a creator who interacts in various ways with the creation. For example, light is both the clothing of God and the first creation, and so it is at one and the same time the creation of God and the revealing and mysterious nature of God. So also heaven is the abode of God, but it is also created. In the creation of light and the creation of heaven, we encounter a view of Creator and creation that understands an intimate tie exists between the two, while

---

[19] On this psalm and for elaboration of some of the points made here, see above, 178–193.

the creator is neither identical with nor contained in the created realities. The two images of the garment of light that clothes the deity and the heaven that houses the deity serve to create a deep connection between the divine and the created orders even as they are distinct and separate.

The work of divine creation and providence is marked by order and purpose; it harnesses the forces of chaotic nature, sending the waters "to the place that you appointed for them" (104:8) and providing a proper place for the different creatures to live. The world God made is a complex but coherent whole, its intelligibility evident to all and sung out in this psalm. The varied purposes of God's creative activity are especially lifted up in this theological poem of praise, as exemplified by the provision of water – for the animals, but also to make the trees grow, so that the birds will have a place to nest and can sing among their branches. "A whole sequence of creative acts has bird songs as its goals."[20]

God's creative work is also a source of beauty and pleasure. The beauty is in the order of a carefully and intricately crafted universe. Its capacity to evoke pleasure is an even more marked outcome of the Creator's work. That is revealed in several ways: in the songs of the birds, in the sea as a place for Leviathan to play, and through wine to gladden the heart. The word for "joy" and "take pleasure in" (*śāmaḥ*) occurs frequently in the psalm. One of the goals of creation, in its details and as a whole, is to provide pleasure and delight. So the psalmist asks: "May the Lord rejoice in his works" (104:31). In other words, this psalm develops in detail the specificity and concreteness the meaning of the divine evaluation in Gen 1: "And God saw everything that he had made, and indeed, it was very good" (Gen 1:31).

A feature of the Ps 104's presentation of God's creative work is that no hint of human domination, of hierarchy in the creation, occurs. The world is a place for humans and animals, and the vegetation that sustains and shelters them. The whole is an intricate and complex creation, one of shared habitation and participation, of appropriate places and times for the well-being of each part of the creation, God is the source of life for all creatures, the breath of life breathed into everyone, animal and human alike. The psalm is an elaboration of the definition of creation suggested by the theologian, Michael Welker, in his reflection on Gen 1 and 2:

[C]reation is the construction and maintenance of associations of different, interdependent creaturely realms. God creates by bringing different creaturely realms into fruitful associations of interdependent relations that promote life. The creature is drawn into and bound up into the process of creation by developing and relativizing itself ... into these

---

[20] Ibid., 97.

associations of relations of interdependence, without which the creature would not exist.[21]

One continues to see in all of this something of the character of God, and not only God's creative and sustaining activity. For the psalmist, creation is particularly a testimony to the wisdom of God. That wisdom is often associated theologically with creation is not surprising. Ps 104 offers grounds for this view. The whole creation is a testimony to the wisdom of God, to the sensibility and order, to the skill and intelligence and practicality of the Lord.

Much more could be said about the way in which this psalm works to spell out the substance of a doctrine of God the Creator, that is, to elaborate the specifics of the first article of the Apostles' Creed. I will mention, however, only two other matters. One is what the text identifies as elements of human life: "wine to gladden the human heart" and "bread to sustain the human heart" (104:15). The terms are parallel and so are clearly brought into conjunction with each other. This evokes two observations: One is that these elements are presented as basic elements of life so that God's provision for human existence can be seen to incorporate both the daily sustenance of our lives and a more festive libation for our enjoyment and relaxation. When the Christian community later incorporated these same elements into its central ritual, it was not only because of their symbolic potential to represent body and blood but because they are what God had provided for human life. The elements of life become the elements of the church in its sacramental life.

A second observation about the Creator's provision of bread and wine is that these are products of nature and culture, products of divine origin and human productivity. The text does not specify seed and fruit but wine and bread. Human activity – cultivating, harvesting, preparing, cooking, or aging the stuff of God's creation – is a part of God's creative work. This is a clear example of the interdependency of associated creaturely realms, as Welker puts it, as well as an indication that the creaturely realms are both natural and cultural, that God's creation cannot be understood as nature on its own apart from cultural involvement with nature.

Finally, one hears at the end a somewhat abrasive note: "Let sinners be consumed from the earth and let the wicked be no more." The realism of the psalmist's praise of the Creator is alert to the reality of evil and wickedness in this beautiful and orderly world. Psalm 104 thus echoes Gen 3 as

---

[21] Michael Welker, *Creation and Reality* (trans. J. F. Hoffmeyer; Minneapolis: Fortress, 1999), 13.

well as Gen 2, and, like Ps 103, knows that iniquity is present and capable of shattering the beauty and order and good of the world God made.

The book of theology that is the Psalter thus gives us a chapter on the character and work of the Lord whose rule is celebrated in the preceding psalms. The two psalms that make up this chapter go a long way to inform the community in its own praise of the nature and character of the divine rule. The works of the Lord are manifold and complex: creating, sustaining, providing, redeeming, forgiving; they are righteous and just, loving and compassionate. One may not flee the hard realities of human life with its injustice and oppression, its evil and wickedness, its sickness and death, into a cosmic praise unrelated to the way individual and communal life is actually lived. However, the one who redeems and heals the sufferer, who forgives the gravest of sins, is the very one who stretched out the heavens and built up the mountains and who provides for the continuities and processes of nature and culture. And all of that theological understanding of who God is and what God does is worked out in the context of praise. Theology as doxology is what the Psalter as a book is all about. Poetry and music are its medium.

15. What is a Human Being?[1]

The Anthropology of the Psalter I

"What is a human being?" That is the anthropological question in any context and by any mode of inquiry – theological, sociological, philosophical, biological, anthropological, and the like. It has been with us and always will be. At least part of the answer to the question is that human beings are *those who ask who they are* and try to answer that question. They may respond in very theoretical modes, as, for example, Descartes' claim to find the human in the rational (*cogito ergo sum*), or Rousseau and Kant's discovery of the essence of the human not in a physical nature but in the moral, or Karl Marx's economic answer. Or one may answer the human question in more personal terms, as in the anguished tones of Jean Valjean's famous "Who am I," soliloquy in the musical *Les Miserables*, where the answer has everything to do with his neighbor and whether or not he is defined by his own name and identity or by an oppressive force outside himself that has renamed him with the numbers of a convict: 24601.

In our own time, the question is sharply present, if not always so identified, in the psychological and physical sciences, especially in the latter case, neuroscience. In the former instance, the issue of the human revolves around concepts of the self; in the latter instance the focus of attention has been heavily on the mind and the brain. The two have been joined nicely in the title (and substance) of the book by the philosopher Karl Popper and the neuro-scientist Sir John Eccles, *The Self and Its Brain*.[2] Clearly, these are avenues into the search for the particularity of being human, of knowing ourselves, avenues down which theology should be eager to go in its continuing efforts to account for what it means to be human, that is, to ask the anthropological question as a theological one.

In the conversation between theology and science, however, one must be aware of both dangers and limits posed by these different routes to

---

[1] In this essay, I am significantly dependent upon two sources that have helped me think about this topic. They are: James L. Mays, "What is a Human Being? Reflections on Psalm 8," *Theology Today* 50 (1994), 511–520 (available online at http://theologytoday.ptsem.edu/); and Brevard S. Childs, *Biblical Theology in Crisis* (Philadelphia: Westminster, 1969), 150–163. An earlier form of the essay was presented as one of the Ryan Lectures for 2002 at Asbury Theological Seminary.

[2] New York: Springer International, 1977.

knowledge of the human. One danger is the assumption that notions of the self can serve fully to account for the reality of the human, thus producing a depiction that takes its orientation from a secular beginning point rather than from a theological one. That is immediately evident when one begins to explore the way in which language of the self has largely replaced language of the soul.[3] Fear of dualistic modes of analysis and a vague sense that soul language is archaic and uninformed by scientific ways of thinking have contributed to a handing over of the language of human individuality to a more secular vocabulary. Indeed, the decline of soul reference may itself reflect an unease with a definition of the human that seems from the very beginning to characterize human existence in terms of something outside itself. That is, soul language by definition suggests some connection to the reality of God, or, as Karl Barth put it, the one "who lives by the Spirit of God."[4] Neither Freudian notions of the ego nor contemporary psychological descriptions and investigations of the self can take one very far toward a more theological understanding of the human, though their analyses may provide significant insight into the nature of the human.

Neuroscience has opened the door to fathoming the mysteries of consciousness and the operation of the brain, so that the mind and its functioning are no longer a matter of purely philosophical or psychological inquiry. The profitable, even necessary, conjoining of the scientific and the philosophical in understanding the workings of the mind is signaled by the conversation between Eccles and Popper referred to above. Happily, that conversation reflects some resistance to a reductionistic understanding of the mind as something whose reality can be dealt with by a deeper examination of neurons or brain waves. Knowledge of the more technical aspects of the working of the brain should help us understand more fully the *mechanics* of human thinking in its mental and emotional dimensions. That is a part of who and what each person is, and the personality in its fullest sense is an outgrowth of those mechanics. So matters as central to human nature – and playing their part in theological interpretations of the human – as memory and the experience of beauty have their seat in the workings of the brain.[5] Here, again, however, the language of the soul is a reminder

---

[3] For further elaboration of this point, see P. D. Miller, "Whatever Happened to the Soul?" *Theology Today* 50 (1994), 507–519 (available online at http://theologytoday.ptsem.edu/)

[4] Karl Barth, *Church Dogmatics*, (Edinburgh: T. & T. Clark, 1961) III/4, 386.

[5] John Eccles tells of a distinguished musician who told his doctor that he had lost all appreciation of music, that while he could still play the piano, "…it means nothing to me. I have no thrill, no emotion, no feeling. I've lost the sense of beauty, of value." Eccles reports that this loss of "the sense of beauty, of value" was due to a not very extensive vascular lesion in the superior temporal lobe on the right side of the musician's brain (*The Self and Its Brain*, 483).

that there is something in the human reality that transcends the most complete analysis of the physiology and neurology of the human being.

The answer to the question, "What is a human being?" however, is surely not a matter of adding something to the modes of analysis of the human that other fields of inquiry produce. Resistance to talk about the "soul" is appropriate if that is simply an addition to something else. I would suggest that another avenue of inquiry may be found in pursuing the anthropological question as it is asked rather directly within Scripture itself. The responses to that question one finds there can contribute to our thinking about what it means to be human.

The place in the Christian tradition where this question is most pointedly and directly raised is in the Psalms, most famously in Ps 8. But the question does not arise only there. It is asked again in a royal prayer for help, Ps 144, and one further time in one of Job's laments (Job 7:17–18), which belong to the psalmic tradition of lament and complaint against God. All three of these biblical formulations of the question "What is a human being?" and the responses they give to the question are dimensions of Scripture's answer to the anthropological question.

I will look at each, but I need to begin with an observation of the most obvious feature that is characteristic of each formulation. I would describe this feature from three different angles: a) The question is never simply "What is a human being?" there is always more to the question; so b) The answer to the question that is offered in each instance is indirect in that it is in response to the more specific formulation of the question rather than to a generalized and abstracted request for a definition of human existence, of human being; and c) The very asking of the question makes the answer, that is, the effort to define the human in some way, by definition, a *theological* matter.

For in each instance, the question is "What is a human being *that you...?*" "What is a human being that you regard/care for/think of/test/visit?" The question is never asked abstractly, never posed as a theoretical question. It is always asked in the dialogue with God, and its formulation is a basic clue to the fact that the Psalms are not going to answer the anthropological question about who and what we are as human beings except in relation to God. One of the things to be noted about the way the psalmists take up this question is that their responses are largely assumptions about the nature of the human that are *not peculiar* to biblical or even religious thought but are common to human experience generally whether perceived within a religious context or not. The critical difference is that the question of the human in the biblical context is also always a question about *God's way* with the human.

My assumption is that if the psalmists ask the question, one should stick around to see what sort of answer they give, before going off to other sources one might expect to be productive of meaning and insight. The starting point, naturally enough, is Ps 8. This psalm is best known for its speaking about the human, but that speaking is totally wrapped in a speaking about and to God. It begins and ends in the exclamation: "O Lord, our Lord, how majestic is your name in all the earth. The psalm intends only to express praise to God and never departs from that. All that it says about the human is part of its "Wow!" about the Lord. Indeed, it is only in awe before the created universe as the work of the fingers of God that the psalmist even thinks of man and woman, of human life.

But what this reflection on the universe as reflective of the glory of God does is precisely to raise a question about the place of human life in the cosmos. And at this point, the psalm uncovers what is surely a basic human anxiety, not a peculiarly Jewish or Christian one, but the fundamental human experience of feeling insignificant in the face of the vastness of the cosmos, whether it is perceived as God's creation or as a happenstance. The intrusion of the first person "I" in the psalm at this one point is, I think, not accidental: "When *I* look at your heavens." The rest of the song is a *corporate* expression, "Oh Lord, *our* Lord" and *generalizes* about human beings, but in this verse a single voice speaks out. I think that is a reflection of the fact that this human sense of insignificance in the universe is not a theoretical conclusion from scientific analysis, though it may be that also. It is a very personal recognition that, somewhere along the way, every one of us encounters. The "I" of this psalm is what makes us aware that the general question, "What is a human being?" is fundamentally a question, "What am *I*?" and what possible meaning and significance can *I* or any other human being have in the midst of this cosmos that seems to have no end in time or space. (Whether that is a correct scientific perception, does not matter. It is how I feel it – and so do you.) To be human is to experience a kind of fundamental anxiety in the face of the universe. That is something that distinguishes human beings from other sensate beings. The psalm reveals that this is not a modern phenomenon. It has always been thus. In our time, such anxiety before the cosmos has a new prominence as cosmologists talk about the fate of the universe, the death of the sun in five billion years and the ultimate end of the universe in a fiery conflagration or in trillions of years of slow and unending evanescence into cold dead silence. Our own experience so conforms to that of the psalmist that we know we are onto something about ourselves. As James

Mays has put it, "To be human is to be afflicted with the capacity for this subliminal glimpse of the significance of our insignificance...."[6]

As the question, "What is a human being" is asked, a further claim is raised about the human reality: What is a human being *that you have been mindful of such a one, that you have taken note of or paid attention to him or her?* Insignificance before the universe has raised the question of the human, but the bigger issue than what is this speck of dust in the vast cosmos is what is this speck of dust before the one who created that vast cosmos. The claim that is being made here is not simply that we are created, like the rest of the universe, or even that we are as human beings dependent upon the Lord of the universe, though both of those things are true. It is rather the implicit claim that being human means to be the *recipient of God's attention*, to be noticed and regarded by the Creator of the universe. To be human is to be regarded, attended to by some other and not to be ignored and disregarded. In Arthur Miller's great drama, "Death of a Salesman," Willy Loman's wife says to her sons these words about her husband, an ineffective, failure of a father and a salesman who has lost the touch:

He's not the finest character who ever lived. But he's a human being, and a terrible thing is happening to him. So attention must be paid. He's not to be allowed to fall into his grave like an old dog. Attention, attention must be finally paid to such a person.

That is Miller's fundamental anthropological claim in his play: This human being, however ineffectual and problematic he or she may be, is one to whom, by virtue of his humanity, attention must be paid. In Miller's play, it is a plea on the part of one of these human beings in behalf of another. Ps 8 makes the daring claim that it is our very nature to be attended to by the Almighty, that we are remembered and regarded simply and precisely because we are human beings.

This is not a casual claim. It becomes the ground on which the outcry of the troubled sufferer appeals to God. The reader of Ps 8 goes on to hear in the next psalm that: "[The Lord] does not ignore the cry of the afflicted; He who requites bloodshed *is mindful of/remembers* them." And Jeremiah, when he cries for help in one of his laments, expresses his plea in exactly the words of the Psalmist's query: "O Lord, you know; *remember* me and *visit* me..." (Jer 15:15).

And even as science sets sharply before us an awareness of our insignificance as human beings in the vastness of the universe, so science has its own form of this second insight. It is found in the anthropic principle, an indication in the nature of the universe that it has been fine-tuned for

---

[6] Mays, "What is a Human Being?", 513.

life. That is, the universe is so formed that if it were even slightly different, younger or older, hotter or colder, more or less dense than it is, that is,
if any of the chemical and physical properties of matter were changed even
slightly, life and intelligence would not exist in the universe, at least not
life and intelligence as we know it. This is anything but a theological
claim, but it is a non-theological way of suggesting that somehow the creation was made for us. In its theological expression, as we find it in Ps 8
and the Christian tradition more broadly, it is the assumption that to be
human is to be known and attended to by the Creator.

There are complex ways through election and covenant that God's special attention to the descendants of Abraham and Sarah is claimed, but that
is a different matter. What the psalmist speaks about is a kind of divine attention and regard that belongs to being human, not to being a child of
Abraham. The forms of that attention merit further exploration, for it
seems that there is a corollary to this definition of the human as the creature attended by God. That is, it seems to belong to *the nature of God* to
care about the human. The biblical narratives and the psalms join in expressing this attention by telling us that the ears of God are "fine-tuned" to
hear the cries of the human in pain.[7]

The third claim of this psalm about human existence is as astonishing as
the second one. Indeed it is the psalmist's recognition of what the divine
attention means for human nature. What it means is a place in the world we
inhabit that can only be described in royal and divine terms: crowned with
glory and honor and only a little less than divine. Over against the awareness of human insignificance in the universe is a claim that human life is
given a role to govern the world of which we are a part, that part of being
human is the responsibility to organize, control, care for, and govern the
world in which we live out our lives: "You have given them dominion over
the works of your hands, you have put all things under their feet." Human
beings may and do muck it up, but it is a part of the human identity "to
create its own world of culture out of the world that is there."[8] Ps 115
makes the same point in a slightly different way: "The heavens are the
Lord's heavens, but the earth he has given to human beings" (v. 16). It is a
religious and theological claim that "You" have given human beings dominion over the works of "your hands," that human rule of the natural order is a divinely given vocation. It is also a part of general human experience that being human means turning nature into culture, seeking to tend
to, control, and use the natural order. So the psalmist once again answers

---

[7] See P. D. Miller, *They Cried to the Lord: The Form and Theology of Biblical Prayer*
(Minneapolis: Fortress, 1994), 173–177.

[8] Mays, "What is a Human Being", 514.

the anthropological question in a way that connects with common human experience.

There is a critical difference, however, precisely because the question has been asked as a theological question and in relation to thinking about the glory of God. The awareness of insignificance before the vastness of the cosmos does not finally lead to a despairing nihilism because that cosmos is "*your* heavens, the moon and stars that *you* have established." We do not contemplate a meaningless void that just happened but a creation that was made good by the God who has also created us and called us into being. So also the human rule over culture is not destined to be an anarchic self-interested exploitation of the natural world around us but a divine vocation symbolized by the righteous and just rule of a king whose responsibility is the well being of his subjects. To place the anthropological question entirely in the context of the praise of God is to perceive the human reality in a way that makes it neither ultimately despairing nor ultimately chaotic.

Before leaving Ps 8 and indeed as the taking-off point for going elsewhere, we should observe the literary context in which this psalm is placed and its somewhat abrasive fit among the psalms of which it is a part. Ps 8 belongs with a group of psalms that begins with Ps 3 – after the introduction to the Psalter in Pss 1 and 2 – and concludes with Ps 14. All of these psalms are prayers for help, commonly called laments, with the exception of Ps 8 and the first part of Ps 9. Ps 8, as a more hymnic poem thus stands somewhat apart from its context. The reason for its inclusion here is not difficult to see. At the end of Ps 7, a fairly typical cry for help, we hear the vow to give thanks to God when deliverance comes, a typical element of the lament. The last line is: "I will sing praise to the name of the Lord, the Most High." Ps 8 is offered, then, as the mode of expression of such praise, as it begins with exaltation of the name of the Lord: "Oh Lord, our Lord, how majestic is your name in all the earth." The repeat of that expression of praise at the end of Ps 8 then leads us into the beginning of Ps 9, with its line in verse 2: "I will sing praise to your name, O Most High" and takes us into the praise and thanksgiving of the first part of that psalm before we are plunged again into the cries for help of the suffering and afflicted ones (9:13f.) whose voices have dominated this first part of the Psalter.

Ps 8 thus makes its claim about the royal nature of the human, the godlike character of human existence, in the midst of quite other voices who cry out in the face of oppression, sickness, and suffering. These other voices also ask the anthropological question. One hears it again in Ps 144, in a voice that may be that of the king. Just before a strong petition for the Lord's help, the psalmist as king addresses God and asks again: "What is a human being?" The question is similarly formulated: What is a human being that you regard such a one, or a mortal that you think of him or her? (Ps 144:3) The answer this time, however, is different. It is not: "You have crowned him with glory and honor. " Rather it is: "He or she is like a breath; their days are like a passing shadow" (v. 4). The psalm then goes on to call upon the Lord to come down and "set me free and rescue me from the mighty waters" (v. 7). So the answer to the human question this time is different. All that is said is a claim about our transiency. Like Ps 8, there is an awareness of our insignificance, but here it is not so much finitude as the sense that we are really almost nothing, and especially that we are so briefly around that we are no more than a quick breath of air. The question about the human in relation to God brings forth once more a generalized statement about human life. But this time, it points to our limitation, our mortality, our transiency. And there is no other word in response to the question here, except again the assumption that in our mortality and transiency we are still regarded; we are known by God; we are attended to by another. The Creator pays attention to the creature; the infinite to the finite; the eternal to the transient. And the psalm that so thoroughly underscores the human condition as fleeting and transient, Ps 90, makes a *claim* and a *prayer* that belong to what the Psalter teaches us about who we are: The *claim* is simply this: "Lord, you have been our dwelling place in all generations." And the *prayer* is this: "Teach us to count our days" and "establish thou the work of our hands." Help us to know our limits and make our time count for something.

The claim that God pays attention to human beings is the point of continuity with the final asking of the question "What is a human being?" in Scripture, this time in the mouth of Job. Indeed Job rings the changes on the question and underscores this fact of human existence as the reality of being visited and paid attention to: "What are human beings that you make so much of them, that you set your mind [fix your attention] on them, visit them every morning, *test them every minute*?" (Job 7:17–18).

Job shares with Ps 144 the answer implicit in the question, that human existence is marked by divine attention. But Job's experience identifies that aspect of human reality as a *problem*, so much so that he does not answer the question. The only answer to the question is in the question itself. The human *reality*, which is to be regarded by the divine, to be known by God, is the human *problem*. The "visiting" of God in Scripture is always an ambiguous matter. It may be for good or ill. God's attention is a constant searching and testing of human life. Better no attention at all. So Job says: "Will you not look away from me for a while" (v. 19). If this is who we are, and Job once more testifies that it is so, then human life, human existence, is not worth a bucket of warm spit, as Job says, in effect, in the

next line: "Will you not look away from me for a while, let me alone until
I swallow my spit" (v. 19).

James Wharton has characterized Job's view on this essential feature of
human existence as follows:

In his desolate suffering, Job has experienced God's "inordinate attention" as a nightmar-
ish terror that makes death preferable to such a "life." God's unaccountable claim on Job
has become a burden he would gladly be spared for the last, brief days of his life (7:13–
16). The glad hymn of Psalm 8:4 is here transformed into a cry of lamentation. The Hebrew word translated "visit" here and "care for" in Psalm 8:4 has nothing to do with
"dropping by." Rather it indicates what God "metes out" to human beings whether for
good (Ps 8:4) or for ill (Job 7:17).[9]

Even as we listen to Job's words, we realize that we have not left the Psalter and the answer to the question that is to be found in its pages. For they
are filled with the laments and cries for help for Job and his human con-
freres. In that same Ps 90, the people declare:

[7]For we are consumed by your anger;
    by your wrath we are overwhelmed;
[8]You have set our iniquities before you,
    your secret sins in the light of your countenance
[9]For all our days pass away under your wrath;
    our years come to an end like a sigh.

There is no more constant voice in the Psalter than the one that cries out in
torment and suffering to God. We know it at its most radical in Job. But
one hears this voice again and again in the Psalter. Sometimes, as in the
psalms around Ps 8, that is about all one does hear, whether it is the voice
of a king or simply one who has been afflicted, faint and pleading before
the Lord, as the superscript of Ps 102 says. The experience of suffering
looms large over the Psalter and seems to be the primary human experience. The one who is crowned with glory in Ps 8 is also a creature of suffering; the one who is *astonished* by God's attention as making us kings
and queens is also one who is *undone* by God's attention, an attention experienced as testing and undoing. Or, in other psalms, the human creature
is undone by God's *in*attention that means no help in the face of the destructive forces of life that take away one's humanity. It is not necessary to
try to create a theological consistency between the experiences of God's
disturbing and destructive attention and God's *abandoning inattention*. In
both instances, the human reality is finitude, transiency, and suffering; and

---

[9] James Wharton, *Job* (Westminster Bible Companion; Louisville: Westminster John
Knox Press, 1999), 50–51.

in both instances the anthropological significance once again depends upon God. If one cannot make claims about the royal place of the human in the creation without that being seen in relation to the mystery of God, one also cannot deal with the reality of pain and suffering without that also being seen in relation to the mystery of God. Neither the psalmist nor Job knows how to speak about the human apart from the reality of God.

One could legitimately stop at this point in our probe of the Psalms' answer to the question: "What is a human being?" There are some things we know now, and they fit with our experience; they connect with things that others outside the community of faith claim about human life.

But the anthropological question is asked one more time in Scripture, and perhaps our reflection on its meaning would be incomplete without attention to the final instance, which is in fact a quotation of Ps 8. It is to be found in Heb 2:6–9.

Three things are immediately noticeable about the appropriation of Ps 8 in this New Testament passage:

1. The presence of the expression *ben ᵓādām*, traditionally translated as "son of man" but in the NRSV as "mortal," has led inexorably to a hearing of this text as not simply about humanity in general but about the one who was known as the "son of man." It is important, however, to recognize that the NRSV translation is not misleading at this point, that the term "son of man" means and is best translated as "a human one." This title is the most anthropological of all the christological titles. It is a way of speaking in titular terms of the incarnational reality that this one was truly human and representatively human.

2. The Greek translates the Hebrew *ᵓĕlōhîm* as *anggeloi*, "angels" rather than "god(s)."

3. The term "a little lower" has been read through the Greek as "for a little while," a legitimate interpretation of the Greek at this point. So the expression refers not to the status of the human being described in these verses but to the *temporality* of "his" status, that is, to a brief period of time in which this representative human being was lower than the angels.

All of this leads to an important christological understanding of the answer to the question, "What is a human being?" That is, there is an *incarnational* answer to the anthropological question also. The human being under whom all things have been made subject (so Ps 8) is the one who emptied himself, being born in human likeness (so Heb 2). The writer to the Hebrews hears in the Psalms the word that whatever we say about the human reality has got to take into account the face of Jesus Christ. The New Testament underscores this in spades when it makes Ps 22, the model lament, the interpretive key to understanding the passion and death and resurrection of Jesus Christ. For as it constantly interprets what is going on by means of the verses of Ps 22, it makes clear that the one on the cross identifies with all those who cry out in the words of Ps 22 or in laments like that. If suffering is a part of the *human* reality, it is also necessarily at the heart of the incarnational reality. Heb 2 recognizes how fully that is the case when it notes that we do not yet see everything in subjection to him. There are still powers and forces at work to do in the human creature. That is true, whether the human being in view is humanity in general or the incarnate one. But then the Hebrews writer says the critical words: *"But we do see Jesus."* "We do see Jesus, who for a little while was made lower than the angels, crowned with glory and honor *because of the suffering of his death*, so that by the grace of God he might taste death for *everyone*." The suffering and death that belongs to our humanity is not the last word. Nor is it a trumping of the glory and honor, turning them into dust and ashes. Hebrews says that it was precisely in the suffering and death of Jesus that he was crowned with glory and honor. What therefore is to be said about the human cannot be confined to general statements about humanity apart from God. It cannot be said apart from the discovery that in Jesus Christ we see who we are and we also see God for us. And what is said about the human cannot be said as a general statement that assumes that what we see now is all there is to see. The answer to the question about who we are is finally eschatological, where tears are no longer part of the human reality, where joy is the order of eternity, and where our transience disappears in the disappearance of death. We cannot see that yet. But we do see Jesus. That will have to do. I think it is enough.

16. The Sinful and Trusting Creature[1]

The Anthropology of the Psalter II

The Sinful Creature

Significantly absent from the treatment of the anthropology of the Psalter in the previous essay is any suggestion that the answer to the question "What is a human being" might be "A human being is a sinner." The silence on that matter in that context is intentional and appropriate. None of the texts that ask the question "What is a human being?" answer by identifying human existence as sinful. That is not the first answer or the dominant answer to the question as far as the Psalter is concerned. In fact, it could be argued that the Psalter does not see sin as a large issue for human life, that is, if one looks at the expressions of confession and repentance. The penitential psalms of the Psalter number only seven, and in some of those the acknowledgement of sin is fairly modest (Pss 6, 38, 102, 143), dominated more by outcries against the suffering inflicted by the acts of others. Talk about one's existence and experience as sinner is not very extensive in the Psalter. So where does that leave one on this issue?

I would suggest that the Psalter points in two different but related directions when one asks about what place sin and guilt play in understanding the nature of human existence. One direction is evident in light of the Psalter as a whole, that is, as one looks at the many cries for help or laments that sound in its pages. The experience of sin about which the psalmists speak most often is *the sin of the neighbor*. If one were to ask the ones who pray these prayers of the Psalter, "Who is your neighbor?" the answer is complex but very emphatic. He is the one who lies in wait to do me in. He is the one who speaks lies against me and uses deception to oppress and destroy me. (The violation of the Commandments most often attested in the Psalter – at least with regard to the second table – is the sin of false witness, the lie against the neighbor.) She is the one who taunts and mocks me in my condition, who betrays my trust. The reality of sin is, in fact, large in the Psalter. It is present in that ubiquitous group called the wicked or the evildoers. These are not necessarily heinous sinners who murder and

---

[1] This essay originated as one of the Ryan Lectures delivered at Asbury Theological Seminary in 2002.

rape and kill, though they may do that. They are the ones who covet and lie and steal, who may use the courts to get at and get from their neighbor, who may withhold wages or repossess property or call in collateral. They are the ones who hide themselves from their neighbor's economic endangerment. They are the ones who turn away in the face of the psalmist's need and leave him or her alone and without community and support.

So here is one indicator of the reality of sin as a part of human existence and one direction that the Psalter gives to the question about the way in which sin is definitive or not for human life. For the "I" of the Psalms, it is there in the acts of her neighbor who is not her neighbor. The one who cries out in these angry and despairing and troubled laments is in Jesus' parabolic language "the one who fell among thieves" along the Jericho road. Human existence encounters thieves and robbers who oppress and Levites and priests who pass by. The Psalter talks less about sin than it articulates the effects of sin upon others. Indeed in the laments that pray for God's help and deliverance, the psalmist sometimes protests his or her moral innocence and so claims God's justice as well as God's mercy (e.g., Ps 17:1-5; 139:1-3, 23-24).

There are places, however, in which the Psalter articulates the reality of sin as something in one's life that is so overwhelming that it cannot be comprehended simply as the experience of the victim. It raises its ugly head directly in the life of the righteous so that one has to ask how much, in fact, human nature is under the sway of sin. The place where that is most evident is in Ps 51. So I would like to turn to that psalm to see what may be discerned from it.[2]

The psalm appears to have two major parts, the first being verses 1–9 [Heb. 1–11] and the second verses 10–17 [Heb. 12–19]. The first part is held together by several features: the creation of an inclusio, "blot out (*māḥâ*) my transgressions/my iniquities," in verses 1 and 9 [Heb. 3 and 11]), the repetition of the words "wash" (*kābas*) and "cleanse" (*ṭāhar*) in verses 2 and 7 [Heb. 4 and 9], and especially the repeated use of terms for sin, iniquity, transgression, and wrong.[3] None of this language reappears in the second part of the psalm except with reference to *others* as sinners and trangressors (v. 13 [Heb. 15]). Reference to "spirit" and "heart" cre-

----

[2] The following discussion draws upon the author's essay "Preaching Repentance in a Narcissistic Age: Psalm 51," *Journal for Preachers* 21 (Lent, 1998), 3–8. I am grateful for permission to use some of the material from that earlier piece in this essay.

[3] For a discussion of how the poetic pairing of the words for sin achieves a result "in which one is overwhelmed with the poet's sense of sin but not dulled by a monotonous repetition," see Patrick D. Miller, "Studies in Hebrew Word Patterns," *Harvard Theological Review* 73 (1980), 87–88.

ates an inclusio holding together the second part of the psalm, verses 10–17 [Heb. 12–19], helping to confirm the final two verses (18–19 [Heb. 20–21]) as an addition to the psalm.[4] Thus the first part of the psalm focuses upon "the seriousness of the disorder" while the second part attends to "the possibilities for new life" with language of cleanliness, restoration, newness, a right/holy/willing and broken spirit and the language of teaching and praise.[5] This does not mean that none of the language of one part is to be found in the other but that the focus shifts from the depth of the sin to the possibilities for restoration, joy, and the praise of God for God's deliverance. Let me then make several observations about the psalm.

1. It is in the first part of Ps 51 that one confronts the terrible reality of sin and what is possible in the face of sin. The poignant plea of the psalmist heaps up the language of sin. Something wrong has happened and the praying one of this psalm is acutely aware of that and of his or her accountability – the superscription says this is David – of his or her sin-iniquity-transgression. The psalm thus sets itself in a single context; but one that has much flexibility, much elasticity. That single context – David's sin – is the unmistakable fact of wrongdoing that not only cannot be denied or suppressed but obviously has taken over the very soul of the wrongdoer. The elasticity of the psalm is that while the superscription connects to David and to his very specific sins of coveting, adultery, and murder, the psalm itself does not, in fact, describe any particular sin at all, and no particular time. Its language is very open and available to whoever knows the overwhelming sense of guilt for wrong-doing that is articulated in its words.

2. This sinner's prayer arises less out of the sense of a *general* condition of sin than out of an acute consciousness of specific, terrible misdeeds. Verse 5 [Heb. 7] is the one place in the psalm that seems to suggest a more pervasive sense of sin, with its intimation of original sin or being born sinful: "Indeed I was born guilty, a sinner when my mother conceived me." It may be possible to read the verse as indicating a kind of original sin, though there is no echo of that elsewhere in the Psalter. It is more likely that these words about being born a sinner are an expression of the depth of the sinner's conviction of sin. The whole of this psalm is a powerful expression of an overwhelming sense of guilt. The cry of verse 5 is less an

---

[4] For further discussion of the linguistic indicators and characteristics of the two parts of the Psalm, see, for example, Erich Zenger's discussion in either F.–L. Hossfeld/E. Zenger. *Die Psalmen. Psalm 51–100* (Die Neue Echter Bibel; Würzburg: Echter Verlag, 2002), 333–334; or F.–L. Hossfeld and E. Zenger, *Psalmen 51–100* (Herder's Theologischer Kommentar zum Alten Testament; Freiburg: Herder, 2000), 46–48.

[5] Walter Brueggemann, *The Message of the Psalms* (Minneapolis: Fortress, 1984), 102.

analysis of the human situation than it is the feeling of one whose sense of sin is so great that it seems to have been there always. Such an overwhelming feeling is truthful but not generally descriptive of the human condition.

That this is the case is reinforced by the superscription, which is offered as an interpretive indicator of the context in which these words are to be understood. They are the outcry of one who was both "a man after God's own heart" (so we are told about David in 1 Sam 13:14) and an adulterer-murderer. Generally when the community of Israel or the individual within that community, confessed their sins, the heart of the confession was, as it is here, the words "We/I have sinned," and that acknowledgment regularly referred to a specific act of transgression described in the narrative or the text that leads into the formal confession. It is rare that such a confession is made as a general claim. It is customarily in reference to a quite identifiable act.[6]

One notes further that generally the words for wrongdoing in the psalm are in the *singular*. While the singular can refer to a broader reality, it suggests primarily the specific sin that has elicited the prayer of confession. There is a repeated plural form, "my transgressions," in verses 1–3 [Heb. 3–5] (cf. v. 13 [Heb. 15]). When that is seen in relation to the superscription, it suggests that the multiplicity involved is not to be understood as a vague, undifferentiated assortment of sins great and small. Rather "my transgressions" are the quite specific concrete, interacting, and interrelated complex of acts around David's taking of Bathsheba – at a minimum, acts of coveting, adultery, and murder, but in fact encompassing also misuse of royal power, sexual assault, conspiracy, and betrayal. The psalm invites one to that searching of the soul that is not content with a superficial acknowledgment of a propensity for sin or sins generally, but a confession of the very real and often complicated acts that have betrayed and undone another, a neighbor – one close at hand or far away.[7] That suggests the psalm is to be read and learned not because it is always applicable to identify a general sinful state but in order to have it at hand when the soul has truly and specifically sinned and is stricken with that recognition.

3. The problem that sin presents in this text is *wholly* a *problem with God*. In apparently stark contrast to the information provided by the superscription, which alludes to David's acts of adultery and murder, the psalm speaks of a sin that is *only* against the Lord (v. 4 [Heb. 6]). But the disjunction between the superscription and the text is only apparent, not real.

---

[6] See in this regard, P. D. Miller, *They Cried to the Lord: The Form and Theology of Biblical Prayer* (Minneapolis: Fortress, 1994), chapter 7.

[7] That is, "near and distant neighbors," to use the terminology of Karl Barth in *Church Dogmatics* III/4 (Edinburgh: T. & T. Clark, 1961), 285–323.

The connection of the text to the David and Bathsheba story is precisely through the line "against you, you alone have I sinned" (v. 4a [Heb. 6]; cf. 2 Sam 12:13) "and done what is evil in your sight" (v. 4a [Heb. 6]; 2 Sam 12:9). It is in Nathan's judgment speech against David that the sin against Uriah and Bathsheba is seen as a despising of the *Lord* and the word of the Lord (2 Sam 12:9).

The need for repentance rests in the fact that transgression and sin, however heinous the effects on human beings, are at root a terrible violation of the person's (or community's) relationship with God. If earlier ages have seemed to overstress the reality of sin and guilt, they have at least done so in the certainty that God grounds our life and it is not self-grounded.

The *repentance* for sin that is the subject of this psalm is different from reconciliation and restitution. The latter, reconciliation and restitution, are more comprehensible to the modern spirit, which tends to assume that the deepest relationship is with the neighbor and so focuses on mending that relationship. But this psalm echoes Ps 8 in arguing that we cannot speak about the human without first speaking about God and there is no dimension of human existence that is not first a matter of our relationship with and dependency upon the one who created and redeemed us. The thrust of Scripture is that reconciliation is fundamentally God's work in Jesus Christ and God's overcoming of the gap in the relation between ourselves and God that our sins have created (2 Cor 5:8).[8]

The problem of talking about confession and repentance, therefore, is in direct proportion to the conviction that human life is really grounded in God. Without that operative assumption, all talk of sin and repentance is perceived as anachronistic, a "preacherish" way of talking about our problems. Preaching that evokes repentance is prepared for by preaching that confronts the congregation in inescapable ways with the reality of God and the reality of God as the most important thing to say about the human, about ourselves.

---

[8] See in this connection the comment of Donald W. Shriver in *An Ethic for Enemies: Forgiveness in Politics* (New York: Oxford University Press, 1995), 29: "On the surface, to say that David's adultery with Bathsheba was sin against God and God 'only' is to reduce to trivial importance the multiple damages done to human beings in the incident. But the narrative associated with the later psalm (II Sam. 11–12) does not permit such an interpretation: there a child dies, a king suffers public humiliation at the hands of a prophet, and the future of his kingship suffers too. The point of Psalm 51 is that the God of Israel takes its sin more seriously than it does. As with the Greeks and many other religious traditions, God and the gods are protectors of the moral order, springing into actions of judgment and punishment when it suffers violation. But in the Hebrew case, the sense of personal affront to the divine is stronger; the one God of Israel is never on vacation from attentiveness to its sins."

4. The sense of sin articulated by the psalmist is a real and terrible experience. It has taken all joy out of life (v. 8 [Heb. 10]); so one great need and petition is the restoration of joy (v. 12 [Heb. 14]). It has created a sense of being stained of being so marked by the sin that one is dirtied (vv. 2, 7 [Heb. 4, 9]); so another great need is to feel and know oneself clean and pure and fresh again (vv. 2, 7 [Heb. 4, 9]). The sin does not need to be pointed out in this case. It is real and its reality is doing in the psalmist. If the usual problem of the psalmist is his or her situation, this time the problem is the psalmist.[9]

No lament against enemies and oppression carries any more pleading and beseeching tone than does this one. The verbs convey this tone in the most poignant way: have mercy, blot out, wash me, cleanse me, purge me, wash me, let me hear joy, hide your face, blot out, create, put a new spirit, do not cast away, do not take, restore, sustain, deliver. The depth of the psalmist's awareness of his or her sin is matched only by the sense of need it has created. As much as any other lament, this psalm is a cry for help. The destruction of this soul, however, is not by any external forces. It is by the terrible weight of the committed sin and the way it stares him or her in the face constantly. And so the psalmist cries out in desperation. Here is no intoned general confession of sins never thought of until read out loud from the order of service or liturgy. This is trauma, desperation, a terrible burden that must be lifted. Because the problem is "me," then the need is not simply to do something about the *sin* – blot out, hide your face – something needs to be done about "*me*"; *I* need to be purified. *I* need to be created anew. *I* need a new heart and a new spirit.

5. It is the *prophetic preaching* of Nathan, however, that opens David's eyes. That context suggests there is a role for the preaching of the word that may, as indirectly as Nathan's parable about the poor man's lamb, create the ground for an apprehension of sin on the part of those who listen. The reading and interpretation of the psalm may break through the self-protecting veneer that every one wears in order to allow the *mea culpa* to come forth when it has not, when the sin is really there but buried beneath or covered over by the veneer. One should be wary, however, of a sweet intonation of the psalm in singing that removes its sting and thus suppresses its capacity to evoke the harsh reality of one's sin and the consequent repentance of heart and spirit.

Such preaching will carry with it the critical teaching of this psalm, that the transformation of the soul and spirit, the cleansing from the sense of

---

[9] J. L. Mays, *Psalms* (Interpretation; Louisville; Westminster John Knox Press, 1994), 202.

stain – a powerful image not to be easily discarded as an outdated way of speaking – is God's act. If this psalm is a powerful confession of sin, it is more radically a fall upon the grace of God. The imperatives listed above make one aware that repentance in this psalm is not a merely human act. Indeed, repentance here is only implicit though very real. The focus of this psalm is on the plea for God's grace and compassion. It is Israel's oldest confession of faith that the God it worships is merciful, compassionate, and full of steadfast love (Exod 34:7). That is the starting point of this psalm in verse 1 ("Have mercy on me…according to your steadfast love."). It is the "way out" for the sinner who is overwhelmed by the weight of the wrong that she has done and knows that the only hope is for God to create a new and right spirit.

The Trusting Creature

If the reality of human sin is not the first or dominant word about human nature and human life in the Psalter, it is also not the last word. There may not be a last word, but there is still a word about the human creature that needs to be said, and I will take one particular psalm to illustrate the point, even though it permeates the Psalter. The point is simply this: What carries human existence through thick and thin is *to live in constant trust in the Lord's care and the goodness of God*. That point is made in so many places in the Psalter. It is most familiar from the words of Ps 23. It has powerful expressions elsewhere in the Psalter, one of those being Ps 62.

Like Ps 23, this psalm is a psalm of trust. From beginning to end, its point and intention are found in the confidence that God delivers, that God can be trusted by those who are in terrible need but lack the resources within themselves or from the community to overcome the dangers that threaten them. A close look at the psalm uncovers several features that belong to the way in which the Psalter teaches us about the human.

1. Trust in the Lord and the Lord's willingness and power to deliver is not an inherent, innate dimension of human being.[10] It is a stage that has been reached only out of the *struggle of the soul*. The prayer begins with the words "my soul waits in silence". The silence here might have in mind a kind of meditative trust. There are places in the prayers of Scripture

---

[10] One may not easily infer from the Psalms an answer to the question as to whether trust in God is something that may be presumed for some prior state of innocence in the human condition. The Psalms speak of the human creature as she or he is.

where one encounters a meditative dimension. Indeed, the psalm immediately after this one, Ps 63:6 [Heb 63:7], refers to such meditation.

In this instance, however, it is unlikely that meditation in silence is meant, though such meditation may accompany the prayer. Here silence is the calm after the storm, the resignation and calm that comes after one has struggled mightily, cried out in anguish to God. While this psalm begins in quiet confidence, it has not gotten there easily. At least the trust of this petitioner has not been a quiet patient waiting. The word that is used here for "silence" only occurs a couple of other places in the Old Testament. One of them is at the beginning of Ps 22, in the midst of the most despairing and anguished cry of affliction preserved in Scripture:

[1]My God, my God, why have you forsaken me?
   Why are you so far from helping me, from the words of
      my groaning?
[2]O my God, I cry by day, but you do not answer,
   and by night, but find no silence.

That is, no calm, no rest, no ease. In Ps 62, we hear now the voice of one who has found such calm and rest out of the anguish and despair described in Ps 22. The prayer is not unlike Ps 131, that wonderful short prayer of a woman who has gone through something of the same thing. At least she has experienced some struggle of the soul, and speaks with the same vocabulary as this prayer: "I have calmed and quieted my soul" (v. 2). She has probably gone through a different sort of struggle, but the end result is not unlike the prayer of Ps 62. One who has struggled, has reached a calm dependence upon God.[11]

There are indications also that the struggle reflected in Ps 62 may not be entirely over. That is suggested by two features of the text:

a. Immediately after the opening verses of confident waiting, the psalmist opens up again in attack on his or her enemies and lament over what they try to do (vv. 3–4 [Heb. 4-5])

b. And immediately after that, the words of the opening verse are repeated, but this time with a very slight but significant modification. The NRSV has made the two verses exactly alike, but they are not. The first verse is a declaration: "My soul waits silently for God." The second is an address to the soul: "O my soul, wait silently for God." We are now into the dialogue of the soul and see something of the struggle. It is not unlike

---

[11] On this interpretation of Psalm 131, see Patrick D. Miller, *They Cried to the Lord*, 239–243.

the dialogue one hears in Pss 42–43, where repeatedly the petitioner says to herself:

Why are you cast down, o my soul,
  and why are you disquieted within me?
Hope in God; for I shall again praise him,
  my help and my God. (42:5–6, 11; 43:5 [Heb 42:6-7, 12; 43:5])

And then:

My soul is cast down within me. (42:6 [Heb. 7])

So also here, the psalmist says to himself: "Be still, my soul." The struggle still goes on, but it is shaped primarily by confidence and trust and that is the primary word the prayer has to offer.

2. And it is indeed a word to offer. That is, this is not simply a prayer in the closet, a quiet expression of trust to God. God does not even get addressed until the last verse of the psalm! That does not mean that it is taken out of the realm of prayer. What it does mean is that this prayer of confidence functions very much like a song of thanksgiving. It is as much testimony to others as it is an expression to God.

So the psalmist turns and addresses the congregation with the most memorable words of the prayer (v. 8 [Heb 9]): Trust in God at all times, in every situation…God is a refuge. What the praying one has learned in the situation of suffering, in the anguish and struggle of the soul, is a word that is proclaimed to others. In the songs of trust, such as this psalm, the *congregation* is called to live a life of confidence in the strength and salvation of the Lord. Those who hear this testimony to the source of hope and salvation are encouraged to learn from this prayer, to find an attitude of faith in its words that is indicative for all.

3. According to the psalm, the manifestation of that trust is precisely *in prayer*. The psalmist says, "Pour out your heart before God" (v. 8 [Heb 9]). That, of course, is a way of speaking of the prayer for help, the cry to God for salvation and deliverance. It is the way Hannah, the mother of Samuel, describes her prayer in the sanctuary when she is so depressed that she can do nothing but cry and won't eat anything. When Eli thinks she has been drinking because he hears her talking in the sanctuary, she says, "I am a deeply troubled woman. I have drunk neither wine nor beer, but I have been pouring out my soul to the Lord" (1 Sam 1:15). The heading of Ps 102 describes such crying out as a prayer of "one afflicted and faint who was pouring out his complaint before the Lord." Those who trust in the Lord at all times know that they can pour out their soul before the

Lord, and that pouring out of the deeply troubled heart, of the afflicted and persecuted soul, of the sick and dying body is itself an act of trust.

The equation of the human creature's crying out in trouble and distress with trust is underscored in the lament of the psalmist in Ps 22:

4In you our ancestors *trusted*;
   They *trusted*, and you delivered them.
5To you they *cried*, and were saved;
   In you they *trusted* and were not put to shame.

The repetition of the verb "trust" three times in four lines is a powerful emphasis on the character of the act of the ancestors remembered by the psalmist. The one difference in the four lines is the verb "cried," clearly to be understood in the poetic parallelism as a synonym for "trusted." The cry of a person in trouble may be understood by others or in other contexts as a reflex action. And perhaps it is at times. The Psalms know that such a way of being and responding is what it means to be human. Indeed the very articulation of the cry in the form of lament is a part of being human, giving voice to the hurt but not simply crying in the dark. It is a voicing of the hurt that is always lifted up to the one who can help. That is the meaning of trust, the conviction that in the deepest distress of human existence, God is receptive to the cry for help. That the words of the psalmist in Ps 22 may also be a kind of struggle of the soul in dialogue with itself is a further reflection of what is learned from Ps 62. Trust is not something that comes after all is tidied up. That is a kind of evidential certitude. Trust is indeed there because of the experience of God's deliverance. That is what Ps 22 claims from the family story. But in the new situation of trouble, the one in distress prays because of the conviction that life is under God's care and the ears of God are receptive to one who trusts enough to cry out. The Chronicler reports such a mode of being in a succinct narrative account of a war of the Reubenites, the Gadites, and the half-tribe of Manasseh against the Hagrites and others: "...for they cried to God in the battle, and he granted their entreaty because they trusted in him" (1 Chron 5:20).

4. The claim of the psalm, that one may trust in the Lord at all times is developed in various ways in Ps 62.

a. Three images cluster together to describe the way the psalmist sees God and his or her relationship to God. They are "rock," "fortress," and "refuge." All of these are frequent images for God in the psalms and often found together, as is the case here, for they express a common, single point – security. They tend to do that from two angles. One is the sense that one is protected from all harm by God's strength and power, that one is secure from the danger of enemies, protected in a mighty fortress that can not be breached by whatever forces are at work to destroy one. Martin Luther's great hymn of the Reformation is rooted, of course, precisely in this theology: "A mighty fortress is our God, a bulwark never failing." The particular psalm that triggered that hymn was Ps 46, but it is echoed in this and many other psalms whose theme is "God is our refuge."[12]

The "rock" imagery, which elsewhere is a virtual title or epithet for the deity, says the same thing, but it adds another dimension to the sense of security, and that is its image of solidity, of a firm place to stand. That point is made explicitly in the psalm when the ascription of the images to God is followed by the expression, "I shall not be shaken." Or as in other translations, "I shall not be moved." Here is one of the psalmic roots of that familiar and much loved American gospel hymn, "I shall not be moved." This is one of the most common expressions of security in the psalms: The one who trusts in God shall not be moved, shall not be shaken, shall not totter and fall (e.g., Ps 15:5; 46:5).

Here, therefore, is a cluster of powerful non-human images for God. They are rich and to be appropriated rather than ignored in the common tendency to focus heavily upon personal images for God. They are not meant to convey an impersonal notion. Indeed, Deut 32 speaks about "the Rock that bore you" (v. 18). But they point us to other features and alleviate some of the difficulties that arise when all one's conversation and theological discourse about God is dependent upon personal images. Not least is that the case because these images do not become easily literalized, much less idolized, tendencies that are too much evident or at least possible, for example, in the discussion about "Father" as image for God.

b. The claim that one may trust in the Lord at all times is developed secondly in contrasting the strength and power of God, the reliability and trustworthiness of the Lord with the ephemeral weakness of all human beings and of all sources of confidence in human terms.

[9]Those of low estate are but a breath,
    those of high estate are a delusion;
 in the balances they go up;
    they are together lighter than a breath.
[10]Put no confidence in extortion,
    and set no vain hopes on robbery;
   if riches increase, do not set your heart on them.

---

[12] On the extent of this imagery in the Psalter and its function in the shaping of the theology of the whole, see Jerome F. D. Creach, *Yahweh as Refuge and the Editing of the Hebrew Psalter* (JSOTSup 217; Sheffield: Sheffield Academic Press, 1996).

Put all the human beings together in the world, big shots and little folks, kings and street people, and they are no more solid and reliable than a breath of air, weighing nothing on a set of scales. So also, there is no final security in wealth and the accumulation of riches, whether by legal or illegal means. Here the text sets a direct counter word to the one about trusting in the Lord. One is not to "trust" in extortion, in wealth accumulated by coercive and oppressive means. But the verse goes even further: "If riches increase, do not set your heart on them" (v. 10 [Heb 11]). It is an anticipation of Jesus' words about not being able to serve both God and mammon. One is inclined to think that if one invests in anything and one's wealth grows, there is one's security. Not so says the psalmist. Do not put your heart there. A bit of practical wisdom: A bear market is soon to follow. In other words, "consumer confidence polls" are wrong-headed from the start and those who are sweating out their retirement investments, for example, need to sit with the Psalms for a while and learn wherein to place their trust. It surely is not in the stock market, which may be one of the best lessons of the past few years.

c. Finally, the claim that one may trust in the Lord at all times is developed in the repeated use of a little-noted particle that conveys in a more *affective* or *feeling* way than substantively the confidence of the psalm. That particle is the small Hebrew word *'ak*, a word that has a double meaning or is capable of being used in two different ways. It appears six times in the first nine verses, though not all of those are indicated in the translation. Insignificant as the small word may be, one can hardly ignore its frequency here. Although it appears more than 150 times in the Bible, in no other text is it repeated as often as in this psalm. Where one sees the word "alone" or "only," it is a reflection of this particle. For one of its meanings, and the one most often reflected in the translations of this psalm, is that restrictive meaning, "only, alone." In this sense, the psalmist sets up the contrast again between God as a source of security and confidence in the face of life's disasters, threats, and contingencies and all other possible places of refuge or secure standing ground. *Only* God, says the Psalm, God alone is my salvation and refuge. That is the only secure rock I know. Its christological interpretation is in the old hymn "On Christ the solid rock I stand; all other ground is sinking sand."

And then with regard to human beings, the particle appears twice more: "Their *only* plan"(v. 4 [Heb. 5]) – those who oppress and persecute and batter a victim – is to bring someone down, to lie and destroy, to undercut hypocritically. And then, again, human beings (v. 9 [Heb. 10]) are *but/only* a breath. The only sure foundation is God and the thing this psalmist knows about human beings is that they are only a breath and some of them have no purpose or intention but to undo others. The small particle sets up the contrast in strong terms.

But this particle has another meaning. It can have emphatic force, "indeed," "surely." So some have translated, "Indeed/surely my soul waits in silence for God." "Surely they plan to bring down a prominent person." And it may be that the particle means "only" in some instances in the psalm and "surely" in the others. One translation, however, has seen this emphatic affirming meaning as consistent throughout the passage and translated it as follows:

Yes, my soul waits calmly for God,
Yes, God is my rock where I am secure;
Yes, despite being a person of high status, they plan
    to push him down,
Yes, calmly wait for God, O my soul,
Yes, God is my rock where I am secure.
Yes, ordinary people are only a breath.

In other words, the particle is that liturgical refrain known and used in low church and black church tradition: Yes! My soul waits calmly for God – Yes! God is my rock and my salvation – Yes! Trust in God at all times; human beings are only a breath – Yes! The particle thus serves as a kind of repeated affirmation of trust and conviction, underscoring everything that is said about God and in contrary fashion about the unreliability of the human creature in comparison.

Old Testament Theology

17. Constitution or Instruction?

The Purpose of Deuteronomy[1]

Few studies of the book of Deuteronomy in the last twenty-five years have been as significant for or as influential on the study of the book as Dean McBride's sharply honed analysis of Deuteronomy as a kind of constitution or polity for ancient Israel.[2] His essay differs sharply with the more common reading of Deuteronomy as having a primarily instructive function, as being a form of proclamation and/or teaching. Indeed McBride's intention was to challenge this reading (or misreading) of the book in favor of its character as a formal and precise presentation of a divinely authorized social, political, and religious order that was meant to be operative in Israel. This careful and forceful presentation has raised afresh the question of what it is that we have in Deuteronomy, and McBride's analysis has not been without its respondents. His work has caused others to revisit the issue. It is appropriate in this context to ask whether there is a way through this conflict, or possibly a way of viewing the character of the book that does not set these understandings simply in opposition to each other.

Some review of the options is necessary on the way to seeing how they can profitably engage each other. In this context, those options will be reduced to two, although any student of Deuteronomy knows immediately there are variations and nuances and indeed other ways of describing the character of the work than will be described here. The fundamental debate, however, centers, in my judgment, in the options posed in the title, a point that seems to be recognized clearly by McBride as well as by others.[3]

The view of Deuteronomy as essentially a homiletical or sermonic presentation of the law, whose aim is primarily to encourage obedience to the divine will, is especially associated with Gerhard von Rad but has been

---

[1] It is a great pleasure to offer this essay to Dean McBride, whose friendship and scholarly acumen have been a great gift for many years. In all matters Deuteronomic he is my constant guide.

[2] "Polity of the Covenant People: The Book of Deuteronomy," *Interpretation* 41 (1987), 229–244.

[3] "Is Deuteronomy constitutional law, more or less closely related to the everyday life of Israel, or is it teaching?" (A.D.H. Mayes, "On Describing the Purpose of Deuteronomy," *JSOT* 58 [1993], 15).

picked up or recognized by many others.[4] Von Rad also focused attention upon the character of the book as a covenant document and saw in it a liturgical sequence as well as a collection of sermons.[5] Indeed the book presents itself as sequence of three speeches or addresses by Moses (chaps. 1–4, 5–28, and 29–32) together with a conclusion (chaps. 33–34), which is also primarily a speech by Moses. The highly hortatory character of all of this material leads to viewing the speeches as serving a sermonic function, a kind of preaching as much or more than promulgation of law. It has become common to hear Deuteronomy referred to as "preached law."

Such a reading of the character of Deuteronomy has had two concomitant features. One is an implicit and sometimes explicit resistance to seeing the book as in any way a legal or socio-political code. That is reflected in von Rad's *Old Testament Theology* when he says:

Indeed, in reducing all the profusion of the commandments to the one fundamental commandment, to love God (Deut 6:4), and in concerning itself so earnestly with the inner, the spiritual, meaning of the commandments, *Deuteronomy rather looks like a last stand against the beginning of a legislation* (italics mine).[6]

Further on, von Rad writes: "Deuteronomy does not set out to be civil law – none of the legal codes in the Old Testament is to be understood in this way."[7] Noth also argued against seeing Deuteronomy as a reflection of state law. Rather it is the basis for the covenantal relationship.[8] An even more explicit rejection of the notion of Deuteronomy as a juridical work in favor of understanding the book as preaching and teaching is found in the comment of G. Ernest Wright:

Deuteronomy is not a juridical book prepared for the use of the judges, kings, and priests of Israel, whose task it was to administer law. It was written for the community, for the "church" of Israel, as a whole. It is a preaching, a proclamation and exposition of the

---

[4] See also the work of Martin Noth on Deuteronomy in his monograph "The Laws in the Pentateuch: Their Assumptions and Meaning," in *The Laws in the Pentateuch and Other Essays* (Edinburgh: Oliver and Boyd, 1965), 1–107. I have focused attention upon the homiletical character of Deuteronomy in my commentary (*Deuteronomy,* [Interpretation; Louisville: John Knox Press, 1990]).

[5] The discussion of von Rad rests upon several of his works including his commentary (*Deuteronomy* [trans. Dorothea Barton; OTL; Philadelphia: Westminster, 1966]), his Old Testament theology (*Old Testament Theology* [trans. D. G. M. Stalker; 2 Vols.; New York: Harper, 1962]), his early collection of essays (*Studies in Deuteronomy* [SBT 9; London: SCM Press, 1953]), and his extended dictionary presentation of the book in *IDB*, (New York: Abingdon, 1962), 1:831–838.

[6] Von Rad, *Old Testament Theology,* 1:201.

[7] Ibid., 1:228.

[8] "The Laws in the Pentateuch."

faith of the nation, which includes the law as the expression of the will of God which must be obeyed, but which in itself is not primarily a law. It is a gospel of the redeeming God who has saved a people from slavery and has bound them to himself in a covenant. . . . There can be no doubt ... that the original purpose of Deuteronomy was not to impose a legalistic system upon the Israelite community, but rather to convey the Mosaic "teaching" or "doctrine."[9]

This is not all that Wright had to say about the purpose of Deuteronomy (see below), but the accent is the same as von Rad's.

The other and even more significant feature of the homiletical way of viewing Deuteronomy, as McBride recognizes at the outset of his study, is an understanding of *tôrâ* as it appears in Deuteronomy as "*instruction*" or "*teaching*." The term *tôrâ* is quite important for understanding the purpose of Deuteronomy. "This *tôrâ*" or "this book of the *tôrâ*" appears at several key places (e.g., 1:5; 4:8, 44; 17:18, 19; 27:3, 8, 26; 28:58, 61; 29:21, 29; 30:10; 31:9, 11, 12, 26) as a way of referring to the Decalogue, the Shema, the exposition of the Decalogue and the Shema in chapters 6–11, the code in chapters 12–26 (together with the curses and blessings that are sanctions to secure obedience to the *tôrâ* and identify the consequences of disobedience), and to the book of Deuteronomy as a whole. Much has been made of the possibility of understanding this term as it appears in Deuteronomy as not simply referring either to a priestly decision or to law as it is customarily understood, but as having to do generally with teaching.[10] That seems to be especially the case with Deuteronomy, where a strong emphasis on teaching and learning is present, and where Moses functions very much as a teacher of the divine will.

It is just this issue, the proper meaning of *tôrâ* in the book of Deuteronomy, that is the jumping off point for Dean McBride in his challenge to the reading of the book as teaching and proclamation.[11] His point, however, is

---

[9] "Deuteronomy," *The Interpreter's Bible* (Nashville: Abingdon, 1953), II, 312, 313. It is apparent in Wright's comment that one of his concerns, as seems regularly to be the case with treatments of Old Testament law and particularly Deuteronomy, is a *legalistic* reading of the book. The notion of preached law and of teaching is a way of combating this tendency.

[10] Here the work of Gunnar Östborn, *Tora in the Old Testament: A Semantic Study* (Lund: Hakan Ohlssons, 1945) has been formative, as well as Barnabas Lindars' study of the word in Deuteronomy, "Torah in Deuteronomy," in *Words and Meanings: Essays Presented to David Winton Thomas*, ed. P. R. Ackroyd and B. Lindars (Cambridge: Cambridge University Press, 1968), 117–136. Lindars summarizes the results of his study in these words: "תורה, then, is the word employed by the Deuteronomic editors to convey their concept of the code as a complete expression of the will of God, having the same binding force as the Decalogue, recorded especially for the welfare of the people, to be learnt and pondered by them. The term retains its didactic overtones, and to say 'the book of the divine instruction' might represent the real meaning better than the usual translation 'the book of the law'" (131).

[11] See "Polity of the Covenant People," nn. 9 and 10, in which McBride critiques some of the scholarly interpretations of *tôrâ*.

not to return to the more customary understanding of *tôrâ* as "law." He takes his cue from one of the oldest interpreters of Deuteronomy, Josephus, who speaks of Deuteronomy as containing the divine polity (Greek *politeia*) delivered by Moses at the end of his life. McBride argues that the use of *politeia* rather than *nomos* is a self-conscious, indeed polemical choice of terms. Such language indicates that Josephus understood the purpose of Deuteronomy as setting forth the socio-political order for Israel's life, an order that had priority over Greek and Roman claims to have the most sublime forms of polity of any nation state. The book of Deuteronomy thus provides a kind of constitution for the nation of Israel, "the divinely authorized social order that Israel must implement to secure its collective political existence as the people of God."[12]

As McBride's programmatic essay is included in this volume, there is no need to describe his argument in detail. Some summary, however, is necessary in order to build upon his work. He notes the frequent reference to the *written* character of the book and the fact that it is the one book that is referred to and cited elsewhere in the Old Testament.[13] The words of the Deuteronomic *tôrâ* are not simply admonitions and guidelines for the faithful but "sanctioned political policies"[14] to be obeyed as one would expect to obey any constitutional provisions. Those provisions, promulgated by "the legislative agency of Moses"[15] are set forth in the "decrees" (Decalogue) and the "statutes and ordinances" (the Deuteronomic code of chaps. 12–26, called by McBride "constitutional articles"[16]), and they are formally adopted in a ratification ceremony involving a mutual swearing of oaths (26:16–19). Provision is made for formal deposit and rereading of the constitution and an elaborate list of sanctions (blessings and curses) is included (chap. 28).

McBride argues that Deuteronomy is something totally new at this point in the character of its polity. It is "a comprehensive social charter"[17] for a "constitutional theocracy"[18] that is highly democratic in its substance. The radical developments of this constitution include its insistence on an egalitarian justice that is rooted in its view of the God who is the authority be-

---

[12] McBride, "Polity of the Covenant People," 233.

[13] For a recent focus on the significance of the written character of Deuteronomy and of writing within Deuteronomy, see the monograph by Jean-Pierre Sonnet, *The Book within the Book: Writing in Deuteronomy* (Biblical Interpretation Series 14; Leiden: E. J. Brill, 1997).

[14] McBride, "Polity of the Covenant People," 233.

[15] Ibid., 234.

[16] Ibid., 234, n. 14.

[17] Ibid., 237.

[18] Ibid., 238.

hind the constitution (10:17–19), the responsibility of the people for choosing their political (17:15) and judicial leaders (16:18), and the role of the king, whose election is democratic (17:15), whose prerogatives are limited (17:16–17), and whose only responsibility is to insure that the constitution is carefully attended to and followed (17:18–20). In its specific provisions, the Deuteronomic polity seeks to protect "above all the sanctity of life and the worth of individual personhood."[19]

This interpretation of Deuteronomy as a polity or constitution setting forth a socio-political order in the context of a religious community, effecting in this case a kind of constitutional theocracy, is of no small moment. The book of Deuteronomy is not simply instruction for faith and ethics. Rather, McBride argues, it is "the archetype of modern western constitutionalism."[20] Indeed, "the Deuteronomic model of theocentric humanism"[21] remains a model in the continuing struggle for social justice and human rights. The political character of the book is as important as its religious character.

The canonical position of the book of Deuteronomy at the conclusion of the Pentateuch further underscores its purpose as a constitution. Deuteronomy rounds off the Mosaic era with comprehensive Mosaic legislation for the future life of the community in the land. Whatever the historical locus for this constitution – and McBride does not really address that question[22] – it is presented now as the polity for the community throughout its life in the land. That sanctions do not appear elsewhere in the Pentateuch undergirds the claim of this polity to control the social order of the community.

The new era under Joshua begins with the Lord's commissioning of Joshua to lead the people into the land and conquer it. But to that is added a very specific word with reference to the Mosaic *tôrâ*:

[7]Only be strong and very courageous, being careful to act in accordance with all the law that my servant Moses commanded you; do not turn from it to the right hand or to the left, so that you may be successful wherever you go. [8]This book of the *tôrâ* shall not depart out of your mouth; you shall meditate on it day and night, so that you may be careful to act in accordance with all that is written in it. For then you shall make your way prosperous, and then you shall be successful. (Josh 1:7–8)

---

[19] Ibid., 242.

[20] Ibid., 243.

[21] Ibid., 244.

[22] One should note, however, his brief comments on these matters in his introduction to Deuteronomy in *The Harper Collins Study Bible* annotated edition of the NRSV where he says: "Many of the characteristic provisions of the book find a close correspondence in the reforms instituted by [Josiah]. Yet in its received form the editing of the traditions points to an exilic setting – when the older Mosaic constitution may have been set within an expanded frame of Moses' valedictory addresses to Israel."

The way in which the Deuteronomic polity was to shape the life and order of the whole community is further underscored when Joshua erects an altar to the Lord on Mount Ebal, specifically citing the Mosaic instruction in the "book of the *tôrâ*." The whole of the *tôrâ* is written on the stones of the altar and then read to "all Israel" (Josh 8:30–35). Emphasis is placed upon the whole assembly being present for this writing and reading of the *tôrâ*, including women, children, and resident aliens (*haggēr hahōlēk bĕqirbām*), an implicit indication of the authority of the polity for each member of the community.

Finally, the evident correlations between the provisions of the Deuteronomic Code and the Josianic reform evidence a signal moment when the book actually functioned as a political and religious charter for ordering the life of the community. Although, in this instance, the reading and writing of the *tôrâ* was especially important for the religious life, it was no doubt a highly political matter for ancient Israel, as evidenced by the way in which the Deuteronomic Code begins with attention to the "unique institutional locus of Israel's communal life."[23]

McBride's reading of Deuteronomy as a constitution is not new, as he himself argues vigorously with reference to Josephus. Other scholars have so understood the book. S. R. Driver suggested viewing Deuteronomy as a kind of "manual" for life in the land.[24] But such a descriptive term does not really point to the socio-political character of the book and suggests more a handbook or how-to guide: an analogy that, while not inappropriate, lacks the precision of the notion of polity. Like McBride, Moshe Weinfeld has suggested that Deuteronomy "has the character of an ideal constitution representing all the official institutions of the state."[25] Similarly, Jacob Milgrom says that Deuteronomy "fashions a national constitution under state-controlled officials."[26] Even G. Ernest Wright, who championed a view of the book as proclamation and exposition also saw in it "a revealed order of society," suggesting that these counter views are not inherently incompatible.[27]

But while McBride's masterful development of the constitutional character of Deuteronomy and its significance has persuaded many, it has not

---

[23] McBride, "Polity of the Covenant People," 240.

[24] S. R. Driver, *Deuteronomy* (ICC; New York: Charles Scribner's Sons, 1895), xxvi.

[25] Moshe Weinfeld, *Deuteronomy and the Deuteronomic School* (Oxford: The Clarendon Press, 1972) 168.

[26] Jacob Milgrom, *Leviticus 17–22* (AB 3A; New York: Doubleday, 2000), 1356. See also his argument with regard to the Pentateuch that "the Torah's laws, far from being a guide for behavior, were, at least in part, the living code of Israel" (1348).

[27] Wright, "Deuteronomy," 313.

won the day.[28] One of the most vigorous and articulate counter voices to McBride's interpretation has been that of Dennis Olson in his study of Deuteronomy titled *Deuteronomy and the Death of Moses*.[29] Olson agrees that *tôrâ* is indeed the key term for describing the book but argues that it refers to a program of "catechesis" rather than to a polity. Further, he believes that McBride's interpretation of Deuteronomy as a constitution comes closer to understanding the book as a whole than such interpretations as covenant, sermon, or law code. Indeed, Olson says:

> The proposal that Deuteronomy is a constitution comes closest among all the preceding proposals in laying out its form and function. Deuteronomy is intended to be the basis for a community's identity and life. The book does provide a succinct and condensed summation of what the community is to be. Some interest in the structures of governance is evident as would be expected in a constitution.[30]

But Olson claims that the instructional and teaching character of the term *tôrâ* as well as of the book as a whole is much more prominent and not really reflected in the constitutional interpretation. As Olson puts it:

> [T]he identification of *tôrâ* with "constitution" misses the connotations of "teaching" and "instruction" that are part of the semantic range of *tôrâ* and part of the central didactic concern of the present form of Deuteronomy. A constitution is not so much taught as it is legislated and enforced. The present book of Deuteronomy does not legislate as much as it teaches.[31]

Olson properly picks up the book's large interest in passing on the story, law, and covenant from one generation to the next. He notes the frequent presence of terms meaning "teach" and "learn," and suggests that in the

---

[28] A.D.H. Mayes' essay ("On Describing the Purpose of Deuteronomy") seems to have been inspired by McBride's work, though Mayes himself takes another approach, drawing upon Habermas. According to Mayes, Deuteronomy arose out of the stresses and strains of the monarchy, and out of growing relation to the larger world of nations, specifically Assyria with its worldview and culture. His analysis is helpful and makes some sense. However, his conclusion, that Deuteronomy "is to be understood as a resource not in itself a constitution or piece of state legislation, but rather a resource to give objective grounding to such a constitution or legislation" (30), is a rather weak outcome and not really a derivative of the employment of Habermas' categories. The distinction between resource and constitutional outcome of resource is not clear, nor is it clear why the former takes priority over the latter in describing the purpose of Deuteronomy. For further discussion of the recent literature on this issue, see Mark A. O'Brien, "The Book of Deuteronomy," *Currents in Research: Biblical Studies* 3 (1995), 105–108.

[29] *Deuteronomy and the Death of Moses: A Theological Reading* (OBT; Minneapolis: Fortress, 1994).

[30] Ibid., 10.

[31] Ibid., 10.

Deuteronomic mode catechesis implies some corollaries beyond interest in educating or socializing a new generation in the community's tradition. These include the fact that Deuteronomy is a kind of systematic theology, forged out of the community's experience; it is an ongoing and adaptive process, with a core in the Decalogue to which the rest of the book is secondary interpretation. Mechanisms are set up in the book for ongoing teaching and interpretation. As catechesis, Deuteronomy is able to incorporate various genres and thus use a variety of methods and forms to achieve its goals. Further, unlike a law code, the Deuteronomic catechesis attains its power not by enforcement but by persuasion and conviction. Finally, Deuteronomy is oriented toward the community, concerned with how individuals relate to others within the community and also shaping the structural and institutional forms of life for the community.

While there are many interpreters who have commented on these matters, the relatively recent seminal and thorough studies by McBride and Olson serve as well as any to illustrate and dramatize the issue. What is Deuteronomy about? What does it seek to do, whether one is speaking about that in relation to earliest forms of the book or to its continuing function as a scripture for a community of faith over many centuries? Who is right in this argument? Is one to read the book as a charter for a political form of communal life or is one to read it to be instructed in the ways God would have the community to live its life? If these are related, how is that so? Does one of these understandings represent the dominant intention of the book while the other one is a recognizable, but not a dominant, strain? A simple response to these questions would be to acknowledge the possibility of multiple purposes to Deuteronomy. That is certainly plausible. To some degree I have argued elsewhere for that sort of flexibility as being built into the very nature of Deuteronomy.[32] A case can be made, however, for a greater integration of these two perspectives. The degree to which both McBride and Olson have identified major shaping and determinative dimensions of the book suggests that these are to be seen as deeply involved with one another. McBride and Olson have each acknowledged there is some truth to the other way of perceiving Deuteronomy, but have claimed that the other way does not really get at the main character and purpose of the book. Choosing between constitution and instruction may be a false option, however. Deuteronomy's significance and purpose lies precisely in the joining of the two.

It is not possible to ignore the character of the book as setting forth a large and comprehensive social order, a polity for the people of God, and

---

[32] See the introduction to my commentary on Deuteronomy.

indeed one that has profound influence upon western constitutionalism, as McBride argues. All of McBride's arguments are cogent, and his point is to be recognized. Indeed, the point may be pressed even further. The distinction between the Decalogue and the Deuteronomic Code is universally recognized. It is Deuteronomy that makes the most of this difference, first in its *narrative* account of the people asking Moses to go and listen to the rest of what God has to say after giving the people the ten words, because they are afraid they will not live if they encounter God face to face again, and then in its reiterated *distinction between the commandments* given directly to the assembly at Sinai and *the later Mosaic teaching* of the rest of the divine instruction, that is, the statutes and ordinances, on the plains of Moab (e.g., 4:12-14; 5:1; 6:1; 12:1). What many have recognized is that if Deuteronomy is to be understood as the polity for the people of Israel, specifically as that centers in the Decalogue and the Deuteronomic Code, in a sense one can argue that the constitution per se is the Decalogue. The Deuteronomic Code specifies and illustrates the force and meaning of these constitutional guidelines in all spheres of Israel's life, much as contemporary law in the United States is developed out of the guidelines in the U.S. Constitution.[33] The fundamental decrees or principles represented by the Commandments continue throughout and are presented twice, in Exodus and Deuteronomy. In each case, they are followed by a body of case and apodictic law that often reflects or specifies the force of the Commandments in particular instances. But this latter material differs significantly between the Book of the Covenant in Exodus and the Deuteronomic Code. The specifying goes on in different ways in different times and places, but the basic decrees perdure in every time and place. Deuteronomy represents a formulation of the polity in a particular time and moment, but one that

---

[33] For an argument that the Deuteronomic Code in 12–26 is set up in a sequence of statutes reflecting the sequence of the Decalogue in chap. 5, see Stephen A. Kaufman, "The Structure of the Deuteronomic Law," MAARAV 1 (1978–79), 105–158; and Georg Braulik, "Die Abfolge der Gesetze in Deuteronomium 12–26 und der Dekalog," in *Das Deuteronomium: Entstehung, Gestalt und Botschaft*, ed. N. Lohfink (BETL 68; Leuven: Leuven Univ., 1985), 252–272 [trans. as "The Sequence of the Laws in Deuteronomy in 12–26 and in the Decalogue," in *A Song of Power and the Power of Song: Essays on the Book of Deuteronomy*, ed. D. L. Christensen (Sources for Biblical and Theological Study 3; Winona Lake, Indiana, 1993), 313–335]. Braulik has offered a more extended study in his monograph *Die deuteronomischen Gesetze und der Dekalog: Studien zum Aufbau von Deuteronomium 12–26* (SBS 145; Stuttgart: Verlag Katholisches Bibelwerk, 1991). This kind of connection between the Decalogue and the Deuteronomic Code, even if not always precisely as Kaufman and Braulik argue it, has been recognized from very early stages in the history of interpretation. See above, 3–16.

has been preserved and shaped in a way that is meant to be a guide for the social order for the community throughout the generations.[34]

The polity and constitutional character of the book is thus evident in the way in which it presents a comprehensive set of fundamental guides for the life of the community – its authority relations and its internal relations, its religious life and its moral life – and then in a systematic way works out the various aspects of the community's life in various specifics. The subject matter of these specifications further underscores the constitutional character of "this *tôrâ.*" It deals with basic institutions and centers of the community's life (the temple), relation to authorities – beginning with the deity but including the various political and juridical and religious authorities – the practices of war, relationships to other states, economic regulations, matters of legal asylum and sanctuary.[35] Even the issue of amending the constitution is taken up. The requirement that nothing be added to or taken away from the Mosaic teaching (4:2; 12:32 [MT 13:1]) may be seen as a canonical formula, but before that it is a *constitutional* formula. So also the Deuteronomic characteristic of referring to the members of the community regularly as *ʾaḥ* ("brother/ sister") rather than the more customary *rēaᶜ* ("neighbor") is a more formal and technical reference to the citizens of the commonweal. This term assumes a formal, familial relationship, not simply one of proximity.

So the constitutional character of the book as a charter for the divinely appointed socio-political order of Israel seems very clear. It is also the case, however, that the constant and unique references to teaching and learning that fill this book together with its rhetorical forms and style are a major part of what the reader confronts in the book. There are seventeen uses of the verb *lāmad*, having to do with teaching and learning, in Deuteronomy (4:1, 5, 10 [2x], 14; 5:1, 28; 6:1; 11:19; 14:23; 17:19; 18:9; 20:18; 31:12, 13, 19, 22). This verb does not appear elsewhere in the Pentateuch. That is a remarkable and inescapable pointer to a deep concern for instruction and teaching. But alongside those explicit references to teaching and learning, various and obvious dimensions of rhetoric and form confirm a preaching or hortatory dimension to this book that is fundamen-

---

[34] Dennis Olson has argued this point in an even more extensive way. He sees in the present form of Deut 5, whose primary substance is the Decalogue, a "miniature version of the structure of the whole book...the *torah* of Deuteronomy *en nuce*" (*The Death of Moses*, 15). He thus follows the line of Kaufman and Braulik, arguing that "the rest of Deuteronomy is visualized as extended and secondary commentary or exposition of the primal Decalogue" (16–17). Olson has a valuable presentation of some of the discussion of this issue in the contemporary literature on 63–64, n. 3.

[35] See Article IV of the United States Constitution, which deals with people fleeing from one state to another to avoid prosecution.

tal to its character, however one translates the key word *tôrâ*. Some of these are: (1) frequent reference to "this day" or "today," (2) the use of "we" in the credos and elsewhere, (3) frequent emphatic use of second-person pronouns ("you"), (4) repeated summons to hearing, (5) numerous vocatives, (6) appeal to memory as a way of actualizing the past in the present, (7) use of threat and promise to motivate hearers to respond, (8) appeal to heart and mind, and (9) use of illustrations (cf. Deut 19:5 and Exod 21:12–14).[36] To these may be added the frequent use of the expression "observe diligently" (emphatic constructions of *šāmar*, "keep," or "observe," or *šāmar* + *ᶜāśâ*, "carry out," e.g., 6:3, 17-18, 25; 7:11, 12; 8:1; 11:22, 32; 12:32 [Heb. 13:1]; 26:16).[37] That there are more motivational clauses attached to Deuteronomic statutes than in any other body of legal material in the Pentateuch serves further to underscore the intent to reason, urge, encourage, and instruct in a way that enhances learning and obedience.

All these rhetorical elements and the concern for teaching and learning are not, however, to be separated from or set over against the constitutional function of the book. Against Olson's assumption that a constitution is not so much taught as it is legislated and enforced, this constitution or polity is indeed to be taught and learned and pressed upon the people. In an important essay on Deuteronomy, Georg Braulik argues for the character of the book as theology, as "theoretic-systematic expression of Israel's symbolic universe." [38] But this is clearly a "political theology."[39] In his presentation, he makes the cogent comment:

The rediscovered Torah-document presented itself as a textbook. If it were to be implemented as *constitution of the state* on account of God's covenant, it would require *a system of theoretical schooling* (my italics). In order to bring about the transformation of society towards favouring the faith in Yahweh, people now for the first time in the history of Israel actually started to *'learn'* in a technocratic sense. Within the advanced civilizations of the antique world, Deuteronomy therefore became a *'paradigm for cultural mnemonics'* (italics are from Assmann).[40]

---

[36] Miller, *Deuteronomy*, 12.

[37] There are variations on these expressions that express the same kind of urgent demand for keeping the constitutional order, e.g., 12:28.

[38] Georg Braulik, "'Conservative Reform.' Deuteronomy from the Perspective of the Sociology of Knowledge," *Old Testament Essays* 12/1 (1999), 15.

[39] Ibid., 17.

[40] Ibid., 20. The reference to Assmann is to Jan Assmann, *Das kulturelle Gedächtnis: Schrift, Erinnerung und politische Identität in frühen Hochkulturen* (Munich: Beck, 1992). Assmann includes an important chapter on Deuteronomy in his study of cultural memory.

The paranesis of Deuteronomy and its emphasis on teaching and learning, Braulik argues, is not aimed at raising an elite. Addressed to "all Israel," its aim is "the formation of a culture of conversation and remembrance for all generations, both men and women." The process is one of internalization and meditation, speaking and remembering and passing on in order to bring about "the complete internalisation of the Deuteronomic model of society."[41]

This joining of a strong hortatory and instructional dimension to the presentation of a model socio-political order, indeed a constitution, is a particular contribution of the Deuteronomic polity, but not peculiar to it.[42] This is something that McBride has clearly recognized, though not with much emphasis, perhaps in order to make his point about the constitutionality of the book as strongly as possible.[43] There were in ancient times, and are still today, differences of opinion about the degree to which juridical and political formulations are simply to be presented and promulgated or to be inculcated, urged, and taught. Seneca did not want reasons for obedience, simply to be told what to do.[44] Plato, however, argued that the laws will accomplish their purpose, and thus render the state prosperous and happy, partly by persuasion and partly by chastising. Deuteronomy understands both positions. On the one hand, it uses significant rhetorical features and motivational clauses to persuade; on the other, it sets up sanctions that are aimed primarily at chastisement for disobedience. At one point in his laws, Plato says: "I would wish that the people would be as persuadable as possible with regard to virtue; and it's clear that the law-

---

[41] Ibid.

[42] With its proliferation of motive clauses, Deuteronomy separates itself from most other ancient Near Eastern legal and political documents. While B. Gemser may have overdone it in his categorical claim that Near Eastern law had no motive clauses, in a more extended comparison of biblical and Near Eastern law, R. Sonsino, while acknowledging that there are some motive clauses in the latter, speaks of "the relative scarcity of motive clauses in cuneiform laws and their greater frequency in biblical legislation" and concludes that "motivation is not characteristic of the ancient Near Eastern law corpora." See B. Gemser, "The Importance of the Motive Clause in Old Testament Law," in *Adhuc loquitur – Collected Essays by Dr. B. Gemser*, eds. A. van Selms and A. S. van der Woude (Pretoria Oriental Series, 7; Leiden: Brill, 1968), 96–115; and R. Sonsino, *Motive Clauses in Hebrew Law* (SBL Dissertation Series 45; Chico, CA: Scholars Press, 1980).

[43] See "Polity," his last sentence of n. 9 and especially n. 22, where he sees Deuteronomy already setting forth Plato's ideal of a law or constitution preceded by explanatory prefaces and statements of persuasion with the sentences themselves.

[44] In his criticism of Plato, Seneca says: "I censor Plato, because he added justifications to the laws. Let the law be like the voice that reaches us from heaven. Command and do not argue. Tell me what I have to do. I do not want to learn. I want to obey." (quoted by D. Halivni, *Midrash, Mishnah, and Gemara: The Jewish Predilection for Justified Law* (Cambridge: Harvard University Press, 1986), 5.

giver will also strive to achieve this, in every facet of his legislation."[45] In other words, persuading the community to keep the social order in all its details as set forth in the laws and statutes is as much the aim of the legislator as setting forth the laws and statutes themselves. For Plato, the legislator had two instruments to use in legislation: persuasion and force.[46] The former was to be manifest especially in preludes or preambles, which would serve to prepare the soul to receive the law.[47] But he saw that each law itself might have a preamble to encourage obedience.[48]

Learning the polity of a community's life is a necessity for those who are responsible for leading the community. So it is that those who govern in a religious denomination are required to learn (and often be examined on) the polity of the denomination, so that they will know it and act according to it in all matters having to do with the governance of the different branches and institutions set forth in the polity. Many will keep a copy of the denomination's polity close at hand for reference when needed. In Deuteronomy, the whole assembly learns the polity, because one of the features of the social order is its highly democratic character and its concern for the well-being of each individual in the community.

But there is another kind of learning also, and that is *learning the story and the basic tenets* of the political order of the community's life. This is certainly a significant reason why the teaching of the nation's history is an important part of the curriculum for children in American public schools, so that they may learn the form of government of the country and be encouraged to abide by it. They may not learn all the details of the US Constitution, but they will learn its main points, and they will also be taught the story that evokes it and tells them what it means. They are taught that the nation's future well-being depends upon its citizens knowing and living

---

[45] *The Laws of Plato* (trans. Thomas L. Pangle; Chicago: The University of Chicago Press, 1988), IV:718.

[46] *Laws,* IV:722.

[47] Plato compared these preludes to musical preludes: "What I wish to say is this: all speeches, and whatever pertains to the voice, are preceded by preludes – almost like warming-up exercises – which artfully attempt to promote what is to come. It is the case, I suppose, that of the songs sung to the kithara, the so-called 'laws' or *nomoi*, like all music, are preceded by preludes composed with amazing seriousness" (*Laws,* IV:722).

[48] "...the lawgiver must always provide that all the laws, and each of them, will not lack preludes..." (*Laws,* IV:723). See also his earlier comment: "So then, is the one who is to have charge of our laws going to pronounce no such preface at the beginning of the laws? Is he just going to explain straightaway what must and must not be done, add the threat of a penalty, and turn to another law, without adding a single encouragement or bit of persuasion to his legislative edicts?" (*Laws,* IV:719–720). It is in this context that Plato makes his comparison between rough and gentle doctors, those who brusquely prescribe and go on, and those who talk to their patients.

by the polity it sets forth. It is thus not surprising to see such high interest in the education of the children in the Deuteronomic polity. That is the way in which the ideals and the particulars of the constitutional order are maintained and carried forward into the future. A community of remembrance is continually being formed and maintained, one that meditates on and internalizes the basics of the nation's polity.[49]

Finally, one may note that all of the constitutional order and all of the learning has an ultimate goal that is articulated again and again in Deuteronomy. In five of the seven instances of the verb, *lāmad*, "to learn" – that is, on most of those occasions when Moses tells the people that they are to learn something – what they are to learn is not "the statutes and ordinances" (as is the case in 5:1).[50] They are to "learn to fear the Lord your God" (4:10; 14:23; 17:19; 31:12, 13). Such learning, however, is clearly connected to the polity, its formal promulgation and its reiteration. Deut 4:9–14 is critical in this regard. The first reference to "learning" is a recall of the Sinai moment when the people were assembled expressly to "hear... and learn to fear me..." The reference here is explicitly to the giving of the Decalogue. Hearing those words is understood as in order to learn to fear the Lord.[51] So the constitution has this large goal, the inculcation, the training in the fear of the Lord. It is not only the promulgation of a socio-religious-political order, which indeed it is, starting with the Decalogue. That order, however, is put before the people to help them learn how to fear and serve and worship and live properly under the rule of God. The ultimate goal of this order is not in itself, but in its being a vehicle for the community's life in fear of the Lord. The point is underscored by the further word that the people are to "teach their children so" (4:10). That requirement, which has already been anticipated in the preceding verse and so is emphasized by its being repeated here, further confronts us with the importance of the teaching of the constitution to the community and to future generations. Then at the conclusion of this section, we are told that Moses has a divine commission to "teach" the statutes and ordinances to be observed in the land. They are not simply promulgated but from the start are taught to the people. The Mosaic instruction, beginning at Deut 6,

---

[49] Braulik, "'Conservative Reform'."

[50] Deut 18:9 is the one other use of *lāmad* as "learn," and there the point is that the people are not to learn the abhorrent practices of the Canaanites. This is the negative version of learning to fear the Lord your God. The people are not to "learn to do according to the abhorrent practices of those nations." Cf. Deut 20:18.

[51] In 6:13, as widely recognized, the fear of the Lord is a positive formulation of the First Commandment. Thus one of the ways in which the community demonstrates its obedience to the First Commandment is in its learning and keeping (see 5:1) the polity set forth in Deuteronomy.

makes explicit that the Mosaic teaching of the statutes and ordinances and the Lord's giving of the Ten Words have the same ultimate goal: that the people learn to fear the Lord. Echoing the point that has been made vis-à-vis the commandments when given at Sinai, Moses says with regard to all that now follows:

> [1]Now this is the commandment – the statutes and the ordinances – that the LORD your God charged me to teach you to observe in the land that you are about to cross into and occupy, [2]so that you and your children and your children's children may fear the LORD your God all the days of your life, and keep all his decrees and his commandments that I am commanding you, so that your days may be long. (Deut 6:1–2)

One may presume that as the community is taught by Moses and as the community is instructed in emphatic terms to "make them known to your children and your children's children" (4:9–10), we are given a large clue about the purpose of Deuteronomy itself, to be the vehicle for the teaching of the social order, of the polity that governs and orders the life of the people of God, a teaching whose ultimate goal is to instill in each member of the community, as they live in this way, by this specific order of existence and communal life, a proper fear and worship of the Lord their God.

The remaining uses of "learn to fear the Lord your God" confirm this emphasis on learning the polity as a learning of the proper fear of the Lord. The king's only responsibility is to have a copy of "this *tôrâ*" at all times, reading in it constantly (and so learning it) "so that he may learn to fear the Lord his God, diligently observing all the words of this *tôrâ* and these statutes" (17:19). In just this way, the king becomes the model Israelite. Then at the conclusion of the book, Moses orders the writing down of "this *tôrâ*" and calls for a regular reading of it in the future. This is to be an assembly of the people as was the case at Sinai and a reading of "this *tôrâ*" "so that they may *hear and learn to fear the Lord your God* and to observe diligently all the words of this law" (31:12). Again, careful observance and implementation of the constitutional charter is the vehicle for instilling the fear of God. Hearing the polity set forth teaches how one may fear the Lord. And, as was the case at Sinai, the polity is to be taught to the children, who otherwise will not know it, so that they may "hear and learn to fear the Lord your God."

One may suggest, therefore, that it is precisely in the conjoining of the constitutional and catechetical aspects of the book of Deuteronomy that one may find its distinctive intention. Deuteronomy gives to the community a concrete form for its life, setting forth and teaching a model of social existence that is not only spelled out in broad principles but also illustrated and specified. Its character has been well described in Dean McBride's careful analysis of the Deuteronomic polity. If the community embodied in this book is a neighborhood, it is also a commonwealth. For the community to live in fact by this pattern, by these institutional forms, and by these prescriptions for neighborly life among the citizens of the commonwealth, the polity must be preserved, read, remembered, and taught to future generations. Its desirability is underscored as modes of persuasion and reason are incorporated into the constitution. The appeal of living this way is evident throughout the book. The exhortation and the learning, however, is not simply to make good citizens. It is to bring about a community of those faithful to the Lord, who demonstrate in the totality of personal, communal, and institutional life their devotion and their proper reverence.

18. "Slow to Anger"

The God of the Prophets

It is to the prophetic books especially, though not only to them, that Christian theology – in its more sophisticated forms and especially in popular theology – owes its tendency to depict the God of Israel or the God of the Old Testament as a God of wrath and judgment, a kind of Janus-faced deity, sometimes turning toward Israel or humankind in wrath, sometimes turning in mercy and compassion. The former seems to be heavily the tone of the Lord's dealing with Israel in the time of the prophets, but the more loving aspect is acknowledged as also present at times.

Such a depiction of God misrepresents the prophetic word and has so distorted the revelation of the God of Israel as to undermine in significant ways the theological standing of the Old Testament in the Christian community, an outcome that is reflected in the absence of the Old Testament from preaching, theology, and liturgy (apart from the Psalms) as well as a consequent misreading of the New Testament as a revelational corrective of the Old Testament's view of deity.

A proper understanding of the God of the prophets needs therefore to focus particularly on this issue, for all else flows out of it or is shaped by one's understanding of the judgment of God. A coherent but complex perception of the wrath and judgment of God within the message of the prophets needs to recognize several things.

God's Wrath

God's anger and judgment are real and a large part of the prophetic word. One cannot underplay this dimension of the prophet's oracles, especially those in the pre-exilic period. Text after text speaks "the word of the Lord," often in first person speech with vivid and disturbing imagery, about God's intent to destroy the people, and sometimes other peoples. For example, the Lord declares:

[13]My anger shall spend itself, and I will vent my fury on them and satisfy myself; and they shall know that I, the LORD, have spoken in my jealousy, when I spend my fury on them. [14]Moreover I will make you a desolation and an object of mocking among the nations around you, in the sight of all that pass by. [15]You shall be a mockery and a taunt, a

warning and a horror, to the nations around you, when I execute judgments on you in anger and fury, and with furious punishments – I, the LORD, have spoken – [16]when I loose against you my deadly arrows of famine, arrows for destruction, which I will let loose to destroy you, and when I bring more and more famine upon you, and break your staff of bread. [17]I will send famine and wild animals against you, and they will rob you of your children; pestilence and bloodshed shall pass through you; and I will bring the sword upon you. I, the LORD, have spoken. (Ezek 5:13–17)

Or in the words of another prophet:

[17]I will bring such distress upon people
    that they shall walk like the blind;
    because they have sinned against the LORD,
their blood shall be poured out like dust,
    and their flesh like dung.
[18]Neither their silver nor their gold will be able to save them
    on the day of the LORD's wrath;
in the fire of his passion
    the whole earth shall be consumed;
for a full, a terrible end
    he will make of all the inhabitants of the earth. (Zeph 1:17–18)

Such texts could be multiplied greatly, for the reality of judgment, expressed theologically as God's wrath or anger, is a constant subject of prophetic proclamation. The language is harsh, hyperbolic, disturbing, and relentless. The resultant picture of God as cruel and unbending, as jealous and vindictive, leaves the hearers of the word disturbed. Such language is meant to match the equally disturbing pictures of the sin of the people and of the nations, also articulated again and again in the prophetic preaching. That correlation is critical and the reason why it is not theologically proper to encounter these images of judgment and take them on their own apart from the larger context.

A God of Justice and Righteousness

The God of the prophets is not a God of judgment but a God of justice and righteousness. The confusion of these two, that is, of judgment and justice, is one of the problems. The reality of judgment is not to be denied, but it is momentary, transient, occasional, and situational. Judgment is not a divine attribute. Justice, however, as a mode of being and acting belongs to the very character of God and is experienced in all sorts of ways, including judgment. One of the most powerful indicators outside the prophets of the centrality of justice for the character of God is Ps 82, where the other gods, the gods of the nations, are condemned to mortality, that is, to the loss of divinity on one ground alone: their failure to insure justice for the weak and the poor and their partiality toward the oppressors of the poor and the fatherless. Justice is not simply one of a list of divine concerns; the cosmos depends upon it.

The point is sharply made in Jeremiah when the Lord says that properly to "understand and know me" is to understand and know that "I am the Lord; I act with steadfast love, justice, and righteousness in the earth, for in these things I delight" (Jer 9:24 [Heb. v. 23]). *Ḥesed, mišpāṭ,* and *ṣĕdāqâ* are what the Lord does in the world. The *mišpāṭ* (justice) may involve judgment, but the sequence indicates clearly that the great things God is doing in the world are loving, just, and righteous. Even the judgment against one party may be the vehicle for the justice of God to be enacted in behalf of another party. The justice of God is in behalf of the "right" (*ṣaddîq*). In contemporary parlance, the "judgment" of the courts is not regarded as an inherently negative thing or as a reflection of a harsh and oppressive attitude toward the subjects of the court. On the contrary, the "judgment" of the courts is the public citizen's last best hope for the triumph of justice in the human community. It is thus no accident that the administration of justice in the courts is one of the items at the top of the prophetic agenda of indictment as well as of recommendation. Without trying to make direct connections, I would argue that that human situation is a reflection of what the community knows about the source of justice and the way in which God deals with the human community.

The wrath of God, a motif indeed prominent in the prophets, is an anthropomorphism, or better, anthropopathism, for conveying the highly negative response of God to human sin and to the disobedience and wickedness of God's people or of other nations (for example, see Isa 5:25; 9:12, 17, 21; 10:5–6; 13:3, 9, 13; 30:27–28; Jer 4:8, 26; 7:20; 10:24–25; 12:13; 30:23–24; Hos 8:5; Ezek 5:13, etc.). It is therefore a way of speaking of divine judgment. But that judgment, whether described in terms of the wrath of God or not, is in behalf of God's righteous and just way in the world. This point is made again and again by the way in which the prophetic oracles effect a correspondence in their judgment oracles between the sin for which the people are indicted and the punishment that is to be announced. The prophet calls attention to the justice of God's judgment by the device of "poetic justice." The ubiquity of this schema in the prophets is a testimony to the degree to which divine judgment is an effecting of divine justice and righteousness.[1] The correspondence is specifically asserted

---

[1] For an extended discussion, see Patrick. D. Miller, *Sin and Judgment in the Prophets* (SBL Monograph Series 27; Chico, CA: Scholars Press, 1982).

by the Lord in various places, as, for example, in Ezekiel's sermon on
Amos 8:2:

[3]Now the end is upon you,
   I will let loose my anger upon you;
I will judge you according to your ways,
   I will punish you for all your abominations.
[4]My eye will not spare you, I will have no pity.
   I will punish you for your ways,
   while your abominations are among you. (Ezek 7:3–4; cf. vv. 8–9)

One may not like the judgment that comes, but the problem is with the
human community, not with the God who judges in order to bring about a
cosmic, human, and cultural order in which justice is normative and not
spasmodic. A telling articulation of just this point occurs in Isa 26:7–10.

[7]The way of the righteous is level;
   straight is the track of the righteous you make level.
   Yea, on the path of your judgments, O LORD, we wait for you;
   your name and your renown are the soul's desire.
[8]My soul yearns for you at night;
   yea, with my spirit within I seek you longingly.
[9]For as your judgments are wrought on the earth,
   the inhabitants of the world learn righteousness.
[10]Should the wicked person find mercy,
   he will not learn righteousness.
   In a land of uprightness he acts wrongly
   and does not see the majesty of the LORD. (author's translation)

The way the Lord makes in the world is characterized by righteousness,
and such righteousness and justice identify the path that human creatures
are to walk. The degree to which this is the case is evident in the "judgments" of God in the world. Through them, the inhabitants learn righteousness. The anticipation and expectation of the community is "on the
path of your judgments." That is, hope is not against judgment but on the
way of judgment because the community has no hope apart from the justice of God. The point is reinforced by the claim that mercy will not show
the wicked the way of righteousness. That is learned only in a divine order
that is itself characterized by righteousness and justice.

Thus divine judgment is a part of the instruction of the community so
that its *imitatio dei* is a reflection of all of God's moves to effect justice in
the human community, including those moves that are characterized as
judgment because they put down the forces of wickedness and disobedience and sin – that is, the persons and communities who stand against the
will of the God of Israel to effect a just order in the world and a moral
ground for comprehending the Lord's way. So it is that the salvific act in

behalf of justice for oppressed slaves in Egypt is an act of judgment against the oppressor Egypt and its king. The prophets do not flinch from daring to claim that in the *realpolitik* of their times, God was at work to bring about justice in and through the agencies of nations and rulers. Their task was to interpret what was going on not as simply unfortunate circumstances but as the activity of a righteous God to deal justly with the human community, an enterprise that involved stopping the various kinds of unrighteousness and injustice operative in the community. That such moves were perceived as punishment was appropriate to the covenantal character of the relationship.

Such punishment=judgment=divine justice and righteousness was always affected by the nature and character of God to show compassion and steadfast love, a claim that was central to the oldest and most common confession of ancient Israel (Exod 34:6–7). While this confession, frequently alluded to in the Psalms, is not a dominant note in the prophets, it does appear in several places (Joel 2:13; Jonah 4:2; Nah 1:3) and lies behind many of the prophetic interpretations of the divine intent and action. In his study of "The Character of God in the Book of the Twelve," Paul R. House comments, "[T]he depiction of God in the Twelve does not differ significantly from that of earlier books, nor from earlier summary texts such as Exod 34:6–7."[2]

The priority of the Lord's compassion is indicated in various ways. One sees it, for example, in the vision reports of Amos when, on two occasions, Amos sees a vision of divine judgment and intercedes, first beseeching God's forgiveness (Amos 7:2) and then a second time simply asking God to stop the judgment (Amos 7:5). The appeal that Amos makes is, "How can Jacob stand? He is so small!" The significance of that particular appeal is immediately evident. The prophet knows the inclination of the God of Israel to care for the little and the weak and the insignificant. To the extent that he is able to make a case for Israel/Jacob to be viewed in the eyes of God that way, he can expect a merciful response. This inclination is what is fundamental to the God of the Old Testament, as persistently so in the prophets as anywhere else in that literature. The intercession of the prophet works precisely because it is grounded in the character of God who is bent toward mercy and compassion, not toward anger and punishment. There are, of course, two more vision reports that indicate the judgment will come (7:7–9; 8:1–3). One notes, however, in these instances there is no intercession on the part of the prophet. It is surely not acciden-

---

[2] Paul R. House, "The Character of God in the Book of the Twelve," in *Reading and Hearing the Book of the Twelve*, eds. J. D. Nogalski and M. A. Sweeney (SBL Symposium Series 15; Atlanta: SBL, 2000), 145.

tal that after the vision of the plumb line by which God measures the faithfulness of the people, the prophet does not seek further relief. From the
image one learns that the people are found to be "out of plumb" and so incapable as such of being the "house" that the Lord needs to be God's people in the world. The walls will need to come down and the house be re-
built if God's way is going to be carried out in the world. So judgment
comes, with defeat and exile, not because God's word is finally judgment
but because God's way cannot be manifest in the world with a people
whose life is so counter to God's justice and righteousness.

The Openness of God's Judgment

The judgment of God is constantly open to the intervention of the prophets. The intercessions of Amos are indicative of this openness, but they are
not particularly novel in this regard. Several texts indicate that the prayer
for God to hold back judgment is a part of the prophetic calling, expected
not necessarily by the people, though they may on occasion seek the
prophet's prayers in their behalf (e.g., Jer 42:1–3), but *expected by the
Lord*. That is, God assumes, expects, and even desires prophetic intercession to appeal to God's compassion and mercy. The exception to this rule
simply proves the point. In Jer 14:11, the prophet is told, "Do not pray for
the welfare of this people," and then in the next chapter the Lord says,
"though Moses and Samuel stood before me, yet my heart would not turn
toward this people" (Jer 15:1; cf. Ps 106:23; 1 Sam 12:23). As in the case
of Amos, the situation is so far gone that God's purposes require a punishment. The people have resisted correction again and again (Jer 5:3), and
now the Lord must move against them. But the assumption is that the heart
of God is fundamentally merciful and affected by pleas in behalf of the
people. There is a sense in which God is afraid for Jeremiah to pray for the
people because the Lord knows there is an inclination within the heart of
God to be moved to mercy by the prayers of the prophets.

Furthermore, the prophetic texts indicate that this vulnerability is not
simply something that God puts up with but that it is built into the character and expectation of God so that when there is not intercession that will
shift God's judgment to mercy, something is wrong and prophecy is failing
in its task, again not because the people say so but because the Lord so declares. One of the responsibilities of the prophet is to stand in the breach
and repair the breach, to mend the relationship between God and the people, an act defined as standing in their behalf so that God will be drawn to

mercy (Schroeder, 1998).[3] Again, one must stress that this is *God*'s understanding and expectation (Ezek 22:30–31). The prophet is, in effect, appointed to appeal to the mercy of God (Ezek 13:5) or to represent the people by exposing himself or herself in behalf of others (cf. Isa 58:9b–12). As Christoph Schroeder has pointed out, standing in the breach is not a manifestation of God's insistence on some violent act to turn away the divine wrath.

God's wrath is not directed against a scapegoat; it is not even directed against the one who stands in the breach. It is rather directed against those who refuse to step into the breach against those who neglect justice, who try to protect their lives instead of risking them for others. God's wrath is not an expression of divine arbitrariness and temper; it has a moral dimension. It is poured out; it breaks out when social cohesion and solidarity break apart.[4]

The point is that even when divine punishment is just, when the actions of the people merit the wrath of God, there is an openness and an expectation that the prophetic voice will intercede, appealing to the mercy of God.[5]

The openness of God to a "change of mind" is in no sense a characteristic divine capriciousness or inconsistency on the part of God. All the instances in which the texts report such a change of mind, a relenting on God's part, have to do with situations where divine judgment is an appropriate way of responding to the acts of the people. In nearly all of the instances, as is the case with the vision reports of Amos mentioned above, the change of mind is from judgment to mercy and the deliverance of the people (e.g., Exod 32:14; Jer 18:8; [but see 18:10 for the reverse movement] 26:3, 13, 19; Joel 2:13–14). That is, there is a divine propensity for merciful response to the people even in the face of their sin and their unwillingness to be corrected. Judgment is a feature of divine justice, but even justice is subject to being overruled by mercy. It does not always happen, but even when the point is made that God will not relent, the tendency of God so to do is emphasized indirectly (e.g., Jer 4:28; Ezek 24:14; Zech 8:14). In one instance, the Lord speaks of having become "weary of relenting" (Jer 15:6), an indicator that such relenting is the operative tendency, enough so as to wear out God because circumstances, that is, the

---

[3] Christoph Schroeder, "'Standing in the Breach': Turning Away the Wrath of God," *Int* 52 (1998).

[4] Ibid., 20.

[5] For a fuller discussion, see Patrick D. Miller, "Prayer and Divine Action," in *God in the Fray: A Tribute to Walter Brueggemann*, eds. T. Beal and T. Linafelt (Minneapolis: Fortress Press, 1998), 211–232; repr. in Patrick D. Miller, *Israelite Religion and Biblical Theology: Collected Essays* (JSOTSup 267; Sheffield: Sheffield Academic Press, 2000), 445–469.

people's sin and stubbornness, bring such change of mind into play so often.

God's Ambivalence about Judgment

The wrath and judgment of God are thus marked by considerable ambivalence and resistance on God's part. Many of the divine speeches in the prophetic oracles reveal this ambivalence and the degree to which the Lord resists the judgment as long or as much as possible. The signs of such resistance are varied and indicative of the fact that judgment is not simply a matter of divine decree but the outcome of a complex process of divine wrestling, anguish, attempted overtures to the people, calls for repentance, warnings that keep the door open, and the like. The divine soliloquy in Hos 11 is indicative of the wrestling within the heart of God and the way in which God's holiness is the ground not only for judgment but also for mercy.

> [8]How can I give you up, Ephraim?
> 　　How can I hand you over, O Israel?
> How can I make you like Admah?
> 　　How can I treat you like Zeboiim?
> My heart recoils within me;
> 　　my compassion grows warm and tender.
> [9]I will not execute my fierce anger;
> 　　I will not again destroy Ephraim;
> 　　for I am God and no mortal,
> 　　the Holy One in your midst,
> 　　and I will not come in wrath. (Hos 11:8–9)

The Lord's bent toward compassion is a part of what it means to be God, not just an option among other possibilities. The definition of deity in the prophets is, as throughout the Old Testament, not a logical extrapolation from an a priori definition of the category but a revelation from the story of God's way with Israel. The prophetic understanding is thus consistent again with the ancient revelation: "The Lord, the Lord, a God merciful and gracious, slow to anger..." (Exod 34:6; cf. 33:19). Such reticence to wrath in favor of compassion is what it means to be the Lord.

Jeremiah's prophecy is one of the places where the wrath and judgment of God are rampant. Even there, and maybe especially there, one encounters the divine resistance to judgment on the people and all kinds of indications of God's frustration and despair at the way the people continue to sin. Chapters 4–6 ring the changes on the announcement of divine judgment, but they are also filled with indications that God seeks in various ways to avert the judgment and agonizes over the failure to accomplish that end. We hear about Judah refusing the correction and discipline of God and instead making "their faces harder than rock" (5:3; cf. 2:30; 7:28; and see below). Further, there are the call to look for the good way (6:16) and the various queries to the people: "Do you not fear me?" (5:22). God's search for just *one* person who acts justly and seeks truth (5:1) is reminiscent of the conversation with Abraham over whether there is anybody righteous in Sodom and Gomorrah, a conversation that, like this prophetic oracle indicates God's openness to mercy rather than judgment if there is the slightest human inclination toward righteousness. The one just and truthful person becomes like those who stand in the breach, whose presence in prayer and righteous action is not only capable of averting divine wrath but is what God seeks always in order not to have to come in judgment. Judgment does not come easily for the Lord of Israel. On the contrary, there is a divine anguish reflected in the inner dialogue within the mind and heart of God that comes to the surface not infrequently and very clearly in these chapters. So the Lord says, "Shall I not punish them for these things?" an address to self or to the prophet (5:9). God's inner anguish is even more evident in Jer 4:19–22, which ends with the first person voice of God in the sentence "my people are foolish, they do not know me (v. 22)." But there is no reason to assume that the earlier first person cry, "My anguish, my anguish! I writhe in pain!" (v. 19) cannot be the voice of God as much as the voice of the prophet, especially as that outcry flows so clearly out of the preceding divine speech.⁶ The anguish and complaint of the prophet is a reflection of the anguish and complaint of God. Judgment is no less unsettling for God than it is for those who view it. Human shrinking in horror from the devastating and destroying wrath of God is already anticipated by the one who so acts.

The mix of divine grief and wrath, of lament and judgment, is evident elsewhere in Jeremiah's prophecy. The divine soliloquy of 5:9 is repeated in 9:9 [Heb. v. 10] as the Lord asks the question, "Shall I not punish them for these things?" and answers with both tears and anger, the former in v. 10 as the Lord says, "I will take up weeping and wailing for the mountains, and a lamentation for the pastures of the wilderness," and the latter with the announcement in v. 11: "I will make Jerusalem a heap of ruins, a lair of

---

⁶ For a full discussion of the case for seeing God as the one lamenting in these texts, see J. J. M. Roberts, "The Motif of the Weeping God in Jeremiah and Its Background in the Lament Tradition of the Ancient Near East," *Old Testament Essays* 5 (1992), 361–374; repr. in *idem*, *The Bible and the Ancient Near East: Collected Essays* (Winona Lake, IN: Eisenbrauns, 2002), 132–142.

jackals."[7] This same complex assortment of responses of anger and sadness is evident also in Jer 12:7–13, which is primarily an announcement of judgment but whose pathos is evident in the frequent references to "my house," "my heritage," "my vineyard," "my portion," and especially in the words "I have given the beloved of my heart (*yĕdidût nafšî*) into the hands of her enemies" (v. 7). Hidden in that sentence are all the words about divine election rooted in God's faithfulness to the promise and God's love for Israel in Exod 19:3–6 and Deut 7:6–11 and 9:4–5. Again, the divine voice is probably present once more in Jer 8:18–9:1 [Heb. vv. 8:18–23] in the same mix of grief, sadness, and anger at the plight/fate/judgment/punishment of "my poor people." And in Jer 14:17, the prophet is told to lament for the people:

You shall say to them this word:
    Let my eyes run down with tears night and day,
    and let them not cease,
for the virgin daughter – my people – is struck down with a crushing blow,
    with a very grievous wound.

The prominence of God's sadness and tears in the midst of anger is an appropriate motif in the prophecy of Jeremiah because it is there also where one encounters extensive use of the metaphor of marriage and divorce as a way of speaking about faithfulness and unfaithfulness. Whether on the human plane or in the heart of God, grief and anger are both present in the face of marital unfaithfulness.

A Responsive God

The judgment of God is responsive to the human situation. The point may be an obvious one, but it is central to the whole discussion. In relation to God, judgment is to be understood as an outcome of God's justice, righteousness, and steadfast love (see Jer 9:24). But it is also and totally an outcome of what happens on the human plane. The only modification of that is by the way in which God's compassion may relent from the judgment appropriate to the human situation. The prophets, however, readily point to the flexibility of the divine word and the divine decision, indicating in various ways the openness of the divine activity, so that God's response is

---

[7] For a discussion of the textual issues and the choice of the MT with its first person verbs rather than the LXX with its imperative, see Patrick D. Miller, "The Book of Jeremiah," in *The New Interpreter's Bible* (Nashville: Abingdon Press, 2001).

deeply dependent upon human response to God's work and God's way. Isaiah's word to Ahaz contains a critical "if": "If you do not stand firm in faith, you shall not stand at all" (Isa 7:9). Ahaz faces a choice, and the choice he makes determines God's response. So also the name of his son, "Shear-yashub," is a symbolic name whose force depends completely upon how the people act. Will it be "[Only] a Remnant Shall Return," or will the name of the child be an indicator that "A Remnant Shall [Indeed] Return" (Isa 7:3; 10:20–23)? In Jer 42, the people ask Jeremiah to pray to the Lord for them and promise that whether God's response is good or bad, they will obey it. Jeremiah does so and reports God's response, which is to the effect that the people themselves will determine completely whether the divine word is good news or bad news, deliverance or disaster. Their decision to stay in the land or to go to Egypt will determine the divine response, for good or for bad.

This same flexibility on God's part is evident in the interpretation of the potter with the clay when Jeremiah visits the potter's house. The Lord says, "Look, I am a potter shaping evil against you" (Jer 18:11). But the point of the text is that the Lord will shape the pot according to the response of the people. At first glance, the Lord's speech seems to show a kind of whimsy: "At one moment I may declare concerning a nation or a kingdom, that I will pluck up and break down and destroy it… And at another moment I may declare concerning a nation or a kingdom that I will build and plant it" (vv. 7–9). What follows each of these statements indicates that the decision is totally dependent upon whether a nation turns from its evil or decides to do evil. There is nothing capricious at all about the momentary decision of the Lord. The way the people act evokes God's response. That such openness is available to the nations of the earth is evident from Jer 12:14–17.

Surely part of the reason so much prophecy of judgment is preserved in the books of the Old Testament prophets is to argue the case for the primacy of justice and compassion over wrath and anger, to make the point that again and again the people went their own way, did not do the will of the Lord, said no when reproved, continued in their sinful ways when specifically called to obedience by the prophets. These oracles heap up not only the words of divine judgment but a virtual catalogue of willful disobedience and resistance to the divine pleas, to the anguished call of God to walk in the good way and to live as "my people" are called to live. Isaiah's repetition of the words, "For all this his anger has not turned away, and his hand is stretched out still" (Isa 5:25; 9:12, 17, 21; 10:4) is accompanied by the repeated indictment of the people for their iniquitous ways.

God's activity vis-à-vis the nation or the nations may be planned or pur-
posed (e.g., Isa 14:24–27; 23:6–9; 46:10–11; Jer 29:10; 49:20; 50:45), but
it is not deterministic or irrevocable, at least up to a point (see, e.g., Amos'
final two vision reports in Amos 7:7–9 and 8:1–3). There is a malleability
comparable to the malleability of clay in the hands of the potter. Human
acts and decisions significantly shape the future of God with the people.
The sovereignty of God is nowhere compromised by the degree to which it
implies freedom and takes account of the human way.

Never the Last Word

The judgment of God is not the last word of the prophets or their largest
word. There may be some exceptions to this claim, but it is the dominant
tendency in the prophetic texts. It is expressed in a variety of ways. The
word of God that "I will not make a full end" of the people is repeated in
Jeremiah (4:27; 5:10, 18; 46:28). While its force is not altogether clear, it
does appear to be a kind of divine caveat in the very midst of the word of
judgment. It does not reduce the pain of the judgment; it does qualify its
finality. The devastating and unavoidable judgment will come to a disobedient and stubborn people, who have failed to respond to God's prior discipline and correction. But even that will not be the final end. That such a
word about not making "a full end" is God's open door to a future for the
people whose conduct and way does not merit it is underscored by its presence in a salvation oracle in Jer 30:11, where the text is explicit about real
punishment not being the end of Judah.[8]

Other texts reveal a God who is not only slow to anger but whose anger
is not forever. Indicative of this strain in the prophetic portrayal of the
Lord of Israel is the word in Isa 54. The proclamation of the prophet of
good news to the exiles comes to a close with his interpretive words:

[7]For a brief moment I abandoned you,
    but with great compassion I will gather you.
[8]In overflowing wrath for a moment
    I hid my face from you,
but with everlasting love I will have compassion on you,
    says the LORD, your Redeemer. (Isa 54:7–8)

---

[8] This text indicates there will be a full end of the nations among whom the Lord has scattered the exiles, but that word receives frequent qualification, as, for example, in Jer 12:14–
17, where the Lord promises to deal compassionately with the nations if they will "learn the
ways of my people."

The experience of judgment is real and devastating. It is reflective of the anger of God, the "overflowing wrath" that has consumed this people, resulting in the destruction of their leadership, their loss of land, and their exile in a foreign land. There is no escaping the reality of the judgment. The prophet, however, speaks the voice of God that terrible as such experience of the divine wrath is, it is nowhere like the "everlasting love," God's compassion for this people. The abandonment is brief; the gathering an act of great compassion. One cannot diminish the terror of the judgment, but the prophet says that it cannot compare with the greatness of God's compassion and love. They are both the final word and the larger word.

This is not unlike the divine word in Jer 3:11 when the Lord calls for repentance on the part of the northern kingdom:

Return, faithless Israel,
    says the LORD.
I will not look on you in anger,
    for I am merciful,
says the LORD;
I will not be angry forever.

This text echoes the similar word of the psalmist, alluding to Exod 34:6–7:

He will not always accuse,
    nor will he keep his anger forever. (Ps 103:9)

A Judgment that Renews

The judgment of God is a part of renewing and reshaping a people for God's own way. God does not give up. Judgment is a stopping place on the way to the reassertion of blessing out of God's compassion. While God's judgment is clearly understood as punishment (e.g., Isa 40:1–2), there are numerous indicators that the punishment serves a larger purpose, to wit, the reshaping of the people toward the intended relationship with their God. A number of notions and images convey such an understanding of divine judgment, for example, the frequent reference to God's "correction" or "discipline" (*mûsar*) in Jeremiah (2:30; 5:3; 7:28; 17:23; 32:33; cf. 6:8; 30:11; 46:28; Isa 26:16). One may compare illustratively the oracle in Jer 31:18–20, where Ephraim is quoted as accepting the divine discipline and becoming ashamed and repenting, resulting in the divine announcement, "I will surely have mercy on him," with the oracle in Zeph 3:1–13, where Jerusalem is depicted as not listening and not receiving correction from past judgments and so experiencing once again the judgment of God. Similar prophetic indications of punishment intended to serve a corrective function

and bring the people back to a true and faithful relationship with the Lord
are more indirectly indicated in such texts as Isa 1:5–9; 9:8–21 [Heb. vv.
9–20]; Amos 4:6–11. In Jer 30:11, the Lord promises to chastise the people
but not to destroy them, to punish but not to make an end of them. Indeed
this word is in the context of an oracle of salvation.

The image of the Lord as the potter molding the clay also suggests the
place of judgment in the divine plan (Jer 18:1–12). The process of judgment may itself be the remolding of the clay. The spoiled clay is remolded
in the potter's hand as Jeremiah looks on. That becomes a metaphor for
God's handling of Judah/the clay. The pot will not work and is flawed as a
container until the potter reshapes it to what it is meant to be or to do "in
the eyes" of the potter [lit. "as was right in the eyes of the potter to do";
NRSV: "as seemed good to him"]. This malformed, misshapen vessel will
be reshaped so that it is right in God's eyes.

An equally prominent image is that of the refining fire that tests and re-
fines. In some instances, the refining fire in the smelter seems simply a
powerful image for judgment (Jer 6:27–30; Ezek 22:18–20), but elsewhere
the image clearly indicates a refining in order to purify and reuse the silver
or metal (Isa 1:24–26). The Isaiah text may suggest that the image in all its
contexts implies a melting of the dross to refine and purify the metal, again
a correcting of the elect people by the fires of judgment so that they are
reformed, literally.

Another image of God's judgment to effect a reformation of the people
rather than a destruction of them is to be found in the image of the plumb
line (2 Kgs 21:13; cf. Isa 28:17). The dimension of reforming the people is
only implicit in this image, but it is there in the sense that a norm or standard of judgment is being suggested, against which the people do not
measure up. The construction will not work; the wall is out of plumb. The
Lord, therefore, will have to tear down the wall because it cannot work
when it is out of plumb. Implicit in such an image is the notion of rebuild-
ing the wall, starting the process over with a wall or construction that is
properly constructed.

Finally, there is the image of the dish that is wiped clean, turned upside
down, and placed back on the shelf:

[L]ike the image of the plumb line there is a functional or utilitarian dimension that
points beyond the judgment and has a larger aim than simply eliminating the food in the
dish. It is in order to render the dish, which has a use or purpose, usable again, to make it
clean so that Yahweh may use it according to his purpose, may fill it anew. The present
food in it is spoiled and rotten. Jerusalem is the dish Yahweh will clean and use again.

The image fits perfectly with the historical fate of Jerusalem—wiped clean, turned on its face to be kept till Yahweh is ready to use it once more.[9]

Such understanding of judgment as effecting change and renewal needs to take account of a related but different strain of thought found in some of the prophets, an understanding of God's work of renewal growing out of the experience of exile. It is evidence of a kind of tension between the language of repentance and the language of determinism, between a notion of virtuous moral selfhood that assumes and expects the capacity for moral decision in favor of the good and so a turn around from bad ways to correct ways and a sense that "people are inherently incapable of acting in accord with the good."[10] This tension has been worked out in some detail with regard to the Book of Ezekiel,[11] but it is present elsewhere, for example, in the prophecy of Jeremiah and in Deuteronomy, which probably at this point reflects a prophetic origin. For Deuteronomy it is the move from the call to the people to "circumcise, then the foreskin of your heart, and do not be stubborn any longer" (Deut 10:16; cf. Jer 4:4: 9:26; a related image is that of washing the heart as in Jer 2:22 and 4:14; see also Ezek 36:25) to the declaration that "the Lord your God will circumcise your heart and the heart of your descendants, so that you will love the Lord your God with all your heart and with all your soul, in order that you may live" (Deut 30:6). While it is unclear whether these two passages reflect a temporal distance, this latter passage certainly reflects the experience of the exile. This may also be the case for Deut 10:12–22, so the difference should not be assumed to be a matter of temporal shift. The tension may be within the same context. Both Jeremiah (see 24:7; 32:39; cf. 31:33) and Ezekiel (see 11:19–20; 36:26–27) speak of God's gift of a new heart and a new spirit that will enable the people to keep the statutes and ordinances. The assumption is at least implicit that only by the Lord's action will the capacity for being and living differently be possible. In like manner, the vision of the dry bones having God's spirit put within them and coming to life reflects this same side of the tension (Ezekiel 37). In the face of the people's complaint that "Our bones are dried up, and our hope is lost; we are cut off completely," the Lord announces the divine intention to bring them up out of their graves and put the spirit of life in them, that is, to transform them from death to life.

---

[9] Miller, *Sin and Judgment in the Prophets*, 137.

[10] Jacqueline E. Lapsley, *Can These Bones Live? The Problem of the Moral Self in the Book of Ezekiel* (BZAW 301; Berlin: de Gruyter, 2000), 185

[11] See Lapsley, *Can These Bones Live?*

Here, therefore, is a significant shift from the images of correction and re-shaping out of punishment to the divine gift of a new being. The God who has punished a recalcitrant people will be the means by which the people are able to live in true and faithful relation to the Lord and the Lord's way. But the change is not a matter of taking correction, finally being repentant, but of receiving a new being and a new will as God's gift beyond the judgment.

The Case of Jonah

The Book of Jonah is a critique of the misreading of God's character and the misunderstanding of God's judgment. The primary function of this story is not to add to the collection of prophetic oracles out of Israel and Judah's history but to provide basic clues to the character of the God of the prophets and especially to fight the misunderstanding of God as primarily aimed at effecting judgment, especially of the non-Israelite peoples. The attack of the book on Israel's xenophobic propensities is evident and well-recognized, but the deeper word is about the character of God and the way in which that character is so heavily oriented toward mercy and compassion that the clearly deserved judgment of Israel's greatest enemy, the hated Assyrians, can be averted. The book presumes significant misunderstanding of the character of God. Repentance takes place, so one would expect, according to the message of the other prophets, that God would withhold judgment. But Jonah assumes, on the one hand, that God's judgment of Israel's enemy brooked no holding back while fearing, on the other hand, that the Lord of Israel even with a hated enemy might act in character, that is, according to the ancient confessional understanding that affirmed the Lord to be compassionate, slow to anger, abounding in steadfast love (Jonah 4:2). The hero of the book of Jonah is the Lord, and the intention of the book is thoroughly theological. It is a revelatory corrective of the propensity to see God's ultimate aim as judgment and to see the elect people's enemies as God's enemies.

The Cross and God's Judgment

To misunderstand the judgment of God as deeply related to the mercy of God and the vindication of the just and righteous purposes of God is to misunderstand the meaning of the cross as well as the continuing words of judgment that belong to the New Testament. The death of Jesus on the cross is preeminently God's act of judgment, but it is also preeminently

God's act of compassion upon humanity. In Christ's emptying of self and obedience unto death, God's way is seen to be so clearly marked by the abundance of steadfast love that it is willing to go even unto death. That the judgment of God is penultimate and not ultimate, a part of the larger purposes for blessing and realization of God's righteous and just rule, is evident in the outcome of Jesus' death. Good Friday and Saturday remind us of the depth of human sin and the terror of divine judgment. There is no escaping that any more than in the prophet's announcements of judgment against ancient Israel. But those days are not the final days any more than the prophetic judgment speeches are the last word about what God was doing with Israel. There is the new life that is given by God and the resurrection from the dead:

[24]It will be reckoned to us who believe in him who raised Jesus our Lord from the dead, [25]who was handed over to death for our trespasses and was raised for our justification. [1]Therefore, since we are justified by faith, we have peace with God through our Lord Jesus Christ, [2]through whom we have obtained access to this grace in which we stand; and we boast in our hope of sharing the glory of God. (Rom 4:24–5:2)

Such a way of understanding God's work in Christ is already anticipated in the story of the way of the suffering servant of Isa 53. It is God's way, a way that does not end in judgment but assumes that the consummation of God's purposes in this world is completely shaped by the character of God, long ago revealed to Israel and persistently insisted upon by "his servants the prophets."

19. What the Scriptures Principally Teach

What the biblical texts say about homosexuality is a matter of some debate. But the larger issue for discussion is less about what the texts say than it is about what we do with that, how we take the textual material as a guide or direction for thinking and acting about sexual relations. Indeed, the church's debate about homosexuality is a particular and significant piece of an ongoing discussion about sexual relationships and ethics and the role that traditional Christian perspectives, shaped by a long history of interpreting scripture, play in determining how Christians should behave and do behave, which are not necessarily the same thing. In what follows, I will suggest issues that seem appropriate to our discussion of how the church is to regard homosexual conduct and what place persons who engage in same-sex activity have in the community of faith.

The Teaching of Scripture

There is not much biblical direction on the matter of homosexuality. Only in the Holiness Code of Leviticus (18:22 and 20:13) do we have actual directives or commands, that is, formal instruction about same-sex conduct. In both instances, sexual relations with a person of the same sex are prohibited in the context of other prohibitions of unacceptable sexual relationships. In the New Testament, the topic comes up primarily in lists of vices that are enumerated in the context of some other topic, for example, lawsuits (1 Cor 6:9), the proper use of the law (1 Tim 1:10), and Paul's argument in Rom 1:26–27 about the corruption of human nature as testified to in various forms of immorality that are outgrowths of idolatry (homosexual activity being one of these). There is some serious debate among New Testament scholars about how to read the New Testament texts and how explicitly homosexual activity as we customarily think of it is in view.[1] But even if one assumes that the texts do indeed speak of same-sex relationships as we customarily think of them, there is not much to build upon here

---

[1] There is much discussion about what forms of sexual activity may be in view in the biblical texts under consideration – pederasty, male prostitution, heterosexual participation in homosexual acts, homosexuality in general, male, female, or whatever.

in terms of direct address of the topic. Two things are clear from the merest review of the direct evidence of scripture: Homosexual relationships are not a matter at all to the fore in scripture, but to whatever extent they are discussed, they are condemned as unacceptable, abomination, or wicked.

In terms of indirect scriptural guidance, one may cite the creation story in Gen 1–3 where male-female relationships are addressed. From this, one might infer something about what is fitting and proper for sexual activity.

With reference to both kinds of evidence, the Old Testament illustrates the elusiveness of the biblical material and the difficulty of reading instruction directly from it. The believing reader of the laws of the Old Testament is met by a kind of dialectic or tension that cannot be dissolved easily and is discernible in a close look at the laws, their order, sequence, and interrelationships. The present shape of the law, as well as what we can discern of its formation, point us to a dual reality – a core of perduring, foundational law or instruction and a congeries of specifics or particularities of that foundational law that are worked out over the passage of time and changing circumstance. The "core" is clearly the Decalogue, or Ten Commandments. The commandments have been placed first in both accounts of the revelation of the law at Sinai (Exod 19–Num 10:10). They are essentially the same in both formulations.[2] The Ten Commandments are explicitly separated off from the rest of the Torah, and both Exod 20 and Deut 5 give an account of that separation, reporting that the Decalogue was given directly to the people while the rest of the legal material was given by God to Moses for him to teach to the people. In other words, the very shape and formation of the laws of the Old Testament mark out the Ten Commandments as foundational and unchanging, the touchstone to which all other laws are to be connected – enduring, adaptable, and effective for life in all situations.

The rest of the law is specific in spelling out of those commandments. That is not always self evident; nor can one say that it was always the motivation behind the law. But, especially in Deuteronomy, it is possible to see that the rest of the specific laws are arranged in the order of the Decalogue as an elaboration of its force in particular details and precedents.[3]

---

[2] The differences between the formulations of the Decalogue in Exod 20 and Deut 5 are relatively minor when compared with differences in the rest of the laws where parallels of some sort exist. The primary difference is in the formulation of the Sabbath commandment where Exodus and Deuteronomy give different motivations for keeping the commandments. Other Deuteronomic stylistic features are present in Deut 5.

[3] In the Holiness Code, for example, one of the prohibitions of same-sex relationships is placed in a series that begins by reiterating the commandment against adultery, suggesting

That means we can look seriously at and draw upon the rest of the law for guidance in understanding the fundamental instruction of the Lord as given to us in the Decalogue.

But none of the specifics have the force of the original. They have themselves arisen in different times and under different circumstances, so that the specifications of Deuteronomy are not necessarily like those of Exod 21–23[4] and neither of those legal codes are the same as those of Leviticus and Numbers, themselves composed of more than one set of Torah instructions.[5]

The present form of the Torah materials of the Old Testament, therefore, present us with several implications for the way we receive and attend to the divine revelation therein. There is clearly a basic law, the Decalogue, that continues the same and is the primary obligation for the community that lives in obedience to this God. There are many specific laws that help us see some of the particulars of the basic obligations. They are instructive but not necessarily obligatory in the same fashion. In some instances, they have high moral impact upon the contemporary community of faith without being carried out; for example, the gleaning laws and the laws of sabbatical and jubilee release (Lev 25 and Deut 15). In other cases, even in laws that are formulated – like the Decalogue – in apodictic or prohibitive fashion, the contemporary community of faith does not find the particular specification as binding or morally desirable. So many cases of these are found in Leviticus and Deuteronomy that there is little need to list them here.[6] These specific formulations help us see in particular times (though we are not always sure exactly what those times were) how the primary obligations were spelled out. The laws of Lev 18 and 20 in some sense represent a move from the commandment about adultery into the whole sphere of sexual relationships and the seriousness of these. There is much that we can and do learn from that. But these laws do not bind in a

---

that the series is to be seen in relation to that commandment (Lev 20:10f.).

[4] For a succinct presentation of the parallel material in Exod 21–23 (the Book of the Covenant) and Deut 12–26, together with some discussion of how these collections seem to represent different stages in the life and economic history of the Israelite community, see G. von Rad, *Deuteronomy* (The Old Testament Library; Philadelphia: Westminster, 1966), 12–15. On the relationship of the various bodies of legal material to one another, see now F. Crüsemann, *Die Tora: Theologie und Sozialgeschichte des alttestamentlichen Gesetzes* (München: Kaiser, 1992), translated as *The Torah: The Theology and Social History of Laws in the Hebrew Bible* (Minneapolis: Fortress, 1996).

[5] For the most recent detailed proposal concerning the character and setting of the different collections of legal material in Leviticus and Numbers, see Israel Knohl, *The Sanctuary of Silence: The Priestly Torah and the Holiness School* (Minneapolis: Fortress, 1995).

[6] For examples, see the essay by Choon-Leong Seow (see n. 15).

different fashion than other Levitical laws that we have set aside in practice. One cannot simply read from the two prohibitions in Lev 18 and 20 a final and binding moral word about same-sex relationships in the same way that one can read a final word from the prohibition against adultery in the Decalogue, though those prohibitions, along with others in the lists, can be instructive for developing an ethic of sexual relationships.[7]

So in our moral deliberation, we are, like the earlier community of faith at different times in its history, faced with having to determine what God wills of us in our time and how the fundamental guidelines work out in specifics today. That process has been going on throughout the history of the church. For example, restrictions on who may be ordained that were operative in the Levitical laws and in later times are no longer operative in our time. We have decided on various grounds – theological, moral, pragmatic, and the like – that the specifics of the law of the Old Testament no longer bind us and restrict who may be ordained. In our own time and con-

---

[7] There is a long history in the church of seeking to distinguish between laws that were seen as binding and those that were not. Various approaches may be discerned in that history. Acts 15 seems to indicate a difference between Jewish Christians who kept the whole of the law (v. 5) and Gentile Christians who were expected to maintain certain abstentions identified in the law (v. 20). In the second century, Christian polemic against the Jews maintained that the laws given after the incident of the golden calf were only binding upon a disobedient Israel, that is, the Jews (I am indebted to Dean McBride for calling this to my attention). Calvin identified the moral law with the Decalogue and Jesus' summary of it and saw that as the fundamental law clearly applicable to Christians. This moral law was the most important, but other laws functioned in relation to it in different ways. Some of the law he saw as precepts "which are not found in the Two Tables, yet differ not at all from them in sense; so that due care must be taken to afix them to their respective Commandments in order to present the Law as a whole." In addition to these, there were "supplements." He explains the "supplements" as follows:

"...with respect to the First Table, the Ceremonies and the outward Exercises of Worship; with respect to the Second Table, the Political laws, for the object of both these parts is merely to aid in the observance of the Moral Law; and it is not a little important, that we should understand that the Ceremonies and the Judicial Ordinances neither change nor detract from the rule laid down in the Ten Commandments; but are only helps, which as it were lead us by the hand to the due Worship of God, and to the promotion of justice towards men.

...therefore it follows, that nothing can be wanted as the rule of a good and upright life beyond the Ten Commandments." (J. Calvin, *Commentaries on the Four Last Books of Moses, arranged in the Form of a Harmony* [Edinburgh: The Calvin Translation Society, 1852], Vol. 1, xvi–xvii).

Interestingly, Calvin puts the homosexuality laws of Lev 18 and 20 only in the supplements, and in one case in the "political supplements." He associated them with the commandment against adultery as further prohibitions against "all sins which are repugnant to the modesty of nature itself" (Vol. 3, 73). There is no doubt that he thought these directives were guides for the Christian life.

text, we have to work out the specifics of obedience to the fundamental commands.

The earlier specifications are not to be ignored. They continue to be instructive, though they vary considerably in the degree to which we pay attention to them. What is clear is that we do not place them all on the same level, even as time-specific reflections of the basic commands of the Decalogue. One can point rather easily to spheres of conduct where the church has made a different moral judgment than what one may find in specific texts of the Bible. Scripture permits some things to which we say "no" – most obviously slavery and male domination of women. We are convinced that our restriction of scripture's apparent permission is faithful to the gospel and, indeed, is ultimately directed by what we have learned from scripture. Scripture also prohibits many things that we permit. The laws of the Old Testament are full of examples. But, in the case of divorce, for example, the church has interpreted scripture against scripture – even against the very specific words of Jesus – to permit divorce and remarriage after divorce.

The *indirect* evidence of the Old Testament relevant to the sexual relationship between different and same sexes is found especially in the picture of the created order as encountered in Gen 1–3. That depiction clearly joins man and woman together in responsibility for filling and ruling the earth, for procreating and controlling God's creation. The image of God is found in the human being as male and female. I take that Genesis story very seriously. But here, in these chapters, is one of the places where in some sense we say "no" to what we hear in scripture and do so in the light of our whole understanding of scripture. I am speaking particularly of the divine judgment in Gen 3. The history of the church and of the larger society is one of resistance to the circumstances announced by God as outcomes of the human sin recounted in Gen 3. We do everything we can to overcome the pain and travail of childbirth. In like manner, much of the economic history of the human race, a history much supported and influenced by the church, has been an effort to overcome and reduce the pain and toil of human labor to feed ourselves – to make it easier to extract bread from the earth. Such efforts are generally judged as morally very positive, except as they represent actions that lead to oppression of others. And finally, in our own time, we are making much headway in overcoming the subordination of female to male, of wife to husband, that is announced also in Gen 3. We do not take these etiologies of the human condition, which place their causality in the divine sentence of judgment, as normative. That is because of the larger scriptural conviction that God moves to deal graciously with us and offers us possibilities of life that do not depend upon pain and anxious labor. We also do not take them as normative because of the other words of scripture and of God that set man and woman together to rule the creation.

Indeed, often it is where scripture seems to fix the way relationships must be and roles must be set – woman subordinate to man, man to cut his hair and woman not to, woman not to speak out in the church, slaves to be submissive to their masters and obey them in fear and trembling as they obey Christ – that the church has heard in the gospel and in the prophetic and liberating words of both Old Testament and New Testament a counter word that does not fix people in roles and relationships and does not let cultural and social mores in this regard become final definitions of who and what we are in the church and the kingdom.

The Genesis stories picture an ideal of enduring companionship of man and woman – one that has sexual relationship for procreation – as central to the human story.[8] That tells us something very fundamental about who and what we are. The defining relationship in the human community is man and woman. That relationship often is manifest in the establishment of a commitment between a man and a woman that perdures and is fruitful in every respect. Of course, for many human beings that particular ideal is not their experience. They may be single and so do not know the man-woman relationship as one of enduring and intimate companionship, sexual and otherwise (or at least not necessarily so). They may be barren and so do not know the procreative fruit of the relationship that God intends. They may be homosexual and so do not know the experience of existing in sexual relationship with a companion of opposite gender. Yet all of these persons, whose numbers are legion, are truly members of the human community God has made and of the community of faith. As persons who in their varied ways and relationships live out lives of service to God, lives of faithfulness, love, and justice, caring for one another and loving God, their place in the community of faith and my judgment of them are not determined by their roles and relationships.

In his final and posthumous work, Paul Lehmann acutely perceived the different possibilities for receiving and drawing upon the Genesis account of the creation of man and woman. His comments are indicative of the fact that what the text says does not yet tell us what it teaches; that happens only when the text is perceived from some angle of vision. For Lehmann, as it should be for all of us, that angle was the gospel, which is, in his now-familiar formulation, what God was and is doing to make and to keep human life human. That definition of God's work in the world is particularly

---

[8] This is not, by the way, the ideal that Paul sets forth for the Christian community.

apropos for this issue, and Lehmann's angle on the Genesis account is worth citing:

[A] divine ordination is not a *limiting* instance, but a *foundational* one. As a limiting instance, the divine ordination to sexual otherness and reciprocity is put forward as the normative mode of sexuality, in relation to which variants are excluded as deviants from the heterosexual norm. As a *foundational* instance, the divine ordination to sexual otherness and reciprocity becomes the liberating instance in relation to which divergent possibilities may be pursued and assessed. As a *limiting* instance, heterosexuality necessarily excludes homosexuality from the divine purpose of and for human fulfillment. As a *foundational* instance of otherness in differentiation and commitment, inequality and heterogeneity, reciprocity and fidelity, heterosexuality becomes the liberating occasion and sign of human fulfillment in relation to which homosexuality may also be affirmed. Just as in Scripture and tradition, a central and indispensable correlation between monotheism and monogamy has been discerned and affirmed, yet without requiring the instantaneous and intransigent rejection of concubinage, polyandry or polygamy, or even interracial and/or interfaith marriage as a test case of the obedience of faith, so the foundational and liberating instance of heterosexuality as a parable of human fulfillment does not require an intransigent rejection of homosexuality as a test case of the obedience of faith.[9]

The Rules of Faith and Love

Interpretation of scripture in the church should not happen without attention to the rule of faith and the rule of love. The former suggests that our individual interpretations are placed against the community's understanding of scripture in past and present. In the Reformed community, that interpretive backdrop is found particularly in the creeds and confessions, though not only there. The subject of homosexuality has not been a specific focus of attention in these documents, though the Heidelberg Catechism quotes 1 Cor 6:9 in one of its questions and interprets homosexuality as one of the sins that keeps one from inheriting the kingdom of God. The tradition thus places the present interpreter in a kind of tension. On the one hand, there is inattention to the issue; on the other hand, where the tradition has dealt with the matter in or out of the confessions, it has generally condemned the practice of same-sex activity. In that context, it is important that the present interpretive activity of the church be a communal one, that our efforts to think about this issue afresh and in reference to what has been thought already be a corporate engagement and not simply a matter of

---

[9] P. Lehmann, *The Decalogue and a Human Future: The Meaning of the Commandments for Making and Keeping Human Life Human* (Grand Rapids: Eerdmans, 1995), 174. The completion and publication of this work is due significantly to the labors of Nancy Duff, whose introduction is helpful for understanding Lehmann's perspective on law and commandment.

individual proposals for reading texts, although we may start at this point. Our interpretation happens in community, and what the community experiences in faith is more significant than the experience of any individual. What we say and do together is more to be attended to than idiosyncratic readings of texts by one or a few individuals. This means listening to a broad range of interpretive judgments in the church, including its gay and lesbian members.

Thus, one of the tasks of the church in the moment is to seek the guidance of the Holy Spirit in reading these texts. The rule of faith has made us reluctant to view same-sex activity as other than a sinful mark, but neither scripture nor the confessions has lifted this topic up for major attention. The very struggle of the church – the large attention that homosexual practice is receiving in the moral, theological, and interpretive discussions of the church – indicates that the rule of faith is properly under scrutiny and that the church is listening for direction from the Holy Spirit. The rule of faith is not fixed, but it is also not changed by any individual. It is my sense that in the matter before us, faith is rethinking its understanding and is attentive to both what the church has said in the past and also to what it is thinking and saying now. The Scots Confession says: "We dare not receive or admit any interpretation which is contrary to any principal point of our faith, or to any other plain text of scripture, or to the rule of love" (chap. 18). It is the phrase "any other plain text of scripture," that appears to give us undebatable clarity on how we judge homosexuality, but the other criteria of the Scots Confession may take us in other directions. We are not, in fact, dealing with "any principal point of our faith" in this regard, and we may be in significant conflict with the rule of love as a guide to how we read and respond to the scriptures.

That rule of love reminds us that our interpretation of scripture stands under the divine command to love God and neighbor. Thus, what we hear from scripture should not lead us away from the expression of love for others. Or, in the words of the document "Presbyterian Understanding and Use of Holy Scripture," adopted by the General Assembly of the Presbyterian Church (USA) in 1983,

all interpretations are to be judged by the question whether they offer and support the love given and commanded by God. When interpretations do not meet this criterion, it must be asked whether the text has been used correctly in the light of the whole Scripture and its subject.[10]

---

[10] "Presbyterian Understanding and Use of Holy Scripture," (Louisville: The Office of the General Assembly, 1992), 19–20.

One of the classic Reformed statements, that of the Synod of Berne in 1528, puts it this way:

> But where something is brought before us by our pastors or others, which brings us closer to Christ, and in accordance with God's Word is more conducive to mutual friendship and Christian love than the interpretation now presented, we will gladly accept it..."[11]

The interpretive comment of the "Presbyterian Understanding and Use of Holy Scripture" statement at this point is very revealing, particularly in light of the fact that it was not written with any reference to the church's hermeneutical debate about the appropriate regard and judgment of persons who engage in same-sex love. That document says:

> No interpretation of Scripture is correct that leads to or supports contempt for any individual or group of persons either within or outside of the church. Such results from the interpretation of Scripture plainly indicate that the rule of love has not been honored.[12]

To the extent that such a test of our interpretation by the rule of love can be made, the church has fallen far short in its use of the texts dealing with homosexuality. Our record on this is all too clear. Exceptions are notable, but the history is generally one of the church's rejection and contempt of those identified by themselves or others as gay and lesbian. It is not simply that we have precluded their holding positions of leadership, which indeed we have done, but we have not welcomed them fully into the fellowship of the church. And the church by its influence and the power of its religious character has been complicit, sometimes in very open fashion, in the larger oppression of homosexual persons by society. Our judgment that homosexual activity is a sin has controlled the way we have behaved toward Christians who are homosexual.[13] The rule of love, which says that our interpretation is correlative with the way we live, raises serious questions

---

[11] Quoted in "Presbyterian Understanding and Use of Holy Scripture," 20.

[12] Ibid., 20.

[13] The phrase "who are homosexual" implicitly introduces the large and much-discussed question of whether or not homosexuality is at all genetic, a trait of being and personhood in some sense, or only a practice that is adopted and can be set aside, even with difficulty. However, that discussion moves – and it is dependent upon all sorts of continuing studies and varying anthropologies – there is no doubt that many homosexual Christians have found their homosexuality something that is a part of them and, in some cases, would gladly have given it up if they could, if for no other reason than the hostility of church and society toward them. Staying "in the closet" is an act of those who protect themselves from a pain that other Christians have and do inflict, in no small measure because of how we have read and followed scripture.

about what we have done with the plain sense of scripture. If it is a means by which we inflict pain and put down other Christians – or other human beings of any stripe – then our interpretation is under question.

At this point, then, one needs to ask about the preeminence of the gospel and of the grace of God as a guide for our proper response to scripture. That response may not be the same as what the plain sense of some texts would indicate. We are not to lose sense, however, of what it is that "the Scriptures principally teach," as the Catechism puts it.[14] The *answer* to that question is what we are to believe concerning God and what duty God requires of us. It is no accident that the verses undergirding this answer that are cited in the scripture proofs accompanying the Westminster documents are Micah 6:8, John 3:16, and John 20:31. These are fundamental formulations of the gospel, of the love of God revealed in Jesus Christ, and of our responsibility to "do justice and love kindness and walk humbly with your God." It is precisely the manifestation of justice and kindness that in this, as in all instances, is a fundamental criterion of our interpretation of scripture. What is ultimately at stake is the triumph of grace in the church.

Knowledge and Experience

Finally, a word needs to be said about the place of knowledge and experience. In another essay in this volume, Choon-Leong Seow properly calls attention to scripture's own acknowledgment that we learn the way of obedience and love, at least in part, by means of our experience and new knowledge that is gained from it.[15] The way of human discernment and reason's sensibility in the light of the complexities we encounter is not something foreign to scripture or disdained by scripture in favor of a simple reading of texts. It is scripture itself that teaches us the importance of new knowledge, of the investigation of science, of the proven wisdom that comes from experience and is a part of our fear of the Lord. We tend to set the revelation of scripture condemning homosexual acts over against our human desire to be open to the homosexual person and over against our sense from experience that homosexuality is not finally reducible simply to the category of sin. But that tendency to trump experience with revelation comes up against scripture's own valuing of the wisdom of experience and

---

[14] The Westminster Shorter Catechism, Question 3.

[15] "A Heterotextual Perspective" in *Homosexuality and Christian Community*, ed. C.-L. Seow (Louisville: Westminster John Knox, 1996), 14–27.

its insistence that those who fear the Lord are to take account of what knowledge and wisdom teach us.

Such learning from experience is not meant to be idiosyncratic; that is, experience is a shared phenomenon, something that each of us gains individually but that belongs to a body of learned knowledge checked and confirmed by the experience of others. Nevertheless, experience, by definition, is something that comes to us out of the living of our lives and what we learn from the living that others have done.

I cannot avoid a personal word about my own experience regarding this point. My construal of scripture and my response, both theologically and practically, to this and other issues is strongly shaped by the experience of growing up in the southern United States between 1930 and 1960, in an ethos in which persons were excluded from normal participation in the society – church or otherwise – because of who they were. The fundamental wrongness of that exclusion, the terrible sin that we committed in perpetuating that exclusion in a segregated society and a segregated church, has made me forever question any moves in church and society that judge and exclude persons for who they are and rule them out of full acceptance and participation. The church has a long history of similar sinful activity for which it is accountable in excluding from acceptance and loving attention those who are homosexual. That personal experience has thus stamped me in a certain way, affecting how I deal with this issue. I am willing to let my experience, which is shared by many other Christians, and the conclusions I draw from it be criticized and to listen to others who would do so. But I cannot fail to be affected and shaped by my experience. For me, it is no less than the power of the gospel in the church that is at stake.

20. Theology from Below

The Theological Interpretation of Scripture

"Biblical Theology"–The Usefulness of Ambiguity

The multiple meanings of the term "biblical theology" require a constant clarification as to the enterprise under consideration when the term comes into play as well as a continuing debate about the "proper" meaning of the term.[1] Rather than this ambiguity being a problem, however, the variety of understandings properly develops out of the different possibilities for connecting "biblical" and "theology." That is, the work of biblical theology has several aims:

1. One is to effect a discipline or *sub-discipline within biblical studies*, the delineation of a discipline within the field that has to do with a comprehensive presentation of the theological character of the biblical literature. This is the most common contemporary use of the term, though, in practice, biblical theology comes to expression primarily in a theology of one of the Testaments rather than a theology of the whole of the Bible. Within this particular form of the enterprise of biblical theology, there are large continuing issues that have to do with the descriptive or normative character of the discipline, the structure of an Old/New Testament theology, its relation to other disciplines, and the like.[2]

2. Another meaning of the term "biblical theology" is the characterization of a *point of orientation*, that is, the interpretation of biblical texts that attends primarily to their theological productivity or the formulation of theological doctrine that attends primarily to its biblical roots and directions. Here is where the terms "theological exegesis" and "exegetical theology" have their meaning. From the Scripture side, one may point to the recent multi-author volume, *A Theological Introduction to the Old Testament*[3] or the various monographs in the "Overtures to Biblical Theology"

---

[1] On the various meanings of the term, see now Michael Welker, "Biblische Theologie. II. Fundamentaltheologisch," in *Religion in Geschichte und Gegenwart*, Band 1 A–B (Tübingen: J.C.B. Mohr, 1998), cols. 1549–1553.

[2] See briefly, Patrick D. Miller, "Biblical Theology," in *A New Handbook of Christian Theology*, ed. Donald W. Musser and Joseph L. Price, Jr. (Nashville: Abingdon Press, 1992), 67–69.

[3] Bruce C. Birch, Walter Brueggemann, Terence E. Fretheim, and David L. Petersen, *A Theological Introduction to the Old Testament* (Nashville: Abingdon Press, 1999).

series, for example, Terence Fretheim's *The Suffering of God*.[4] From the side of systematics, a contemporary example of such a concept of biblical theology is suggested in Welker's *God the Spirit*, though this work is distinctive in the degree to which exegetical theology is in thorough dialogue with philosophy and culture as well as consciously working against the misdirections and traps of much modern theology.[5]

3. In this latter case as in other instances, biblical theology exercises a *critical* function vis-à-vis theology. This has been in some sense the task of theological interpretation of scripture or the task of biblical theology from the Reformation onwards. The *sola scriptura* principle is a form of the Protestant principle that places all theological formulations under the judgment of scripture and seeks to find the biblical grounds for them. Thus it reflects both the orienting and the critical function of biblical theology. The critical aim is found also as biblical theology offers a "critique of abstractions"[6] as well as correctives that are brought against both systematizing that ignores tensions or depends upon formulations or understandings that are counter to the best interpretation of the biblical materials. One finds such a critique in Welker's study of creation and particularly in his rereading of Gen 1 and 2, as indicated, for example, by his response to the insistence of some of his theological colleagues that theology's task is to identify, articulate, and preserve the distinction between God and the creation. To the contrary, Welker argues in his close re-reading of Gen 1 and 2 that the biblical traditions identify all sorts of interdependencies and interrelationships between both God and the creation and parts of the creation.[7]

Related to biblical theology's critique of abstractions and distortions is its capacity also to *surprise*, that is, to produce the unexpected, especially with regard to assumed truths and propositions. That happens, for example,

---

[4] Terence E. Fretheim, *The Suffering of God: An Old Testament Perspective* (Overtures to Biblical Theology; Philadelphia: Fortress, 1984).

[5] Michael Welker, *God the Spirit* (Minneapolis: Fortress, 1994) [Translated by John F. Hoffmeyer from the German edition, *Gottes Geist: Theologie des Heiligen Geistes* (Neukirchen-Vluyn: Neukirchener Verlag, 1992].

[6] See in this regard, the comments of Welker in *Creation and Reality* (Minneapolis: Fortress, 1999), 18–20 [Translated by John F. Hoffmeyer from the German edition, *Schöpfung und Wirklichkeit* (Neukirchen-Vluyn: Neukirchener Verlag, 1995), 32–35]. Such critique is not the outcome of biblical theology alone. Insofar as philosophy of religion, for example, is conceived of as a hermeneutical enterprise, it may serve a similar function as has been argued recently by Ingolf Dalferth, "Erkundungen des Möglichen: Perspektiven hermeneutischer Religionsphilosophie," in *Perspectives in Contemporary Philosophy of Religion*, edited by Tommi Lehtonen and Timo Koistinen (Schriften der Luther-Agricola-Gesellschaft 46; Helsinki: Luther-Agricola-Society, 2000), 50–53.

[7] Michael Welker, *Creation and Reality*, 6–20 [*Schöpfung und Wirklichkeit*, 15–35].

in Welker's identification of the manifold interdependencies between God and creation[8] or in the writer's uncovering of the character of prayer as an act of persuasion.[9] A more famous case would be Luther's biblical studies and the surprising discovery of the grace of God that justifies the sinner. One might argue that this is a proper understanding of the hermeneutical circle, that is, as the part serves to make one rethink and adjust one's understanding of the whole.[10]

4. While some biblical theology may serve only a critical function in regard to doctrine and systematics, more often there is a *constructive* aim at work also. That is, the biblical theologian is after an understanding of God and the world that will make sense of other data than the Scriptures and so will think in a large fashion about the way specific and concrete texts illumine fundamental realities.

It is a common assumption that the primary issue between biblical and systematic theology is how they differ.[11] That question, however, assumes implicitly that there is a sharp difference and perpetuates the notion that insofar as they are disciplines they are separate entities that have boundaries, each not to be crossed by the other. Thus is created the naïve but common picture of biblical theology as an enterprise that gets straight what the Bible says and then hands it over to systematic theology. The systematic theologian awaits the true/pure word from the biblical interpreter, and the biblical interpreter washes his or her hands of the material once it has passed into the hands of the theologian. This may be a caricature, but it is an all too common operating assumption, one against which, I assume, this conference is self-consciously set.

In fact, the relationship does not work that way, except in a very narrow and small sense. Systematic theologians do not wait for biblical theologians to hand them the theology of the Bible or a theological interpretation of the whole or parts before they begin their task. Nor do biblical theologians refrain from taking their theological exegesis as far as it will go, often engaging the tradition, particularly at its high points, such as Augustine,

---

[8] A lay study group reading Welker's book was genuinely excited by this surprising discovery.

[9] Patrick D. Miller, "Prayer as Persuasion," *Word and World* 13 (1993), 356–362.

[10] Note the reference to "discovery" on the part of the editors of the biblical-theological study group on power, powerlessness, and the divine as a way of describing a major outcome of the work of the group. See William Schweiker and Michael Welker, "A New Paradigm of Theological and Biblical Inquiry," in *Power, Powerlessness, and the Divine: New Inquiries in Bible and Theology*, ed. Cynthia L. Rigby (Atlanta: Scholars Press, 1997), 18.

[11] See most recently James Barr, *The Concept of Biblical Theology: An Old Testament Perspective* (Minneapolis: Fortress, 1999), 62–76, 240–252.

Luther, Calvin, and Barth. What may happen, more often than not, is the drawing of a de facto boundary by the failure on the part of the biblical interpreter to take his texts into conversation with the theological tradition, philosophy, and the like as well as by the failure of the theologian to set the biblical literature as foundational for theological construction. This may happen for less than reasons of principle or method and more for pragmatic ones having to do with areas of expertise or interest. Crossing the boundary in both directions, or simply making the movement as if there are no boundaries, allows the possibility of a genuine interaction between biblical and systematic theology.

Rather than focusing upon a presumed difference, one might argue that biblical and systematic theology share more than they differ. That is discernible first of all as one looks at the various meanings of the term "biblical theology" discussed above, some of which have to do specifically with the interaction between the Bible and theology. But that shared sphere goes further. Both have to pay attention to text; both have to attend to coherence; both operate in the convergence of freedom and order. The language and categories of the one can be appropriated by the other in a fundamental way (for example, narrative theology, on the one hand, and the use of a systematic outline in biblical theology on the other). Both disciplines need to attend to the question of major and minor voices and are forced to make evaluations (Pauline or Deutero-Pauline epistles, Deuteronomy or Qohelet) and account for the evaluations. Or to put it another way, both systematic theology and biblical theology must deal with the issue of how to present a picture that is faithful to the manifold and complex presentation of the tradition and one that conveys some sense of a whole, some coherence that seeks to overcome the problem of contradictions while not ignoring tensions and complexities, not suppressing or ignoring some perspectives or some data.

The movement back and forth across the boundaries will probably be most productive when it is the systematic theologian who makes the movement. While the outcome will depend upon the individuals involved, and the biblical theologian is hardly absolved of boundary-crossing responsibility, at least not in the light of all that is said above, the systematician brings to the enterprise a larger store of theological knowledge – by definition – than does the biblical theologian. What this means is that theological exegesis very much needs the engagement of the systematician in precisely a theological interpretation of scripture.

It should be noted that the dissolution of the boundary between biblical or exegetical theology and systematic theology happens regularly in one particular context, the act of *preaching*. The text is there in its concreteness and particularity and in dialogue with other texts. An assumption is shared in the reading and preaching of the word that scripture matters and grounds whatever is to be said. But the context is the modern world and the questions and issues it presents. The context is also a community at worship and thus acknowledging and assuming the reality of God.[12] The congregation belongs to a theological tradition to which the preaching is responsible, and the explicit orientation of that tradition on the task of theological interpretation is not only acknowledged but expected and applauded. Human experience is one of the backgrounds against which the text is heard. Whether in sophisticated or non-sophisticated fashion, the sermon takes account of the problematic of human existence. Every illustrative move is an imaginative attempt to connect the biblical word with the human situation. The enterprise is thoroughly theological in that doctrine, history, pastoral concerns, assumptions about the social context, and the like come to play in the interpretation. The boundary disappears in preaching. Indeed, one may argue that it does not even exist in that context.[13]

Theology from Below

The involvement of the Scriptures in the theological task implies at first glance or in one sense a move "from above," that is, from the authority of the text and its claims to speak definitively in some way about the subject of theology.[14] In another way, however, one may argue that the Scriptures

---

[12] This is why it is necessary to distinguish to some degree between the sermon and preaching. The latter may be in one sense only an oral presentation of the sermon, where the theological work has gone on. But insofar as it is a cultic act, set in the midst of the congregation at worship as it makes its claim to stand before and in praise of God, preaching outruns the sermon in significant ways that insure that in at least one context theology cannot be reduced to thought or idea.

[13] Here also is the reason for being critical of notions of a "hermeneutical gap" between exegesis and preaching, as if there is some move that one makes after exegesis serving to connect the text with the world of the interpreter in a way that is not present in the exegesis itself. Continued articulation of the claims of the text as that evolves out of the interpretive enterprise turns into preaching. Where that turn happens is difficult to tell, and rightly so.

It is surely the case that one may go further from the world of the text to the world of the interpreter and congregation, but the start of that is inherent in the initial engagement with the text. That is especially apparent in preaching that is not dependent upon the lectionary but starts with the interpreter's own choice of text, such choices often having to do with a sense of the prior connection of the text to the present life of the congregation. Even the preparation for lectionary preaching, however, operates without a sharp sense of the boundary between the text and the world.

[14] One might argue that there are other ways in which theology may operate "from above," particularly as it is done on the basis of philosophical categories or concepts, which are brought to the discipline from outside its material basis. In this case, formal criteria control material substance.

provide the "experience" that grounds theology's articulation of the
knowledge and love of God. But this is not some paradigm or structure of
experience. It is a highly complex interaction of personal and interpersonal, social and political, heaven and earth, of family and families, tribe
and tribes, nation and nations. It encompasses the experiences of human
existence in its personal and corporate manifestations including institutions, processes, and systems. Theology is formed out of such comprehensive experience that is regularly understood in relation to the reality of
God. As such, theology can become *concrete, imaginative,* and *realistic.*

a. Theology becomes *concrete* as its material is kept in touch with the
realia of the biblical report about life as it is lived or meant to be lived under God, as it speaks about the words and deeds of the one who has a name
and whose character and activity are made known through the experience
of a community and its people and their interactions with other communities. The abstractness of much talk about God is undercut if the God who is
talked about is Yahweh of Israel. For this deity has a specific identity and
character, a tradition of words and deeds that uncovers that identity and
lets us know what the abstraction "god" means and involves.

The fact that the same word, *ʾĕlōhîm*, can function as both noun and
name opens up the way in which the Scriptures speak about God, both in
relation to a common cultural understanding of deity and with regard to
quite specific words and deeds and traditions that belong to the experience
of a community that itself is complicated in its character and in its longev-
ity through history.[15] Those words, deeds, and traditions both connect with
broader cultural and theological notions and experiences and also stand
against them.[16] There is both congruity and incongruity between the name
and the noun, between the words and deeds tradition associated with Yahweh of Israel and the philosophical, theological, historical, and social understandings of the concept. As name and noun come together, the symbol
"God" is subject to all sorts of reconceptualizations that go on in the culture and have much to do with the viability and intelligibility of the con-

---

[15] On some of that complexity, see Rainer Albertz, *A History of Israelite Religion in the
Old Testament Period,* 2 vols. (The Old Testament Library; Louisville: Westminster John
Knox Press, 1994) [Translated by John Bowden from the German edition, *Religions-
geschichte Israels in alttestamentliche Zeit* (Göttingen: Vandenhoeck und Ruprecht, 1992)];
and Patrick D. Miller, *The Religion of Ancient Israel* (The Library of Ancient Israel; Louisville: Westminster John Knox Press, 2000), chapter 2.

[16] See Patrick D. Miller, "God and the Gods: History of Religion as an Approach to Bible
and Theology," in *idem, Israelite Religion and Biblical Theology: Collected Essays* (Journal
for the Study of the Old Testament Supplement Series, 267; Sheffield: Sheffield Academic
Press, 2000).

cept. Thus theology is attentive to philosophy, psychology, anthropology, and other disciplines to articulate the viability and intelligibility of the reality of God. What theology has concretely, however, is an identity filled with a content that arises out of the manifold and diverse experiences of a community, a community that extrapolates in manifold and various circumstances from that experience to speak about not only its own life, its suffering, judgment, and redemption but about the whole cosmos, its creation, its endangerment, and its fulfillment.[17] In Paul Ricoeur's language, "Naming God is what has already taken place in the texts preferred by my listening's presupposition." It is that naming that biblical theology seeks to hear clearly and in detail in its listening.[18]

The wholeness of scripture is a claim that those words and deeds continue in the revelation of God in Jesus Christ. Jesus Christ is who God always was. Who and what God is and is about unfolds in the story of the life, death, and resurrection of Jesus Christ. The elaboration of the words and deeds of Yahweh in and for – or against – Israel and through Jesus of Nazareth provides the substantive ground for systematic theology's articulation of the faith in conversation with the issues and questions of reason, experience, the world, science, philosophy, and the like.

b. Theology becomes *imaginative* out of the imagination of scripture, bringing together the picturesque and metaphorical and poetic dimensions that infuse the Scriptures with the realm of the imagination and the poetic in human life. It is in this dynamic engagement that theology receives the critique of abstractions and is led into the imaginative. It is in the indirectness of poetic speech that the mystery of God is maintained in the theological enterprise.[19] The allusiveness and elusiveness of biblical poetic

---

[17] Ingolf Dalferth has rightly observed that God is not the subject of theology but a short formula for the concrete perspective in which theology considers all its subjects, including the God question. Even the perspective of theology is not the abstract or philosophical notion of God but God as Creator, Redeemer, and Consummator, precisely because of the identity that is given to the reality of God in the ways and deeds of Yahweh of Israel. See Dalferth, "Erkundungen des Möglichen: Perspektiven hermeneutischer Religionsphilosophie," 55 and n. 19.

[18] Paul Ricoeur, "Naming God," in *Rhetorical Invention and Religious Inquiry: New Perspectives*, ed. Walter Jost and Wendy Olmsted (New Haven: Yale University Press, 2000), 163.

[19] In this connection, see, for example, the author's discussion – drawing on the interpretation of Gerhard von Rad – of the syntactically loose connection without the usual conjunction between the critical sentences in Gen 50:20 ("You reckoned evil against me; God reckoned it for good...") as conveying the mystery of divine providence in the way the two realities indicated in the sentences are to be related to each other ("The Theological Significance of Biblical Poetry," in *Language, Theology, and the Bible: Essays in Honour of James Barr*, ed.

texts or of the generally poetic character of biblical literature become swords against the fixed categories and abstract formulations that can lure systematic theology into making reason, confessional formulation, and experience traps rather than vehicles as well as against the assumption that only descriptive discourse can be referential.[20]

Garrett Green has argued for the significance of the imagination in the theological task in a dual way. "Theology must become imaginative – again, in both senses of the word – for it must understand itself to speak the language of imagination, and it must pursue its task with imaginative creativity: in short, it must articulate the grammar of the Christian imagination imaginatively!"[21] Like Ricoeur's call for the theological appropriation of the poetic, Green's focus upon the imagination is precisely an attention to the particularities, the concreteness, the metaphorical of scripture, to the practice of what he calls an "imaginative literalism." Christian theology, he contends, "should adhere tenaciously to the *sensus literalis* of scripture in the faith that *only here, in these metaphoric images does one encounter the Living God* [italics mine]."[22]

c. Theology becomes *realistic* as it takes up the reality of God and "creaturely reality as intended by God" that is portrayed in the Bible.[23]

Samuel E. Balentine and John Barton (Oxford: Clarendon Press, 1994), 226–227; repr. in Miller, *Israelite Religion and Biblical Theology*, 233–249.

[20] Ricoeur warns against assuming that poetic discourse cannot be understood as having a referential discourse, along with discourse of a descriptive character (scientific, historical, sociological, etc.). Poetic discourse, he suggests, is also about the world but not about the manipulable objects of our everyday environment. "Poetic discourse calls into question …uncritical concepts of adequation and verification. In so doing, it calls into question the reduction of the referential function to descriptive discourse and opens the field of a nondescriptive reference to the world." ("Naming God," 167).

[21] Garrett Green, *Theology, Hermeneutics, and Imagination: The Crisis of Interpretation at the End of Modernity* (Cambridge: Cambridge University Press, 2000), 205. Cf. his earlier work, *Imagining God: Theology and the Religious Imagination* (San Francisco: Harper and Row, 1989).

[22] Ibid., 206.

[23] Welker, *God the Spirit*, x [*Gottes Geist*, 12]. It is important to recognize in Welker's heavy focus on "reality" and "realistic" theology that the reality of which he speaks and that is communicated in scripture is an *intended* reality. This does not mean that the Scriptures do not speak about a present reality. Rather "a realistic theology makes clear that our experience, our worldviews, our moral systems, and our value structures must be enlightened and changed in order to correspond to creaturely reality." (*God the Spirit*, xi). On this notion of a realistic theology, which seems to function as a kind of bridge notion and indeed operates in Welker's case on the boundary or interface between biblical and systematic theology, see *God the Spirit*, x–xi, 46–49 [*Gottes Geist*, 12–14, 49–57]; cf. Bernd Oberdorfer, "Biblisch-realistische Theologie: Methodologische Überlegungen zu einem dogmatischen Programm," in *Resonanzen: Theologische Beiträge Michael Welker zum 50. Geburtstag*, ed. Sigrid Brandt and Bernd Oberdorfer (Wuppertal: Foedus, 1997), 63–83. The bridging has to do not only with the connection between biblical and systematic theology but with the connection be-

That reality, as Welker has underscored, is given to us in a complex of traditions, stories, genres,[24] experiences, or, to use his careful formulation "a complex pattern of interconnected testimonies." Even the use of the term "pattern" may convey a greater coherence than is there, but theology from below in this context does seek to uncover the interaction between the *complexity* of the reality of God and God's way for creation in the biblical story, which constantly breaks open efforts to describe it systematically, and the *coherence* that is suggested in various and indirect ways (for example, the narrative movement discernible in literature that is full of non-narrative traditions, the presence of a beginning and an ending for the whole, the way in which traditions explicitly interact with one another, referring back to and quoting each other,[25] the breadth of usage of the name YHWH – not total of course, as Qoheleth and Esther indicate, and the identification of the name of the Lord of Israel with the Lord of the church, and so on).[26]

The enterprise envisioned above has been summarized in Oberdorfer's discussion of "biblical-realistic theology":

'Biblische Theologie' ... versucht die traditionellen religiösen und theologischen Chiffrierungen und Symbolisierungen biblischer Inhalte von ihrem biblischen Ursprung her zu reformulieren, oder sie rekonstruiert die Bedeutung und interne Vernetzung verschiedener biblischer Begriffe und Konzepte und sucht von da her neue Gesichtspunkte in die gegenwärtige theologische Verantwortung des Glaubens einzuführen, und dadurch starre Begriffskonstellationen aufzubrechen, neue Deutungs- und Kombinationsmöglichkeiten zu eröffnen und damit zur Überwindung der Plausibilisierungsprobleme christlich-theologischer Inhalte beizutragen.[27]

---

tween past experiences and expectations of God and present and future ones. One assumes his resistance to appropriating the term "biblical theology" is in part because he sees in the term a formulation that is generally so confined to the material of scripture that it may tend to indicate only a highly descriptive account of what is in the Bible and not a discipline on the boundary between scripture and theology and the boundary between past and future. The continuing debate about whether or not biblical theology ought to be descriptive or normative suggests his wariness is appropriate.

[24] See in this connection the work of Paul Ricoeur, "Toward a Hermeneutic of the Idea of Revelation," *Harvard Theological Review* 70:1–2 (January-April, 1977), 1–38.

[25] See, for example, the work of Michael Fishbane, *Biblical Interpretation in Ancient Israel* (Oxford: The Clarendon Press, 1985).

[26] The articulation of a biblical-theological inquiry in terms of the interaction of complexity and coherence is particularly formulated by Schweiker and Welker in their essay "A New Paradigm of Theological and Biblical Inquiry." Others have suggested similar interactions as central to the method of biblical theology, e.g., J. Christiaan Beker in his various works on New Testament theology where he speaks of contingency and core as the appropriate poles of biblical theology's method. See, for example, his book *Paul the Apostle: The Triumph of God in Life and Thought* (Philadelphia: Fortress, 1980).

[27] Oberdorfer, "Biblisch-realistische Theologie," 78.

Coherence without Reductionism

In his discussion of a "biblical-realistic theology," Oberdorfer asks about the selectivity and perspectivity of moving out of Scripture into theology or of returning to the Scripture to bring about critique of distortions and abstractions as well as surprising discoveries. Which themes, concepts, and notions out of the Bible are to guide theological understanding?[28]

It is at this point that one may ask if the much-criticized move to find – within the Old Testament at least – a center, a controlling theme, or a set of polarities or tensions that have a governing or dominating force merits further consideration. Much of the discussion in this direction is an outcome of the work of von Rad, who argued for a continuing kerygmatic tradition, a stream of testimonies as the structure of Old Testament theology rather than any single concept. It is safe to say that so far von Rad has won the day, as evidenced not only by the failure of various proposals for a center or basic concept to gain a following but also by the criticism of such moves as reductionistic, a critique that has come from within Old Testament theology and from without.[29]

If, however, there is to be any order and coherence in the theological interpretation of the concrete, realistic complex of biblical traditions, then it may be wise to ask about those perspectives that seem to be guiding, dominant, widely present, etc. as a way of providing some temporary or penultimate control over the materials. The alternatives are not simply one central idea or myriad complex of forms and traditions. It certainly is unlikely that any single proposal for a center will itself be sufficient to incorporate the fullness of the Old Testament or point to all the important dimensions of its theology, much less of the Bible as a whole.[30] Nor should

---

[28] Oberdorfer, "Biblisch-realistische Theologie," 77.

[29] In this regard, note the Old Testament theology of Walter Brueggemann, which does not seek an orienting center or thematic but does take von Rad's emphasis on Israel's testimony as the impetus for a controlling structural metaphor, that of the courtroom and the presentation of the witnesses who help the jury decide what is true. See Walter Brueggemann, *Theology of the Old Testament* (Minneapolis: Fortress, 1997).

[30] One of the problems in the interaction between biblical theology and systematic theology is the timidity of the former in trying to think about the Bible as a whole. There are some notable exceptions, among them Paul Minear's *Eyes of Faith*, published some 50 years ago (1946) and more recently Brevard Childs' *Biblical Theology of the Old and New Testaments* (Minneapolis: Fortress, 1993). Brueggemann moves freely in and out of the New Testament in a way that the writer finds refreshing, suggesting in non-systematic ways where there are resonances between the Old Testament and the New, between God's story with Israel and the work of God in Jesus Christ. By and large, however, thinking theologically about the Scriptures as a whole happens more often from the systematic side of the discussion than from the biblical.

that be expected. That is the point of the reductionistic criticism. But the enterprise that has produced such potentially reductionistic outcomes has also served to identify quite significant structures and traditions, significant for both the Old Testament as a literary document of theological character and indeed significant for the faith of the community out of which that document comes. Some examples will illustrate the point:

- Walter Eichrodt's proposal about "covenant" as the center of the Old Testament has received far more critical reaction about its failure to encompass the whole of the Old Testament than it has recognition of the way in which the covenant relationship between the Lord and Israel is so fundamental to the whole of the Old Testament, so much so that when it is not present, that merits comment.[31]
- Rudolf Smend's identification of the covenant formulary, "I am your God and you are my people," grows out of Eichrodt's perception.[32] Once again, the relationship of Israel as the people of Yahweh and Yahweh as the God of Israel is fundamental to most of the Old Testament traditions.
- Werner Schmidt develops this insight in terms of the First Commandment/Shema, a variation on the above proposals.[33]
- Even von Rad's kerygmatic testimonies point to a tradition stream that is indeed central to the Old Testament and to its theological interpretation. That not everything fits within that is, of course, the case, and so von Rad did his "third" volume on wisdom. But to assume that wisdom does not rest in any way within the tradition of kerygmatic testimonies requires a strangely schizophrenic reading of the faith of Israel.

The point is not that we should go back to seeking a unifying whole but that a perspectival approach requires some assessment and valuation of the complex of traditions and interconnected materials. Are there traditions that hold things together in ways that help identify the things that matter

---

[31] Walter Eichrodt, *Theology of the Old Testament,* 2 vols. (Philadelphia: Westminster, 1961, 1967).

[32] Rudolf Smend, *Die Mitte des Alten Testaments* (Theologische Studien, 101; Zürich: EVA-Verlag, 1970). Cf. Rolf Rendtorff, *The Covenant Formula: An Exegetical and Theological Investigation* (Old Testament Studies; Edinburgh: T&T Clark, 1998) [Translated by Martin Kohl from the German edition, *Die Bundesformel* (Stuttgart: Verlag Katholisches Bibelwerk, 1995).]

[33] Werner Schmidt, *Das erste Gebot: Seine Bedeutung für das Alte Testament* (Theologische Existenz heute, 165; München: Chr. Kaiser Verlag, 1969); cf. *idem, The Faith of Israel* (Philadelphia: Westminster, 1983) [Translated from the German, *Alttestamentlicher Glaube in seiner Geschichte* (Neukirchen-Vluyn: Neukirchener Verlag, 1975).]

theologically and contribute to discerning coherence in the complex?[34] To see the enterprises represented above as simply a search for the "great idea" is partly to misunderstand what they are about. Covenant was not for Israel an idea but a reality that affected all of life, related to kinship issues, politics, and personal relationships. The exclusive worship of Yahweh may be turned into the idea of monotheism, but for Israel it was a life and death requirement realized in continuing cultic activity, undergirding legal and judicial forms and activities, and experienced as determinative for the very fate of the people, anything but an idea.

In similar fashion, biblical theology explores various ways of *structuring* and *ordering* the biblical traditions not for the sake of abstracting a system nor with a view to creating final determinations but precisely to help uncover the manifold ways in which the theological enterprise can bring the traditions together. These may be significantly historical in approach, as demonstrated in the older *Systematic Theology: A Historicist Approach* by Gordon Kaufman (an approach long abandoned by him).[35] Or one may come at the traditions more canonically, as in the recent first volume of Rolf Rendtorff's Old Testament theology. Welker's pneumatology is to some degree a mix of both. The writer's theology of prayer takes its structure from the structure of the experience of prayer as that is recounted again and again in Scripture (cry for help, divine response in the salvation oracle, and human response back to God in praise and thanksgiving).[36] This particular widespread pattern occurs in all sorts of genres, periods, and experiences. It is also seen to be indicative in a fundamental way for our understanding of God and for christology, particularly the meaning of Jesus' death and resurrection. Further, not only can one not reduce what is described in this way to a great idea, it is echoed over and over in the experience of Christian faith in any time as a reality that is felt and perceived as well as understood.[37]

---

[34] The same point could be made with reference to the discernment of significant tensions and polarities at the heart of the Old Testament. These also are clues to basic perspectives that matter theologically. So also the focus of Schweiker and Welker on cultic, prophetic, and legal dimensions within the traditions or the texts (Schweiker) or on cultic, legal, and mercy dimensions (Welker) is a way of overcoming an over-simplified and reductionistic appropriation of Scripture for theology and ethics while identifying primary biblical categories as forms of complexity on the way to coherence. See the essays by Schweiker and Welker in *Power, Powerlessness, and the Divine*, as well as the writer's concluding observations about their papers in the same volume.

[35] *Systematic Theology: A Historicist Perspective* (New York: Scribner's, 1968).

[36] Patrick D. Miller, *They Cried to the Lord: The Form and Theology of Biblical Prayer* (Minneapolis: Fortress, 1994), esp. chapters 3–5.

[37] Very rarely do I talk with others about this that someone does not come to me with a report of a very concrete and often detailed experience that corresponds in sharp ways to the pattern described above.

All such works are experiments in plausibility, and the theologian-critic asks precisely after their plausibility and the degree to which they give order and allow for contingency, incorporate the rich data and effect valuation, hear the varied voices and perceive a melody, recognize dominant streams and give account of the eddies and whirlpools off to the side or in the middle of the ongoing river. To the extent that happens, then plausibility may be acknowledged – but not finality. There are always further surprises.

21. Man and Woman

Towards a Theological Anthropology

The opening chapters of Genesis have played a large part in the history of Christian doctrine, particularly at the point of developing a theological anthropology. That has been especially the case in regard to the matter of the *imago dei* and the "fall" or the question of the origin and nature of sin. I would suggest, however, that the larger anthropological matters in these chapters have to do with the community of man and woman and the interface of humanity with the natural world, but more particularly with the earth.[1]

The Community of Man and Woman

In the first of the creation stories (Gen 1:1–2:4a), the culmination of God's creative acts is the forming of human beings. Very little is said in that context about the human creature. Only two things – the human being is made in the image of God and is male and female. The ramifications of that are large for theological anthropology, for the doctrine of the human. For it is precisely creation of humanity as *man* and *woman* and as woman and man in *community* that is the climax of the story of God's creative work. The story not only is not indifferent to humanity's being comprised of two genders. It specifically sets that to the forefront, but without elaboration, when it tells of the final creative act of God. Despite the fairly common reading of the account as indicating a general notion of relationship or even a concept of sociability, it is much more specific than that. Maleness and femaleness, whatever that may consist of – and one notes the story does not seek to spell that out at all – are not hidden or even *secondary* in the creative purpose. They are *prominent*. Furthermore, it is not the man by him-

---

[1] This essay represents a return to the subject matter of an earlier piece (Patrick D. Miller, *Genesis 1–11: Studies in Structure and Theme* [JSOTSup 8; Sheffield: JSOT Press, 1978]) but with a more theological intent. That is, the essay may be understood as a piece of theological exegesis or exegetical theology. Its presence in this volume is a small expression of my esteem for its honoree as scholar, teacher, and editor and even more of my gratitude for his friendship through the years.

self or the woman by herself. That is, it is not woman and man separate or individually or as distinct but separate genders. It is women and men in community to whom the divine blessing and the human task are given. Once the declaration is made that it is as man and as woman that God has created human beings, then the story speaks of them only in the plural:

[26]"Let them have dominion (male and female)..." [28]And God blessed *them* (man and woman) and God said to *them* (female and male): "Be fruitful and multiply and fill the earth and subdue it (man and woman together) and have dominion (woman and man) over the fish of the sea, etc..." [29]and God said, "Behold I have given you (male and female) every plant... *you* (man and woman) shall have them for food."

This community of woman and man is where the image of God is represented according to the parallelism of the tricolon in Gen 1:27. The image is clearly a ruling function in this text as indicated first in verse 26. The purpose of creating ʾādām in the image of God is that the human creature may rule the earth. That purpose is further indicated in the contextual fact of the way that images of kings were set up in different places to represent the rule of the king in those places. The image identifies who rules there. God's rule of the creation is through the divine image bearer. But that divine image bearer, and thus the ruler of creation, is man and woman together. Not only is there no subordination of the woman in this account, but she is specifically given a ruling task along with the man.[2]

In the divine blessing that follows immediately upon the creation of human life as man and woman, three things are present: (1) One is procreation to bring about humanity on the earth, though this is probably to be understood quite specifically in relation to the creation of nations and communities (see, for example, Gen 17:20 [Ishmael and the Arabs]; 35:11; 47:27; Exod 1:7 [Jacob and the Israelites]).[3] That is, the procreative dimension is also a *culture-creating* activity as well as a biological one. (2) Another part of the blessing is the provision of the fruit of the earth as food for its creatures. The relation of woman and man as the human creatures is thus more complex. The biological dimension with its procreating possibilities for growth is clearly a facet of this relation and a significant dimension, but it is only one. Man and woman are also joined together as a *com-*

---

[2] On the character of this ruling activity, see Walter Brueggemann, "King in the Kingdom of Things," *Christian Century* 86 (1969), 1165–1166.

[3] See in this regard the argument of Norbert Lohfink ("Growth: The Priestly Document and the Limits of Growth" in idem, *Great Themes from the Old Testament* [Edinburgh: T&T Clark, 1982], 167–182) that the word for "subdue" in Gen 1:28 (*kābaš*), may be seen in relation to the peoples' taking possession of their territories, as at the end of the Priestly literature in Josh 18:1 with reference to Israel.

munity of need who live by divine providence. (3) Finally – and it would seem most important because it is a part of the expressed divine intention prior to the act of creating man and woman [Gen 1:26] – is the divine assignment of the human task: the ordering and care of the earth, which is what the image of God is all about, belongs to the community of women and men. The story assumes from the start that it is *together* and *only* together that the human responsibilities for filling the earth with peoples and ruling the earth and its creatures, that is, the tasks that belong to our very being as God's creatures, can be carried out. The human story starts that way and cannot be read or lived as if this beginning is not true in the deepest sense. It is out of this creative intention of God that all the proper notions of cooperation, mutuality, and complementarity between men and women flow forth.

Underscoring the above analysis of the text is the fact that the focus upon woman and man *in relation to each other* and to God is continued *immediately* in the next episode of the story, Gen 2 and 3. Here the narrative form makes man and woman the primal couple. There are some features of that story that are quite important for thinking about the community of men and women:

1. The divine reflection, "It is not good that the creature should be alone" (Gen 2:18), lifts up the relationship between man and woman as God's intention in the creation. Human loneliness and isolation are not a part of God's plan, and the primary form of companionship and relationship in the creation is that of woman and man. Furthermore the relationship and companionship between woman and man is distinctive and fulfilling in a way that is not the case between woman/man and other parts of the created order. Gen 2 tells of the creation of the animals as an outcome of the divine judgment that it is not good for *hāʾādām* to be alone, but that outcome is insufficient for the fundamental companionship that belongs to human existence. Nor does the Yahwistic story identify the creation of woman as for the purpose of procreation. Companionship and sexual union (2:24) are what the story focuses on in its account of the creation of the woman to join the man. Procreation, which is part of the blessing of God upon the man and woman in Gen 1, comes into the Yahwistic story but is not at the center of the divine intentionality.

2. The mutuality and complementarity of male and female is accented in the clear indication that woman and man need each other ("a helper as his partner" – Gen 2:18). Coming together in community, whether in the intimacy of a loving relationship or in other more extended ways is not reducible to biological urges and marriage, though that is certainly part of being man and woman and the Bible affirms both. Nor is it due to the accidents of proximity, but because we find we need each other and our

wholeness is in some sense achieved in the relation of women and men. As many have noted, the expression "a helper as his partner" does not imply subordination, for in the Old Testament the term "helper," often applied to God, refers to the person in superior position, able because of greater strength, and the like, to "help" the other person. The expression *kĕnegdô*, "corresponding to it," indicates precisely what it means: a correspondence or shared identity, mutuality, and equality.[4]

3. The expression "bone of my bone and flesh of my flesh" (Gen 2:23) is a *covenantal* formula suggesting solidarity in weakness and strength, as Brueggemann has demonstrated in a careful study of this formula in the Old Testament.[5] While it is commonly taken that the "help" is either a serving responsibility, which is not the case, or simply a generalized assistance, it is reasonable to presume with Brueggemann that the "help" provided by the woman for the man is in the assignment that has been given to the man, that is, to work and watch over the garden. The solidarity and mutuality implicit in the covenantal formula have to do with solidarity in the human task, the care of the garden (and later the ground – Gen 3:23), a shared responsibility comparable to that articulated in the Priestly account in Gen 1.[6]

4. While the story in Gen 2–3 shows reflexes of the patriarchal context in which it took shape, for example, "the man and his wife," in various ways the story shows at one time the man and at another time the woman as the *attracting center* or the *initiator of action*:

- male – woman made out of the rib from man
- female – man leaves his place and security to cleave to his wife
- female – woman initiates the conversation with the snake and eating the fruit

---

[4] Phyllis Trible, *God and the Rhetoric of Sexuality* (Overtures to Biblical Theology; Philadelphia: Fortress, 1978), 90.

[5] "The key phrase about the relationship in 2:23a is a covenantal formula which does not speak about derivation in a biological sense but means to speak about commonality of concern, loyalty, and responsibility." Brueggemann's analysis is consistent with the above discussion in that he argues that the three main dimensions of this part of the story are the need for a mate, the affirmation of finding a partner, and the implication of this new partnership. Walter Brueggemann, "Of the Same Flesh and Bone [Gen 2, 23a]," *The Catholic Biblical Quarterly* 32 (1970), 532–542.

[6] On the way in which the taking of the woman from the rib of *hāʾādām* indicates both continuity and discontinuity but no more subordination of the former to the latter than is implied in the "taking" of *hāʾādām* from the ground, see Trible, *God and the Rhetoric of Sexuality*, 94–102.

- male – one of the results of the sin and judgment is man's rule over his wife

5. The judgment "to your husband shall be your desire, but he shall rule over you (the woman)" has caused much trouble for women and ultimately has had devastating effects on the community of men and women. A couple of things need to be said about that:

a. This is not divine creative intention but the outcome of human sin and divine judgment.

b. In most cases, the human community seeks to overcome the results of its sinful actions. That is no less the case here. This rule of man over woman and husband over wife is bracketed by two other statements of sinful results: the painful toil and labor of child-bearing and the painful toil and labor of earning a living. In both of these other cases, the human community has done all it can to overcome these negative dimensions of the human condition. And indeed the whole biblical story is oriented toward an overcoming of that final result of human sinfulness – death. The corollary of that history is that male dominance and female submission are to be struggled against as vigorously as human beings struggle to make human work less toilsome and child-bearing safer and less painful. In none of these cases has the human race overcome the punishing outcome, but it surely is going to keep trying.

c. The Bible itself proffers a counter word about the nature of this relationship in the Song of Songs. The expression "your/its desire (*těšûqâ*) is for..." is an unusual one in the Bible, occurring only three times, twice in this story with regard to the woman's desire for her husband that ends up in male dominance and in Gen 4:7 where the desire of sin is for Cain but he is unable to rule over it or dominate it. The only other occurrence of this idiom is in the description of the relationship between the two lovers in Song of Songs. But there the "desire" (*tešûqâ*) is that of the male lover for his beloved, the woman. This desire that carries with it no implication of rule or dominance is then completed by the references to the mutual desire of the woman and the man, though without the technical term that appears in Gen 3–4 (2:16; 6:3). As Ellen Davis has noted, this is an intentional echo and reversal of "the sad ending of the idyll in Eden. No longer, the poem declares, are desire and power unequally distributed between woman and man."[7]

---

[7] Davis comments with regard to the author's frequent allusion to other biblical texts and phrases: "It is her (?) habit to take old words from the religious tradition and set them in new contexts, where they acquire fresh associations. She is consciously rereading the tradition, at the same time creating a continuation and a turning point in that tradition. She is witnessing to the new possibility that she sees God creating with this man and this woman" (*Getting Involved with God: Rediscovering the Old Testament* [Cambridge: Cowley Publications, 2001],

6. Finally, the story describes a primal breach in the relationship of human and God, and there, too, woman and man are together. It is not so much a question of who acted first, or who is the active, inquiring, aggressive one – surely the woman in this primal story – or who is the passive, acquiescing one – surely the man. It is rather that man and woman are in this from start to finish together. They are both prohibited from eating the fruit; they both eat the fruit and thus disobey. Together they see their nakedness and together they try to do something about their new plight. They both pass the buck when confronted by God. With both man and woman, God deals mercifully in providing clothes to cover nakedness.

The story of the garden as a story of the beginning of the human race makes clear that our life and death are with each other, as woman and man in relationship. It does not ascribe certain characteristics to man or woman. It does not place one or the other totally controlling the relationship. It does not see one as more sinful or more punished than the other. We are in this as woman and man together, and together we live, together we blow it, together we work to overcome the effects, together we are treated mercifully.

Human Beings and the Earth

The *image of God* is a particular dimension of this matter, but as most interpreters of these texts have recognized, the divine image has less to do with some inherent nature of human being and more with the role of the human being vis-à-vis the natural world. That is, the image is a representative one more than it is an indicator of some innate aspect of human life. In the Mesopotamian context, the king was the image of the god and so represented the deity's rule in the particular place where the king ruled. In the biblical literature, that representative rule has been democratized and universalized. The image points to the responsibility for dominion over the earth and its fullness. Thus the *imago Dei* is clearly not a nature but a role, not a characteristic but a responsibility (cf. Ps 8), the rule of the earth and its creatures.

That such a rule of the earth is complex and not simple and assumes all kinds of interdependencies between the human creatures and the earth is demonstrated by the degree to which the history of humanity in its prime-

---

72). See also Trible's discussion of the interplay of the Song and Gen 2–3 (*God and the Rhetoric of Sexuality*, 144–165) and specifically her comment with regard to the repetition of this phrase: "Another consequence of disobedience is thus redeemed through the recovery of mutuality in the garden of eroticism" (160).

val story is an interpretation of humanity's relationship to the earth and the
soil, a point scored by both parts of the creation story, the Priestly and the
Yahwist.[8] In Gen 1 the relationship is articulated in relation to "the earth"
(*hā᾿āreṣ*). All three parts of the divine assignment/blessing have to do with
the relation of the man and woman community to "the earth." They together have the responsibility for "filling it" and for "ruling it." But the
earth also is the source of sustenance for both the human beings – and it is
clear that one really cannot talk about anthropology in terms of "man" but
only in terms of man *and* woman and so must speak of human beings and
not only of human being – and the animate creatures of the earth. At this
point, things are more complex in that such providence, affected by God's
good creation in behalf of the sustenance of man and woman, is shared
with the other sensate creatures. There is a complicated interdependency
that is evidenced in the *ruling responsibility* of the man and woman and
the *provision* that is shared by man and woman and the different animal
creatures of the earth.[9] One may presume that at least a dimension of the
ruling responsibility is a caring for and ordering of the earth, that is, the
man and woman's responsibility to see that this shared interface with "the
earth" and its produce is possible and works. But there is a tension here.
The provision of sustenance is a differentiated gift to all the sensate beings
that God has made and not a part of a hierarchical order. What the man and
woman do in their rule of the animal world does not involve appropriation
of or control over the provision that God has "given" to the animal world.
The Lord says, in effect: "See, I give you this and the animals that" (Gen
1:29–31).

The interdependency of the creation and the human creature, implicitly
understood as man and woman, is echoed in Ps 104, though without the
notions of dominion or rule that are explicit in Gen 1 and without the differentiated understanding of the human as man and woman. The sense of
the shared creation and the provision for life as a part of the creative work
of God is developed in an even more elaborated way there as the poem
speaks of providing place for all the animals (e.g., vv. 16–18), time for
animals and humans to do their work of finding food (e.g., vv. 19–23), and
a differentiated provision of food for the animal world and for the human
world (though these are not formulated in the same way in Gen 1 and the
Psalm). The responsibility of the human creature for caring for the earth,
ordering it, and making it work is implicit in the way that the human provi-

---

[8] Thus the "yes, but" playing off of the Priestly and Yahwist creation accounts is unnecessary, as Michael Welker has vigorously argued on other grounds (*Creation and Reality*, 61–
64).

[9] See in this regard the discussion of Welker, *Creation and Reality*, 70–73.

sion is described in Ps 104. For while the provision for the animals is grass and herbage (and, of course, water), the human provision is not grain and grapes and olive trees but bread and wine and oil, products of culture, of human activity.

In the Yahwist's account in Gen 2–4, the complicated interdependency and interaction of the human creature with the earth is developed in a different and more narrative fashion. This point is obvious in the wordplay between *ʾādām* and *ʾădāmâ*, 'human being' and 'ground'. But it goes much further than that. The account of creation, of life under God and rebellion against God, of creaturely existence, of sin and judgment, of human vocation and community is a story of the intricate relationship between *ʾādām* and *ʾădāmâ*. The pre-creation state is when there is no *ʾādām* to till the *ʾădāmâ*. *ʾādām* is taken or created from the *ʾădāmâ* and in death returns to the *ʾădāmâ*. *ʾādām*'s vocation is to work the *ʾădāmâ* even when sent from the garden. From the *ʾădāmâ* comes the sustenance of human life. When *ʾādām* sins, the earth is also affected; the consequences involve the natural order, the ground, and humanity's involvement. And the relief that is given to human existence under the judgment of toilsome labor is given by an *ʾîš hāʾădāmâ*, a man of the soil, Noah, who by his name is seen to be the one who provides relief from the work: "Out of the ground (*hāʾădāmâ*) which the Lord has cursed this one shall bring us relief from our work and from the painful toil of our hands" (5:29).

The evidence for this complex interdependency is even more substantial than the above summary indicates. This is sufficient, however, to suggest that in multiple ways human existence exercises its dominion over the natural world at the same time that it is related to that world in origination, vocation, and destiny. Hierarchical relationship is a facet but not the whole.[10] Insofar as Christian anthropology attends to and takes its cues from Gen 1–11, a rich source, it requires at its center an understanding of the human as oriented around both the differentiation of man and woman as well as the complex but highly productive and dangerous interdepend-

---

[10] The play on *ʾādām* and *ʾădāmâ* forces the discussion around the one designated *ʾādām*, but the way in which that term moves back and forth from its reference to the male to its reference to the human being as both male and female (particularly in the expression *ben ʾādām*) and the covenantal, helping relationship between the woman and the man indicate that the term resists a simple designation with reference to the male. That is further confirmed by the different ways in which the connections clearly involve both the man and the woman even when the story distinguishes between them (taken out of the *ʾădāmâ* and returning to the *ʾădāmâ* sent from the *ʾădāmâ* to work the *ʾădāmâ*). The role distinctions arise in the breakdown of the human enterprise and the judgments that are placed on man and woman. They are not placed as central to the relationship as God created man and woman. For more detailed elaboration of the interplay of *ʾădāmâ* and *ʾādām*. See Miller, *Genesis 1–11*, 37–42.

encies of men and women and the interdependencies – hierarchical, providential, and otherwise – of man and woman with the earth/ground and with the creatures who also inhabit it.

Place of First Publication

1. "The Place of the Decalogue in the Old Testament and Its Law"

   Interpretation 43 (1989), 229–242

2. "The Sufficiency and Insufficiency of the Commandments"

   Unpublished

3. "Metaphors for the Moral"

   Unpublished

4. "The Good Neighborhood: Identity and Community Through the Commandments"

   The Character of Scripture: Moral Formation, Community, and Biblical Interpretation,
   ed. William P. Brown (Grand Rapids: Eerdmans, 2002), 55–72

5. "The Story of the First Commandment: The Book of Exodus"

   American Baptist Quarterly 21 (2002), 234–246

6. "The Story of the First Commandment: The Book of Joshua"

   Covenant as Context: Essays in Honour of E. W. Nicholson, eds. A. D. H. Mayes and R.
   B. Salters (Oxford: Oxford University Press, 2003), 311–324. Reprinted by permission of
   Oxford University Press

7. "The Psalms as a Meditation on the First Commandment"

   Revised and expanded paper read to the Society of Biblical Literature International Meeting in Cambridge 2003

8. "The Commandments in the Reformed Perspective"

   Paper read at a meeting of Reformed exegetes and theologians at the University of Stellenbosch 2001. To be published under the auspices of the Center of Theological Inquiry, Princeton, NJ

9. "'That It May Go Well with You': The Commandments and the Common Good"

In Search of the Common Good, eds. Dennis McCann and Patrick D. Miller (New York: T & T Clark, 2005)

10. "The Ruler in Zion and the Hope of the Poor: Psalms 9-10 in the Context of the Psalter"

David and Zion: Essays in Honor of J. J. M. Roberts, eds. Bernard F. Batto and Kathryn Roberts (Winona Lake, IN: Eisenbrauns, 2004)

11. "The Poetry of Creation: Psalm 104"

God Who Creates: Essays in Honor of W. Sibley Towner, eds. William P. Brown and S. Dean McBride, Jr. (Grand Rapids: Eerdmans, 2000), 87–103

12. "The Hermeneutics of Imprecation"

Theology in the Service of the Church: Essays in Honor of Thomas W. Gillespie, ed. Wallace M. Alston, Jr. (Grand Rapids: Eerdmans, 2000), 153–163

13. "Prayer and Worship"

Calvin Theological Journal 36 (2001), 53–62

14. "The Psalter as a Book of Theology"

Biblical Texts in Community: The Psalms in Jewish and Christian Traditions, eds. Harold W. Attridge and Margot E. Fassler (Leiden and Atlanta: Brill and SBL, 2003), 87–98

15. "What is a Human Being: The Anthropology of the Psalter I"

What About the Soul: Neuroscience and Christian Anthropology, ed. Joel Green (Nashville: Abingdon, 2004). Reprinted by permission of Abingdon Press

16. "The Sinful and Trusting Creature: The Anthropology of the Psalter II"

Unpublished

17. "Constitution or Instruction? The Purpose of Deuteronomy"

Constituting the Community: Studies on the Polity of Ancient Israel in Honor of S. Dean McBride, Jr. eds. Steven Tuell and John Strong (Winona Lake, IN: Eisenbrauns, 2004)

18. "'Slow to Anger': The God of the Prophets"

The Forgotten God: Perspectives in Biblical Theology, ed. Andrew A. Das and Frank Matera (Louisville: Westminster John Knox Press, 2002), 39–55

19. "What the Scriptures Principally Teach"

Homosexuality and Christian Community, ed. Choon-Leong Seow (Louisville: Westminster John Knox, 1996), 53–63

20. "Theology from Below: The Theological Interpretation of Scripture"

Reconsidering the Boundaries Between the Theological Disciplines ed. Friedrich Schweitzer and Michael Welker (in press)

21. "Man and Woman: Towards a Theological Anthropology"

Reading from Right to Left: Essays on the Hebrew Bible in Honour of David J. A. Clines, eds. J. Cheryl Exum and H. G. M. Williamson (Sheffield: Sheffield Academic Press, 2003), 320–328. Reprinted by permission of The Continuum International Publishing Group

Scripture Index

Old Testament

New Testament

Subject Index

Forschungen zum Alten Testament

Edited by Bernd Janowski, Mark S. Smith
and Hermann Spieckermann

Alphabetical Index

Forschungen zum Alten Testament

Perlitt, Lothar: Deuteronomium–Studien. 1994. *Volume 8.*
Podella, Thomas: Das Lichtkleid JHWHs. 1996. *Volume 15.*
Pola, Thomas: Das Priestertum bei Sacharja. 2003. *Volume 35.*
Rösel, Martin: Adonaj – Warum Gott 'Herr' genannt wird. 2000. *Volume 29.*
Ruwe, Andreas: „Heiligkeitsgesetz" und „Priesterschrift". 1999. *Volume 26.*
Schaper, Joachim: Priester und Leviten im achämenidischen Juda. 2000. *Volume 31.*
Schenker, Adrian (Hrsg.): Studien zu Opfer und Kult im Alten Testament. 1992.
    Volume 3.
Schmidt, Brian B.: Israel's Beneficent Dead. 1994. *Volume 11.*
Schöpflin, Karin: Theologie als Biographie im Ezechielbuch. 2002. *Volume 36.*
Spieckermann, Hermann: Gottes Liebe zu Israel. *Volume 33.*
Steck, Odil Hannes: Gottesknecht und Zion. 1992. *Volume 4.*
Stuhlmacher, Peter: see *Janowski, Bernd.*
Weber, Cornelia: Altes Testament und völkische Frage. 2000. *Volume 28.*
Weippert, Manfred: Jahwe und die anderen Götter. 1997. *Volume 18.*
Weyde, Karl William: The Appointed Festivals of YHWH. 2004. Volume II/4.
Willi, Thomas: Juda – Jehud – Israel. 1995. *Volume 12.*
Young, Ian: Diversity in Pre-Exilic Hebrew. 1993. *Volume 5.*
Zwickel, Wolfgang: Der Tempelkult in Kanaan und Israel. 1994. *Volume 10.*

For a complete catalogue please write to the publisher
Mohr Siebeck • P.O. Box 2030 • D-72010 Tübingen/Germany
Up-to-date information on the internet at www.mohr.de